S'.ffo'.

04

5

THE LIFE AND THOUGHT OF AUREL KOLNAI

The Life and Thought of
Aurel Kolnai

FRANCIS DUNLOP
Honorary Lecturer
University of East Anglia, UK

Ashgate

Published by
Ashgate Publishing Limited
Gower House
Croft Road
Aldershot
Hampshire GU11 3HR
England

Ashgate Publishing Company
131 Main Street
Burlington, VT 05401-5600 USA

Ashgate website: http://www.ashgate.com

British Library Cataloguing in Publication Data
Dunlop, Francis
   The life and thought of Aurel Kolnai
   1. Kolnai, Aurel 2. Philosophers - England - Biography
   I. Title
   192

Library of Congress Cataloging-in-Publication Data
Dunlop, Francis.
   The life and thought of Aurel Kolnai / Francis Dunlop.
      p. cm.
   Includes bibliographical references and index.
   ISBN 0-7546-1662-2
   1. Kolnai, Aurel. 2. Philosophers--England--Biography. I. Title.

   B1646.K7774 D86 2001
   192--dc21
   [B]   00-065040

ISBN 0 7546 1662 2

Printed and bound in Great Britain by MPG Books Ltd, Bodmin, Cornwall

Contents

Acknowledgements		*vi*
Introduction		*viii*
1	Family and School (1900-1918)	1
2	Political Development (1916-1919)	19
3	War, Revolution and Counter-Revolution (1918-1920)	36
4	Kolnai's Psychoanalytic Episode (1920-1926)	51
5	Early Days in Vienna (1920-1924)	65
6	University Studies and Related Publications (1922-1930)	86
7	Political Journalism or Philosophy? (1920-1930)	109
8	Fighting for the West in Vienna (1930-1937)	130
9	Peripatetic (1937-1940)	154
10	New York and Boston (1940-1945)	179
11	Quebec (1945-1955)	203
12	England or Spain? (1952-1961)	229
13	England - Early Difficulties (1958-1964)	253
14	The Last Fifteen Years (1958-1973)	272
Appendix: Kolnai's Attitude to the Catholic Faith		301
Notes		*305*
Select Bibliography of Kolnai's Published Works		
and of Works about Kolnai		*330*
Index		*337*

Acknowledgements

I have received much help and encouragement over at least a decade in writing this book. I would like first to thank the following people, who have helped me in various ways as private individuals: Prof. Elizabeth Anscombe, Prof. Leslie Armour, Mr Peter Ayrton, Mme Catherine Back, Dr A. De Tószeghi, Prof. Léon Dion†, Mrs Joanna Dodsworth, Dr Judith Dupont, M. Ferenc Fejtő, Mrs Jean Flood CBE, Brother Francis SIHM, Prof. Dr Rafael Gambra, M. Claude Germain, Miss Lisbeth Gombrich†, Mr George Gömöri, Dr Donald Grant, Mrs Irene Grant†, Frau Dora Haag-Keller, Dr Karin von Hámos, Prof. Alice von Hildebrand, Dr Endre Kiss, Prof. Brian Klug, Prof. Nicholas Kurti†, Dr Alan Lacey, Dr György Litván, Dr David Lloyd-Thomas, Miss Sarah Lumley-Smith, Prof. Pierre Manent, Prof. Bernard Mayo, Dr Alfred Missong, Mrs Cate Mullins, Prof. Dr Juan Miguel Palacios, Prof. D.Z. Phillips, Mrs Mária Schmidt, Prof. Emeritus Francis Seton, Miss Esther Simpson† OBE, Mr George Szirtes, Senator Arthur Tremblay†, Mrs Pauline Tremblay, Mrs Doreen Vaughan, Prof. David Wiggins, Prof. Bernard Williams, Mme Claude Winkler, Prof. Tom Zolnay.

Special thanks are due to the following: Prof. Dr Miguel Ayuso (who acted as the representative Prof. Dr Victor Marrero† in Madrid, and gave me valuable comments on the Spanish chapter), Dr Zoltán Balázs (who gave much informative help over Hungarian matters), Prof. John D. Beach and Mrs Sunny Beach (who, as well as sending me Kolnai's letters, entertained me in their house in Spain), Prof. Thomas DeKoninck (jnr) (who helped me with the Quebec chapter and made available to me copies of Kolnai's written communications with his father), Mrs Susi Lanyi (who wrote me so many friendly and informative letters, entertained my wife and myself in Oberlin, and provided hundreds of letters written to her late husband, George), Prof. Jeanne Lapointe (who, as well as corresponding and suffering an interview, sent me annotated books Kolnai had sent her from England), Mr Csaba Nagy (who gave me permission to copy Bela Menczer's Memoirs), Dr Nicholas Nathan (whose encouragement was crucial in getting this book published), Miss Szylvia Tóth (who discovered things for me in Budapest, and whose parents put me up during my visits to the city), and Mr Robert R. Vámbéry (who answered a great many questions about his old friend with enormous thoroughness and sent numerous Kolnaian letters). I would also like to thank the following for giving me copies or letting me see their collections of Kolnai letters: Frau Annegret Hartmann, Mrs Eszter Kelemen, Ms Judit Kinszky, Sr D Salvador Pons and Mrs Cynthia Read.

Libraries where I have consulted and copied documents and letters include those of Columbia University, NY, Concordia University, Montreal, the Dokumentationsarchiv des Oesterreichischen Widerstands 1934-45, Vienna, Laval University, Quebec, the Pet⇒fi Irodalmi Muzeum, Budapest, and the Vienna University Archives. I have also been helped by M. Laurent Tailleur, Archiviste du Séminaire de Québec, and by Miss Jill Duncan, Librarian of the Institute of Psychoanalysis, London.

I must acknowledge here permission to quote material from the Kolnai files of the Immigration department of the Home Office, and the archive of the Society for the Protection of Science and Learning in The Bodleian Library, Oxford.

Thanks are due, finally, to the Philosophy Department of King's College, University of London, for a photocopying grant.

Introduction

Aurel Kolnai was born to Jewish parents in Budapest on December 5th, 1900. He died in a London hospital of a heart attack on June 28th, 1973. During those seventy-two and a half years he lived, successively, in Budapest, Vienna, Paris, New York, Boston, Quebec and, finally, London. Kolnai is primarily known in English and American academic circles as a moral philosopher and conservative political thinker, though in Vienna he is perhaps better known as a member of the Psychoanalytical Association, and then again as a Christian leftist journalist. Although he never held or tried for political office, he was engaged on the fringe of the 1918 "Chrysanthemum Revolution" in Hungary, and then again as part of the Christian democratic movement in Austria, when the country began to move towards Fascism. Apart from that, he was always active as a philosophically inclined writer on politics, with special attention to National Socialism in the thirties, and then, during the early years of the Cold War, to Communism. His experience of university teaching was very limited, and the only full-time post he ever held was at the Catholic Laval University, in Quebec, from 1945 to 1955. In London he never managed to obtain more than a part-time post, lecturing at Bedford College from 1959, with temporary visiting fellowships at Birmingham, England and Milwaukee, Wisconsin.

Kolnai's life was dogged by bad luck and what he himself diagnosed as simple "failure". Three of his books were never finished (two being "overtaken by events"), one was lost in the war before it could be published, and another was not printed because the publisher went bankrupt. He was never able to settle in an environment conducive to the full working out of his fundamental insights, and the formation of a "school". But, in any case, his character was such that he would never have accepted a flock of disciples, and his "failure", if it really was failure, was to a large extent the result of his own lack of balance and practical wisdom. But his philosophical work, in moral and political philosophy, especially in the diagnosis of the "utopian mind", is of enormous interest and importance, as the academic community is gradually beginning to discover. Several works have now been posthumously published and others are being translated and reprinted. But because his work is so scattered, being written in five different languages and appearing in rather more countries, a general awareness of it is bound to be a slow and laborious process. But the relevance of his best work is perhaps greater than ever, as the Western world ever more wholeheartedly embraces the subtler forms of totalitarian tyranny, which Kolnai so clearly understood.

Quite apart from the importance of his philosophy, Kolnai was an extraordinarily interesting man, who made a very strong impression wherever he was known. He was a fascinating conversationalist and raconteur, with a wonderful memory, powerful sensitivity and a grotesque sense of humour. He was also a great letter-writer, and, as he put so much of himself into his correspondence, the survival of many hundreds of letters to his friends goes to make up for the fact that he had no Boswell at his elbow to remember and record the things he said. He also left behind a few very interesting youthful diaries, and other material which, together with the letters, and often copious marginal comments in his books, yields a full picture of his life and character.[1]

I have so far said nothing about Kolnai's own account of his life. These memoirs were to have been published in 1956, but the project was abandoned. Many attempts were made by Mrs Kolnai, after her husband's death, and then by Professor David Wiggins and others, to get them published, but nothing ever came of it until 1999, when Lexington Books brought out Francesca Murphy's edition.[2] So the question arises: "Why a biography, when we have Kolnai's own memoirs?" Quite apart from the stock answer to this: that a person is not always the best writer of his own life, there are several reasons why a biography is needed. Firstly, the memoirs only extend to 1952, leaving the last twenty-one years of Kolnai's life unaccounted for. Secondly, Kolnai says himself that they do not constitute an autobiography in the usual sense; rather, he uses the story of his life as a thread from which to hang a series of essays.[3] Thus, he says very little about certain periods of his life which are, in fact, of great interest, and which are covered by some exceptionally revealing letters. Thirdly, the style of Kolnai's memoirs is not always very accessible. For the most part they lack the "lighter" moments even of some of his philosophical papers, and, despite Kolnai's extraordinary self-objectivity and frankness, conceal certain aspects of his personality. For these and other reasons, I believe that my book, even as biography, will form a valuable complement to the memoirs.

But there is another reason why the present work is needed. Kolnai says very little about his own writings, apart from sketching out the main themes of the most important of them. But that leaves a great deal unaccounted for. I have therefore tried to include in my study some account of nearly everything he published, including his journalism, and much of what still remains unpublished. Since I have not been primarily concerned with an assessment of his thought, but have included an account of what he wrote in an account of his life, some readers will perhaps find that I have not tried to do as much as they would have liked in the way of tracing lines of development, both within Kolnai's work, and in relation to those who influenced him, or in passing judgement on it and relating to it current concerns. I have not neglected these things altogether, but, in accordance with my purpose, I have aimed at giving the reader a conspectus of what Kolnai wrote, and showing the place it held in his life. What the present work may the more easily do, therefore, is give the reader valuable orientation in Kolnai's *oeuvre*.

I have already mentioned that Kolnai wrote in five languages. They are Hungarian, German, English, French and Spanish. I have had to learn enough Hungarian to read and translate passages from Kolnai's publications, letters and diaries in this language. Luckily I already had at least a basic knowledge of the other languages. But all the translated quotations are my own work. I can hardly hope there are *no* mistakes, but I trust there are not many serious ones.

Chapter One

Family and School
(1900-1918)

Aurel Kolnai was originally named Aurél Stein. His parents, Ármin (the Hungarian version of Hermann) and Valéria (née Glück), were both Jews. He was born on December 5th, 1900, at 10 Báthory St, Budapest. This is a street of large apartment blocks, built towards the end of the century for the newer bourgeoisie,[1] just east of the magnificent Hungarian houses of parliament. The block containing number 10 was destroyed in the 1939-1945 war, and replaced with an ugly utilitarian building. But, probably about six years after Kolnai's birth, the family moved to an apartment at 92 Aréna Ave (now Dózsa György Ave), a spacious and well-appointed flat in a house originally built in Art Nouveau style.[2] It still stands, though much altered, near the corner of Andrássy Ave, with views of Heroes' Square and the City Park. On the left-hand side of the square is the Museum of Fine Art, and beyond that is the zoo, where Kolnai spent many happy hours communing with his favourite animals. When Kolnai was born, this area of the city was where the richest and most respected Hungarian Jews lived.[3] The move to Aréna Ave would have symbolised a definite step-up in the world.

This is the material side of the feeling of "solid security" which, Kolnai tells us,[4] pervaded his childhood. His father was a wealthy bank-manager, and his mother also came from a prosperous family. He was, therefore, brought up in an atmosphere of wealth and bourgeois comfort, which lasted unthreatened until the end of the First World War. Much of Kolnai's life thereafter was characterised by poverty and the effort to find a regular source of income, but through all these vicissitudes we can glimpse the faint but lasting feeling on Kolnai's side that he was in some way entitled to enjoy the good things of the world (in moderation) and to indulge a taste for specific luxuries.

Another aspect of the "vital tone" of Kolnai's childhood was, he tells us, "virtual estrangement from (his) home milieu".[5] We shall look at the estrangement shortly, but we should look first at the milieu. Despite the general integration into the wider society of Budapest and other Hungarian Jews, the extended family, including a great number of more or less distant cousins, was still extremely important in Kolnai's parents' social world, and in that of their friends. The "home milieu" therefore represented something extensive but exclusive. When Kolnai eventually reached the United States as a penniless refugee, he found several relations from whom material help could be successfully sought.

Budapest Jews tended to be liberal, with hardly any of the characteristic religious beliefs or rituals of Orthodox Judaism, but rather more of the traditional moral and social practices of the community, such as organised charitable giving to the poor. Kolnai tells us that, during his childhood and early youth, he never knew anyone, whether Jews or Christians, for whom religious beliefs and practices were a living thing, but his parents regularly helped certain poor relations in the early twenties.[6]

His parents were both "first generation" Budapesters. His grandparents all lived in Northern Hungary, in the region of present-day Slovakia which took its tone from Pozsony, or Bratislava, rather than the Hungarian capital. But Kolnai has only this to say about his grandparents: "My father's father, a prosperous tailor or cloth merchant in Slovakia, who died before I was born, was a 'zealot', a very rigorous orthodox Jew".[7] József Litván, a first cousin of Kolnai, says a little more, describing grandfather Saloman as

the long established leader of the Jewish community in Nitra, a tall, thin, man, revered as a saint by his family and community. He died aged 94, and on that year's Day of Atonement the synagogue was full throughout the twenty-four hours.

Of his (and Kolnai's) grandmother Vilma, née Sgall, Litván says:

She was short and plump, and directed the affairs of her scattered family as though the whole world's energies flowed through her. Her first two girls were married at fourteen, and died as victims of their own infirmity. Of the fourteen children she bore, six girls and one boy survived.

Litván's own memoirs, the source of these quotations, contain a photograph of "grandfather Stein" in the prime of his life, with short beard and moustache and longish hair, and a fine embroidered cap on his head. He looks very slightly unkempt, and has an expression that seems to combine the far-off look of a mystic with a down-to-earth pugnacity.[8]

Kolnai, then, had six aunts and no uncles on his father's side. All the aunts married, and had dowries, which brought them educated husbands. Litván says that "two out of the six daughters married journalists, one a lawyer, two civil servants and only one a businessman." … "The succeeding generation", Litván continues, "produced, besides Kolnai, Jenő Gömöri, who founded and edited the Modern Library" (quite an institution among the bourgeois book-buying public in Hungary), "also engineers, lawyers and a doctor".[9] Among the husbands of his father's sisters was Zsigmond Schiller, an editor of the *Pester Lloyd*, the most famous German-language daily of Budapest. He was also a noted botanist, and his collection of specimens is, or used to be, in the National Museum. Another of his aunts married a man whose son or grandson was a ballet dancer and later directed the theatre at Győr. Litván's own aunt, his father's sister Irma Mendl, had the more dubious distinction of being one of the first victims of the Russian Bolshevist system of arrest to be named in Solzhenitsyn's *The Gulag Archipelago*; she was taken in charge by a "boy-friend" at the Bolshoi theatre and shot in 1926 for being "too close to Bukharin".[10] Kolnai's mother seems also to have come from a family of some social standing. One of Kolnai's cousins on this side was György Széll, who made the Cleveland Symphony Orchestra into a world-famous ensemble; another was Pál Winkler, who became the very rich founder of Opera Mundi, a worldwide publishing venture based in Paris.

Liberal Jews in the Hungarian half of the Dual Monarchy, or "Austria-Hungary", tended to think of themselves as Hungarians of Jewish ancestry. Their families might be the descendants of Jewish families who had been settled within the frontiers for several generations, many of whom eventually gravitated to Budapest, which tripled its population between 1875 and 1900, and was the fastest growing city in Europe.[11] With its sophisticated intellectual and cultural life, it represented the liberal strand within Hungarian Jewry, as opposed to Pozsony, which stood for orthodoxy. In so far as Hungary possessed a bourgeois class, Jews very largely constituted it. Quite a few were members of the Hungarian parliament, and some were ennobled, so that one can speak truly of a genuine assimilation, consistent with the liberal traditions of Hungary since the middle of the nineteenth century. Nevertheless, the assimilation was not complete. Boys like Kolnai tended to have few, if any, friends who were not fellow Jews, and to a great extent Budapest, especially its large Jewish minority (about 20 percent of the city's population at the turn of the century, as opposed to 5 per cent in Hungary as a whole), was regarded with suspicion by those outside the capital. During the First World War the Jewish population of Pest was much increased by Galician Polish Jews displaced by the Russian army's incursion into the Austrian area of South Poland, and these refugees, often extremely poor and still wearing the traditional gabardines, were much more conspicuous than the longer established Jewish families. The sheer intellectual and cultural energy of the Budapest Jews also meant that they were among the foremost revolutionaries in 1918 and 1919 (95 per cent of Béla Kun's government were of Jewish descent), and the "White reaction" of 1919 and subsequent years took the lid off a seething anti-Semitism - though, as Kolnai stresses, it was worlds apart from the systematic and cold-blooded hostility of the Holocaust.

Although Kolnai made a few affectionate-nostalgic references to his father towards the end of his life in letters to people he knew very well, I have seen no references to his mother apart that in this summarising passage in the memoirs:

> To my parents I owe an ingrained sense of honesty and respect for Capitalism which in spite of countervailing moods and arguments has never really left me … To my mother, in especial, I owe a hard backbone of character, a certain sense of tragedy, a tendency not only to shun but to hate wrong and to hate not only wrong but rosy illusions.

(It is clear from a short fragment among Kolnai's papers that the "rosy illusions" his mother hated were often those of his father.) "To my father", he goes on,

> [I owe] a primary preference for compromise and a first impulse to yield - which on further reflection I may correct into a kind of Dutch courage - as well as a virtually "objectivistic" knack for easy-going detachment and indifference, of which my mother had nothing.[12]

It is tempting to conclude from this slender evidence that, despite the feeling of security his mother offered, with her inflexible moral integrity, she - at the very least - found it difficult to love him. However, Kató Back, whose mother was a first cousin of Ármin's, and used regularly to accompany her in her childhood when she called on Kolnai's parents, remembers her as good-hearted and generous. Kolnai himself says:

> My parents were certainly not just to me, and I am equally certain they did love me, largely in a false way, but by no means in the sense of merely pretending to love me; their love was not a mere "mask of possessiveness".[13]

But another passage from the Memoirs is worth citing in this connection. Kolnai is recalling the books that made the greatest impression on him as a child, and singles out especially *Gulliver's Travels* and *David Copperfield*:

> These are my first experiences of great literature, and also of feminine love, for I immediately fall in love with Princess Glumdalklitch - not a little envying Gulliver for being her pet - and then, in a more sublime key, … with Miss Trotwood, alias Aunt Betsy, that radiant type of the British Maiden Aunt.[14]

It is not difficult to see a mother-substitute in both imaginary objects of his affection - an interpretation reinforced by the fact that the great love of his mid-twenties was old enough to be his mother.

György Litván, son of the József already mentioned, recalls seeing Kolnai's parents in the late thirties in their little house in Moszkva tér (a great comedown from 92a Aréna Avenue). He remembers his mother as a rather "mouselike" figure in relation to her more expansive and excitable husband. It seems likely that, as a dutiful wife, Valéria supported her husband in all essentials, yet devoted considerable efforts to damping down his sudden enthusiasms. It is worth adding that this psychological contrast was quite contrary to the physical difference between them. Kató Back remembers the mother as a handsome matronly woman, whereas he was slim and dapper.

Although he had good reason to regret his father's ill-judged attempts to get him to follow in his footsteps, there is no doubt that Kolnai felt a deep kinship with his father of a different order from the impersonal moral passion he shared with his mother. When he was nineteen, the family spent some time in the mountain spa of Trenčianske Teplice, where Kolnai vented his frustration at being cooped up in their rural retreat by writing a little dialogue.[15] The characters are his parents, himself, and the Haasz and Ledowski families, and they are at table. Messrs Haasz and Ledowski are obsessed with business; the females enthuse about clothes, or attend gushingly to the small children also present, while passing reference is made to the end of the Empire and pogroms in Budapest. Food is another major concern, and the piece, "Still Life at Trenčanteplice", starts with Kolnai offering his mother the skin of the meat he is eating:

> *Mother*: Give it here, then, you useless thing, it's the best part!
> *Father*: Oh no you don't! Auluschka [affectionate form of Aurél], you little donkey, do you love your father?
> *Mother*: Really, Mani [short for Hermann], talking to the big lad like that in front of others!

It seems clear that Kolnai's father, who was at least forty years older than Kolnai, did love his son in his own breezy, tyrannical and inconsistent way (elsewhere Kolnai calls him "kindly, selfish and easy-going"), and this accounts for the affectionately nostalgic references Kolnai makes to him in later life, when he recalls forceful and pithy remarks and comments he made in his "accurate" German and not very accurate Hungarian, his favourite phrases, eccentric pronunciations, and his habitual verbal responses to certain situations. Yet "the bloody crimes of parents are monstrous",[16] he pointedly writes, and recalls the occasion when, in the Kovács' big flat in Váci St, he made a significant impression on the company with the remark: "I'm afraid of my parents ... but they're also afraid of me."[17]

We must now attend to the "virtual estrangement from (his) home milieu"[18] alluded to above, which he describes elsewhere as an "inner breach", though this, he hastens to add, never actually led to a complete severing of relations with his parents. To Kolnai the general reasons for this "inner breach", or "virtual estrangement", crystallised around two issues, his attitude to animals and, more importantly, his attitude to the First World War - though we shall have also later to note his family's opposition to his pursuit of a career as a writer. This is what he says on the question of animals:

> Love of animals, my strongest emotion, ... meets with cold antipathy from my parents; animals are alleged to be "carriers of germs" and my grave diphtheria-like illness in the summer of 1909 is quite gratuitously

attributed to my previous contact with two little dogs, but I know there must be some other, baser, motive: our very outlooks on the world seem to clash here. (There was, first, the lingering Mosaic horror of pagan animal-worship; secondly, indignation at my squandering love on creatures whom it could not in any way be "useful" to oblige.)[19]

The love of animals went very deep in Kolnai. When young, he gave names to his "friends" in the zoo, and to the end of his life his letters and occasional writings are peppered with exultant references to sightings of and sometimes encounters with, especially, dachshunds and cats. His parents' attitude must have deeply affronted him, particularly as their opposition may have been unconsciously strengthened by the feeling that his love of animals was to some extent a substitute for human love. Their utilitarian objection can be usefully compared with a marginal comment Kolnai made in one of his books. The author, discussing the biblical book of Job, says that in the ancient world misfortune was taken as a sign that one had offended God. Kolnai comments:

> This is still very common among Jews today. My parents assumed that every piece of misfortune was somebody's "fault" (e.g. if one had a sore throat one must have "stood in a draught": this was both one's "own fault" and possibly also the "fault" of the person who had left the window open, etc). [This was] one of the most important factors in my breach with this social world.[20]

This attitude suggests a prevailing concern with both mental and physical management of things, and thus fits well with the utilitarianism expressed in the approach to animals. If this was a cornerstone of their *Weltanschauung*, then it is clear at least why they often found it hard to understand their son, who was, in the physical-material sense, impractical, and much more interested in passively absorbing the essences and values of things than of controlling them.

Before I discuss the issue of the First World War, one or two other observations should be made. The animal example already quoted implies that Kolnai's parents had some reason for their concern about his behaviour. He was in fact always getting ill, his life a long succession of illnesses, medical examinations and operations. Parental worries on this score, though often justified, can be irritating, and lead on to arguments and rows. No doubt this accounted for much mutual vexation. But Kolnai was, over and above this, a very difficult person to deal with. He tells one most revealing childhood anecdote about himself in another marginal annotation. This note is sparked off by the author's account of the Russian armies who "spilled into Europe out of the remote plains and impenetrable forests from which Napoleon had roused them" by his unsuccessful invasion. "Like beings of a different species they ... performed their natural functions in parlours".[21] Kolnai, who was always much better disposed towards Czarist Russia than might have been expected, and liked to think he had inherited Slav blood from his paternal grandfather, expresses some solidarity with the invading barbarians as follows:

> I did this for three or four months when I was nine and a half. Aunt Bertha came to visit us in her fine new brown frock, and I immediately urinated on her. Once I pissed into the pots on the fire in the kitchen.

The young Kolnai can hardly have been an easy child.

Kolnai also had a brother, László, usually known as Laci. He was the black sheep of the family, imprisoned for financial irregularities, and not above stealing from his mother when he needed to top up his generous allowance. He was about four years older than Kolnai, though less gifted. Like others of the gilded youth of the day he paid to have his own indifferent verses published, using for the purpose the pseudonym Szent Sebestyén (St Sebastian). He was tubercular when young and spent some time in Alexandria. Around 1918 he was living in his own flat in another part of Pest. His imprisonment and general untrustworthiness caused his parents, and Kolnai, much distress, and Kolnai hardly ever referred to him in adult life. But there was in fact a strong psychological affinity between the three male members of the family. One way of expressing this is to say that all of them were unusually ready to flout rules and conventions, and to be indifferent to the suffering of others. In Kolnai's case this aspect of his character was considerably modified by his sense of justice, respect for truth and marked timidity in the face of established authority. His father's business sense, and almost certainly stricter upbringing, seems to have kept him within the law, whereas László was badly spoilt, and, as a result, adopted the life of a playboy. He was also a great survivor, living through both his tuberculosis and the Second World War, when a great many members of the family were victims of the Holocaust. In the late forties Laci wrote for help to his brother and other relatives in the USA, and his wife's cousin asked Kolnai whether he was really a bad man, or just foolish, or mad. In Kolnai's view he was "deeply neurotic, physically sick and also a bad man", adding that his conduct was a good imitation of senile imbecility.[22] Laci clearly did get help in various forms from at least some of those he approached (certainly up to 1953), though others of those who knew him best advised against sending anything. When Tom Zolnay met him in Budapest in the early fifties, trying to arrange some financial assistance from a charitable Jewish organisation, he had "an extremely poor hunched-over posture" and seemed "almost like a figure out of some Dickens novel - a sort of Fagin?"[23] Eventually he found himself a wife, Dora, who looked after him until his death in 1972.

The spoiling is clearly implicit in Kolnai's description of his father's views about the upbringing of his children:

> My father's educational principle was that in place of strictness and threats it was better to appeal to reason; but he meant by this that a man should address his children thus: I'm appealing to your reason, can't you see, Auluska?[24]

Kolnai follows this with a little incident he recalls:

> Once about 1927-8 [on a visit from Vienna] I was still yawning in bed around 10.00 a.m., bored and depressed. Papa said: Up, Aurel! I replied with conviction: I haven't the slightest intention of getting up. He answered, in wickedly provocative style: Next time you'll be giving me a box on the ear![25]

Like László, Kolnai also found the increasing restraints of civilised life difficult, at least when young, and expresses this fact several times when he tells us that, during his teens, he often wanted to be a child again. This nostalgia for childhood, Kolnai says, began as early as the age of ten.

We come now to the matter of the First World War, and of Kolnai's support of the Entente, in opposition to his family. As already implied, this difference of attitude was not the origin of his inner breach with his family, but led to serious quarrels, and in some sense definitively confirmed it. Nor was his decision to support the Allies against Germany (and hence Austria-Hungary) made at the outset of the war itself, but in 1913, when he was twelve and a half. Kolnai, always very impressionable, had already visited Berlin and other parts of Germany with his family, as well as Vienna and other Austrian cities. He makes it clear that the essence of his great choice did not spring from "any bias against my country ... [or from] any doctrinal rejection of patriotism"; he simply espoused "the cause of the 'Entente', which (he) knew to be the 'enemy' cause, as against Germany".[26] In precocious self-examination after the first few months of the war, on the eve of the impending Russian victory in Galicia against the Austro-Hungarian army (in which relations or personal connections of his were certainly fighting), he found the basis of his choice to be this: Germany represented "the hegemony of one 'technically' superior nation guilty of moral anarchism, smitten with self-worship and the cult of power as an absolute", whereas the Entente - especially France, England and Russia - stood for "mankind ordered in freedom and manifoldness".[27] This professed concentration on "the qualities of the belligerents alone" at the expense of historical considerations, is an early instance of what is perhaps Kolnai's most persistent and prominent element as a political thinker, his tendency to see all issues in moral or spiritual terms.

Among his family and friends, Kolnai says, he stood alone during the first two or three years of the war, with the single exception of József Litván, his cousin, who much admired Kolnai's greater intellectual maturity, and was quickly won to the cause. One or two prominent Jews were against the war from the start, but by and large, especially in the early days, most Jewish Hungarians behaved as patriotically as their Magyar compatriots. The implication of unpatriotic behaviour did trouble Kolnai a little in middle and old age, and he admits that his decision was morally questionable, writing in his memoirs that his choice represented heresy rather than apostasy; there were undoubted pro-English and pro-French strands in the liberal culture of Hungary, on which it had long prided itself; the situation, therefore, was not absolutely clear-cut.

The family tensions brought about by Kolnai's attitude came to a head on the way home from the German island of Nordeney, where their 1914 summer holiday was interrupted by the dramatic events that ushered in the war. Writing in early 1919 he says he "hated the Germans from the bottom of [his] heart", and "still remember[s] the night when there was a howling gale on the island, and I tossed and turned in bed, longing for a similar gale to break out all over Europe."[28] There were rows with his parents. After many days of excitement and tension in the holiday crowd in the hotel, a telegram announcing Russia's mobilisation was read out in the hall. Soon they were on their way home, but they had to take a very roundabout route. "At Cologne cannons are being mounted on a tower. I eat a banana; good God, I've not eaten one since! We travel on. I don't like Basel." They had to break their journey here for two or three days, and something of great moral significance happened to him in this half-Swiss, half-German city, within a very short distance of the French frontier. He was clearly greatly upset by his parents' response to his views. Perhaps his mother's "vexed and grieved" conduct could have been borne, but his father was simply unable to cope with this "wayward and problematic little intellectual", and treated Kolnai's pro-Entente speeches and arguments as play-acting and bluster. For him, as for many of his fellow-Hungarians, such an unthinkable attitude could not be taken seriously. His account of the journey proceeds: "At last I read, plastered on a shop-window: War! Germany has declared war on Russia, France is mobilising."

Referring many years later to these momentous days he says:

(I) could easily have reached the French frontier, crossed it and asked to be taken on in the Foreign Legion. But I was only thirteen and a half, didn't think of it, probably didn't have the facts, and was above all too comfort-loving, for which I can never forgive myself.[29]

In another letter he refers to his "Original Sin at Basle", and to the "essential and irrevocable breach with [his] parents", which occurred a few days later.[30] It seems hardly credible that Kolnai reproached himself for not having gone to France and volunteered for the Foreign Legion. It was probably the fact that he didn't think of doing so, or didn't feel regret that he couldn't usefully do so, that he recalled with guilt. It should be noted here that he was not in the habit of speaking or writing lightly of what he considered to be moral inadequacy.

What form did the "breach" with his parents' world actually take? Was there anything more than an uneasy sense that his own life must be lived according to other standards and in response to other models? His rejection of Hungary itself didn't occur until the failure of the bourgeois liberal revolution became apparent in 1919. One minor expression of the "breach" may have been his adoption of the surname Kolnai on February 13th, 1918 (it was apparently culled from Ferenc Molnár's juvenile story *The Paul Street Boys*). However, this practice was common among the many non-Hungarians living in Hungary and, as an act of disassociation, requiring his father's consent, it could only have had private significance. Perhaps the fact that his brother did not "magyarise" his name made it more symbolic than it would otherwise have been. The real significance of the breach for us must lie not in its expressions but in what it reveals of Kolnai's mind.

What for almost all other children would have probably have remained a dull feeling of difference and alienation from his "home milieu" was raised by Kolnai - in highly characteristic fashion - to the level of a clear-eyed and irrevocable moral decision.

As has already been implied, Kolnai was extremely precocious, reading and writing things that would hardly be expected of a considerably older child. He tells us that at six he "knew half of the Central European Bradshaw by heart", an accomplishment recalled by Pál Winkler, his cousin, and retailed as a prodigious curiosity to his own children many years later.[31] József Litván first met Kolnai in 1911, when they were both ten. He writes in his memoirs that Kolnai already had well-developed intellectual interests (two or three years before this he had been devouring ancient history), and made a tremendous impression on his young cousin, seeming "almost like a grown-up". Already he was fascinated by the physical appearance of his friends and relations and the "ancient mystical aspects" of places. Litván, who had only just moved to Budapest, continues:

> The eccentric extravagance of his ideas, his explosive impulses and the many-sidedness of his talents made him also rather isolated, and so we got to know each other quickly. Despite his intellectual superiority our friendship was a solidarity of equals. What he respected in me was probably my relative normality, and the balance he lacked himself.[32]

It should perhaps also be added here that Kolnai's juvenile interests were not all intellectual. In 1964 he recalled "the magic world, reminiscent of Blues and Greens in Byzantium, of the two or three great football clubs and their prominent players in B[uda]p[est], c1910", and the "excited and bitter party loyalties and enmities" they aroused.[33] From adolescence onwards, however, Kolnai was the last person to be suspected of an interest in sport.

I have already said something about the prematurely abandoned family holiday on Nordeney in 1914, and the first stages of the circuitous homeward journey. His account also reveals that, though there is no record of his having any lessons in Italian (apart from his native German and Hungarian he had been learning French since the age of nine), he could read it well enough to decipher the inverted headlines of newspapers people were reading in the tram in Milan: "Germany threatens France through Belgium"; "The brutal militarists commence their deeds of blood"; and finally, on the morning of our departure, the great, long-awaited, news: "England has declared war on Germany". I become absorbed with a beautiful grey cat in the hotel.

The end of this, no doubt to his parents nerve-racking, journey from Milan is also worth recording:

> We leave, and a mere hour or two later realise we're going towards Genoa, not Venice. Back to Milan. Off again next day; at the last moment we get aboard a train still going as far as Trieste [then still part of the Austrian Empire]. I am excited to read pro-Entente analyses in Italian papers. At last we reach Trieste, and, after about ten days there, Budapest. With Trieste I associate incidents from the beginning of the war: Liège, the conquest of Togo, the bloody partiality of our papers, braying donkeys in the market square, losing my way in the outskirts, Kropotkin's Memoirs - and a twenty four-hour rather mystical journey home.

Back in Budapest he uses his toy cannon to shoot holes in the pictures of the German leaders.[34]

***

Kolnai's education was characteristic of his class. For most of the time until he was fourteen he was taught by governesses and then private tutors, though for about one half year before this he attended the Lutheran gymnasium in which he had enrolled in September 1910. This abortive attempt to establish him in the school may well have been called off because of his delicate health. In any case, he used to go to the school to take the examinations needed for promotion to the next class, and attended regularly from the autumn of 1914. His school, "The Evangelical Gymnasium of Augustan Confession", was one of the best gymnasiums, or grammar schools, in Budapest, and therefore in the country.

Despite the Christian and Protestant foundation of this school Kolnai tells us that

> there was barely a trace of confessional discrimination and, outside religious classes, little or no emphasis on religion, except in the negative sense of eschewing all questioning of it and all reference to ticklish

subjects like evolution or "higher criticism". God was mentioned seldom and perfunctorily only; Providence or the destiny of the soul, not at all, Christianity or its Founder, not unless the historical context made it necessary.[35]

No attempt of any kind was made to convert Jews to Christianity, though baptism was not uncommon in career-minded or socially ambitious Jewish families, and though about half Kolnai's fellow-pupils ("many of them prosperous and most of them 'aspiring'") were from Jewish families. The school's religious instruction, given by local rabbis, was mechanical and perfunctory, and did nothing to counteract the atheism inculcated by one of his family tutors.

Kolnai's class was clearly above average, since Jews "furnished the ablest scholars", and well over half of his classmates were Jewish. Kolnai must in fact have been one of the brightest boys in the school, since he had an awesome reputation among his contemporaries, yet one fellow pupil "constantly came above me in all subjects, and a couple of others might rival or surpass me". Of the non-Jews, he adds, only a single Lutheran, "with a German name, ranked close to us". As for his best subjects, he always felt confident of success in Greek and Mathematics, "and to a lesser degree, Latin; whatever had to be 'crammed' rather than construed or thought out, like history or geography", caused him difficulty and worry, especially if it didn't interest him.

Kolnai only makes particular mention of three of his class-mates. The first was a fellow anti-war propagandist, Andor Berei, of whom he says he was especially fond. "He was a delicate and meek Jewish boy, poor but refined, highly intellectual, shrewd and prone to irony", employing this weapon on Kolnai himself. He also mentions György Kovács, whom he always refers to as Caesar, describing him as "a socialist of the Bevanite shade, yet an Anglophile endowed with a delicious sense of humour".[36] There is also mention of the well-known novelist Francis Körmendi. Two of his teachers impressed themselves particularly on him, Kálmán Tóth and László Rácz. Tóth was the classics master,

a gaunt, rough-hewn petulant Calvinist in his fifties, strict but just - indeed, a heart of pure gold encased in a rough shell - a bachelor and, as rumour had it, a former cavalry officer; his hatred of smugness, hypocrisy, embellishment and slacking would almost seem Prussian, in the older and best sense of that term.

Rácz, on the other hand, a mathematics teacher,

> was one of those rare persons who are beloved of everybody, and for the right reason; universally popular because of their genuine worth. A mathematician of repute he had at the same time the looks, the carriage, the voice, the manners and the character of a true gentleman.

Kolnai recalls with particular pleasure the time when, shortly after the closure of the Galilei Circle (see chapter 2), he and some fellow-leftists were making very heavy weather of what he describes as a not particularly difficult problem. Rácz grew increasingly irritated until:

> We heard him mutter in a low but angry voice, while still walking across the class-room: "Want to reform society ... set up a new social order ... create the world anew ... redeem mankind ... can't cope with a function of the fourth degree." I grinned shamelessly, conceited young ass that I was ...[37]

Kolnai hints that he was a thorn in the flesh of many of his teachers - not, of course, out of high spirits or sheer rebelliousness, but for moralistic or ideological reasons. We can gauge the strength of his trouble-making potential from the following story he tells of himself. At fourteen years he was a subscriber to *Juventus*, a schoolboys' magazine written in Latin. In September 1914 the editor rashly described the Serbs as *populus immundus barbarorum*, "a filthy barbarian people". The young Stein, as he was then, at once cancelled his subscription.[38] In his last year he seems to have provoked the school authorities by making public his contempt for the Hungarian literature course, where some of the writers held up for admiration and imitation seemed to him to have been selected on purely nationalist, or sentimental, "folksy", grounds.

The change to regular attendance at school seems to have done great things for Kolnai. Among his miscellaneous personal papers are three loose pages from a notebook in which he records the period of his "greatest intellectual development", from 1915 for about a year.[39] Until then, he tells us, he had been intellectually preoccupied with the war, and with algebra. But now he embarked on some serious philosophical reading (Bergson and Ferrero), and, with Litván and Imre Kinszky, another first cousin (neither of whom was at Kolnai's school), he made plans to publish a hectographed magazine, which eventually ran for several months under the title *A két oldalon* (On both sides). The contents sound impressive, a mixture of stories, comments on current affairs, and articles of a more general interest which suggest the high intellectual level of his fellow pupils. But the literary competition sheds interesting light on Kolnai. In the late sixties he had some correspondence with an old class-mate of his, Gáspár Soltész, who reminded him that he had been the winner of this competition. He remembered the whole business very well, still treasured the prize (a two volume edition of Gottfried Keller's *Der grüne Heinrich*), and recalled a good proportion of Kolnai's magisterial comments in the magazine:

> The result of the competition was lamentable ... Of 14 entries I could not call one good ... But G.S.'s two-act play stands out from the rest ... There is no proper plot, the language is far too schoolboyish, but it definitely shows talent ...

Soltész, himself an extremely able man, goes on to say that he used to read this report over and over again, and "thought a lot about the fact that you were the first person in my life to say about a work of mine, that 'it definitely shows talent'".[40] Outside the context of the magazine Kolnai was writing for his own delectation about electrical circuits and on "Authority and Thought" as sources of knowledge, coming to the balanced conclusion that human beings need both. He also started his study of Freud and of mysticism, and began his collection of inks.

His sense of intellectual blossoming reached a high point at the beginning of 1916, when he made a reading plan for his own general education, to fill up the gaps in the school curriculum. At the same time he was still producing stories and poems, and something he calls an "Agonology", based on a chess match, which he discussed for some time with a professor at the Technical High School, though failed to get it published. In March he "founded" his library. Then he wrote an essay on mysticism himself and one on the "characteristics of the DC electrical circuit", interspersing these literary labours with numerous walks, and a study of the layout of Pest - not to mention his ordinary schoolwork.

Also in March - we must remind ourselves that Kolnai is still not sixteen - he entered the school literary society competition for an essay on the national spirit. His entry was entitled "On the Preservation of our National Character". This is what he says about it:

I was walking on Lehel St and there, at the corner of Aréna Ave, in a little Teresa district stationer's, I bought some commercial writing paper, on which, in double copy ink, I wrote the study which later won the smaller twenty crown prize. The unusual smell of the ink has remained from that time, uniting my copy with Lehel St and those days.[41]

The Easter holidays came, and he fell ill with 'flu, having just bought Poe's *Tales of Mystery and Imagination* and Anatole France's *Garden of Epicurus.*

I had already felt out of sorts that morning. In the afternoon I walked out on Egressy Ave as far as Róna St. An unforgettable walk, with the onset of fever and trembling in my limbs. Lying in bed with a temperature of 38C, I wrote my poem "The Nation's Night" and the very short "Dramatic Scene on Üllői Ave".[42]

During the late spring he played a lot of chess, and wrote a treatise on the philosophy of chess, making much use of the Budapest City Library. In the summer he became interested in "the Jewish question", and his interest in the war revived, thanks to the Russian offensive. He began a game of postal chess with Sándor Zinner, which he eventually lost in November. His study of Mach's philosophy began, and he read Binet's *Child Psychology*. So ended his great intellectual leap forward. His record ends with the promise that he will write again on the subject towards the end of 1917. This piece, if ever written, has not survived.

Kolnai's record, *1915-1916*, also mentions the "District wars", an imaginary topic which would keep him occupied far into his Vienna period. As a quasi-logical result of, on the one hand, his temperamental attraction to conflict, and, on the other, his comparative atmospheric or "mystical" research into the various districts of the city, to which his many walks were dedicated, and his study of its layout, came the idea of clashes and antagonisms breaking out into real wars. These he wrote up in the form of war reports, with battle plans, alliances and re-alliances, and poems celebrating major incidents and famous generals.[43] The notebook fragment just referred to also contains the earliest passages in "Uj-Portugués", a made-up language with echoes of Latin, Spanish and other romance languages. There are many traces of this (for example, translations of poetry) in a later notebook.

The early months of 1918 see Kolnai beginning to revise for the *Abitur* exam which took place in the early summer. At some point he was also summoned for an army medical along with Berei and Kovács, but was rejected as unfit because of his deafness - the result of childhood illness.[44] He approaches the actual exam with a mixture of confidence and mistrust. He suddenly panics over history and frantically mugs it up, but in the event answers practically all the questions with ease. Kovács tries to make him laugh in the exam room as they are waiting for the oral questions on Greek literature, but, in general, he feels he has done well - as indeed he did, though he is a little sore about not getting any prizes or scholarships. Kolnai's *Testimonium Maturitatis*, which showed him eligible to go on to university, was issued in both Hungarian and Latin. He achieved final marks of excellence in all the school's main subjects: Hungarian, Latin, History, Mathematics, Physics and Greek. In the lesser subjects: Religious doctrine, German, Elementary Philosophy, Natural History and Geometrical Drawing, he was also classified as excellent, but fell down in Geography, for which he could only manage a mark of "good".

The family, who never missed their summer holiday during the war, returned from Lake Balaton to Budapest in the autumn. Kolnai began to prepare for the university, where, astonishingly, he was going to read medicine, along with several of his friends, including Kovács, Litván and Steinitz. Despite his life-long interest in medicine he switched "after a few days" to the faculty of law - though whether there was any kind of family battle behind all this, there is nothing in the records to say. There was also a psychoanalytical congress to attend during these months, where he saw "Freud, Ferenczi, Varjas, Ophuysen, Rank, Sadger", and others. Meanwhile the allied victory was inevitable, yet:

> I only recall an evening visit to our relatives in Kárpát Street, where they [as good patriots] despairingly sketched out the unfavourable situation. "They increase in number every day, and we grow fewer."[45]

He does not recall whether or not he managed to keep his feeling of triumph to himself.

Chapter Two

Political Development (1916-1919)

So far I have said very little about Kolnai's developing political interests. I shall, therefore, say a little more about this aspect of his life during the war years, prefacing it with a brief account of Hungarian liberalism, and the main institutions which helped to form the young radicals of Kolnai's generation.

The feeling of being the "master race" of East Central Europe was still widely shared by the Hungarians of Kolnai's youth. Indeed, when he was asked to write about the Hungarian Uprising of 1956 even Kolnai himself emphasised the Hungarian love of liberty, and the "aristocratic traditions" of the people.[1] The survival of the Hungarian language, a non-Indo-European tongue, in an area also inhabited by Slavs, Germans and Romanians, is alone enough to suggest Hungarian predominance. Besides this, the nation had enjoyed long periods of flourishing independence, with its own constitutional liberties, in the Middle Ages. The semi-independence of Transylvania, ruled by Hungarian princes, had enabled the great traditions to outlive the Ottoman invasion and Turkish rule, which at one time seemed to threaten the whole of Europe. Nor did the Magyars think any less of themselves after incorporation into the Habsburg domains. If Rákóczi's revolt of the early eighteenth century failed because most of the power was now in the hands of Habsburg beneficiaries, that of the liberal Lajos Kossuth in 1848, which evoked much interest and moral support in liberal Europe and the United States, could only be put down with Russian help.

This failed attempt to regain independence was answered by Habsburg "Neo-absolutism", administered by Alexander Bach. But then came the battle of Königgrätz, when Austria was defeated by Prussia. Under the leadership of Ferenc Deák, Hungary was in 1867 able to negotiate the famous *Ausgleich* - the constitution of the Dual Monarchy. Questions of finance, war and foreign affairs (now concentrated on alliance with Germany) were settled jointly in cabinet with the Emperor, or, as he was to Hungary, the King. In all other spheres the Hungarian parliament was autonomous. The serfs had been freed. Hungary now gave Croatia semi-independence and legislation was soon introduced which was to give far-reaching equality to the other "nationalities": the Slovaks, Ruthenes, Romanians and Serbs who also lived within the borders.

From 1867 until 1918 the liberals of Hungary enjoyed a period of almost uninterrupted power, and it might have been expected that the state would evolve along similar lines to the states of Western Europe. Yet aspirations for progress still clashed strongly with the desire to cherish national distinctiveness, and the bogey of further Russian interference seemed to justify putting a brake on the full emancipation of the "nationalities". There were also divisions between the (mostly conservative) agricultural and the (mostly liberal) industrial magnates, and very few were far-sighted enough to make cooperation with Austria more than grudging. Meanwhile, the still overwhelmingly rural society of Hungary was changing with increasing rapidity. The great estates of the magnates continued to grow, the lesser nobility, or gentry, were increasingly forced to sell their land and to join the already swollen band of civil servants, the great army of landless rural peasants plunged deeper into destitution, many of them either emigrating abroad or moving to the slums of Budapest. The land problem was acute, yet no really effective measures were taken by the liberal government, who were more interested in building up an industrial base.

When Kolnai was old enough to take note of these things, no socialist or radical deputy had been elected to the Hungarian parliament; the franchise was still extremely narrow, and the secret ballot was still only a desideratum; the "nationalities" could only take a full part in public life if they would consent to be "magyarised" in language and culture; and very little had been done to help the rural and rapidly increasing urban poor. Social unrest in Budapest began to make itself increasingly felt. There were loud demands for an extension of the franchise and a secret ballot. Between 1906 and 1914 the main concern of governments seemed to be not to yield on these points. Eventually the Emperor himself stepped in. Alarmed by Hungarian aspirations for a separate and wholly Hungarian-speaking army (the common Austro-Hungarian army used German), the government was pressed to introduce a Law of Electoral Reform, but the details of the bill imposed on the house were a calculated insult to all who stood to benefit from it.

All through these years, Kolnai writes, the ruling classes continued to use the "comfortable and high-sounding liberal phraseology"[2] employed by their genuinely liberal predecessors of the first seventy years of the nineteenth century. There was accordingly a sense of bourgeois confidence in Budapest and other cities, a response to growing prosperity. Yet it was possible for gymnasium pupils at the end of the century to be ignorant of the nationalities' very existence.[3] But both "1848" and "1867" grew out of liberalism, "though certainly a nationalist and gentry brand of liberalism",[4] and the pre-war regime, despite its corruption, was not wholly without genuinely liberal features. Magyarised Slavs and Romanians could, like assimilated Jews, achieve great things in Hungary. But Oszkár Jászi's scornful description of the regime as a "pseudo-liberalism" was eagerly taken up by young radicals, and Kolnai's own later modification - "a liberalism gone sour" from over-defensiveness and a lazy refusal to look the real situation in the face - does not mark a very great reassessment, despite the fact that his later comments on the Hungary of his boyhood are made in full awareness of the horrors that were to succeed it.

***

Although there was always something original about Kolnai's thought (recall his love of mathematics coupled with his childlike and "passive" but highly sensitive taking in of phenomena), it is hardly surprising that his early social, ethical and political writings are heavily influenced by the intellectual milieu of Budapest progressivism. In effect this was an alternative and more extensive Jewish world (in his maturity he refers to it as "the progressive ghetto"),[5] but it had windows opening on the advanced countries of Western Europe and gave him something he could not find in the "pseudo-liberal" and conservative *Orbis Hungaricus* of family and school. At the same time, Kolnai was never a genuine Marxist socialist, and his longing for "progress" was always more a desire for tried and tested changes than for genuine revolution. As he put it in the early fifties:

> What we meant by reaction was, partly at least, ... the reluctance of the Hungarian ruling class ... to recognise Western standards as self-evidently obligatory; in other words, their insistence on the peculiar circumstances and, correspondingly, the special requirements of Hungarian state-life.[6]

He explains also that what "we" moderates meant by socialism was "the transformation of (our) own country into an intellectually advanced democracy, based on foreign models already accomplished and apparently above criticism".[7]

As already intimated, to some extent his eager embracing of this intellectual atmosphere, which included psychoanalysis and Herbert Spencer's positivism, was a way of giving more substance to his rejection of his family milieu. Much of Kolnai's youthful literary output suggests an author shackled by theories, from whose restrictions he is unconsciously striving to extricate himself. Even his attitude to the First World War began to impose a persona on him. At first it generally counted either as a piece of wilful perversity or as a piece of highly dubious eccentricity. But, as the war progressed, and more and more leftist and progressivist thinkers came to oppose it, or at any rate Hungary's place in it, Kolnai's opposition was associated more with leftism as such, and this tended to drive him further towards the left or radical side than if he had held a more conventional view.

Another aspect of traditional, nationalist, "gentry" Hungary mentioned by Kolnai in his memoirs is the unusual level of intellectual corruption wrought by "pseudo-liberalism", with its refusal to look unpleasant facts in the face. Yet for all its "fixing" and cynicism the pre-war regime still tolerated a great deal of criticism and dissent. Thus, since it was virtually impossible for radicals and progressivists to achieve any real power in the state until the Hungarian collapse of October 1918, the radical thrust against the status quo was chiefly intellectual. Towering above all other critical thinkers and writers of the time, and probably the most important personal influence on Kolnai's life, was the figure of Oszkár Jászi.

Jászi was born in 1875 in a nationally mixed area of Transylvania. His father was a doctor, of Jewish descent, who became a Calvinist to improve his children's chances. Oszkár studied law at Budapest, and was much impressed by Gyula Pikler,[8] who became a symbol of the struggle for academic freedom in the university. Without accepting his unorthodox naturalistic theory of law, Jászi took from him a deep interest in sociology and a scientific approach to social and political problems. He taught for a time at the University of Kolozsvár (now Cluj, in Romania), and then worked unpaid at the Ministry of Agriculture in Budapest, getting to know the facts about the land problem. From 1905 to 1906 he studied in Paris, whence he visited England, and sat at the feet of many prominent leftists and liberals in both Paris and London. During the next few years he made it his business to get to know some of the most prominent statesmen of the Austro-Hungarian "nationalities", including Maniu of Romania and the great Masaryk of Czechoslovakia (a future hero of Kolnai's).

During all this time Jászi took the leading part in the formation of a new radical intellectual generation. Around 1900 he co-founded the Sociological Society and the famous journal *Huszadik Század* (Twentieth Century). By 1907 he had come to believe that pure scholarship was a luxury Hungary could not afford, and that his two new institutions should not shrink from attempting a truly liberal transformation of the intellectual and political atmosphere - though as a result he was nearly dismissed from the Ministry of Agriculture. Accordingly, the Sociological Society, which was now run in collaboration with prominent socialists, started a "Free School", initially aimed at opening the eyes of the working classes to the world around them and to their condition within it, but then adding advanced lectures for university students.

Finally, Jászi started his own political party, the National Citizens Radical Party, shortly before the First World War. Jászi's aim was to bring the classical liberalism of the early nineteenth century up to date, free of its later distortions. The party, especially its hospitality to middle class intellectuals, inevitably attracted elements he disapproved of, both to his right and to his left. But his political description of himself and his immediate circle is of a group of "free socialists", "increasingly alive to the errors and inadequacies of Marxist orthodoxy":

> We disagreed with the Social Democrats in our belief in the primary importance of brainwork to society, in our view of the land system as the prime factor in the capitalist order, in our advocacy of free co-operation and decentralisation in opposition to the State Socialism of the Marxists, and in our disapproval of their doctrine of the class war.[9]

Jászi was at this time attracted to the ideas of the American "single-taxer", Henry George. Under his influence he thought that the most vital need in Hungary (and other countries of comparable economic development) was the elimination of capitalist surplus value and unearned income, since this would release land for those who at present had no chance of owning it and solve the social problems brought about by the vast estates. His other great political theme was the problem of the nationalities. Jászi did not believe that Hungary could be held together simply by giving the nationalities equal rights within the existing state. Instead, especially during the war, he refurbished and championed the idea of a confederation of autonomous Danubian nations held together by a common allegiance to the Crown. This became known as the "Eastern Switzerland" conception of postwar Danubian order, and, having being frustrated by the collapse of the Empire during 1918, was revived during the Second World War, when Kolnai again felt drawn to it.

I have already emphasised Jászi's determination to found political solutions on science, which largely meant a scientific method, or even a scientistic ideology, applied to society. But he remained at heart a moralist, and this is undoubtedly what attracted Kolnai. Jászi's strong moral sense, inherited both from his Jewish ancestry and from his partly Calvinist upbringing, led him to deplore both large-scale Realpolitik and the petty and dubious compromises of the Hungarian Social Democrats; they also led him to criticise systematic thinkers of the stature of Marx, Freud, Bentham and Huxley, on moral grounds. His strongly puritan attitude to sex must also have greatly attracted Kolnai, as was his readiness to raise and discuss the "Jewish Question" - especially the moral problem of unregulated usury and those arising from the intellectual brilliance of people not historically rooted in the general cultural substance of the country they lived in. But above all Jászi was an "open" thinker, keenly receptive to new ideas, but always ready to criticise them in the light of a solid ballast of moral values. His personal influence was enormous; he was undoubtedly the leading intellectual radical of the pre-war period in Hungary.

To complete this picture of the progressivist world Kolnai moved in from about 1916 to 1919 we should say something about the Galilei Kör, or Circle, and its first president. It was founded in 1908 in the aftermath of the "Pikler affair" as a branch of the "Hungarian Association of Freethinkers"; Jászi gave it his blessing but was not actively involved in it. But its first president, Karl Polányi - another student of Pikler's - was also an important influence in Kolnai's life, though, by the time Kolnai joined the Circle, Polányi was a cavalry officer in the Austro-Hungarian army, and it had begun to deteriorate. Kolnai only got to know him in Vienna in the early twenties.

Karl Polányi,[10] who was born in 1886, always remained much more of a leftist than either Kolnai or Jászi, but was never an orthodox one. He was another original thinker (though Kolnai never rated him as high as Jászi) with a deep and incorruptible moral sense, who almost worked himself into the ground to earn money for the family after the death of his father in 1906, while continuing his study of law at Budapest University. In all his work he attacked the determinism of Marx, and emphasised individual responsibility. His economic work is shot through with the idea that "being economical" is not a policy forced on us by our understanding of economics; human beings have a choice as to how they will live. They are not at the mercy of economic laws.

Polányi says that in his day the Galilei Circle had about 2,000 members.[11] They were mostly Jewish, uniformly proletarian and often very poor. The Circle was not tied to any political party and kept itself apart from the conventional political and career groupings characteristic of university students. As Polányi's daughter later wrote, very much in the spirit of its founders, it constituted "a challenge to the backward and reactionary character of the University and the general pervasive morass of clericalism, corruption, opportunism, privilege and bureaucracy".[12] The result was a large group of socially committed youth with no particular politics, slightly hostile to the merely theoretical discussions of the Sociological Society. Polányi later wrote that there were no serious internal conflicts in his time; the membership - continually changing to avoid ossification - was united in service of "the cause": to spread the scientific world-view and bring a new moral seriousness into the university and society generally.[13]

During the war the circle seems to have undergone considerable changes, for example in the social composition of the membership and the political commitment of its members. It seems clear now that, though the society was officially neutral in politics, there was a very definite bias towards the left;[14] what perhaps distinguished the Galileists from other socialists was their openness to different possible forms of socialism. But it seems no accident that the Galilei Kör proved a fertile recruiting ground for the army of young officials employed by the Soviet regime of 1919, when the Circle, re-opened in late 1918 under Michael Károlyi, was once more closed. Kolnai wrote in his memoirs that the Galilei Kör provided him with his first experience of the totalitarian mentality.[15]

Such, then, were the main institutions of the radical, scientistic, intellectual opposition in pre-war Hungary, associated with Oszkár Jászi and like-minded thinkers. There were also "radical", or progressive, institutions on the literary and artistic front, and many individuals had a foot in both worlds. *Huszadik Század*'s literary twin was *Nyugat*, in which Kolnai himself tried in vain to publish in 1920. We should not forget also the more aestheticising and "modernist" form of revolt of the "Sunday Circle", whose centre was the young György Lukács, Hungary's best known Marxist theorist and philosopher, and long an ornament (if a decidedly unorthodox one) of the post-Second World War Hungarian Communist regime. The philosophical inspiration of Lukács and his friends was originally German Idealism, rather than the scientific empiricism of Jászi and his colleagues. They too were inspired by a moral disgust at traditional society and politics in Hungary. But, instead of setting out to "redefine and rejuvenate" the once flourishing liberal tradition with the help of scientific method and foreign models, they wanted to "transcend" it, believing that liberalism was everywhere defunct, and that the way forward lay through the evolution of personal consciousness.[16] There was, of course, much contact between individuals belonging to these various groups. But, for Kolnai, it was the world of Jászi that really counted. As he says in his memoirs, Jászi came near to taking the place of "a personal deity in my atheistic universe".[17]

***

The main forum for the development of political views at Kolnai's school was the *önképzőkör*, literally the "self-educating circle", usually glossed as "school literary and debating society". This was a traditional institution of the Hungarian gymnasium, and a place where clever pupils could acquire considerable status among their fellows. Kolnai made his first speech there in March 1916, and, in 1917, he writes, "with a few others of my ilk ... carried on a good deal of subversive and anti-war propaganda".[18] By this time practically all leftists and radicals wanted Hungary to withdraw unilaterally from the war, but Kolnai's gymnasium seems to have had a relatively permissive policy concerning the public expression of such views.

But there was a limit to this, and it is highly likely that this "anti-war propaganda" was the main cause of the "rows" at school he looks back on in his brief account of the October revolution. Much light is shed on the matter by a *Bildungsroman*, translated as *The Happy Generation*,[19] by Kolnai's class-mate Francis Körmendi. It seems highly probable that the author drew heavily on his own experience in writing it.[20] The novel gives a very good sense of what it must have been like to be at school in Budapest during the First World War, and includes a fair amount about the Galilei Circle, to which Kolnai (who joined in 1916) and some of his fellow gymnasiasts belonged. Although the circle had a subversive reputation among conservatives, increasingly justified as the war went on, Kolnai's own school did not forbid its pupils to belong to it, as some other schools did. Körmendi recounts that towards the end of 1917, "the 'moderates' [in the circle] began to complain that the Society was overdoing it". Instead of studying democracy and "advanced political sciences", or pacifist and humanitarian education, it "was now carrying on activities that savoured of Bolshevist propaganda", by trying to take away the country's will to fight. This led to "a series of quarrels which developed into such a violent feud between the supporters and opponents of the Society in the school that eventually the teachers were forced to take notice of the matter".[21] There are echoes of these Galilei Circle disputes in Kolnai's correspondence with Imre Kinszky. It sounds as though Kolnai and Andor Berei, together with another friend called Imre Steinitz, tried to set up a moderate "gymnasium bloc" within the club; by August 1917 they had begun to lose heart.[22] These cards also show that, as well as hearing invited lecturers from outside, members themselves sometimes spoke formally at meetings. Béla Menczer, who became a life-long friend of Kolnai, records in his memoirs his first meeting with him in 1917. The occasion was a meeting in Budapest at which he was to speak, Kolnai being his chairman. "In the schoolboy there was already something of the old wise man, of the erudite master and great authority".[23]

In November of that year he took part with other Galileists in a local electoral campaign in the first district of Budapest, comprising the castle area of Buda and surrounding streets. The Radical party were putting up Dr

Géza Supka as their candidate against the right-wing "Independentists", or nationalists, and the young canvassers had to distribute literature and try verbal persuasion as best they could. Kolnai's reminiscences are characteristically mixed. On the one hand, he nostalgically recalls

> those misty early winter weeks previous to the election, spent in exciting wanderings and tramway journeys through the dreamy streets of the delightful southern boroughs on the 'Buda' side,

strongly flavoured as they were for him with the lyrics of Milán Füst, whom he had just discovered. On the other hand, there is the indirect reference to the extreme shortage of fuel in Budapest at the time (which meant that much of the "literature" was used for heating), the story about the man who seriously asked how much his vote was worth (Kolnai "took fright and ran away"), and the political perceptions of the inhabitants (for one man, anyone who opposed the Independentists must be an extreme rightist, qua supporter of Habsburg absolutism, for another, any vote for a bourgeois party must mean betrayal of the working classes).[24]

Galilei politics came to a head in January 1918 when the little, and entirely unofficial, group of revolutionary socialists in the circle tried to spread their anti-war views among serving soldiers, by printing leaflets and conveying them into army barracks. The government took this extremely seriously, closed the club down and instituted an early-morning arrest of all committee members. Kolnai was included, as one of about six gymnasium student representatives, and taken along to the Central Police Commissariat to be questioned. In fact, he had known nothing of this private initiative, and, after a long and weary day spent at the commissariat with his gymnasium and university fellow-members, he was allowed to go home. The two main ringleaders were later sentenced to two or three years in prison, only to be released in the early days of the October revolution.

Kolnai recounts this incident in his Memoirs as his only serious brush with the police, and adds that it brought down the wrath of his parents upon him, but says nothing about the school's reaction. But Körmendi tells us that the authorities instructed the schools to deal severely with all Galilei Circle members. About sixty or seventy boys were given a stern reprimand and two were expelled. Some of the other boys refused to speak to ex-Galileists and sympathisers, and for long called them Bolshevists.[25] Kolnai's official position in the Galilei Circle, together with his outspokenness and conviction of being in the right, are probably the reason why, despite his excellent record of work, he was not given any school prizes or a scholarship for university study. It is hardly suprising that his parents were angry at his political involvement.

Although Kolnai was instinctively critical of any leftism with a Marxist flavour, he was certainly not averse to considering other positions than the Jászian Radicalism he mainly identified with at this time. He was an assiduous attender of lectures, and had many political discussions with Berei, who, though himself a Jászian moderate at least up to early 1918 (Kolnai and he took a walk one day to get a sight of Jászi's villa), later became a Bolshevist and an important member of the Hungarian regime after the Second World War. For six months from the autumn of 1916 Kolnai joined the youth branch of the Social Democrats, and, in a card to Kinsky of August 1917,[26] says he will probably attend a "socialist" group meeting, probably in the Galilei Circle. But two months before that he had seen a performance of Ibsen's play *Rosmersholm*, and was deeply impressed by it, especially by Rector Kroll. This character, he wrote in his memoirs, "neither a saint nor altogether ... wise, ... a borné pedestrian ..., capable of using ... even underhand methods", nevertheless possesses moral greatness, because he "defies crime and folly, and stands for the Good; for a high tradition not lightly to be cast overboard". This dramatic performance stood out in his mind in later years as "the first great experience of (his) attraction towards conservatism".[27] The Radical Party was his real political home at this time, and Kolnai reports a "beautiful" speech by Jászi at a party meeting in the summer of 1917, and, in his account of the publication of his first article and the "bourgeois" revolution, writes as follows:

Overwhelming enthusiasm reigned at the unforgettable congress of the Radical Party, two weeks before the revolution broke out ... The leading figures of the congress - Krejcsi, Jászi, Szende and, ah, Biró! - float before me in semi-delirium, since after the congress I had Spanish 'flu. After the 'flu came the news of the final disintegration and legendary resignation of Dr Wekerle and the democratic administration. After that came the revolution.[28]

One other matter is worth pausing over here, because it remains a constant in Kolnai's political writing. Kolnai's friendship with his cousin József Litván reached a peak in 1915. They met daily at this time, going for walks, playing chess and discussing the world's problems together. "Kolnai and I", he says, "lived in what was almost an intellectual symbiosis". During those few years, before they drifted apart, "he influenced my whole life".[29] But Litván moved much further to the left than Kolnai. His father died at the beginning of the war, and he had to give lessons to eke out his mother's meagre pension while attending school himself. One of his pupils had a father who was manager at a coalmine, and Litván was persuaded to go and stay for a time during the holidays in the mining village where he worked. At his request he was taken down the mine, and saw with his own eyes the dreadful working conditions of the miners. We may link this with another reference to Francis Körmendi's *The Happy Generation*, where the hero, like Kolnai, is accustomed to take long walks around Budapest. As the war progressed the streets became ever fuller of war-wounded, of hideously mutilated men, and of virtually starving refugee or orphaned families. The main character of the book (who presumably represents Körmendi) feels horror at all this. But Kolnai never writes about the ugly sights to be seen around him in the city; his highly developed sensitivity for the atmosphere of its different regions did not lead to any account of their human inhabitants. Nor are his later socialist political writings conspicuous for emphasis on the "welfare" aspects of politics. Kolnai's personalism led him to interpret political situations largely in terms of what promoted fully personal life, as opposed to the animal life of habit and sensual enjoyment; the idea that a certain material standard of welfare may also be necessary if the average man is to be able to live a life of personal responsibility is not prominent. He certainly does record in his diary notes around the beginning of 1917 "walks begin to nauseate me", and this may have been for the same reason that they did Körmendi. It remains true that the kinds of things that impressed Litván and Körmendi, and strongly contributed to their political attitudes, are, for whatever reason, passed over in silence. There is, perhaps, a hint of them in a reference to the Budapest general strike in June 1918, which was a desperate call for material help in a war increasingly seen to be meaningless (Russia had long since ceased to fight), and was savagely put down by the police. It was, writes Kolnai, "pitiable, yet heroic, in its utter defeat." But he immediately adds: "And I remember the beautiful, sombre, summer morning, walking with Berei in the City Park, and the bitter tone of our discussion".[30] The fact is, Kolnai's mind was such as always to emphasise what he considered the root of the evil. Whether or not he felt sympathy with the poor and wretched, the important thing was to address the political conditions, which ignored the question of personal being. Hence his support for Jászi and the bourgeois Radicals, who had little contact with the Proletariat, but for whom "brain-work" was important.[31]

***

Let us now return to the publication of Kolnai's first article, in the prestigious radical journal *Huszadik Század*. Kolnai's diary-like account of this, which also records some of his reactions to the war, the Bourgeois Revolution and first two months of the Hungarian Republic, was written out in a former mathematics exercise book in the early days of 1919. The publication of the article was an important landmark in his life. Hence the minutely detailed narration - and its preservation. In the middle of February 1918, he wrote, he had been reading *Huszadik Század* a lot and "began to phantasize about writing for it (him)self". He had always wanted to publish his writings, but hitherto, he says, his sights had been set no higher than book reviews, for which his "father's influence" (such as his family connection with the editor of *Pester Lloyd*) might prepare the way. Like Kolnai, his friend and cousin Imre Kinszky was also in the habit of writing things, and

> one Sunday evening, when I was accompanying Imre to the tram terminus on Damjanich Street, I asked him slyly to send in one of his articles. (In such matters I was always supremely self-interested: if he doesn't succeed, too bad!; if he does, then I'll have a go myself.) But Imre didn't toe the line, and said: send something in yourself, before stepping on to a 33 with a derisive grin.[32]

A week later, "on the afternoon of Sunday March 3rd", he and his brother are out for a walk with Kinszky, who says he has something to show them when they have found somewhere to sit. So they turn into the zoo, sit down near the pheasant house, and, after a bit of desultory chat, Imre produces a couple of letters from his pocket. "The gist of the second letter was that [editor Jászi] would be pleased to publish the interesting polemical piece on apathy as soon as there was space". "Fantastic!", writes Kolnai:

> It is clear that Aurél must write now as well. But discretion vis á vis the family! So what about? Activity and Passivity will be best. But will he publish it? Out of the question! Of course he'll publish it. Impossible to tell. But all this is nothing to the question of presentation. What sort of paper, what form of address, how do I sign it, how long should it be? - I was driven almost mad as these questions rattled about in my head all afternoon.[33]

After a period of panic - "what I have to say won't fill a single side" - he pulls himself together and starts to think methodically about it. Luckily, he hasn't a lot of schoolwork on at the time, and luckily again he "succeeded in keeping the real nature of what (he) was doing from (his) mother". On the fourth day he has completed his piece and takes a tram to his brother's flat to show it to him. Problems arise over the accompanying letter:

There was one expression I felt wasn't sufficiently deferential, but Laci encouraged me to be more forceful. When I couldn't decide between "Professor" and "Mr Editor", Laci suggested the terse and pithy solution "My man". He had no success here, but it was due to him that I became an "obedient servant", not a "humble" one. [There follows the text of the letter.] I had written "gratefull" thus, with two 'l's, and corrected it; the whole thing looked very childish, and the address got a bit smudged. But "79 Pasaréti Avenue" was clear enough, thank God. Well, that's it. Goodbye! Down below I drop it into a letterbox (maybe in Pannónia Street, or Visegrádi Street). Back at home I consult the encyclopedia to see whether Jászi is really a Senior Lecturer (since Imre didn't insert this in the address) ... yes he is, so let's go to bed! The waiting begins.[34]

Indeed, he found the waiting to be long and agonising (though in reality a mere three weeks). He reproaches himself for not having registered the letter, and for having posted it in "a remote, perhaps completely disused, letter-box in the Outer Leopold District!" Then he succumbs to bronchitis and is confined to his room:

The whole business had become known in the family as well, as a result of some gossip in Imrc's household. The situation was not pleasant. Laci sometimes teased me about it. Mother went to Baden for a few weeks; so they kept a close eye on me under the direction of the family doctor.[35]

Eventually he telephones the office, not daring to ask for the editor, to enquire whether his article ever arrived. He is told to ring again when the editor has come in. Later, he writes:

I took up the receiver again with foreboding. I put my question to the typist Emmy once more, and this was her answer: You have still not been good enough to tell me your name! Then I thought: Nothing matters any more, *pereat mundus*, and answered: Aurél Kolnai. Emmy said something like "just a moment" and left the telephone. I wait with a heavy heart. For a minute or two. My presentiments of disaster become stronger still. A colossal bang. I calmly contemplate death. The telephone clinks. I attend. "Hullo. Oszkár Jászi here!" I commend my soul to God.[36]

He notes Jászi's "surprisingly shrill telephone voice", and adds: "For this conversation, see copybook VIII, green, hard cover 2" - which has not, alas, survived.

Eventually, he had a very encouraging letter from Jászi, and felt free to tell his mother and the rest of his friends. He met Jászi at the office by appointment with Kinszky, and Jászi later suggested an expansion and some reference to Vierkandt and Lévy-Bruhl. The article eventually appeared on Christmas Eve.

Here is what Kolnai says about his paper in his memoirs:

> I concocted and submitted a paper bearing the title "Activity and Passivity in the Evolution of Civilization" - conceived in the spirit of Spencer's "Differentiation and Integration" theory, the mainstay of my official world-view, and seasoned rather arbitrarily with some bouts of political radicalism.[37]

Despite these and other self-deprecatory comments, there is no doubt that this youthful paper has a balance and poise more characteristic of an older and more experienced writer. In fact the paper's relative merits are certainly on the side of its more formal, logical, features than on the side of content. Kolnai himself said that, once he had passed the stage of fact gathering (exemplified in his mastery of the Central European Bradshaw) his penchant for "rules and structural analysis" came to the fore, and dominated all his literary output.

There is also a pleasing clarity about the paper, with its neat definitions of activity and passivity in both theoretical and practical contexts, and remarks such as "To see things objectively means to see them differently where this is called for". We also find, in the analysis of their interplay, a foretaste of Kolnai's sense of the complexity of things. Parts of the paper certainly make us pause and think - despite its crudely scientistic aspects.

Herbert Spencer, and other positivist social thinkers, were popular among the radicals in Hungary because they suggested the inevitability of progress away from social relations in thrall to superstitious tradition and irrational custom and towards a more rational and perspicuous set of social and political institutions. The key idea was evolution applied to society as such, with the assumption that sociology and psychology are simply branches of biology (itself a branch of physics). Hence Kolnai's paper is full of Spencerian scientistic terms such as structure, function, system, adaptation, and of course differentiation and integration. Hence, too, its assumption that the evolution of species, approvable cultural change, the individual's growth to maturity and the neurotic's recovery of mental health are really all manifestations of the same laws, and mental illness itself, together with war, for example, are "regressions". All this enabled Kolnai to display his general knowledge, and weld together some of the ideas of L.F. Ward, Vierkandt, Binet, Lévy-Bruhl and Freud in a skilful synthesis.

The key Spencerian idea is, of course, that life evolves through differentiation, including the perception of differences in things, and integration, which includes practical adaptive activity.

Kolnai's reasons for choosing this topic for his extremely rapidly written paper were almost certainly political, as he hints in his summary above. The topic was clearly one he had been thinking about, and we know that he had recently been involved in Galilei Circle politics, trying to defend the more moderate Radical position against the Marxist revolutionary conception of social progress. At the same time, the Radicals believed in thinking about society, whereas there had always been a tendency towards "activism" among Galileists, who were apt to despise the pure scholar and the religious thinker (Kolnai, in Comtean fashion, is happy to give religion a transitional function in society). The passivity of knowledge is a central theme of the paper; real knowledge implies mental passivity vis á vis the environment, instead of actively making up stories about it at the prompting of feeling. Only if one passes through this stage of passivity (taking in the real differences and regular connections between distinct phenomena) will one's activity be truly adaptive to the environment, and thus produce a true material or social integration. Otherwise it is likely to be childish or like that of "primitives". He certainly had the impatient activist type of revolutionary in mind here.

At the same time, of course, Spencerian scientism is very like Marxism in its belief that progress is bound to come about. The determinism implicit here really applies just as much to his favoured progressive thinkers as to Marx. At this stage he had not found a reconciliation between his belief in progress and his strong sense of moral responsibility and of the intrinsic, as opposed to merely "functional", value of personality.

The above interpretation of the real occasion of the paper chimes in both with Kolnai's life-long belief that thought is for action and also with the fact that when he was in Czechoslovakia with his parents in the summer of 1919, as described in chapter one, he wrote out a short passage of this paper in his current note-book. There is nothing to explain this action except the content of the passage, which deals with the primitiveness of revolution, when carried out by only a part or class of society, in contrast to the deliberate restructuring of society at the will of all. He now saw that Hungary, with its Bourgeois Revolution and Communist successor, exemplified the more primitive state, whereas Masaryk's Czechoslovakia was an example of the true "sociocracy" which marked the culmination of social progress.

When Kolnai's paper appeared, *Huszadik Század* had only a few months left to run. It was banned by the "White" counter-revolutionaries seven months later, and in any case Jászi and most of the main contributors had left the country or were either in prison or under threat of it. Kolnai did not contribute another full-length paper, but, apart from reviews and briefer notices of at least fourteen books, he wrote two or three discussion papers for it. In one of these he discusses the possible relationship between a "final end programme" in politics and a "transitional programme".[38] His concerns are primarily logical or structural, to suggest criteria for the distinction and to establish the proper relation between them. He suggests - here he is still moving in a Spencerian world - that a "final end" can only be one towards which there is a strong natural or developmental tendency in any case. The question is: is the socialist (Marxist) one of this kind, or is a more likely candidate the new social order promoted by Henry George (and at that time supported by Kolnai, following Jászi)? As for the relationship between this and transitional programmes, the latter are primarily constitutive of the former, they do not stand in a means-end relation to it, as another participant in the discussion had maintained. He also insists that no final end can be "absolute"; the new social order must at least in part adapt itself to circumstances. Kolnai's life-long interest in anti-utopianism and the logic of practice is already apparent here.

In a slightly longer article, written probably in December 1918, he discusses "The psychology of continuity and change in political positions".[39] This paper was clearly inspired by the fact that so many people who had hitherto supported the established Imperial Government rather quickly transferred their support to the Hungarian "National Council" and the revolutionary coalition of Count Károlyi in the autumn of 1918 (Kolnai himself emphasises with pride in his "Notes on the Revolution of 1918" that his own principles did not change during this time). He first discusses the general question whether, constitutionally speaking, there is more value in the permanence or the changingness of a politician's standpoint. He soon shows that constancy is an essential virtue of social life; without it there can be no trust, or acting on principle; all would be a matter of surrender to impulse. Nor can there be political policies or programmes without it. However, constancy can represent mere rigidity (something mechanical), and where it is legitimate, it is distinguished by its "organic" character. In his discussion of changeableness he first examines the notion of compromise, "the most important restraint on constancy", concluding that it need not amount to a change of view; it is sometimes the way to achieve "the best possible". But true change must be legitimate sometimes, since circumstances change. But again we must distinguish, say, change influenced by the mere "success" of a viewpoint (in the sense of the number of its adherents), or "mechanical switching between two ready-made points of view", and the "organic development" of someone who deliberately adjusts himself to new facts. This is not a profound paper, and it is still confined by the irritating straitjacket of sociologism (here Durkheim is added to Spencer), but it is sensible, well worked out, and shows Kolnai using his gifts as a writer and thinker to make sense of the world around him. Considering that he was still only a little past his nineteenth birthday it is a considerable achievement.

Chapter Three

War, Revolution and Counter-Revolution (1918-1920)

When the First World War broke out many Hungarians of the ruling classes thought that it would quickly bring to an end the period of general social and political unrest which preceded it. A rapid victory over the Serbs and their Russian and other allies, while Germany dealt, if necessary, with France and England, would restore the prestige of the dual system and bring back the stability of the late nineteenth century. But the opposite happened. The war went on and on, and the Austro-Hungarian armies suffered enormous losses, and had to rely more and more on the Germans. There were serious shortages of food and fuel at home, and social unrest increased. After the Russian revolutions of 1917, and Russia's withdrawal from the war, many Hungarians saw no point in continuing it. But it still dragged on, and became ever more brutal and hopeless. Hungary now had to contend with internal revolutionary threats, and with prisoners of war from Russia who returned full of Communist propaganda. The position began to get out of hand.

The Empire seemed also to be splitting apart geographically as the various nationalities tried to go their own way. At the outset of war their representatives issued declarations of loyalty to the Dual Monarchy, but as its issue became doubtful they became more cautious. Once the Entente began to talk about a complete abolition of the Habsburg monarchy in any form, the ideals of independence initially harboured by the few gained more and more support. By the summer of 1918 there were strong currents among the nationalities in favour of absolute independence. As the war neared its end it also became apparent that the Entente had made certain commitments to some of them in return for military or other support.

The forces in Hungary opposed to the Habsburg regime now began to prepare for momentous political changes. In 1918 there were defeats by the Italians, and on the Western Front. The Nationalities began to set up their own "national councils". In September Bulgaria surrendered, soon followed by Turkey, and the German military command recommended acceptance of the American President Wilson's "Fourteen Points". At the beginning of

October the Empire asked for an armistice according to the Wilsonian programme, but by this time it was too late to save it intact, as the new states of Czechoslovakia and Jugoslavia had been all but officially recognised. On October 17th the great strong man of Hungarian politics, István Tisza, admitted publicly that the war was lost. This had an immediate effect on the already demoralised army, and mutinous soldiers began streaming back from the front.

Faced with this crisis, the Hungarian ruling classes, still thinking along dualist lines, had nothing new to offer, and seemed almost paralysed. Accordingly, the leftist and progressive forces in Hungary set up their own National Council. Its leader was Count Károlyi, one of the richest aristocrats in Hungary, who had taken over the leadership of the "left-wing Independentists" during the war, since he was convinced that Hungary could only find a proper future for itself if it embarked on a democratic course freed from the dual system and the German alliance. Politically speaking the National Council was an alliance of Károlyi's Independentists, Jászi's bourgeois Radical Party, and the Social Democratic Party, but it also contained representatives of the newly-formed Soldiers' and Workers' Councils, and some other prominent individuals of a leftist or radical persuasion. Despite the bitter hostility to the Council of some tradionalists, who saw its inauguration as a revolutionary act, it seems to have been a genuine expression of the public desire both to salvage something from the exhausting war, and also to ward off complete social chaos. A great number of prominent groups and individuals, including the police and even Tisza himself, eventually either joined it or gave it their blessing.

Meanwhile, with the threat of anarchy and revolution growing ever stronger, as more and more leaderless and penniless soldiers rampaged menacingly around Budapest, and demonstrations became the order of the day, the King and his advisers hesitated. The National Council's political programme - still in the form of a demand to the King - included a new government, independence for Hungary, an end to the war and the German alliance, new universal suffrage and the secret ballot, and a Wilsonian nationality policy based on the right of self-determination. The King and his advisers could not accept this, especially as the National Council representatives were a completely untried and inexperienced political group, and Károlyi was thought to be a turncoat by the old ruling classes. The King would not take the risk of nominating him, and asked the conservative Count Hadik to form a government. Hadik, who had no party and no policies, counted on the help of the military, and on Károlyi's unpopularity in parliamentary circles. While he also dithered, the Czechs, Croats, Slovaks and Ruthenes were moving further down the road of secession. On October 30th he formed his government, provoking riotous demonstrations from the Soldiers' Council and the left-wing Socialists. Hadik ordered troops to the Astoria Hotel, the National Council headquarters, to take the situation in hand, but the soldiers refused to obey orders and tore the royal insignia off their uniforms, substituting white chrysanthemum flowers, on sale at the time because of the approaching All Souls' Day. The National Council leaders sat tight in the hotel, expecting to be arrested at any moment. There was shooting all around them, nobody really knew what was happening, but in the early hours Károlyi was summoned to the Royal Castle in Buda to take over as Prime Minister.

So began the "Chrysanthemum" or October Revolution, which seemed to Kolnai and many others an almost incredible fulfilment of their dreams. Its one casualty in the capital was the great István Tisza, bitterly hated especially because of his prosecution of the war, who was shot in cold blood in his own house. This crime was never cleared up, possibly never even properly investigated. In some parts of the country the peasants spontaneously revolted and attacked the property of the rich, and order had to be restored at the cost of considerable bloodshed. But the absence of any general fighting increased popular support for the Károlyi government, and more and more people hurried to give it public acceptance.

From the outset, the new regime, almost wholly lacking as it was in political experience and, to a great extent, political skills, was faced with some extremely grave problems. The first revolved around the question: what was Hungary's status now in international and territorial terms? It had not only now separated from its equal partner and fellow Habsburg subject, Austria, but was also now in a completely uncertain relation with the Slovaks, Ruthenes, Romanians and Croats who were loudly proclaiming their independence. And yet these peoples did not each occupy some neatly delimited territory which could be simply detached, but had for centuries, and in varying proportions, lived alongside Hungarians. The first problem was partially solved when, on November 16th, the government proclaimed Hungary a republic. But the second was a great deal harder. One reason why some people supported Károlyi was because of his connections among the ruling classes of the West. It was thought that he, if anyone, could secure favourable territorial deals at the peace conference. This trust was disappointed, and, despite all that Jászi, as minister of nationalities, could do in the way of negotiation with the nationalities themselves, Hungary was eventually deprived of over two-thirds of her territory. The difficulties were compounded by the fact that Hungary remained almost entirely isolated diplomatically until the Peace Treaty was signed in June 1920.

The second main problem was the composition of the government itself, and the nature of its political base. Károlyi's own party was small and eclectic; being in its origins a splinter-group of protest from the traditional

Independence Party, it had attracted a very mixed bag of supporters. Jászi's bourgeois Radical Party was also composite. The central core was made up of non-Marxist "free socialists", many of them Jewish intellectuals like himself; to their right was a group of advocates of land reform who defended industrial capitalism, and to its left were various socialist and Marxist elements who could not feel at home in the very anti-intellectual and largely anti-bourgeois Social Democratic Party. As a whole it was an idealist party of talent and moral earnestness, but with very little popular base. Only the socialists had this. They were the only substantial organised power in the state after the disintegration of the army, but had little conception of a common good beyond the bounds of their own class. They too were split into a Trade Union-orientated right wing, and an increasingly activist left, which proclaimed the class war and demanded more of the traditional leftist goals. Agreement on important matters was thus extremely difficult. The bourgeois Radical group began to break up as early as December, when the right wing seceded, and Jászi resigned in January, since nothing had by then been done about the agrarian question.

In *Revolution and Counter-revolution in Hungary*, Jászi is very bitter about the Social Democrats, attributing the eventual collapse of the "Octobrist" government largely to their failure to take a wide view of things. And yet, with the full support of Károlyi and the Radical Party, the government allowed the foundation of the Hungarian Communist Party by Béla Kun on November 24th. This was a fateful step. Kun, who had been a Russian prisoner of war and was among the first to accept the Bolsheviks' invitation to be instructed in the revolutionary creed, had been specially trained to carry this to Hungary. From the start, the presence of the Communists proved a standing temptation to the more extreme Socialists, who felt hampered by the demands of coalition government, and to the many industrial and agricultural workers for whom the revolution did not appear to be bringing them the plenty they had fondly imagined. But in truth, the economic situation was extremely bad, and the government could not really cope with the increasingly radical demands of the workers. In January, in response to pressure from the Workers' Council of Budapest, the socialist representation in the government was increased, and even the Radical Party found itself moving leftwards.

So far there had been no time for elections, but the appointed day was now approaching. The Communists and left-wing Socialists broke up the meetings of their less extreme colleagues and of the new rightist bloc, and caused mayhem in the streets. Eventually the government felt it had to neutralise the Communist party to make elections possible, and also to distribute some of the largest estates among the peasants, a measure opposed by the extreme left because it wanted to transfer the estates intact to public ownership. On February 21st the government took the chance offered by a Communist riot and arrested Kun and about one hundred other Communists. As luck would have it, Kun was very badly beaten by the police, and there was a liberal outcry. With the additional incentive of a Russian threat to unrepatriated Hungarian prisoners of war, many Communists were released, and the conditions of the others' incarceration much alleviated. But the pre-election intimidation was by no means over, and, as the election approached, the Radical party withdrew its candidates, saying that parliamentary government was now impossible, and advised its supporters to vote Socialist. On the following day Colonel Vyx, of the French military mission, delivered his famous note, from which it appeared that Hungary was going to have to cede even more of its territory to Romania, and the leaders and people began to panic. The only salvation seemed to lie in the East, in Russia, and, after rejecting the Vyx note, the government handed power to the Socialists, on the understanding that they would share it with the Communists. But the left-wing of the party had struck a secret bargain with Kun and his colleagues, and, as they had agreed, the dictatorship of the proletariat was proclaimed on March 21st. Károlyi, the President of the Republic, only discovered this by chance after the event. The peaceful transfer of power had been accomplished over his forged signature.

The Kun regime enjoyed about four weeks' grace before it too was beset by insoluble problems. But, in a whirlwind of extravagant legislation, "industry, agriculture, trade and finance" were taken into public ownership, the state also assuming "control over apartment houses, the bank deposits and jewelry of individuals, courts, newspapers, the entire cultural life of the country, and private schools".[1] Naturally this could not proceed very far, but it pleased the workers, now reunited, and also a great number of young and progressive intellectuals, who were offered interesting and challenging jobs in education, the arts, and propaganda. As Kolnai wrote to Jászi twenty five years on: "there were very few of us who did not lose our heads" during this time.[2] But inevitably these and similar measures could not please everyone, and the extreme shortages of food and materials could not be overcome.

Then came the Hungarian Red Army campaigns against the Romanians in the east and the Czechs in the north, in a desperate attempt to defy the harsh boundary decisions of the Entente and thus gain credibility for the regime. There were some surprising but temporary successes, especially in east Slovakia, but the Romanians could only be held back eventually by a word from the Entente, internal opposition was growing, and there was an unsuccessful attempt by the "rightists" in the government to gain more power at the expense of the left. There was also an unsuccessful counter-revolutionary rising in the capital in June, and a "White" army was formed in the South of the country, at Szeged. Certain villages attempted to undo the effects of the revolution, and these and similar attempts were met by the sanguinary visitations of Tibor Szamuely's dreaded "terror units". Anti-Semitism also became more pronounced, owing to the enormous proportion of Jews in the government. Kun and his colleagues eventually resigned on August 1st in favour of a more moderate Trade Union regime, as the Romanian troops, with the agreement of the Allies, advanced towards Budapest. Kun had all along trusted that the Soviet Red Army would eventually come to the aid of the Revolution, but when this was obviously not going to happen, most of the Reds, including Kun, took refuge in Vienna. On the 4th the Romanians occupied the capital, and supported a rightist coup d'état on the 6th. The Habsburg Archduke József then asked István Friedrich, in the name of the King, to form a counter-revolutionary government, and the nine-month bipartite revolution was at an end. Meanwhile, the white National Army, under Admiral Horthy, moved nearer to Budapest to keep an eye on things.

The main priority of the new regime was to get rid of the Romanians and to form a coalition with which the Allies would negotiate. There was systematic "official" plundering by the Romanians, who refused to budge until the frontiers agreed with the Allies in 1916 were guaranteed. In the event, the new coalition was far more rightist than the Allied Commissioner, Sir George Clerk, had intended, but, since the real power would be in the hands of the National Army once the Romanians had left, the *fait accompli* was accepted. So the new government was recognised, the Romanians withdrew and the Whites entered Budapest. The terror, hitherto largely confined to areas within reach of the army, was now unleashed on the capital. There had been several hundred deaths at the hands of the Reds, but the killings had been far less systematic. Now there was a cold-blooded retributory factor in the killings, and, in the four months from the beginning of August, about 5,000 people were executed. In addition, about 70,000 were gaoled or interned, and thousands emigrated. The retribution was meted out not just to those thought to have supported the Bolshevik regime, but also to those directly associated with the "Bourgeois" revolution as well. There was a very strong anti-Semitic element in all this, and the new "Christian Course" of the "Awakening Magyars" and similar movements played a strong part.

Nevertheless, the Entente had insisted on multi-party parliamentary government, a legitimate left and guaranteed civil rights. The leftist opposition in fact stopped well short of socialism, and anything that could be interpreted as encouragement to revolution was ruthlessly suppressed, the Communist party being finally banned in 1921. There had been much nationalist enthusiasm for monarchy, but this was prohibited by the Entente. So, in a parliament occupied by officers of the National Army, Horthy was elected Regent, with considerable powers. Even so, there was some sort of political life, within these limits, and, after Teleki's traditionalist government was formed in July 1920, the illegal terroristic activities of certain extreme rightist groups began to be brought under control. Intellectual life, on the other hand, suffered considerably from the *Numerus Clausus* law of the autumn of 1920, which limited the number of university places for Jews to their proportionate representation in the population, and there was also savage censorship of books and periodicals.

***

Kolnai had welcomed the October revolution with wild enthusiasm. As he later put it in his memoirs:

> There was something blissful, psychologically speaking, about this chaotic and improvised emergence of a "new freedom", the release of tension and "outbreak of peace" that went with it, the vague promise of a sweeter world in sight and the end of our justly hated vassalage to Germany.[3]

But this mood was short-lived: "I was immersed in a trance of silly beatitude", he writes, "which was soon to yield to bewilderment and anguish, and at the end of winter, to black despair".[4] On a more practical level:

> With a few friends and new acquaintances, I tried to set up a "Students' Organization" of the Radical Party. It very soon became conspicuous that some of the young men were only using the "bourgeois radical" mask for purely "bourgeois" reactionary purposes: in due course, we parted company. A little later, the remaining leftists appeared to discover, one by one, that Radicalism (together with Henry Georgism, which some of us cherished at the time) was rapidly becoming "obsolete" and that Communism was "the force of the future" - and therefore the proper lodestar of progress.[5]

One of these leftists was his old friend Andor Berei, and when he attended meetings of the Galilei Circle that autumn, he was laughed at for his praise of democracy. He describes his position at this time as that of a "staunch old-fashioned positivist", and notes that this outlook was far less characteristic of his fellow-intellectuals who went over to Marxism and

Bolshevism - notably the group around Lukács and Mannheim - than the various varieties of Idealism. He also records the fact that the Lukács group had made a point of "declar(ing) for democracy and against Communism" after the Revolution, yet by January they had thrown in their lot with Kun.[6]

Despite Berei's drift towards Communism, Kolnai and he, with the help of György Kovács, were still together involved in a not directly political intellectual enterprise which began earlier in the year. Béla Menczer refers to it in these words:

> In that summer of 1918, I remember that Berei gave me a roneographed advertisement of something called "The Problem Bureau", signed by him and Kolnai. "Tell us your problems in philosophy, psychology, the social sciences, biology, etc., and within a week we will send you all the possible solutions, with ample bibliographical documentation etc. etc."[7]

Kolnai himself refers to his "Problem-solutions" once or twice in his youthful notebooks, and it seems that the "firm" was still going in the late winter of 1920. There is also an exhaustive list of problem-topics in one of his notebooks, which gives impressive confirmation of the enormous programme of reading Kolnai had taken on himself from his sixteenth year (see above). Whether the bureau actually had paying clients is not recorded, but it seems quite likely that there were students from wealthy families prepared to pay for their help.

In December, as I have already recounted, his first published article appeared in *Huszadik Század*. By this time he had already written other things that later appeared, and was beginning to complain, like an old hand, of the editorial dilatoriness of Robert Braun, Jászi's assistant. The actual appearance of his paper was a relief, since his relations, who could not believe that he would ever be a writer, used to smile whenever it was mentioned. Kolnai had in fact almost stopped believing in its appearance himself. In January his Radical University Students' organisation broke up, and his dismay at the political developments grew deeper. When Jászi proposed on the eve of the Communist take-over that the Radicals should not stand in the forthcoming elections but advise their members to vote Socialist, his "anger and disgust" was mingled with grief that "this act of moral suicide" should have been proposed by his idol. This is how he expresses the feelings he felt after "the dictatorship of the proletariat" had actually been proclaimed:

> Thus ended, on that dismal eve of March 21st, the fool's paradise ushered in by the chrysanthemums of October; thus did I fall, from a spurious heaven whose taste had long turned sour, not back into a

humdrum terrestrial valley of tears but down into the chasms of a most real hell on earth.[8]

Kolnai was still enrolled in the university faculty of "Law and Political Science". But the Communists soon closed the faculty, and he had to enrol yet again - this time in the "philosophy" faculty, to study French and German. Though he never quite got over his shock at Jászi's "moral cowardice", a few days after what he then called the "Red Counter-revolution" he saw Jászi in the garden of his villa, where they together bewailed the new turn of events. But his memories of the few months of the Kun regime are fuller of personal touches than those of the Octobrists. He recalls the flourishing of gallows humour among the bourgeoisie, and rather enjoyed having to call everyone "elvtárs" (literally "comrade of principle"); when registering for his new university course he entered his father's profession as "finance institute worker", inwardly chuckling at a vision of the dapper paternal figure scrubbing the palatial stairs of the bank - where, despite the state take-over, his financial expertise was still needed. He also recalls meetings with Berei and Litván. Berei, now full of moralistic revolutionary zeal, indignantly quoted (without naming him) his wicked "counter-revolutionary" utterances in a letter to the *Vörös Ujság* (Red News), and Litván, now under the influence of "the Lukács-Mannheim group", could not share his indignation at the government's regularly printed invitation to "denounce immediately to the Red Guards whomsoever they overheard, in the tram-cars or elsewhere, criticizing the decrees of the Soviet Government".[9] Berei, as we have said, never looked back in his Communist career, whereas Litván, like some other of Lukács's followers, gradually retraced his steps towards a more "Octobrist" position. Kolnai also visited Karl Mannheim with a friend some time during this period, but found the conversation rather uninteresting because of his own ignorance of philosophy.

Kolnai writes that, when total power was handed to the Hungarian Communists on a plate, as it were (he always thought that this could have been prevented), he was convinced that "the whole of the continent, if not of the world" would rapidly be submerged in "the Red flood".[10] On April 23rd he signed a paper authorising Imre Kinszky to use any of his books or "non-official papers" he might choose while he was away. It is clear that this was a precaution taken when his family were about to flee from Budapest. But, he explains in the Memoirs, "the World Revolution lagged unexpectedly". The German socialist government had resisted the slide into Communism, and put an end to the Bavarian Soviet regime. The Whites were also having temporary success in Russia. Kolnai therefore dissuaded his parents from leaving. But when Béla Kun's government effortlessly put down the revolt of the Budapest Military Academy cadets, he changed his mind and began "feverishly" urging his parents to escape. They may possibly have also reckoned with the anti-Semitic outburst which was bound to follow once the now foundering regime collapsed. Be that as it may, the family probably left on or shortly after July 15th, when Kolnai actually made his books over to Kinszky, surrendering all right to them, in what purports to be a legally binding document. This receives illumination from the remark in the memoirs that, in those days, he "in some essential sense ... ceased to be a Hungarian", and began to get used to the idea that he would live "in exile". Accordingly, the family left Hungary (legally) for the new state of Czechoslovakia in a "Norwegian train", and spent a fortnight or so in "the beautiful old trilingual city of Pressburg" (the German name for Pozsony and Bratislava), at the Carlton Hotel in Hviezdoslav Square. Here, for the first time in many weeks, they could eat a decent meal - goulash and roast goose in place of continuous "barley and vegetable marrows" (which was certainly more than some people were getting in Budapest). Kolnai was greatly excited at the sight of a Scotch Regiment marching down the boulevard in their uniform kilts, and also at the signs of ancient civilisation under orderly bourgeois control. It was like returning to waking normality from some nightmare.

August saw the family in the cooler air of the hills north of Bratislava, at the spa of Trenčianske Teplice, where he felt acutely the loss of the mystical ambience of the old city. This Slovak interlude enabled Kolnai's father to establish contact with his many relations living in the area. By September they had moved on to Austria, where they seem to have spent their time in Baden, near Vienna, and in the old imperial capital itself. Here they stayed in the Erzherzog Karl Hotel, where Kolnai had a room overlooking the courtyard.

On May Ist Jászi had left Budapest in a Red Cross train for Vienna, only arriving on the 3rd. In his unpublished diary he records several visits from Kolnai. Thus: "September 8th. Short visit from young Kolnai". Jászi was glad to note his abhorrence of Communism and Marxism. Kolnai, for his part, recorded that Jászi disapproved of his enthusiasm for the German Socialist Minister of War Noske's resort to military means in dealing with them. His visit was repeated on the 17th, and Jászi records that Kolnai liked his "anti-Marx scheme".[11] On October 17th and 18th he read Kolnai's "interesting work on liberal socialism. But this highly intelligent young man seems so old!" There was another visit on the 21st - presumably to hear Jászi's verdict on his book - and finally he called to say goodbye on 27th November. "So young, yet as wise as an old man." Meanwhile his mother had also called, and had tried to persuade Jászi to talk him out of philosophy and become a bank clerk.[12] It seems that the family returned shortly afterwards to Budapest, judging that it was now safe for them to do so.

Not long after the beginning of the new year, 1920, Kolnai established contact with Sándor Ferenczi, the leading Hungarian representative of psychoanalysis - the beginning of his five or six year connection with the movement. He told Imre Kinszky about this in a card addressed from the Hotel Britannia in Budapest.[13] There is also a reference to Gyula Germanus, the great Hungarian Orientalist, who for some reason was also teaching Kolnai English at this time - the only time he ever had formal lessons. His anti-Semitic wife was a relation of the White Terrorist Héjjas, and would not acknowledge Kolnai's presence in her house. He also refers ironically to "Stein's new book" - presumably his brother's. Finally he mentions that his Vienna relatives have posted off to him his "NG paper", which has not yet arrived.

***

It is time to say something about what Kolnai had been writing during these two years. The "NG paper" is his first published work in German, which appeared in one of the early numbers of the short-lived Viennese weekly *Neue Gemeinschaft*.[14] The title, "Mercy and Justice", alludes to the classic opposition between love and justice, or feeling and reason, taken here as principles of social order. As in his *Huszadik Század* papers, the piece comes from reflecting on recent experiences, in this case the regime of Béla Kun as compared with that of the Octobrists, or rather perhaps that of Masaryk's Czechoslovakia. Communism is here associated by implication with feeling and religion, moderate socialist democracy with reason and "science". His theoretical framework comes again from Durkheim, with the lingering background presence of Spencer. The paper is entirely abstract, with no examples at all; he tries to show the logic of his two fundamental principles, making certain modifications as necessary, but in a still too rigid and formalistic manner. The theme is a favourite one of Kolnai's in one form or other, and, in the purely ethical sections, he makes some good points, but he spoils them by linking them too closely to political principles.

Next to be published were two papers in the Berlin quarterly *Nord und Süd*. The first of these proposes a new electoral system based on proportional representation but which also tries to ensure the personal relation between voter and representative.[15] Kolnai was always interested in electoral systems, and was always holding his own imaginary elections. When he came to live in England he joined the Electoral Reform Society, and favoured proportional representation for the United Kingdom. The paper itself is fairly technical, but, in the eyes of one expert,[16] there is nothing particularly remarkable about it. The other paper, "Are the people mature enough for democracy?", contains another challenge to Bolshevists, who claimed that the people must be ruled through a transitional dictatorship before they are ready to control their own lives.[17] In place of an end-state utopian view of democracy, and a purely formal, procedural, concept, Kolnai defends a "transcendent" concept, which is an "organically developed formation of the life of the people"; it is possible for any group of persons, but it has to be worked for in all sorts of ways.

These published writings can be supplemented by three very battered fragmentary notebooks, which have somehow survived from this period, written in a mixture of ink and pencil, and containing all sorts of material jumbled up together. The first, containing forty pages, seems to have been written during the first half of 1919. Kolnai had clearly been reading *Változtatnod nem lehet* (You Cannot Change It), a volume of poems by Milán Füst; here he places them in five categories from "good" to "outstanding", and singles out their seven "chief characteristics". There are details of a chess tournament, won by Kolnai in his own house, with Berei, Kovács and Béla Székács, giving the results, and analysing the players' "competition psychology". His mathematical interests are catered for in various other graphs and tables concerning district elections and traffic analyses (probably about trams). The "district wars" come in here also, and there are lists of the main communication routes between district headquarters. There are also poems of his own and three lists of headings for papers: "The Concept of the Organic in the Humanities", with sections on Durkheim and Spencer, "Two Different Meanings of Radicalism" and "Logical Thinking".

This notebook also contains the first evidence of his life-long concern with the imaginary future history of a Hungary which had retained its old boundaries in 1918 and gradually developed into a constitutional monarchy called "Ulászló". Here already are the names of some of the chief politicians and statesmen, complete with portrait heads, and some "official" reports of governmental changes (in the year "1956"). Later in his life at least, these imaginary events were not selected in wholly arbitrary fashion but, to some extent, in obedience to a commonsensical "logic of history", the working out of the most likely outcomes, given certain data about the political "material" concerned, and in response to probable events beyond its borders.[18] This enduring fantasy had an astonishing degree of "reality-likeness" for its author, and he used to send certain friends detailed reports of the latest happenings (which included wars and revolutions and all the vicissitudes of a complex political life) in Ulászló, sometimes including them in his ordinary letters alongside reports of his own doings.[19]

The notebook also contains an extraordinary phantasmagoria called "A half hour's journey around moral radicalism", in the form of a dialogue featuring Kolnai himself and nine of his most important friends and acquaintances (including Berei, Kinszky, Kovács, Steinitz and Litván), who all have a very small number of short "speeches". Though nominally about Otto Weininger's moral radicalism, it is, at this level, inconsequential, and yet each of the characters is featured expressing his own characteristic views and riding his own hobbyhorse.[20]

The second notebook ("1919-1920") was begun in Bratislava in July 1919. It reflects his journey with his parents (there is no mention of his brother) through Czechoslovakia and Austria and back home to Budapest in the second half of 1919. There is the same mixture of doodles, poems, stories, dialogues, article and book outlines, little papers, mathematics, chess games, etc, in several languages (including his own "Uj-Portugués"). Again, there are a few faint echoes of wars and political changes in the world outside. The most notable here are, perhaps, the few references to the White Russian generals, with whom Kolnai's sympathies clearly lay, who were fighting the revolutionaries in Russia. Amongst the "jeux d'esprit" are the detailed accounts of "Library elections". Here he imagines his own books as the citizens of a modern republic. This sample of an official report, which clearly reflects some real event, is a good illustration:

A campaign has begun in the Political party [to which Kolnai's political books belonged] to the effect that Somló Bódog's work [title unidentified] should be expelled from the right honourable books because of its author's recent traitorous, reactionary, conduct, and that if Kolnai (as "owner") refused this, there should be a boycott of the book. In the government, ministers Weininger (*Sex and Character*) and George (*Protective Tariffs or Free Trade?*) and secretary Hertzka (*The Social Problem*) supported the proposal, but it was rejected by 25 votes to 11. In the board of enquiry it was thrown out with 19 for and 3 against, but in the General Assembly, after the debate between Rédei and Somló, by 408 for and 92 against. In every case the reason was: the worth of a book is not affected by its author's subsequent behaviour.

The poems in this notebook include a series entitled "Ahasuerus". This tells us a lot about how Kolnai saw himself at the time, since Ahasuerus was the legendary "wandering Jew", accursed for mocking Christ at his crucifixion and compelled always to move on from place to place, "old, bearded, ragged, sad, a harbinger of calamity".[21] These poems do indeed express the dreariness and emptiness of everything, and his own loneliness in the world. Technically speaking, they are relatively sophisticated, but though they occasionally contain some striking imagery and turns of phrase, the inability to sustain a high level of poetic atmosphere betray the writer very much more at home in prose.[22]

Perhaps the most interesting item in the book is a short paper entitled "Courtesy towards Women". In the first part he examines three "psychological" interpretations of this practice. Firstly, it is said to be a mark of respect, based on motherhood and its accompanying dangers and pains. However, soldiers may undergo even greater perils without earning comparable respect, and women's sexual pleasure is surely an adequate compensation for child-bearing. This "respect" - for any woman as such - must then be a primitive "religious" feeling for "humanity" as an undifferentiated unity, from which men, living personal lives, have separated themselves.[23] Secondly, courtesy towards women, which often goes with a kind of jokeyness and the avoidance of anything too "serious", is seen as a way of reinforcing female inferiority, of keeping women only half-personal and making them better "hedonic devices". It is also seen as a way of compensating them for their inferiority as persons, by shielding them from its consequences.

The ethical section begins with the claim that, unless male courtesy is motivated by rational goodness towards the weaker sex it dishonours both men and women, since it presupposes a primitive stage of life (as in the first interpretation) which our culture has outgrown. In showing this irrational courtesy, men allow themselves to sink back into superstition. But women are even more to blame for conniving at this, and "fixing" their inferiority. They find it more flattering to stay in their "beguiling swamps", surrounded by attentive admirers. But they don't have to. Indeed, there is a general moral demand that men should always treat women as persons, putting instinct at the service of personality. We should form an "anti-gallantry association", which would elevate most men, clear the ground for the elevation of women and improve sexual morality.

This little paper was clearly written under Weininger's influence. No thinker, Kolnai writes, apart from Max Scheler, shook him so profoundly. Kolnai and Weininger had, of course, much in common. They were both highly precocious, self-conscious, sensitive intellectual Jews, brought up in a very puritanical atmosphere and - it seems probable - with difficult relations with their mothers. But the shock came from the fact that Weininger's philosophy was in so many respects opposed to Kolnai's youthful world-view. His relation to Weininger, in fact, recalls Wittgenstein's.[24] Both thinkers were immensely impressed by him, but both were also extremely critical of many things (in Wittgenstein's case, most things) he wrote. Kolnai himself later wrote a short article on him, shortly before the tenth anniversary of his death.[25] Here he calls Weininger "the greatest moral thinker of our times", praising him for his championship of a fundamental moral individualism which had nothing to do with selfishness, and for the hitherto unequalled single-mindedness with which he tried "to disclose the connections and meanings within the phenomena" of sexuality. Many people, he says, falsely assumed that his anti-feminism was his central motive. Despite the bias and distortion that had crept into his account of women, his chief target was not really women but sexuality itself, "which contains in condensed form all that is immoral, and all that opposes personality", by breaking down personal boundaries, taking away free will, promoting the use of others for pleasure and promoting the animal in man at the expense of the spiritual. It took his conversion to Catholicism to show him the error of Weininger's claim that all sexual pleasure, within wedlock or out of it, is exploitative and immoral.[26] Already in the *Tuz* paper he rejects the "systematic" elements of Weininger's moral thought; two and a half years later he can see that a major source of Weininger's claims about women and sex was his "blindness for the problem of limitation", with its invariable consequence, "blindness for important concrete principles".[27]

***

In June Kolnai left Budapest with his family for Baden and Vienna, fully intending never to live in Budapest again. There were several reasons for this. Firstly, he could see no future for himself in counter-revolutionary Hungary as the free and independent thinker he aspired to be. Secondly, he knew now that his family would never support him in this role in any case, and needed to get into freer air, and take advantage of the much better chances of living by his pen afforded by Vienna. Thirdly, he simply needed to get away from the haunts of his childhood and youth, now irrevocably tarnished with the failure of his early hopes, with "the whole sadness and the whole bitterness of that decaying world", as Béla Menczer put it.[28] Fourthly, he was still afraid that his very modest role in the October revolution might eventually catch up with him. More to the point, perhaps, he might be tempted into disobeying one of the new laws designed to discourage anything of the sort breaking out again. No doubt he was at one level sad at this departure; but on the whole he was glad, and looked forward eagerly to establishing himself as a leading writer and publicist in what was, he already knew, a much pleasanter and greater city.

Chapter Four

Kolnai's Psychoanalytic Episode (1920-1926)

Kolnai had returned to counter-revolutionary Budapest with his family before Christmas 1919. Early in 1920 he wrote to Sándor Ferenczi, the leader of the Hungarian psychoanalysts, expressing his keen interest in the cultural implications of psychoanalysis and "correcting a misinterpretation of Spencer's philosophy in one of his essays". This elicited an invitation to call, and in early February Kolnai told Imre Kinszky that he and Ferenczi had had a good talk. "Struck by my suggestion", he goes on in the memoirs,

> that psychoanalytic conceptions might provide a spiritual weapon against Marxism and Bolshevism and perhaps against Reaction as well, he commissioned me to write two papers with this end in view.[1]

The first of these, entitled "The Relevance of Psychoanalysis to Sociology", was duly delivered to the Budapest association on April 18th. Kolnai was elected as a member that very day, and Ferenczi lost no time in writing to Freud about his new protégé:

> Today we heard an outstanding paper by a new member called Aurel Kolnai on "Psychoanalysis and Sociology". So much psychoanalytical understanding on the part of a young man with no previous contact with us could not have been foreseen. Since I know you are especially interested in social psychological questions at present I have asked him to send a copy direct to your address ...[2]

The second paper could not be delivered in Budapest because of Kolnai's move to Vienna. Here he quickly established contact with Otto Rank, a lay analyst and editor of *Imago*, the periodical dealing with the cultural as opposed to the clinical and scientific side of psychoanalysis, who soon commissioned several book reviews and another paper, and seems to have taken over Ferenczi's role as his patron. On October 16th the latter wrote to Freud saying how disappointed he was that he "had to lose him so soon after his discovery", and expressing his impatience to know how "he will go down in your own circle". "The Psychology of Anarcho-Communism", the second paper Ferenczi had commissioned, was in fact delivered before the Vienna group on October 29th. On the 31st Freud wrote to Ferenczi as follows:

> Kolnai made a generally good impression in our session the day before yesterday. But really he did little more than translate sociology into psychoanalytic language, and was completely eclipsed by the following speaker, Radó, whose highly intelligent talk showed how analysis could really be used to shed light on sociological phenomena.[3]

Writing over thirty years later, Kolnai clearly expressed the substance of Freud's deflating yet just criticism in his memoirs, and wholeheartedly endorsed it. At the time, however, he was not yet ready to see the matter in this light. In his postcard to Kinszky the day after the meeting he promises to send "a detailed hand-written report of the interesting discussion and humorous incidents arising out of yesterday evening's lecture". Though Freud may have "seen through" him, others were clearly impressed - or at least made allowances for his extreme youth, and looked forward to putting him right in time. The occasion as a whole, with Kolnai passionately defending his interpretations before the assembly of cigar-puffing celebrities, must have been highly gratifying to him.

The two papers had already been printed (in German) as a brochure before the second was delivered, and appeared very soon afterwards as volume nine of the International Psychoanalytical Library, entitled *Psychoanalyse und Soziologie.* "As if that were not enough", adds Kolnai, the booklet was also put into English and published the following year.[4] He got one hundred Hungarian Crowns for the German text and five pounds sterling for the English translation. Negotiations continued well into 1921 with the Dick Press, in Budapest, over a revised Hungarian edition with an introduction by Ferenczi, but these came to nothing in the end.

Here is the psychoanalyst Theodor Reik's account of the little book in a 1921 article about the International Psychoanalytical Library:

> In a programmatic work Kolnai demonstrates the importance of psychoanalysis for a deeper understanding of social problems by tracing back the mass-movements of Bolshevism, Anarcho-Communism, etc., to their unconscious roots, and by trying to display the hidden yet dynamic psychological factors which have influenced the development of these social movements. The new methods that Kolnai looks for in sociological research are marked out by the great importance he ascribes

to psychoanalysis in the scientific understanding of the psychological aspects of the problems.[5]

Kolnai himself also briefly summarised his own work at the time in a short pseudonymous article entitled "Freud, the Social Psychologist":

> Kolnai undertakes to harness psychoanalysis to the wagon of Durkheim's sociology and individualist social reform, and, taking issue with Federn, sees progress in the complete eclipse of the status of the primeval horde.[6]

We may compare this with his mature judgement. In the first part, he says,

> I tinkered at a parallel between the Freudian aim of "raising the mind to a higher level of consciousness" and Durkheim's theory of *solidarité organique* based on the division of labour (as opposed to tribal and religious *solidarité mécanique*) ...

(This, of course, has much in common with "Activity and Passivity in the Development of Civilisation".) In the second part, he goes on,

> [I] "psycho-analysed" the Marxist system as a form of "paranoia", proletarian class fraternity as a "neurotic" expression of "homo-eroticism" (probably the silliest rubbish I ever concocted in my life), and what I called "Anarchist Communism" as a sort of collective "schizophrenia" (religion being, according to Freud, merely a collective "compulsion neurosis") ...[7]

Paul Federn, with whom Kolnai briefly takes issue over "the primeval horde", was the first to extend Freud's line of investigation in *Totem and Tabu* (largely about primitive religion) to social and political questions. As vice-chairman of the Vienna group, with his "stagy-looking (yet genuine) blue-black Assyrian beard",[8] he must have seemed a formidable adversary. There was in fact a contemporary political issue here: how was one to evaluate the Russian revolution? In his book, Federn, writing in 1918, had seen the revolution as "the way of saying goodbye to prehistory", as an advance from a society in which all authority relationships have the emotional colour of father-son relationships to one where all men are equal brothers and rule themselves. His political conclusion was the superiority of the "soviet" or "council" system of government, as opposed to dictatorship of the proletariat, which would mark a return to paternalism.[9] Kolnai, however, identifies the equality of brothers with the anarchism of "the primeval horde". The revolution therefore marked a regression from paternalism to anarchy. The proper solution was to distinguish between types of paternalism, between "the older, despotic, form" ("Feudalism" once more) and "the more progressive, ruling and organising form". Authority-relations are essential in society, but they need to be sublimated. Indeed, since all ought to be property-owners, the true desideratum is not a society where all are brothers, but one where there are "neither fathers nor sons" but only rational persons. When Kolnai delivered his paper, he tells us, Federn

> read into [his] point a reactionary emphasis, and in a tone of friendly banter remarked how surprised he was to see a young man side with the Fathers rather than with the Sons and with the White cause as against the Red.[10]

Kolnai, of course, with his "radicalist" solutions in mind, favoured neither, though after thirty years or so he could write of Federn's "banter": "Bless his soul! I would fain believe that he was not really wide of the mark but in fact read my heart better than I did myself".[11]

Perhaps Freud's dismissive judgement of his second paper made him think a little more about what he was doing. At any rate, by the end of the year he was beginning to have some doubts about psychoanalysis, noting with concern that an article which "very convincingly called in question" a well-known psychoanalytic test ("the experiment of numbers formed at random") was passed over in silence in the official organs,[12] and by February 1921 he could tell Milán Füst that he was "no longer very interested in psychoanalysis by itself".[13] However, five days after writing his letter to Füst he gave a short paper to the Vienna group on sadism and masochism, and attended another session of short papers in May. By this time he also had a close friend of his own age in the society, the Englishman Eric Hiller, with whom he visited Jászi.[14] After the war the *International Journal of Psychoanalysis* was edited by Ernest Jones in London, though printed in Vienna. In order to avoid the problems arising from this double location, Hiller, Jones' assistant, was sent to Vienna in December 1920 to work on the journal there. Kolnai and he soon became friends, and spent many evenings in each other's company. By summer 1921 the two of them were frequently together with Kolnai's cousin, Pál Winkler, who was also interested in philosophy. No doubt his misgivings about Freudism were frequently aired between them.

Eric Hiller found it difficult to work with Otto Rank, who ran the psychoanalytic press, since Rank was becoming more and more neurotic. The growing tension between them may have affected Kolnai's relation with Rank also, and in the summer of 1921 his allegiance to the movement received a serious blow. Sigmund Haller was both a pupil of György Széll, the musician son of Kolnai's mother's cousin, with whom he lodged, and also a patient of Dr Rank:

> When making the acquaintance of Sigmund Haller in the previous winter I had talked to him with imprudent freedom about various subjects, mentioning, for instance, that I thought more of Dr Reik than of Dr Rank; a day or two afterwards, I had seen Dr Rank at his office, and he had warned me with a significant look that it was forbidden to a patient to read psychoanalytical stuff other than that assigned to him by the analyst, or to discuss psychoanalytic matters with anyone except the analyst, to whom, by the way, he was strictly obliged to report, without reticence, all the experiences and thoughts that in any way occupied his mind.

During the summer Kolnai let out something he had heard about Dr Rank to Haller and Hiller, and asked his friends not to let it go any further. Haller immediately announced that he would have to tell Rank, his analyst, thus casting to the winds "the command of gentlemanly discretion", which Kolnai had assumed would override the analyst's precepts:

> Was I not confronted here with a new aspect of totalitarian tyranny? My contacts with the psychoanalytic movement were henceforth few and far between, though I formally left the Psychoanalytical Association in the Spring of 1925 only.[15]

This dawning revulsion, however, did not prevent Kolnai from continuing to write in the official organs, and attending some meetings. It may also have led him to give more play to his "gadfly" activity than his constructive talents - hardly a popular move in a group which had already lost at least two "heretics" (Jung and Adler) and their disciples. There is a suggestion of this in the official report of the meeting of October 26th 1921, where he is recorded as having "put forward some problems over the relation between Ego-drives and sexual drives".[16] A list of Kolnai's awkward questions follows. Such questions are, in fact, of the kind that drove Freud to keep readjusting his own ideas - at any rate as Kolnai reconstructs his thought in his review of *The Ego and the Id*.[17] It is therefore possible that Freud profited from them. Rank seems to have started to turn down written contributions of Kolnai's from about this time, but on March 15th 1922 Kolnai is listed among the contributors to a discussion of Dr Fokschaner's paper on chess, and clearly shared Freud's dismissive assessment of it, as he records in his memoirs. But in the autumn of that year Eric Hiller, unable to work any more with Rank, had resigned, and around this time conversations with Karl Polányi strengthened his growing conviction that there was something morally dubious about the movement.

The question arises: why did he not leave it sooner? Clearly his more trivial reasons for an interest in psychoanalysis (for example, its "debunking" potential and "detective story" aspects) no longer had much hold over him. He was, as we shall see below, very earnestly seeking a faith by which he could live; psychoanalysis was still, perhaps, a more adequate candidate than, for example, the moral faith of the Vienna Ethical Society, which he seems to have tried, and other similar organisations. In any case, he was impressed by Freud himself, and felt, no doubt, that the good side of psychoanalysis outweighed the defects. And his status in the movement may still have given him hopes that he might have a salutary influence on it, by promoting the elements he thought most important both verbally and in print. There was not a lot of scope in his short book notices and primarily reporting role in the *Bécsi magyar Ujság*, in which he wrote four short psychoanalytical pieces;[18] but it is noticeable that he rarely voiced any misgivings in his publications at this stage. This is certainly true of "Psychoanalytical Sociology", which merely summarises Freud's thinking about "Communism and collectivism", "wish-fulfilment in Communism and individualism", and "the psychological difference between anarchism and individualism".[19] It appears as a kind of supplement to Kolnai's own book, and shows hardly any trace of his own special interests. It may be that this is the paper commissioned by Otto Rank in 1920 even before he had delivered his Vienna paper, and that its publication had been delayed.

The atmosphere of "The Cultural Importance of Psychoanalysis"[20] is very different. This commission was obviously something of a coup for Kolnai, since the issue of the journal in which it appeared was a *Festschrift* in celebration of Ferenczi's fiftieth birthday, and Kolnai's fellow-contributors included Ernest Jones, Melanie Klein and other leading psychoanalysts of the day. Kolnai's paper clearly expresses his own views of, say, early 1922, though without the reservations referred to above, and show very clearly what he valued in Freudism. Towards the end of the paper he contrasts psychoanalysis with Marxism, noting:

1) Dogmatic economic monism on Marx's part; a scientific method with far greater potentiality for development and new applications on Freud's;

2) Rational interest as a universal key to understanding (M) vs in-depth investigation of the psyche (F);
3) Assumption of a pre-determined course of development (M) vs speculation confined to the empirical sphere (F);
4) Promise that all mankind will be absorbed into the impersonal proletariat (M) vs strengthening of the position of the critical personality (F).[21]

Kolnai's stress here on the formal, methodological elements of psychoanalysis betrays his reluctance to accept some of the more exotic content becoming established in psychoanalytic circles. But the article also points to factors revealing the superiority in Kolnai's eyes of psychoanalysis over his old Spencerian world view. Certainly Freudism hoped to complete its understanding of man in a biological, rather than a materialist, "synthesis" like the various forms of social Darwinism; but because it seemed to reveal the precise mechanism whereby what was "higher" in man (culture and morality) was built on the "lower" (social Darwinism relying too much on vague general concepts like "differentiation and integration", or mere "survival-value", and so on) it seemed to be much more in earnest in its acknowledgement of different kinds and levels of experience. At the same time, since it was a systematic method, making possible a "ruthlessly" scientific approach even to "the holiest, most secret and most humble" things, it also had no place for transcendent reality, and remained within the bounds of a determinist, or scientifically orderable, world.

Kolnai also makes two other points about psychoanalysis, which look forward to his own later preoccupations. One of these is its opposition to what he later called "departmental Utopianism", to the many cases in which "some natural scientific method or tendency enjoys an exaggerated, from the outset inappropriate, prestige, and, as it were, attains the position of a mystical idol",[22] and becomes the answer to all problems in the relevant department of life. Psychoanalysis, by contrast, despises all simple panaceas, and works through truth, knowledge, critical self-direction and self-control. He also commends it for its many links with popular psychology (wish-fulfilment, mental origin of mental illness, disguised sexual motivation, symbolism, etc),[23] in a way that anticipates his later claim that philosophy must begin with, and keep always in close touch with, common sense. We shall briefly return to the ethical section of this paper below.

Kolnai also published a psychoanalytical analysis of the character of Oblomov, the eponymous anti-hero of Goncharov's novel.[24] While not, of course, having much to do with any literary assessment of the book, it seems to me to be a very helpful analysis, but it is noteworthy that the psychoanalytical apparatus Kolnai uses is strongly biased towards concepts readily understandable in terms of popular psychology. This is less true of his earlier, but still interesting, long psychoanalytical review of a novella by Franz Werfel.[25]

In 1923 Hiller left Vienna. There were not only tensions between him and Rank, but also between him and Freud; Ernest Jones, trying to mediate between Hiller and the Austrians, perhaps inevitably incurred hostility from both sides. Kolnai himself was now being urged by Milán Füst, who later underwent a short analysis, to receive psychoanalytic treatment. I shall discuss the background to this exchange below, simply recording here Kolnai's straight answer: he didn't think it could help him with his two most pressing problems - what to do with himself, and how to live. When Füst returned to the topic he rejoined with some degree of irritation that, even if psychoanalysts could "prove" that "I see my parents, grandparents, brother and (non-existent) sister in a dachshund" it would leave him cold.[26]

By this time Kolnai had embarked on his university studies in philosophy, and discovered Max Scheler, who was to have a powerful and lasting influence on him. It was in fact his reading of Scheler and of Chesterton which proved the decisive intellectual impulse to his turn towards theism, with a Catholic sign, during these years. In November 1924 he delivered a paper to the Vienna group in which he expounded and discussed Scheler's objections to Freud's theory of the ontogenesis of sexual love, which was subsequently published in *Imago*.[27] He shows first that many of Scheler's detailed criticisms rested on a misreading of Freud. He then defends Freud against Scheler in the question - important in the whole business of sublimation - of whether feelings can be compounded of other feelings, or whether one feeling can change into another, which Scheler denied. In all this he appeals to experience, and criticises Scheler's phenomenological method for its inflexibility when it comes to understanding events in the real world. He ends by listing four groups of problems where he says psychoanalysis can learn from Scheler: problems of normality and pathology, of psychological development in general, and of repression, condemnation and sublimation. Closely connected with this last group are the moral problems:

is the relation between psychoanalysis and ethics adequately explained by the claim that the analysand is "given back to himself" and can now so control his drives and desires that there is no longer any possibility of neurosis? Or are some basic moral principles already concealed, taken for granted and used as criteria in the analytical process?[28]

Kolnai clearly thought there were and, in a long footnote, asks first how a psychoanalytical pedagogic could possibly dispense with some moral preferences; if complete neutrality were possible, would it not be bound to involve "repression" of higher mental contents? And how can practising analysts avoid working on psychological material that has a moral origin? Surely they cannot simply "turn away" from this fact? Finally, do not practically all analyses betray, firstly, a rejection of prevailing "social" evaluations, and, secondly, an affirmation of the work of bringing to light and then mastering "the dark corners of the soul"?[29]

The contrast between this challenging ending and the ethical section of "The cultural importance of psychoanalysis" is striking. In the earlier paper,[30] published hardly more than eighteen months before, he had commended psychoanalysis as an adjunct to ethics. There he said that psychoanalysis made ethics more profound; by bringing all its objects to light it made possible "a genuinely comprehensive and informed ethical judgement". Once the repression of certain drives was overcome a real choice between "living them out" and critically condemning them was possible; at the same time the hitherto repressed drives might be sublimated, and an "increase of cultural values" ensue. The freeing of drives from repression would also rob them of their coercive power, since the "reality principle" was stronger than the "pleasure principle". Scheler had helped him to see in detail that his former commendation might well be based on wishful thinking.

He was clearly now on the way out of the movement himself, and keen to let Füst know. A few days after its delivery he wrote that his lecture had been a great success:

> The orthodox [Freudian] Dr Nunberg, who made some attempts to terrorise me, was shouted down by the liberal youth. Nunberg really looked at me as though I were a Soviet dictator.

In the same letter he told Füst with relish that A.J. Storfer, a Hungarian writer on psychoanalysis, told him that the most complete example he knew of a psychoanalytic upbringing was that of the son of the psychoanalyst Dr Hug-Hellmuth, who strangled and robbed his tutor's aunt.[31]

On January 31st 1926 the disappointed Ferenczi, who had first introduced Kolnai to Freud, wrote to him as follows:

> Kolnai has left the association. His reason is that he's about to publish a doctoral dissertation in Vienna in which he is critical of some of the fundamental tenets of psychoanalysis. We are glad to be rid of him.[32]

Kolnai's dissertation reached its final form early in 1926, and was published a year later.[33] "The ethical outlook of psychoanalysis" is one of four ethical theory-types he criticises in the light of his theoretical insights. Its treatment of Freudism carries much further the criticisms he had rather hesitantly voiced in his Freud-Scheler paper of late 1924, and introduces some new ones. His moral critique is summed up as follows:

> The key to the ethical stance of psychoanalysis can be found in its principled unwillingness to take up any ethical stance, although this is inexorably forced on it by the very nature of its transactions.[34]

The key principle, he now says, "is by and large an untenable fiction". Many of the analyst's clients are neurotic, immature, inadequate or even criminal; how can the "will to healing", exercised in an interpersonal context, dispense with suggesting some sort of moral code, even discounting the obvious value to be attached to truth and sincerity? And again, how can the endless prying into the murky corners of the soul, especially the repressed desire for incestuous union with the mother, not in the end suggest that acting out these fantasies, or something like them, is really of no moral importance? Although this eventually boring procedure can take away from sin "the piquancy of the 'Exciting'",

> the basic attitude of ethical relaxation, combined with an intrusive enquiry into the Immoral, must inure us to the habitus of regular "calm" immorality, thriving in the absence of conscience-pangs.[35]

The metaphysical objection could only clearly be raised by Kolnai once he had become familiar with phenomenology and objectivistic philosophy in general:

> The goal of psychoanalysis, to remove the psychic realities which have inserted themselves injuriously between "naked drives" and "ordinary regulative reason", betrays a far-reaching kinship with the formal ethical dualism which we find for the most part (though with quite different nuances) in both the positivist and the Kantian outlook on the world.[36]

It is the result of

> (an) inclination to deny the givenness of values and to combine the general, abstract, construction of values with a likewise "reduced" world-material, scrupulously purged of spirit and value.[37]

Psychoanalysis, however, is uncertain whether it wishes to put the real emphasis on spirit or matter, the higher or the lower. Sometimes it emphasises the lower drives, seeing anything mentally higher in terms of "sublimation", which, he now feels sure, is always a way of making things unreal, of depriving them of their force by wrapping them in obscurity. Alternatively it puts the stress on "regulative reason", at the same time "rehabilitating" the various components of the sexual drive, and raising them to the virtual dignity of directive principles. Psychoanalysis is, in fact, simply a classic case of "that cognitive tendency which prefers to undress things rather than recognise them, and is always squinting about for coarser-grained 'behindities'".[38]

But this was not the end of Kolnai's literary attention to psychoanalysis. As a fairly recent convert to Catholicism, he was to publish two strongly critical papers in the Viennese monthly, *Volkswohl*, which was popular in Catholic trade union and university circles. The first, "An Illusion of the Future",[39] came out in 1928, and constitutes a review article of Freud's book on religion, *The Future of an Illusion*.[40] He starts by stressing Freud's vast superiority over all his disciples, and commends him for his unfashionable defence of human reason in an age beginning to glory in irrationality. After a sketch of Freud's instrumental theory (religion is an illusion, but serves an important purpose in relation to culture, etc), which is, of course, quite unacceptable to him now, he attacks the familiar claim that too much energy spent in hushing up sexual matters in childhood and youth prevents the proper development of the intellect. "Freud", he writes "has no idea of the extent to which there is "crippling of the intellect" within the empire of naturalistic thought, for example within psychoanalysis itself. He also chides Freud for his unprecedented heaping up of "constructions, parallels, interpretations and unmaskings", on which his own "extremely abstruse mythology" (Ego, Id, Super-ego, etc) is based, and, by appealing to the great artistic and intellectual achievements of the past pours scorn on the idea that psychoanalysis can now at last help man to "come of age" and substitute rational for superstition-based culture.

The other paper came in 1929,[41] and is a reply to Thomas Mann's paper, "Freud's place in the intellectual history of the modern mind".[42] Kolnai acknowledges Mann's stature as a novelist, but has no difficulty in showing that he was a confused and simplifying thinker. Mann appeals here to psychoanalysis for roughly the same sort of reasons appealed to by the Kolnai of 1923 in the Ferenczi Festschrift, as a beacon of progress and rationality in a world turning its back on enlightenment, and taking refuge in Fascism and Catholicism. Kolnai quickly disposes of Mann's simplistic "either progress or reaction" schema, and fastens once more on what he now sees as the most important error of psychoanalysis: the idea that increased knowledge about the depths of the psyche will automatically lead to what is higher and better. Indeed, he adds here, some of the contents of these "depths" may even in fact be constructed by psychoanalysis. He acknowledges that Freudism is not a simple philosophy of *Ausleben* (giving the drives their head), but repeats the charge made in his dissertation: its non-moralism is in practice bound to encourage *Ausleben*. Thomas Mann, he suggests, has confidence in Freudism because he is really an evolutionist, believing in some kind of law of human progress. But belief in progress is only rational if the world is regarded in the light of Christian theism.

Despite these hard-hitting attacks, the movement could not quite be rid of Kolnai even yet, thanks to the attention given him in the Soviet Union. For a few years after the Russian revolution psychoanalysis was accepted and disseminated in Russia. But after the Stalinist "Soviet Marxists" got the upper hand over the old Bolshevists of World Revolution, this changed. A new official periodical *Under the Banners of Marxism* was begun, and from 1925 a German edition was published in Vienna. In the first number of this, W. Jurinetz published an article, "Psychoanalysis and Marxism",[43] in which he launched a virulent attack on Kolnai's *Psychoanalysis and Sociology*. He also saw Freudism as an alternative world-view to Marxism; but he wrongly assumed that Kolnai's brisk and confident pronouncements represented the "official" view of his subject-matter, so that his attack on "one of the most zealous pupils of Freud" sufficed, as he thought, to discredit the whole system. Here is his summary assessment of the book:

> [It] is one of the basest lampoons ever published against Marxism and the revolutionary movement of the proletariat ... We hear only the voice of blind malice, so that one puts down the book with a feeling of inexpressible disgust. Some elemental hate has driven the author to heap absurdity on absurdity, to resort to such contradictions that in comparison with them the decay of Kautsky's thought appears as a high-point of logical consistency.

After summarising Kolnai's position he says that other authors (in the same field) "repeat all this, though with less expressive power" - though Kolnai himself says his text "was written in very poor German and but perfunctorily overhauled by the Publisher"! However that may be, Jurinetz's anathema greatly pleased him, especially since every Western European Communist Party member was bound to follow his line, on pain of condemnation as a deviationist. Even in 1930 A. Stoljarov could still end his summary of what Kolnai said about the various forms of leftism with the scornful conclusion: "This, if I may be permitted to say it, is the 'sociology' of Freudism".[44]

***

Before leaving this general topic I must briefly say something about Kolnai's interesting paper "On the Mystical", which he finished in the autumn of 1920.[45] This was not originally written for a psychoanalytical audience at all, but his friendly relations with Otto Rank at the time suggested to him that he could adapt it for *Imago*, by "weaving into [it] a variety of distinctively Freudian threads". Kolnai says that it "deal[s] with the psychology of the 'weird' feeling and the types of objects and situations evoking it" (on an analogy with sadness as both a feeling and a quality of things).[46] The word "weird" is really a stop-gap, since there is no single English word that will fully convey what Kolnai wants to communicate.

When Kolnai was young there was much fashionable interest in mysticism and the great religious and philosophical mystics. But Kolnai is very careful to distinguish the Mystical, as he understands it, from mysticism and the Mystic, as also from a sense of mystery and the Mysterious. In particular he associates mysticism with "a binding of the soul to given mysteries" which does not favour the development of the Mystical in the least. To call someone a "mystagogue", was to condemn him morally in the strongest way possible. To perceive the Mystical behind the surfaces of things requires, by contrast, a wide perspective and initial hospitality to the everyday knowledge of things.[47]

Part of the special interest of the paper to its original audience must have been Kolnai's demonstration that the Mystical forms a neat counterpart to the Comic, which Freud had analysed in *Jokes, and their relation to the Unconscious*. A central case of the Mystical is the phenomenon of slowly encountering something greater behind what is insignificant, whereas in the Comic, what appears significant or great is suddenly revealed in its littleness. Again, the Mystical always contains a feeling of a hidden, superior, power; the Comic goes with a familiar feeling of the object's inferiority.

However, section four of the paper is, in many ways, the most interesting and revealing. Here Kolnai surveys the kinds of object (things, persons and situations) which possess the quality of the Mystical, and briefly explains why. Many of his examples represent his own more eccentric interests, and help us to understand his obsessions. Thus, in the paragraph on "the mystical quality of things", after the easily intelligible "machines", which "seem to be examples of new life-forms", we find listed "the boundaries of cities and wards", which "invisibly determine the lives of enormous defined groups of people", have capricious ground-plans and (often) romantic names. In the outskirts of cities (that is, near their boundaries) there is a "grotesque mixture of old and new, ... a wavering between city and country". He then turns to machines, paying special attention to mills ("something really creative, bringing forth what is new") and is careful to insist that he is not talking about their symbolic value. Then again there are "locomotives, railways as such, which [apart from their life-like aspects], precisely because of their *Gebundenheit* [the fact that they are confined to pre-determined tracks] and the colossal extent of their organisation, are more mystical than cars and aeroplanes, which are usually merely romantic". Finally we must mention "apparatus run by electricity, in which the increased action at a distance and concentration of energy seem so magical". In all these and many similar cases the feeling of the mystical arises, it seems, through a contemplative approach to things, in which what at first appears merely useful, humdrum, or administratively convenient, takes on a much wider or deeper significance, to which we respond in appropriate feeling. It is surely not too fanciful to see here something like that "wonder" which is indispensable for all true philosophy. The Mystical is important because it detaches us from all practical and self-related concerns, enables us to see the world as full of meaning, significance or value in itself, instead of simply as an apparatus for human use. These more general considerations are only implicit in the paper, and only partially realised even by implication. But it seems to mark a new stage in Kolnai's career as a philosopher - though he was not yet 20 when he had completed it.

The paper is also interesting methodologically. Kolnai tells us that he had no knowledge of phenomenology until he began his university studies, but, if we disregard the "psychoanalytical" passages, where "theory" to some extent dictates the proceedings, the paper to a considerable degree anticipates the method of "Der Ekel", his most important phenomenological essay. Even the psychological parts, we should add, are by no means worthless. For example, he points out that there is an element of regression associated with the Mystical, and indeed the way of seeing which reveals it is often associated with childhood, and with those who still retain a childlikeness in their make-up. This anticipates his interest in Chesterton, and the whole approach of the paper seems to me to mark a milestone in his progress towards religious faith.

Chapter Five

Early Days in Vienna
(1920-1924)

Kolnai spent the summer and early autumn of 1920 with his parents. On October 2nd they left the Sanatorium Gütenbrunn in Baden for Vienna's Grand Hotel. Kolnai was determined to stay in the Austrian capital come what may, but it is clear that his parents would only be prepared to allow this if he took determined steps towards becoming financially independent of them in a few years' time.

Quite apart from their knowledge of Kolnai's character - which did not yet reach as far as the realisation that he would never be capable of any but serious intellectual work - they did have good reason for at least wanting to discourage him from making philosophy the centre of his life. Although Ármin Stein was still rich, he cannot have had great confidence in the future after the collapse of the Empire and other recent political upheavals. Apart from the anti-Semitism in Hungary, there was the possibility of further revolution. Vienna itself was still full of ragged and starving victims of the war and subsequent upheavals, many of them political refugees from Hungary, to whom the Viennese government was determined to provide asylum, and although the Social Democratic Party had just lost their leading position in Austrian politics, the official ideology of the party was defiantly Marxist, and the Communists to their left (both Austrian and Hungarian) were busy with plots and disturbances which threatened the stability of the new republic. In addition, there was serious inflation, not properly dealt with until the end of 1922, which obviously added to the air of insecurity. Apart from all this, Kolnai's father, now in his sixties, was now having to support relations in Hungary, and his other son, Laci, was not entirely trustworthy. All in all, it is not very surprising that his parents took the line they did; after all, many university teachers also earned money in extra-academic fields. Wouldn't it be the best insurance for the future to have Aurélka trained in something useful, whatever else he chose to do with his time?

In some respects, the few years of Kolnai's life from 1920 to 1924 are exceptionally well documented, thanks to a very revealing set of letters written by him to the poet and novelist Milán Füst, beginning in early 1921 and continuing at the average rate of about one per month throughout this period. They can be supplemented with more cards to Imre Kinszky, and from brief passages in his Memoirs. It is worth trying to reconstruct the events constituting what he himself called his "struggle" with his parents, since they were enormously important to Kolnai himself. The other major topic for which the Füst letters are a rich source, is the continuing evolution of his political, ethical and religious beliefs.

Kolnai came to Vienna on that October 2nd in the knowledge that his *Psychoanalysis and Sociology* was already in the press. He also had his book on Liberal Socialism, which Jászi had read and which only needed translation into German and some revision; he was also well on the way to realising his sketches for a third book. These facts must have convinced his parents that he should at least be given a chance to prove himself as a professional writer. But, at their insistence, he lodged in the house of György Széll, a cousin-by-marriage of his mother's, where he was to live until he had left university in 1926. Apart from the Szélls, the household also contained their son, also György, who had recently begun his internationally famous musical career, and his first wife Olga.

Kolnai for the most part loved living in Vienna, but the Széll household was all too redolent of that "family milieu" he so much disliked. In a short pencilled dialogue, "Mittagsszene" ("At Lunch"), Kolnai depicts the two older Szélls graciously entertaining their country cousins, the Baruchs, from Miskolc, in Hungary. Virtually the sole topic of conversation is the richness and quality of the food, and Kolnai's attempts to steer it into other channels are unavailing. György Széll pours scorn on his work, and he is the general object of pitying amazement for eating as though he were on a diet. Meanwhile Kolnai grinds his teeth and curses György under his breath. Nevertheless he clearly found something impressive about "George bácsi",[1] as he always tended to do with very successful, larger-than-life figures full of their own importance. To mark this, Kolnai used to call him "The Master of Mariahilf", after the Vienna district where they lived.[2] Their daughter-in-law Olga, whom Kolnai describes as a "mean person", was always complaining bitterly about their treatment, and once suddenly turned on Kolnai in a rage, accusing him of encouraging "delusions of grandeur" in George bácsi because of his nicknames. Kolnai also had a store of anecdotes about him. He had legal training, but also engaged in business. When Kolnai lived with him he ran some kind of a security firm, and both he and his wife were morally affronted when a rival organisation set up in the vicinity. All in all, this was not a household in which Kolnai was inclined to spend much of his time.

Nor was there much need to do so in Vienna because of the wonderful institution of the "coffee-house". Kolnai devotes several pages of his memoir to the Vienna *Kaffeehäuser* of his young manhood,

> (which had) something of the comfort and dignity of an English club, divorced from any idea of formal membership and thrown open to the public, yet without ever degenerating into vulgarity or being submerged by a brawling mob.[3]

Very soon after his arrival in the United States, he wrote a short article, "The Austrian Coffee-House", but failed to get it published. But I shall here insert an extract from a paper by György Litván:

> The role of the coffee-house can hardly be exaggerated in the everyday life of the Vienna emigrants, who rarely lived in decent-sized flats. The only place they could work and meet one another was the café. This is recorded in all their diaries and memoirs.

He then goes on to quote Andor Németh, a well-known Hungarian writer and literary critic, who had spent the entire period of the First World War interned in France, stopped off in Vienna on his way home, where he had relations. "On the very next day", he recalls,

> I began my Viennese life. I walked down Kärntnerstrasse and turned into Herrengasse, since my brother Zoltán told me that this was where the two literary cafés, the Central and the Herrenhof, were to be found. The Café Central was the more serious of the two, and was frequented by the older writers. The waiter pointed out Peter Altenberg's table, then accompanied me into the chess room and introduced me to an old gentleman who, a few years before, used to play every afternoon with Trotsky. From there I went across into the Herrenhof, where I was also shown round by a waiter. He showed me the young writers' usual table, where Franz Werfel also sat; that very evening he read aloud from his poems.[4]

Kolnai himself counted several cafés as "his", and practically everything he wrote during his Vienna period was produced in them. Apart from specialising in the way Németh mentions, most cafés had a selection of newspapers and periodicals representing the predominant interests of the clientèle, and, as well as dictionaries, might even have a complete encyclopedia for the patrons' use.

During his first winter and spring in Vienna Kolnai worked feverishly to get another book accepted for publication. The work on liberal socialism was gradually translated into German in Budapest by Imre Kinszky. In a spate of postcards Kolnai urges him to work both faster and more accurately. As his own German was still inadequate, he got a friend of his cousin Pál Winkler, one Ernő Paulsen, a Viennese medical student, to revise Kinszky's text. As Paulsen couldn't undertake to work on it beyond the beginning of June, Kolnai's appeals to Kinszky became ever more pressing. His own time was almost fully occupied with his "Personalist Ethics", which he had planned some time ago, though he also made an unsuccessful attempt to sell some translations, submitting his version of three of Karinthy's poems for the Rikola Press.

During that first winter he also contacted various important figures who might help him get his work into print. Jászi was an obvious candidate for this, and Kolnai certainly met him from time to time but Jászi himself was, during this time of enforced exile, "in a feverish state of constant inner crisis and mental anguish".[5] In the six years he spent in Vienna before his emigration to the United States, György Litván tells us:

> He wrote an account of the Hungarian revolution and counter-revolution of 1918/19 in Hungarian, German and English. He also attempted to outline his social and economic views in several lengthy manuscripts ... He edited the daily newspaper *Bécsi Magyar Ujság* for three years and wrote hundreds of articles for Hungarian, German and other journals published in the successor states as well as several dozens for the Western Press. [He] made frequent and long trips to meet Mihály Károlyi in Czechoslovakia, Italy and Yugoslavia, and to visit his own family in Slovakia and his friends in Transylvania. In 1923/4 he spent six months on a lecture tour in the United States. Throughout this time, he conducted an enormous correspondence which held together the first political emigration from Central Europe this century. In addition, he kept a diary, which remains an indispensable source for the history of all the post-1918 emigrés, from the Liberals to the Communists, and of their political and diplomatic efforts unmentioned in printed sources.[6]

Jászi was glad to accept Kolnai's contributions for *Bécsi Magyar Ujság*, and no doubt put in a good word for him here and there, but it is not surprising that Kolnai had also to appeal to others.

Accordingly he sought out Wilhelm Börner and Paul Weisengrün, both known to him initially from their books. Kolnai had reviewed Börner's "Peace Education" in *Huszadik Század* in 1918,[7] and was drawn to him by his earnest moralism and his interest in religionless moral education in schools, and perhaps also by the fact that the author had actually been imprisoned for a short time for publishing the views expressed in this book. He found him "a kind and cultured gentleman, with something pastoral about him". As leader of the Vienna Ethical Society, "he organized 'secular Sunday services' with lengthy but well-delivered pacifist sermons and very good chamber-music, and had a regular practice of 'lay cure of souls'".[8] Paul Weisengrün's "Cultural Politics, World War and Socialism" came out in 1920, and was reviewed by Kolnai in *Aurora*.[9] He obviously approved strongly of his anti-Marxism and his stress on the absolute primacy of consciousness; also on the claim that all "economic, political, religious, ethical, civilisational and cultural impulses are the joint product of consciousness and sub-consciousness". Unfortunately Kolnai found him insufferably conceited. He does not mention any tangible benefit resulting from these contacts, though the publishing job which Kolnai was vainly hoping to get in February may have been suggested by one of them.

When Kolnai first came to Vienna he rather "despised" the idea of university study, thinking that he already knew enough. But in April and May he did write to the German universities of Berlin, Rostock, Breslau and Heidelberg, and also to Vevey in Switzerland, to enquire about three-year doctoral courses (as opposed to the four year minimum normal at Vienna). Whether this had his parents' approval is not recorded. But he was also continuing with his Ethics, Kinszky and Paulsen were continuing their work on the Liberal Socialism book, and he was writing letters to numerous publishers, which invariably elicited refusals (however "properly boot-licking" they were, as he described the rejection of Duncker & Humblott to Kinszky). The Kinszky cards also make several references to some "scandal" surrounding his relations with the periodical *Aurora*. The second of two papers he published there certainly does look forward to a continuation which never appeared; there is also a hint that they had perhaps offered him some sort of a job; at any rate, some hopes had been dashed in that quarter, though Kinszky sounds as though he was more indignant than Kolnai.

However that may be, his hopes for the two books, and for the Hungarian version of *Psychoanalysis and Sociology*, having now almost faded away, his parents made him sign up for a three-month commercial course. He passed his exam in the New Year of 1922 and started looking for work. On 1st February he began a two and a half year traineeship with "Gefia", a "Company for Industrial Equipment".[10] Kolnai seems to have spent much of his time working on the firm's card-index, with occasional translation work, during which he learnt a lot about boilers and their constituent parts. The end of April saw him extremely bored with Gefia, and about to leave for a month's trip to Frankfurt and Munich. On his return he asked his parents if he could apply for a three year course in the Frankfurt School of Social and Economic Science. However, they were adamant that they couldn't afford to support him properly at a German university. If he couldn't stand Gefia he would have to work in Budapest. With this end in view they summoned him home to Hungary in mid-August.

Salvation came from an unexpected quarter. His older cousin, Jenő Gömöri, offered him a job starting on the 1st September. This was the more surprising as the last contact Kolnai had had with him was in a letter which he sent him at the end of 1921 more or less breaking off relations. Before that they used to meet occasionally in Vienna. Gömöri spent much of his life in abject poverty, but was always bouncing back with some short-lived way of making money. Kolnai describes him as a "crude and illiterate but ambitious literary manager",[11] though the Hungarian Literary Dictionary says that he taught before the First World War in the Faculty of Arts at Budapest University. He combined this post with founding and running the Modern Library, which lasted for five years from 1910. This was a kind of Hungarian Everyman's, though there was more emphasis on modern works, including some first translations into Hungarian. It published six hundred titles before the war brought it to an end, and was instrumental in introducing many works of modern European literature to Hungary. But as a result of the war and the upheavals that followed, Gömöri lost all his money, and he got Imre Kinszky to offer his beautiful pre-war silk ties for sale to lecturers at the university. After the White counter-revolution he went to Bratislava, and then to Vienna. Here he made a fresh start with the New Modern Library, and brought out a new literary and cultural (but definitely non-political) monthly called *Tűz*, to which Kolnai contributed. Only two issues of this (a double and a triple) seem to have been published, the second showing a marked decline in typography and design over the perhaps unnecessarily sumptuous first. Kolnai's "severing of relations" with Gömöri seems to have been partly caused by his popularising and vulgarising approach, which Kolnai thought did real cultural harm, though many of the authors from whom he commissioned work were in the first rank of contemporary Hungarian writing.

The job Gömöri now offered Kolnai, "in such a way that he has convinced both me and my parents of its suitability", combined the assistant editorship of a revived, weekly, *Tűz* and the post of reader to the New Modern Library. In his letter to Füst of July 25th Kolnai follows up this announcement with a request for contributions, with the bait that "Kosztolányi, Szép and Karinthy" have already assented. Indeed, he appears to have thrown himself wholeheartedly into this work, soliciting contributions from many of his friends and acquaintances, and leaving himself hardly any time for anything else. But it could not last. On November 1st he resigned his job on the now "disgusting" paper, though was persuaded to continue part-time for a little longer. His main reason for leaving was a straightforwardly moral one. As assistant editor, it was his job to send the agreed honoraria to the contributors. But Gömöri held the purse strings. As it turned out, Kolnai had to have a separate fight with Gömöri to get the money in every case. "I am extremely glad that this wretched period of my life is at an end", he writes.[12] We may add here that *Tüz* finally closed in summer 1923. An important cause seems to have been the action of the Budapest government in banning so many of the Modern Library's and New Modern Library's titles (the latter only amounted to six). This reduced Gömöri to penury once more, and he returned to Bratislava at the summons of his Czech regiment. When, during the Second World War, the police came to the ghetto to round him up for deportation to Auschwitz he managed to dash off, despite being shot at as he ran. When asked later what he did when he reached safety, he replied: "I wrote a poem".[13] After the war he lived in Hungary by himself in a wooden hut with nothing but a bed and a table. Awarded a literary prize in 1948, he died in 1967.[14]

Meanwhile salvation had once more come to Kolnai. Old György Széll seems to have understood Kolnai better than his parents did, and suggested to them, with Kolnai's concurrence, that he be allowed to register late at Vienna University for philosophy. This, of course, prompted a visit from Ármin, who agreed, provided that Kolnai went back to Gefia. So from 8 until 1 he worked at his "boring, mechanical, purposeless and mindless" tasks, and spent the afternoon and evening at the university.[15] This continued for the rest of 1922 and for most of 1923, though, by October he was becoming increasingly irked by the arrangement, and toyed with the idea of going to a Swiss university in the Spring. But during November he told Füst that he would definitely be leaving Gefia on December 15th, and spending Christmas in Salzburg. The probable reason for this will concern us below, but it was not one he could easily share with his father, so he was summoned home to Budapest on April 4th 1924 to sort things out, and spent a wretched and exhausting month there. This was, in fact, the first time he had been home since the summer of 1920. In addition to his fears that his modest support of the Chrysanthemum Revolution might be held against him by the authorities, he had meanwhile been attacking the regime in print, and, as an (obviously not infallible) precaution, signing his *Bécsi Magyar Ujság* contributions under the pseudonym of István Lenz.[16] But in the event he was left completely unmolested, and soon saw that these fears had been groundless. But his feelings about the city can almost certainly be glimpsed behind these words of Béla Menczer, who was imprisoned during 1922 and 1923 for organising unauthorised philosophy lectures:

> I hated the lies, the hysteria, the stupid self-justifications of the people in power. I was revolted by their murders, their brutality, their utter corruption, their flippant and haughty cynicism, their servile judiciary, the short-sighted, primitive materialism of the profiteers of a ruined empire.[17]

On the other hand he was now utterly homesick for Vienna, and resolved to seek Austrian citizenship as soon as he could. In the end he seems to have convinced his parents that he could not change on these fundamental points, and that they must continue to support him at the university without his having a job - provided he stayed on at the Szélls - until his graduation as doctor of philosophy in the summer of 1926. This was not the end of his "struggle". But, for the time being, he could study uninterruptedly without having to fight his parents for the means to do so.

***

Kolnai's summarising dismissal of the two books he tried in vain to get published during 1921 and 1922 is characteristically severe:

> (They) were a welter of utilitarian scraps brewed together unconvincingly with moods of "ethical radicalism", Oppenheimerian and similar "liberal-socialist" tenets, and utterly dilettantish "practical" proposals concerning the "cooperative factory" and an enhanced role of "personality" in democracy.[18]

Part of the book on liberal socialism appeared as two papers in *Aurora*, a periodical which filled part of the temporal gap between the cessation of *Húszadik Század* and the inauguration of its successor *Századunk* in 1927, when censorship in Hungary had begun to ease. Perhaps the papers benefited from Jászi's comments,[19] but "The sociological foundation of liberal socialism"[20] shows hardly any advance on the political papers Kolnai was writing at the end of the war, the cast of authorities featuring the usual Spencer, Durkheim, Dániel, Oppenheimer and George, with walk-on parts from two newcomers, Dühring and Weisengrün. "The ethical foundations of liberal socialism"[21] does, however, show a new interest in Utilitarianism, and, though there is no reference to Mill or any other well-known English utilitarian, the Millian themes of basing morality on happiness, each person being the best judge of his own happiness, and the need to distinguish between higher and lower pleasures (here "beatitudo" is contrasted with "felicitas"), does strike a slightly new note for Kolnai; the whole is rounded off with his by now familiar personalism.

But "Elements of Personalist Ethics" seems to have been more interesting. The text of this has not been preserved, but two outline sketches survive. It is possible to see from these what an advantage Kolnai actually had in mingling his early philosophical studies with psychology and the social sciences. These empirical studies, when combined with his natural analytical bent, saved him from too premature a concentration on the question of moral justification, and prompted him to welcome and examine all the main ethical phenomena, in a way that (as in the "Mystical" article) anticipates his phenomenology. Thus, although he is still moving within an ultimately "scientific", or positivist, framework for ethics, in line with his youthful world-view, he insists on the distinctness of moral obligation from moral value, devoting a chapter to what he calls "the ethical norm". The sub-headings suggest that he analysed this as a kind of "non-physical pressure", which, as a brief remark in one of his cards to Kinszky explains, did not remove the individual's autonomy. However, there was no escaping the form of the moral norm, "no further alternative to chaos or cosmos [moral order]". A clash of norms could only be resolved thus, it is hinted: we must be sensitive to "a dynamic degree of given value-content"; if the injustice of a proposed beneficent action - so we may interpret this principle - has sufficient (non-physical) power to outweigh a similar power urging us towards beneficence in the given case, then it manifests itself with the force of a moral obligation. Kolnai is also insistent here that the source of the moral norm is not outside ourselves - it is not a mere "social" pressure. That he was in deadly earnest about all this is confirmed by a short poem which he wrote at this time. Its thrice repeated refrain "I am not my own" encloses two short verses, the one addressed to the authority-figures of "policeman, publisher, banker, doctor", who are trying to make his choices for him, the other extolling the life-giving power of "the crystalline flesh of the Norm", which will guide him on his earthly journey and give him a kind of immortality. All this shows Kolnai's early appreciation of the fact that many of the profoundest problems of ethics arise at the meeting place of fact and value, the Empirical and the Ideal - or however else one may designate that duality which it is impossible to escape in this sphere. Kolnai may be still dependent on other people's theories, but he is also consulting his own moral experience in a way which cannot long be made to seem compatible with his early intellectual allegiances.

Kolnai's three contributions to the monthly *Tűz* need not detain us long. The first is in the form of a longish letter which has recently been reprinted in Budapest in a book subtitled "Selected documents of the Hungarian avant-garde".[22] Here Kolnai hits out at the ideological commitment of the literary and quasi-Dadaist movement, "Ma" (Today), whose émigré members he almost certainly met in Vienna. He derides the mere smashing of rules for its own sake, claiming that art is about "intensifying and sharpening forms of life". His third is a highly favourable review of Füst's short novel *Az Aranytál*.[23] The second, written in early 1922, is entitled "Christianism or Christian Culture?".[24] The official ideology of the Hungarian White counter-revolution of August 1919 was generally known at this time as the "Christian Course". Its confused mixture of anti-liberalism, anti-Semitism, anti-Communism, nationalism, and traditional-ism was an expression of almost blind reaction against the horrors of the previous two years or so. Christianism, Kolnai says, was also blindly reactive, but nearer to certain aspects of contemporary church teaching - a movement away from politics in the vague direction of the primitive Christian "community of love" inspired by such writers as Tolstoy and Dostoievsky. Most of its devotees were disillusioned Hungarian Communists. As such, it was completely opposed to the spirit of Western Christendom:

> Christianism separates itself from the Christian Church and the Christian world. From every world - from all reality and all values, except perhaps from a cloudy poeticism and a mystique with no trace of the Mystical. Nothing is so far from truth, and from the culture of us West Europeans, from industrialism, from the conquest of nature, democracy and the culture of a secular ethos.[25]

In his account of the Chrysanthemum Revolution Kolnai had included a poem in which he called for a "Kulturkampf", a cultural struggle, against Christianity as the inevitable opponent of reason and enlightenment. Now he can say:

> we are Christians, since we are not Easterners or Asians, Marxists or Anarchists, Occultists or Christianists, living thoughtless and superficial lives as opportunist quasi-Europeans.[26]

This new acknowledgement of Christianity as an ally in his fight for a personalist political order informed by sociology is one of the fruits of his triumphant discovery of G.K. Chesterton in 1919.

Kolnai's twenty four articles in *Bécsi Magyar Ujság*, many of them constituting the regular feature "Men and their Ideas", span the period between mid-1921 and mid-1923. We have already said something about the psychoanalytic ones. The other major thread running through these pieces is that of the "Catholic Revolutionary". This is, in fact, the title of his first contribution, a general introduction to Chesterton's thought. Kolnai had now been avidly reading him for nearly two years and, of late, discussing him with Eric Hiller. In his memoirs he devotes considerable space to the extraordinary effect Chesterton had on him:

> There was not present in me the slightest feeling of being swept off my feet by any potent suasion, suggestive appeal or irresistible brilliance ...; what I felt was, not that I was "accepting" anything proposed from outside, but that a stream of thought was entering me which was immediately more at home within me, more in tune with my soul, more my own, than any explicit thought of my own had been so far.[27]

So now he was able to write about Chesterton, as though the idea came from himself, that Catholicism meant not gloomy dogmatism, but

> universal and endless support of the Good and fight against Evil, wherever we are and wherever we find them. It is the duty of all to fight this battle to the end even with weapons of violence.[28]

Chesterton's revolutionary creed, he says, is not anarchism, Communism or even "honey-tongued Christian Socialism" but individualism "in the richest sense of the word". He seeks "the self-imposed order, reason and objectivity of the priceless individual soul". State-socialism is "servile", capitalism produces its own form of servitude, "the answer to the social problem" can only be "a free agreement with a property-owning work-force". "The central meaning of all revolution", therefore, is "the division of great estates among the farm workers who live on them". The famous "Distributivism" of Chesterton and his friend Belloc, which is reflected in the last two sentences, was fairly soon rejected by Kolnai as utopian. But Chesterton's essential legacy remained. Meanwhile, the theme of Catholic Revolution was Kolnai's way of marrying together his long-lingering Octobrist liberalism, with a growing appreciation of Christianity.

The theme emerges again in October 1921. The occasion was the publication by a traditionalist bishop of a book about the famous eighteenth-century revolutionary, Abbot Martinovics.[29] Kolnai points out that, for whatever reason, the bishop judged Martinovics more harshly than previous writers. Was it just a coincidence that Martinovics was an Octobrist before his time (even down to the "Eastern Switzerland" idea)? Whatever his faults may have been he did "care for the moral point of view", unlike today's revolutionaries. Early in 1922 Kolnai returns to the theme in "Merezhkovsky, the Russian Catholic", whose dislike of the Russian Revolution was a consequence of his dislike of the Orthodox Church.[30] "Christ means for him", Kolnai says, "not power and hierarchy, but personality, fuller life, aristocracy for all". The trinity represents the three ideas of the French Revolution: freedom, the brotherhood of thinking men and equality in personal existence. Finally, in July 1922, he discusses the views of Saint-Simon in "Socialist Christianity".[31] Kolnai, with evident approval, writes that, for Saint-Simon, the essential command of Christianity is that "men should treat each other like brothers". As far as there is a social and economic order this means that we should see that men's predominant bodily and intellectual needs are catered for. "Whosoever does not believe this or works against it yet professes himself a Christian, is a heretic".

Many of the elements of Kolnai's liberal socialism, with its Henry Georgian, Dühringian or Chestertonian variations, also occur incidentally in his articles on Spengler, Jordania ("The Bernstein from Georgia"), Henry George himself, Chesterton and Shaw (where there is a brief discussion of co-operatives), Follin, James Bryce, Fourier, Milyukov, and Prentice Mulford; "Book-shortage" is really an attack on the severe censorship prevailing in Budapest; "The Face of the Russian Revolution" (on Russian revolutionary poetry), "Public Life in America", and "Chinese Philosophy of the State" (following the rather disappointing "Bertrand Russell on Europe and China"), are primarily descriptive; only the article on Dühring need briefly detain us here.[32] The occasion of the latter was the appearance of a Hungarian version of Engel's *Anti-Dühring* in 1922. Dühring, a much-hounded socialist "heretic", and fanatical "jesuit" of the moral law, was just the kind of man to inspire Kolnai, with his "blazing hatred of all shams, shortcomings, hoaxes and aestheticisms", and "his belief in the reality of things and the unique and stupendous reality of man". Kolnai has no difficulty in showing how "the nagging and crotchety" Engels, with his "arbitrary, mistrustful, capricious and utterly unreassuring way of arguing", distorted his flawed hero.

***

Kolnai met a good many of his old friends in Vienna. Both Andor Berei and József Litván had gone over to Communism in 1919. The former was imprisoned in 1921, and then sent to Russia on a prisoners' exchange, where he was trained for his future leading role in the Hungarian Socialist Rebublic. But even in 1920, when a friendly sleeping-car attendant consented to take his bundles of dirty washing back to Vienna to hand to his mother, he saw nothing wrong with concealing Communist propaganda in them, and thus risking the innocent man's job and possibly even his life. This was enough to make Litván renounce Communism for ever.[33] Kolnai could hardly keep up his friendship under those circumstances, though he continued to meet the Russian-trained Béla Lándor, and "used him as an object-lesson for studying the Communist mind", while Lándor found him amusing.[34] As for Litván himself, whose medical training in Budapest was interrupted by the *Numerus Clausus* law of 1920, and never resumed, he had by now adopted Christianism, along with a good number of other former Communists, which Kolnai considered merely a foolish aberration.[35] Relations therefore remained good, and they eventually met up again at the end of Kolnai's life.

Neither György Kovács nor Imre Kinszky had become Communists. Despite this, the former was imprisoned for a time and then managed to get into Vienna University to read medicine, and he and Kolnai spent much time together. He eventually became a well-known dentist in Budapest, and, even at a distance, relations between Kolnai and "the eternal social democrat" remained warm. He also remained friends with Kinszky, who followed Litván in having his university education broken off by the white regime and making a career in textiles. He was murdered by the Nazis towards the end of the war.

It seems likely that the Kolnai-Füst correspondence began after Kolnai discussed a poem of Füst's in his article "On the Mystical".There was also a family friendship between Füst and the Kinszkys. Unfortunately, no letters from Füst to Kolnai survive, and Füst does not seem to have referred to Kolnai in any of his published diaries, so we do not know what he thought of him. But the nature of Kolnai's letters, and the fact that Füst kept them, suggest that the correspondence was important to both of them.

Throughout the early years Kolnai continues to address Füst with respectful formality, even when unburdening himself (frankly and objectively) about his personal problems, or forcefully disputing some moral point. Kolnai writes later that, although they met each other occasionally, they never really liked each other much. What drew Kolnai to Füst, apart from the fact that he was "absolutely crazy" about his writings in his youth, was his "mental structure".[36] Both of them shared the objective outlook of the mediaeval philosophers. Thus they were able to discuss without too much mutual misunderstanding, though it gradually became apparent to Kolnai that Füst's world-view was, as regards contents, primarily aesthetic, whereas his own was, as we know, moral.

Milán Füst is better appreciated today in Hungary than he was, though he is still classed by some literary experts as a "minor poet of the *Nyugat* circle".[37] Kolnai always rated him much higher, and in 1958 he finds one of Füst's last prose works to be absolutely first rate both as poetry and as

philosophy. When Kolnai first wrote to him, as a young man only just
turned twenty, he told him frankly, with much highly pertinent detail, that
he didn't usually like the loose rhythms and free form characteristic of
Füst's verse, but that Füst had established a technical position of his own
between form and formlessness, and that, in any case, all this was
redeemed for him by the "*nagyságos*" (grandeur) of the verse.

During 1921 Kolnai's letters are mostly factual, or about Füst's poetry.
But towards the end of the year they start to introduce important moral,
philosophical and religious topics. Thus, on December 20th 1921, Kolnai
responds, still guardedly, perhaps, to Füst:

> About happiness, a difficult question - there is noble happiness and
> noble unhappiness, and if the first isn't possible we must try the second;
> I believe you yourself are a hero of unhappiness,[38] while Gilbert Keith
> Chesterton is the hero of happiness; and he, perhaps the greatest living
> thinker in Europe today, is more monumental while you are more
> extraordinary, since in the end you have attained to a completely refined
> and more philosophical happiness than his, as can be seen in your new
> book.

In the next letter[39] he tries to explain why a messenger of Füst's didn't
succeed in making contact with him, by expatiating on his own character:

> for some reason I can't quite grasp people don't like me, act dismissively
> towards me and avoid any contact with me; so I'm anxious not to appear
> pushy and fawning - sometimes it doesn't work and I seem more like a
> log of wood. That was the case with the friend. I should have tried to
> compensate ...

In these early months of their correspondence there were occasional
misunderstandings on the part of Füst, who was not an easy man to get on
with. After one such occasion Kolnai writes rather fawningly back to say
how much he appreciates Füst's writing to him, and how much he gains
from his letters.[40] The atmosphere is reminiscent of that of some of the
Jászi letters of the early forties. Kolnai clearly experienced Füst as a kind of
authority-figure, as he did Jászi, and was anxious to justify himself to him -
provided he had free rein to say what he felt about things. However, two
months later we find Kolnai himself trying to encourage Füst, who seems
to have been going through a bout of depression, with the thought that the
cultural climate of contemporary Hungary prevents his work being
appreciated as it really deserves; in any case, his poetry is potentially of
much more universal interest than Ady's, since the latter is too closely

bound to Hungarian themes. Then, feeling perhaps that he has stepped out of his proper role, he adds: "but more competent people in your own circle can tell you this."[41]

Shortly afterwards, probably at Füst's prompting, Kolnai sketches out the main problem-points of his life, under six heads.[42] In general, he can never be free from care, and this prevents him being really cheerful, despite his jokeyness and his "fundamental bias towards the pleasures of life". His problems with his parents are by now familiar, but we should note that Kolnai does admit that they have much right on their side. The most pressing problem of all is that of career. He feels sure that he ought to be devoting his life to questions of "ethics, sociology, social reform and related matters", but has "hardly enough cash for pocket-money nowadays". The trouble is he is not adaptable, and his social ideas (summarised here) are completely at variance with his roots. He longs to be independent of his family, which would be easiest if he had a business job, but this brings great conflicts ... The difficulties are compounded by his sexual problems:

> absence of erotic satisfaction reduces my capacity for work and vitality; my physiological life, even more my psychological, is *Zärtlichkeits-hunger* ["longing for tenderness"]. For ethical and dispositional reasons I could only satisfy the two together and monogamously,

for which he would, of course, need money. In any case, he is "not the kind of person others fall in love with". Yet, "if my position were otherwise better, erotic ascesis would make me less depressed". Again, he feels very distant from his family, both immediate and extended, without really knowing why; although he has friends, he sometimes thinks he hasn't, and his acquaintances secretly make fun of him because of his moral scrupulousness. Lastly, he has no time to get things published and to enlarge his knowledge properly. He ends by thanking Füst "for reading this subjective letter".

That Kolnai, deeply impressed by Weininger, would have problems about sex will probably come as no surprise to the reader. In his notebooks he expressed his unease at the fact that many young progressives did not share his strict sexual ethical principles (the revolutionary youth of the Bolshevist regime were notorious for their lax sexual morals), and betrayed an attraction towards the "ethics of ascesis". Béla Menczer records that during the war the old social conventions about sex were still enforced in the kind of social circles he and Kolnai came from, but that there was a marked change of atmosphere from 1919.[43] It is not altogether surprising, then, that when Kolnai removed to Vienna, where bourgeois sexual morality had long been laxer than in Budapest, his private utopian dream was of "a world without women",[44] one, presumably, where discussion was never interrupted on the grounds that things were getting too "serious" for the women present, and where he was not tempted by girls.

But Kolnai's sub-editorial position on *Tűz* raised his morale considerably. He boasted to Füst that after a year his salary would cover at least two-thirds, possibly all of his "life-expenses". When the latter suggested that the weekly wasn't worth his attention, Kolnai lowered his respectful guard for once by fastening on Füst's mention of Ervin Sinkó, former member of Béla Kun's government, with whom, it seems, he would have to deal. "I have an implacable hatred of that pigeon-souled commander of the Kecskeméti Red Army division, more recently, my God, piss-pot bearer to the Soviet executive committee".[45] But, as regards the standing of *Tűz* itself, he, Kolnai, is not so much against "culture", like Füst, as against those who "slobber it to pieces" and always come up with something negative. He still stands by what he wrote on March 20th 1922, that *Tűz* can again perform "an important, indispensable, cultural mission", by promoting what is valuable on the current cultural scene, and providing a common forum both for Hungarian exiles in Vienna and for all the former nationalities of the old Hungary. He, at any rate, will do his best to pursue this policy. In his next letter Füst renewed his attack, saying it would prevent Kolnai from doing what he really wanted to do, and wondering whether he still cared about "an independent scholarly existence". Kolnai had in the end to fall back on the plea: "I have to live", and cited Karl Polányi as one who was also compelled to live as a poor journalist.[46] But by November he had, as we know, crestfallenly to admit that Füst had been right. Next time, he would pay more attention to his warnings.[47]

However, the next few letters show him gaining the moral high ground once more. At Kolnai's earnest request, Füst had been induced to become a regular contributor to *Tűz*, and several instalments of his *Diary Notes* were published in its pages. What neither Kolnai nor Gömöri knew was that he was about to send other self-contained instalments of the same work (with the same title) to a daily paper in Košice. When they saw this announced they had to write to the editor to make sure there would be no duplication of material. But the lack of a previous announcement on *Tűz*'s part did it a certain amount of moral and financial damage. Kolnai first wrote to Füst "in his capacity of *quondam* employee" simply to tell him this.[48] But Füst did not reply with an apology, as Kolnai expected, so in his next letter he went into the matter in detail again. Kolnai never actually demands an apology, though the "moral damage" also affected him in person, and more than once says that the whole matter is not very important, but he will not leave it alone.[49] Füst was obviously put out by this, thinking he had done

Kolnai a favour by supplying *Tűz* with diary extracts, only to have his magnanimity thrown in his face for some trivial business reason, so Kolnai tries to sum the whole matter up in another letter. He grants that Füst is right "from the point of view of moral merit", but insists that he himself is right "from the point of view of procedure". Füst was the greater giver, certainly:

> If I concede this much, I can perhaps defend myself from the grave and serious charge of constructing a rational theory out of miserliness to keep my dyspeptic nature in bounds. The matter is best expressed in some words of Ferenc Molnár ... "Principles should be produced when it's a matter of taking and not when it's a matter of giving". Quite right! - But it doesn't follow from that that we have no principles.

Füst himself must see that his "gospel of beneficence" can't settle every question in life. Indeed:

> I find it very significant that you cannot actually imagine Communism as an ideal order; in despair of this, you resort to the hopeless alchemy of hoping to get from the "heart" what the intellect cannot produce. This is merely an acknowledgement of your own weakness and moral bankruptcy. All irrationality is immoral. Why? Because it's irresponsible, doesn't add up (gives no account of itself). An organized personality must live by principles. Wisdom is the same for all, though there are different regional applications; there's only one logic, with various methods.[50]

Later in the letter Kolnai accuses Füst of inconsistency in his moral advice:

> At first you said I should think more of pleasure, and now you're recommending my cutting down my needs to a minimum, since it follows necessarily from the policy of beneficence and is irreconcilably opposed to the search for pleasure.

Returning to beneficence again, he cites Karl Polányi ("from whom I have learnt so much that is good"). His conception of it is focused on rational responsibility and solving the social question, not on acting "from the heart". And in any case, how could a policy of unlimited generosity be squared with dedication to intellectual or creative achievements?

Kolnai was relieved to receive a reply from Füst in due course, and, keeping him up to date with his "struggle" to get his parents to recognise his true nature, spells out the principles that govern his acceptance of their financial support. However rich they are (in the summer of 1922 his father and brother, together with another colleague, had started a new bank in Budapest), he has no right either to poverty or to riches, though they have a moral duty not to let him starve. This follows from the fact that he was born a bourgeois, and consequently tries to stand free and independently on his own feet. The work his father insists on his performing is not unbearable, as the *Tűz* job was, since it does not dishonour him. "It is a treadmill, not a hell".[51] The 1923 letters also give evidence of an increasing interest in religion. He even asks Füst what he thinks about his entering a religious order (Kolnai was attracted to the Jesuits). A little later he tells Füst that he has abandoned that idea:

> for that matter I'd be reluctant to give up my Jewishness. I could only enter the Catholic church with real pleasure if the whole of Jewry were converted at the same time. My ideal is the Zionism of a Jewry converted to a Hebrew-Catholic religion under the aegis of the Pope. The mission of Jewry could moreover be to work for the mutual discovery of the Church and the Anglo-Saxon world.[52]

However frivolous that may sound, he returned to Vienna in late summer after a trip to Salzburg, Innsbruck and Bregenz, as "an implicit convert" to the Catholic faith.

A new moral problem now presented itself at Gefia:

> I've got a new female colleague, with whom, according to a former piece of advice of yours, I should fall in love, since she's a very attractive and spirited woman, but I can't ask her to have a long conversation about the problems of the history of economic theory.[53]

When Füst took some kind of contrary line in the matter, he adds that there is something boring about his colleague. He had also been in the habit of making funny faces and noises, in order to attract her (elsewhere he says one of his Gefia colleagues "tried to kiss me"), but gradually realised that this was wrong, since this was exactly the kind of approach he would use, say, to a dachshund. He was, in other words, "using" another person "purely like an animal". All might have been in order if she was someone "to whom he was also drawn through psychological affinity".[54] Füst clearly found this an important theme, since Kolnai replied again very soon: "To seek a closer friendship with H.B. would perhaps be a sin; I know similar instances (a friend of mine living here) and maintain the same about them."[55] Next month he returns once more to the subject. Women are "brothers in the Lord", and it therefore behoves men to be very scrupulous in dealing with them. As for Füst's idea that one may "enjoy pleasing stupidity", the whole point of monogamy, with its idea of equal partners, is against it:

> Besides I don't find femininity as such beautiful; a young woman combing her hair in the glass is in general a disgusting sight, representing the emptiness of vanity.

As for the business of making faces, etc, one may "regress" to the position of the pleasingly stupid person with one's equals; to make a real companion of one is not good. There must always be the possibility of rising to a higher level. "We are not pashas, but honest Christians, Europeans, personalist gentlemen; let us behave accordingly."[56] A day or two later he left Gefia for good; he doesn't say why, but it seems very likely that this was his way of avoiding temptation.

Another example of Kolnai's reasoned morality in practice is his attitude to charitable giving. Kolnai's errands for Füst had brought him into contact with one Pataki, some connection of Füst's from one of the "successor states" who was living in poverty in Vienna, and it seems that Füst had asked him to assist this man. Kolnai, writing from Salzburg, first explains that his parents' allowance, and their demand that he account for most of his irregular expenditure, leaves him very little leeway. In the second place, he says,

> my parents do not permit or recommend me to practice charity to any great extent because, apart from my situation in life, it is possible that after a few years I may find myself on my beam ends; and because they themselves are obliged to support other needy relatives.

They therefore think it better that he occasionally treat himself to a visit to the theatre than a friend to a meal. However, once he has more financial independence, he will allocate a certain proportion of his income to charity, in the knowledge that there is very little he will really be able to do for any individual, and that there will be many for whom he can do nothing:

> At all costs I want to avoid what I call silly Russian, non-European, sentimentalism. Charity is an embarrassing, painful and ugly business, people carry it out surreptitiously (like some hygienic operation that takes away one's appetite) and then live normal, individualist, lives founded on the separateness of independent gentlemen, which indeed excludes charity but not giving - in the form of "civility".

The worst situation is one where a man "is dependent for his very existence" on another. But civility, "to procure pleasure for others", is fine and noble, because it doesn't "constrain" them. The crucial question about giving is then: does it create a difference of rank between giver and receiver?[57]

Füst, predictably, took a different line, but failed to convince Kolnai, so he returns to the theme. Füst is right to say that meeting the needs of the poor is a duty, but this leaves the essential points untouched: humiliation of the recipients and distaste for the giver. He was also right to point out that even the giving of gifts between equals contains "a good dose of selfishness". For example, when he gave Eric Hiller two inscribed books on his return to England "I bound the man, who was dear to me, more tightly to me, I put him under an obligation, expanded my personality, as it were". There certainly is in the normal case less selfishness in charity, especially when it is invisible and dispersed. But to conclude that charity is therefore always to be preferred to giving to one's equals leads to absurdity. Indeed, it would prevent our spending anything even on ourselves above what is absolutely needful, and thereby "destroy the constructive values of our lives, without anyone else being able to build up such values":

> From this I infer that charity is to be ruled out as a form of life and that a roughly specifiable percentage of one's income should be directed to such purposes. It is vital here to retain some flexibility in the calculations. Even so, the whole method is inadequate, since we can and ought to try and prevent the need for charity arising. Certainly human dignity can suffer whether we take the way of alleviation or that of prevention. So it is also vitally important to retain a sense of having to choose between evils.[58]

Kolnai was in fact grappling here with real problems in his own life. Béla Menczer was now in Vienna, having left Hungary after a short spell of incarceration, and was extremely hard up. The question of how best to help him was not easy for him. Being the son of a relatively rich man, he was assumed (even by Füst) to have much greater available funds than he in fact had. In addition, Vienna was full of very poor people, each representing a case of genuine need. What we see in Kolnai is a refusal to be swayed by immediate feeling, a habit of looking at issues in terms of his entire moral outlook. The discussions in these letters prepared the way for his doctoral thesis, towards which he was beginning to work, but he still had a long way to go before he was satisfied about the theory of ethics.

The Füst letters start to become less frequent during 1924, and, by January 26th 1925 a new tone seems audible. There is something more relaxed, more "everyday", about them; they are far less full of the tenacious argumentativeness that characterises the letters of 1922 and 1923. Kolnai had by then begun to settle, to enjoy his studies - now freed from the chains binding him to Gefia; he no longer needed Füst as a sounding-board in his search for a creed to live by.

Chapter Six

University Studies and Related Publications (1922-1930)

After telling Milán Füst about his late registration for the Vienna University year 1922-1923, Kolnai says nothing more about his university studies until the following autumn. He then writes that he is registering for his third semester, and that he is finding the philosophy lecture courses, of which he has already attended six, very interesting; during the coming year he intends to be orally examined on six courses, and will be speaking about ethical values in a seminar.[1]

Kolnai had originally hoped to complete his doctorate in three years, as might have been possible for him had he been allowed to study in Germany. But in fact he had to take four years (some took five) to reach this goal, and was "promoted" doctor of philosophy in July 1926. Before being admitted as a doctoral candidate and examined on his dissertation, he had to be "habilitated", and passed fit for university teaching himself (a purely formal qualification, since it was extremely hard, especially for an outsider like him, to gain a university post in Austria at the time). Kolnai's habilitation involved a certain number of oral examinations, most of them based on selected lecture series, and three on seminars, involving his own presentations, which could include book reviews. For each of these exams the candidate was awarded one of four marks. Except for his earliest course, "Philosophy after Hegel", for which he only achieved the second highest mark: "Good", he was adjudged "Very Good" in all the other thirteen examinations.

Apart from the courses in philosophy, Kolnai seems to have registered for two in economics and several in history. His main economics course was Ludwig von Mises' lecture series on "Fundamental problems of theoretical national economy", for which he opted to be examined and got the top grade. He says nothing about Mises in his memoirs, but tells Füst on one occasion that he enjoys "skirmishing with Pofessor Mises over his critique of the idea of homo oeconomicus".[2] Although he took ten history courses, and attended Heinrich Sbrik's Historical seminar, he does not appear to have been examined on any of them. The records show that he concentrated on nineteenth-century history and historiography, with an excursion back to the Reformation and - now increasingly dear to his heart - the British Empire, whose development was expounded by the "distinguished and charming" Anglophile, Francis Pribram.

Kolnai seems also to have sampled other courses for which he was not registered (for example, he went with György Kovács to some of his medical lectures). On October 29th 1924 he wrote to Imre Kinszky asking him to buy at Lántos's[3] on his behalf, out of the funds raised by the sale of his books, the Bordeaux Professor Duguit's *Le Droit Objectif*, which he intended to review at Professor Felix Kaufmann's seminar. Kaufmann, "a stalwart red-haired Jew and manager of the Vienna office of the Anglo-Iranian Oil Company", whom Kolnai "knew slightly, in private", had invited him to attend part of his seminar in the philosophy of law.

The philosophy professors and lecturers who made the most impression on him were Robert Reininger, Heinrich Gomperz, Karl Bühler, Moritz Schlick and Hans Eibl. S. Kornfeld, whose Ethics course he sampled in his earliest student days, O. Ewald and R. Wahle seem to have made little, if any, impact. It is not clear why Kolnai first sampled and then continued to sit at the feet of Moritz Schlick, the famous Logical Positivist, since, Kolnai tells us, "his system had even less appeal to me then than it has today". What is more, Schlick "was surrounded by sectarian devotees of this creed", which dismissed all philosophical questions outside logic and "'unitary science' (i.e. experimental physics) as *Scheinprobleme* [pseudo-problems]", and regarded all metaphysical and ethical concepts and statements as "meaningless verbiage". Kolnai's own name for this "Vienna School" at the time was "The Society for the Elimination of Philosophical Thought". Nevertheless, he appreciated Schlick highly, both as a man ("gentlemanly, handsome and elegant") and as a teacher, taking five of his lecture courses and attending four of his seminars.[4] Schlick also appreciated Kolnai, judging by the top marks he was given for the four courses he selected, and his "very agreeable" reception of Kolnai's seminar paper on Scheler's *Sympathy*.

The ten lecture series of Robert Reininger which Kolnai attended were

> sometimes superficial without ever being shallow, never exciting but not boring either, a little disappointing as they slipped round the core of things but most useful for the learner.[5]

Unlike Schlick's courses, whose titles suggest the more scientific interests of contemporary positivism, the Neo-Kantian Reininger's were more concerned with the history of philosophy, covering Greek, Mediaeval and Indian philosophy, as well as more recent topics. He was "a true gentleman and always scrupulously fair".[6] Hans Eibl, a Sudeten German and violent German nationalist, with beefy frame and "pock-marked face", came near to Nazism in the 1930s without ever being a real Nazi. His lectures on the history of patristic and scholastic philosophy (with a special series on Augustine) seem to have been a major stimulus towards awakening Kolnai's interest in mediaeval thought, "with its emphasis of the reality of distinctions, 'intentional' object-reference[7] and the world as an 'ordered manifoldness'".[8] Unfortunately, he was not able to follow this up at the time as much as he would have liked, being already committed in other directions. Eibl later contributed a preface to Kolnai's book *Sexualethik*.

His favourite in the faculty was undoubtedly Heinrich Gomperz, whose

tall, bulky, somewhat unwieldy figure, his huge aquiline nose and his heavy full beard, his self-assured portliness and the imperious, as it were prosperous, yet at the same time highly civilized and argumentative ring of his voice belonged to the last golden age of Austria.[9]

Gomperz was to be Kolnai's director of studies and thesis supervisor. Though he had a sarcastic turn of phrase, and was not popular with the general run of students, and although he had no sympathy with Kolnai's Catholic or his phenomenological interests, this proved a fortunate choice. Not only did he strongly appreciate Kolnai's exceptional gifts but he proved to be a born teacher, not a flag-bearer for any particular school, but a "pedagogue of philosophical thinking" and an adept at "Socratic midwifery", always aiming to bring out the best of whatever ideas Kolnai produced and helping him towards their better expression. Kolnai attended five lecture-series of his, and five times went to his "philosophical exercises" class. He seems to have remained in touch after leaving the university, and met him in New York during the war.

At the end of his fifth semester, early in 1925, Kolnai had passed all his habilitation exams and, though not ceasing to attend lecture courses and seminars, was now working mainly on his dissertation. In his letter to Füst of 26th January he writes about the increasing pressures of study. Since he had recently received permission to submit his thesis in early 1926 he has had to study even harder, and would be going to Innsbruck at Easter to write a first draft. In February he reports that things are going well with his new intensified regime. The provisional title for the dissertation is "Begrenzung und Abstufung in der Ethik" (Limitation and Gradation in Ethics), and he is putting his whole heart into it. He then goes on to tell Füst about the superiority of phenomenological ethics over other types, its recognition of the complexity and refinement of practice, as against the rigidities and simplifications of naturalist or Kantian theory.[10] It was lucky for Kolnai that the German Karl Bühler had been given a chair in Vienna the year he himself came up. In 1923 he had tried his lectures on "The Mental Development of Man", and in the 1924-1925 session he signed up for his "excellent special course on logic and the theory of Knowledge", largely based on Külpe, Brentano, Meinong and Husserl,[11] on which he chose to be assessed:

> With his bull-like stature and his bawling voice, his sharpness of mind and his remarkable gift of unbiased intellectual appetite, Bühler put a tremendous intensity into his lectures, and perhaps did more to make me settle definitively in the orbit of phenomenology than an express devotee of Husserl, or even the master himself, could have done.[12]

Although Felix Kaufmann also seasoned his jurisprudence lectures with "some ideas borrowed from Husserl", Bühler was in fact the nearest thing the university possessed to an advocate of phenomenology, which was in fact very little known in Vienna in the early twenties (despite its relative popularity in some other Austrian universities). Kolnai had already been greatly stimulated by Scheler's *Sympathy* in Spring 1924, but it was Bühler's, as it were, official sanctioning of his inclinations later in the year that made him first realise the importance of the new movement. He was, of course, already strongly biased in that direction, not only by his recently awoken interest in scholastic thinking, to which the early phenomenologists, and especially their "father", Brentano, themselves harked back, but also by Chesterton ("this Fleet Street Aquinas, this public-house phenomenologist", by far the most "powerful and formative" intellectual influence on him),[13] and before that, by his own native cast of mind trying to assert itself through its gradually disintegrating ideological "skin". Although modern European philosophy had, taken as a whole, come to impress him more and more

> as a disease and a wilful suicide of the mind rather than as a liberating "advance" beyond Scholasticism, the treasures of which had been stupidly abandoned and impatiently thrust aside by the innovators instead of being judiciously sifted and revised or completed and enriched from new sources,[14]

the stimuli received from Eibl and, even more from Bühler, had at last enabled Kolnai to find himself, philosophically speaking, and begin to construct a lasting edifice of thought.

***

Kolnai's dissertation, eventually entitled *Ethical Value and Reality*, was given the mark of "unanimous distinction" by Reininger and Gomperz, despite their lack of sympathy with Kolnai's approach. It was published in expanded form by the prestigious publisher, Herder;[15] Kolnai had to pay them 2,750 Reichsmark for a print run of 1,000 copies, in the hope that he would receive back one mark for every copy sold. The reviews, in a variety of publications, were in general very favourable, but some of them bewailed the unnecessarily obscure, allusive and aphoristic style. "Never have I seen an author so gifted with the power to write well who so abuses his power"; Jost Terhaar, writing in *Gral*, of Essen, Germany,[16] surely spoke for all readers, past and present. And yet it is hard to miss the signs of rigorous, almost remorseless, and authoritative thinking about the details of the moral life.

The extracts from Kolnai's letters to Milán Füst in the previous chapter will have made it clear that Kolnai was passionately concerned to think out concrete moral problems arising in his own life, and that he did so in terms of that great variety of general principles characteristic of subtle and intelligent moral discourse. His dissertation, for all its abstraction (which sometimes creates great difficulties for the reader), does not mark a change to a clearer and simpler moral world. From this time on, a single note can always be heard behind Kolnai's discussions of the classic moral theorists, and their many epigoni. The great systems, for all the partial truths they contain, do not reflect experience as it actually is, but represent a drastically simplified and selective model of experience. And yet moral experience, painstakingly scrutinised for its objectivity, and certainly capable of some formalisation, remains the only court of appeal. If it should turn out to be difficult to capture and systematise, the thinker must simply make the best of it, contenting himself with whatever partial formalisations offer themselves and never deviating from this attitude.

The central theme of the work is the mutual dependence of ethical value and reality. Kolnai. in his search for moral guidance, had studied the classic moral philosophers and found them wanting. Ethics is, of necessity, a theoretical discipline; but Kolnai insists that its relatively abstract treatments of the moral life must take greater account of how people are to be helped to live morally better lives. "The 'turning' of theory towards practice is still part of its content".[17] It is not that the moral philosopher is himself a practical moralist. But he must provide the moral educator and reformer with principles which take account of the general realities of life, leaving it to them to adapt these in their turn to the particular circumstances of their hearers' lives. But the dissertation is not designed as a complete ethics. Rather, it brings to light, and illustrates, certain "essential phenomena of the ethical *concern with reality*".[18]

Herder's blurb was almost certainly written by Kolnai himself. Here we read of "the assumption that the manifold of concrete moral values points towards a value-permeated ethical reality which both exists, albeit imperfectly, and is yet to be striven for". Reflection on morality shows that, in acting morally, the agent is trying to improve a world which is already good in some respects and bad in others. We meet people who are, say, models of justice, but who lack the milk of human kindness, our public institutions contribute to human welfare in some respects, but impair it in others. Goodness and badness are therefore already aspects of the real world we inhabit, and that world also includes ourselves, who also contain both good and bad moral qualities. Perhaps the first requirement of the moral philosopher, then, is to become thoroughly familiar with that great variety of morally significant values already instantiated in reality. Any moral action is action "on" a reality, including ourselves, which is already both good in some respects and bad in others, and certainly capable of improvement.

In the preface Kolnai also sums up his own philosophical allegiances. As the previous paragraph may already have suggested, he identifies with the new "Objectivism" represented by "Brentano, Meinong, [the early] Russell, Külpe, Husserl, Driesch, Geyser, Scheler, and Soloviev". Neither value nor reality is just "in the mind". His own endeavour will be to "complete" the phenomenological ethic of values put forward by Scheler and his follower, von Hildebrand. Kolnai had been enormously stimulated by Scheler's ethics, especially his key idea of the order of "material values", that enormous variety of value-qualities and types of value-qualities arranged hierarchically, and which we apprehend in experience both "in themselves" and also as objectively instantiated in persons, groups, artefacts, situations, works of art and nature, or in parts or aspects of all these and other objects. Kolnai also valued his emphasis on the human person and the personal value-essence,[19] on love, reverence and dedication, and on his identification of the highest Value with God. But Scheler's value ethics denies the independent moral significance of the end or goal of action. For him morally good action was a matter of giving precedence to the higher value (justice rather than self-interest, for example) as a kind of self-expression. This did in fact make one a better person. But he denied that the *goal* of self-improvement was morally good at all; it was blatant Pharisaism. Kolnai points out that all action in the proper sense contains some reference to an end, and that this is nearly always morally significant and sometimes the most significant thing about it. This "one-sidedness" of phenomenological ethics, the result of its "somewhat over-exclusive concern with the world of values 'in itself', and an inadequate treatment of its relations with reality", led Kolnai to think that "some borrowing from the older teleological ethics was absolutely necessary".[20] To quote Kolnai's blurb once more, if one is seriously concerned with reality, "Value ethics turns into an 'ethics of end' (in the neo-scholastic sense) without one's having to give up the advantages of the phenomenological method".

Kolnai introduces three key ideas into his adaptation of value-ethics. The first of these, and the one that gives the least trouble, is that of "limitation". In the first place, values limit one another:

> Theoretical ethics must recognise that, although the Good is unlimited in a dynamic sense, in that it can never be completely realised ..., it does not at all have to be unlimited as regards its particular contents. Peace is a value, but it does not follow that the complete disappearance of struggle is good; chastity is a value, but it does not follow that the complete disappearance of sexual activity is good; sacrifice is a value, but it does not follow that complete disregard of one's own advantage is good.[21]

Moral and political projects and reforms are also limited by the presuppositions of reality. There has to be sufficient ethical will and moral energy. In addition (Kolnai is here summarising chapter 2, which is his first anti-utopian essay):

> The central task in finding an ethical end is the evaluation of expressions of will which are already present but may be undesirable or subject to uncontrollable influences. In so doing it comes up against the following limits: 1. of emphatic constants (the value-essence, existence, rights and desire-structure of *persons*; the existence and character of social unities, especially *civilisations*), 2. of unemphatic constants (psycho-physical make-up, natural "givens"), 3. of relatively unemphatic variants (the sphere of technology, the economy, etc).[22]

Kolnai's introduction of the idea of "moral emphasis" (and its cognate terms) marks another addition to the ideas of value-ethics. Since there are always *gradations* of emphasis, it will be most convenient to consider them together. Kolnai was clearly struck by the fact that there can be agreement on a person's proper moral response to a situation even though there is no single criterion of such appropriateness but perhaps a variety of values or principles summoning the agent in different directions. In each morally relevant situation, then, there will be some value which is emphatic, and, as there is usually more than one, some value which has higher emphasis than the others. As the end of the previous paragraph suggests, some things, like the human person, always have moral emphasis - or moral importance - as "emphatic constants", that is, as objects which must always be respected. It is, then, moral emphasis, and gradations of emphasis, which provides "the essential focus of moral intention". Kolnai assures us that emphasis is "objective": it is a feature of real situations whose presence or nature can be "pointed to", argued about and agreed on, provided there is not too great a discrepancy in people's moral perspective. He also says that emphasis is "devotion to value, being claimed by value ... feeling the presence of value in one's own action, or some moment of it".[23] The presence of emphasis sometimes depends on the individual's value-essence. Here, the idea of "devotion" to value makes obvious sense, as a kind of individual vocation. Where "compulsory values" are concerned, in situations where certain conduct is morally required of anyone, we must assume that what Kolnai calls the "moral need", or "desire",[24] to assert oneself morally in society, is sufficient to make people "give themselves" to the values concerned.

There are many ways in which one may be "claimed by value", not all of which require immediate action, but all responses modify reality somehow, since even the bare acknowledgement of value will contribute to one's own gradual moralisation. Some value emphases are "urgent", requiring an immediate response. Some are "compulsory", as pointed out above, and these will very likely be negative (involving refraining from doing something one might be tempted to do), and may be required of one by others. Others highlight desirable responses, and others simply claim our moral admiration and reverence, as with the saintly or heroic acts we hear about. In this early work Kolnai puts less stress on distinguishing what he will later call "emphatic" morality from "implicit" morality, where the "moral theme" is mingled with other practical interests; here in the dissertation he is happy to contrast morality as the observance of laws with morality as "ethical culture", and to emphasise the latter.

Kolnai's frequent use of the formal idea of graded series of emphasis is the least satisfactory feature of the book. But the following examples give some idea of what he is about. There are, first, gradations between values themselves. "This means that every value implies other values, which have a watered down and, as it were, peripheral presence in our image of the first value".[25] So Justice has its neighbour values (truthfulness and peaceableness) and its consequential values (concern for other's welfare, etc); a just action that disregards these values lacks something of what justice should be. This picture is completed by the idea of The Good, which includes them all. Kolnai's idea is a more subtle form of the claim that all moral virtues are really one. Another example of gradation of emphasis concerns aspects of moral conduct. On every particular occasion of judging a piece of conduct some aspects will have greater emphasis than others, making them more relevant to the assessment.[26] Among the aspects Kolnai mentions are "vaguely foreseeable consequences and consequences intrinsically bound up with the nature of the action", the circumstances of the action (nature and situation of agent) and its consequences, the subjective intention of the agent (his more or less conscious willing) and the objective results (more or less remote) of conduct, self-intention and other-intention. Another example occurs in his discussion of loyalty. From the point of view of loyalty every person confronts mankind as a graded whole, or as a set of gradations; the degree to which we are morally bound to people will probably depend on the life-issue in question.

Kolnai also uses his ideas about gradation to illuminate the question of moral freedom. He shows how the apparently opposed ideas: "Morality on the basis of freedom, and Freedom as a result of morality" are reconcilable if we look at the phenomena in its light.[27] Other particular issues he discusses in the course of the book include the ethics of the formation of ideals, the moral question of how we should treat our own less welcome needs or desires, the relation of extra-ethical to ethical values, the metaphysical world-picture suggested by ethical theories, and general questions of social organisation. One chapter contains illuminating discussions of certain "value-monist and anti-grading theories". The following quotations are representative:

> [Kant's] separation between the "good will" and all other things, notably the ethically uniform crowd of "inclinations", takes the rejection of gradation so far that it becomes a highly precarious undertaking to build a bridge to genuine everyday morality.[28]
>
> The deepest spirit of Communism is, materially speaking, contempt for Mankind, and formally speaking, the abolition of limitation and gradation.[29]

Referring to Liberalism and Utilitarianism, he writes:

> The ethic of the order of justice opposes gradation with a formal ethical dualism, the ethic of regulation with a formal ethical monism. The one says: what is not covered by the (minimally assessed) regulation is irrelevant; the other says: everything is regulated.[30]

It is also worth quoting the following:

> The ideas of permeation and gradation rule out tolerance as a *supreme* [my emphasis] principle, together with its rigid dualism between a spiritual world filled with purely subjective contents and a system of rules to protect it.[31]

In chapter five he presents a formal survey of value-experiences to show the basic ways in which ethical attitudes can intend reality. In so doing he also puts the idea of gradation to use again, since the idea of The Good hardly appears at all in the first type of value-experience, whereas in the fourth it is itself directly apprehended. He begins, then, with the "experience of exclusion", a response to situations where the agent is morally required to reject certain forms of conduct, objects or relations which would automatically threaten the presupposed value of personal life. The disvalues concerned are concentrated around malice, uncleanness and baseness. Then comes the "experience of coordination", which concerns life materials of no special moral significance in themselves. The following explanation makes it clear that these values relate to justice in a broad sense (in this case veracity):

> [This] value-experience ... always concerns intended elements of reality, states of affairs or situations, which the disposition "acknowledges", "respects", to which it "adapts" or "opens" itself, and in this way the object is honoured in its general properties, quite independent of its particular value and disvalue (eg whether a state of affairs one has to communicate is good news or bad).[32]

Next we have the "experience of incorporation", which relates to elements of reality just as they are, either incorporated in a new value-reality, or, when it concerns mental contents, in general devotion to reality. The values concerned are those of various forms of love and achievement. Lastly there is the "experience of directness", in various types of "the concentrated experience of the Ethical as having the solidity of an individual substance".[33] Kolnai claims that, in the end, morality is founded in such points of ethical contemplation, and even mysticism, when we sense that "nothing matters except the absolute Good". These rather formal explications can give little sense of the richness of this chapter, in which Kolnai discusses, among other things, the nature of moral evil, formalistic values (objects of the experience of coordination), the nature and meaning of love, ethics and religion, and other questions. As always, he is ready with pertinent incidental remarks about the classic moral theories.

The publisher's blurb summarises the final chapter as follows:

> Finally, on the basis of the idea of gradation, the author moves towards a theory of person and act, personal responsibility and the personalistic fashioning of life and society as such. The author is especially concerned with the ethical foundation of Christian-democratic social reform...

Kolnai's account of the person is far better conceived than that of his master, Scheler. Reflection, he says, reveals:

> a conjunction of experiences and acts which points to a "substantial bearer" ... and also reveals a constant, as it were, "intra-substantial" order of gradations, in that less emphatic layers are laid around an ethical kernel and *their nature determined, albeit incompletely, by it*.[34]

Thus he can say that the person morally transcends his acts. But the person is also transcended by his act; "as a result there is a counter-gradation from act to person alongside the gradation from person to act." On this basis - compare the locution: "he acted better than he knew" - he elaborates a theory of responsibility which covers "acts which are not in the least mandatory, or taboo, which, therefore, *taken in themselves, do not imply any clear-cut ethical response to the subject*."[35] From the section on the "personalistic fashioning of life and society as such" we may quote the following: "Social freedom does not consist either in organisation or its abolition, but in its right qualitative ordering, limitation and diversification."[36]

***

Kolnai's thesis was closely followed by two highly intelligible ethical papers in German periodicals. "Inclination, duty and cast of mind"[37] was his response to a recent paper on Schiller and Kant. Schiller took Kant to task for making duty-consciousness the centre of his moral psychology, claiming instead that the proper heart of the moral life was the moralisation of "inclinations", so that morally approvable desires became second nature. It seems that the author of the paper had tried to combine these views, suggesting that duty-consciousness and duty-performance constituted a first level of morality, and that moralised inclinations constituted an "advanced" moral superstructure. Kolnai sets out to attack the strict personal dualism which Kant, Schiller and the contemporary writer all shared. He argues for the moral unity of the person, and for the absurdity of an isolated and totally feelingless "duty-machinery" or moral will on the one hand, and a set of inclinations unerringly, and without any need for direction, aiming at the Good on the other. If champions of duty distort the nature of the person, the supporters of feeling magically transform it, by imagining it raised to a "supra-moral" state. The right solution is a moral "Gesinnung", cast of mind, or "-mindedness", which embraces all mental aspects:

a stratified personality where there is room for moral judgement, uninfluenced by affects, as well as immoral tendencies, but where moral biases prevail in that they organically and irrevocably ensure the moral trustworthiness of the person because they present themselves, so to speak, under the sign of that judgement.[38]

The paper ends with some considerations which show the complementarity of a moral psychology embracing the whole person and an ethics firmly anchored in reality.

"The Structure of Moral Intention"[39] goes further into the nature of moral-mindedness by way of the question: what does a moral agent have to have in mind (or intend) in the moral act? The answers of Kant, Scheler and Hartmann are criticised for their one-sidedness, though Kolnai's own proposals draw on all three, and also add new elements. Firstly, there must be some kind of affirmation or willing of the Good as such, as the essential background to value-preference. Only this can make sense of moral decision. There must also be some care for the agent's own goodness (and fallibility), otherwise his action dissolves into mere "intoxication". These two elements are "background" elements of moral conduct of any kind, the first being a "conditioning background", the second an "accompanying background", though they may also come to the fore in certain circumstances. The ethical intention itself comprises five elements, which are "legitimate and as a whole indispensable; ... they are also subject to an order corresponding to the situation".[40] The intention itself is not a general readiness to act morally which is then tacked on to morally indifferent activities, but "the ethically determined concrete intention itself". Everyday examples can be found in, for example, the filling out of invoices as part of a day's work, or reading to a sick uncle. So then, the moral intention is directed to, firstly, particular moral values (an externally well-ordered life, family solidarity), secondly, moral rules of conduct - important when temptations to abandon moral action occur - (do your duty, help those in need), thirdly, "object-goods" (useful undertakings, the person of the uncle) to which the action relates, fourthly, "goal-goods", whose creation is striven for (making a living, keeping up his spirits), and fifthly, any natural, even momentary, impulses or likings which can be fitted in to the ethically guided action (office companionship, affection for the book to be read aloud), so as to prevent its becoming a burden. Kolnai then investigates various forms of "false intention", that is, intentions erroneously claimed to be good, in the light of the five elements just surveyed and the two background factors. A disordered intention is likely to underly these; conversely completeness of intention does provide an applicable standard of conduct, since it is here that the transition from value to reality is clearest. Intention-monism, however, especially when it is deliberate, is the surest formal criterion of ethical error.

***

Kolnai's "promotion" to Doctor of Philosophy was, by some administrative quirk, rearranged to take place on the very day he had fixed for his baptism, July 10th 1926. In view of the eager progress he had made towards Catholicism between, say, 1921 and 1923, it might well have been asked why he delayed this event so long. Kolnai himself implies that he found it difficult to take a step which amounted to rejection of the Jewish religious community;[41] it seems very possible that his relationship with Irma Gémes, which will be discussed below, also stood in his way. Be that as it may, he was in touch during the latter part of this time with individual Catholic clergy, as well as new Catholic friends.

Before that he had been much influenced by Theodor Koppányi, an old friend of Kinszky's. Koppányi was a political rightist and traditionalist, and also a scientist, who managed to get into Vienna University in 1919. Like Kolnai, he contributed to both *Tűz* and *Bécsi Magyar Ujság*. Kolnai spent much time with him, sometimes taking him along on his nocturnal rambles about the streets of old Vienna. When he departed for Chicago in 1923 to take up a research fellowship, Kolnai told Füst that his loss was "irreplaceable". He was the first close friend of his who was also a Catholic, and "brought home to [him] the reality of Catholicism as a concrete and living thing".[42]

Koppányi's place was taken by a friend of his, Hugh Winspear, a Canadian in the process of changing over from the Anglican to the Roman church; Winspear then put him in touch with an English Jesuit, Fr Martindale, with whom he exchanged letters up to the time of his conversion. His letter to Milán Füst of February 1st 1925 shows that these were not confined to religious matters, since he tried, in vain, to enlist the priest's interest in getting Füst's novella, *Advent*, translated into English. Among the "difficulties" Father Martindale dealt with, Kolnai mentions the after-life and the political orientation of the church, which was to occupy him more and more agonisingly during the next dozen or so years. He seems also to have discussed with him the problem of "reluctance to give up (his) Jewishness" unilaterally. Fr Martindale countered with the assurance that "no one had a greater chance of making a good Christian than a former Jew".[43]

But the man who finally gave him instruction and received him into the Church was Fr Georg Bichlmair, another Jesuit, who had a special ministry to academics and intellectuals. He was obviously just the right kind of man for Kolnai,

> a stout, jovial, energetic middle-aged man of peasant stock, learned and of wide intellectual interests but thoroughly practical, a man of firm certitudes but ready to ponder counter-arguments.[44]

He spoke up later for politically leftist Catholics during one of Kolnai's most anti-clericalist periods around the beginning of the nineteen-thirties, and, during the war, organised the rescue of many "non-Aryan Catholics" about to be sent to Auschwitz and other death-camps, before being deported by the Gestapo. When the time came for Kolnai to be baptised he chose Thomas for his Christian or baptismal name. He had in mind St Thomas Aquinas, the great mediaeval Catholic philosopher of the Christian faith. Ironically enough, he later became extremely critical of aspects of Aquinas's thought, and even more of that of his modern followers, the "Thomists", and it may well be that he would then have preferred St Thomas the apostle, who first doubted the resurrection but then gave his absolute and unqualified assent once faced with the evidence of his own senses.

We may pause here for a moment to ask what his conversion meant to Kolnai. He himself tells us that there was nothing sudden about it; it was rather the quasi-logical conclusion of "gradual evolution, stock-taking and clarification".[45] Kolnai's personality was intrinsically passionate and religious; his youthful *Notes* on the Hungarian revolution contain an atheist-anti-clericalist poem in which his longing for rational enlightenment is expressed with great religious intensity. As the political and personal events of the immediate postwar years unfolded, he became aware of an increasingly wide gulf between his "official" world-view and the world as he actually saw it. So he began to see that he could no longer reject theism, together with some religious expression of it; finally he was ready to enter the "Catholic World" - which lacked the ineliminably "tribal" aspect of Judaism - as the only possible framework of dogma and practice within which his life could begin to make sense again.[46]

***

During his university years Kolnai's *Zärtlichkeitshunger* also seems to have found some degree of satisfaction. But because he and his friends rarely discussed their serious romantic attachments, not much can be established with any certainty. However, his close friend Róbert (usually known as "Lolo") Vámbéry recalls that at some time during his university years

Kolnai became engaged to a German girl, and that he occasionally travelled to Germany in order to visit her. Since it was possible for students to migrate between Austrian and German universities during the course of their studies, it is likely that she was at one time a fellow-student in Vienna.

But his great love-affair with Irma Gémes was much more important and significant. The bare fact of it was well known and obviously talked of in his circle, but, again, he does not seem to have discussed it with anyone, so that even the approximate dates must remain a matter of probability. What makes this relationship sound so unlikely at first is the fact that Irma was the mother of Kolnai's future wife Elisabeth (whom he married in 1940), and was at least fifteen years older than him. Her husband, Mr Gémes, was in business, but, by the time the love-affair between Kolnai and Irma took place, the marriage was either legally at an end - the divorce took place in 1927 - or no more than an empty shell.

On July 26th 1925 Kolnai and Irma, together with an unidentified third person, sent a card to Kinszky from Vienna. Kolnai's main contribution consists of a picture of a man dancing and drinking and being pierced by Cupid's arrow, together with a little rhyme, which says:

> Dear Imre, come over here! There's much good wine here, where Irmacska [diminutive of 'Irma'] brought us all! You would do a lover's heart good - come here if you are his friend!

Kolnai is certainly in love with someone, but Irma's six lines (she clearly knew Kinszky well) give nothing away. She and Kolnai are at any rate by this time close friends, but the person Kolnai is in love with might just as well be the German girl referred to above. It is also conceivable that Kolnai is in love with Olga Gémes, Irma's elder daughter, who was a student of architecture in Vienna around this time (though there is no mention of her on the card). Among Kolnai's manuscript poems is a long sequence for New Year, entitled "Silvesterlandschaft", a series of "expressionist" and other visions reflecting many of his favourite themes. At the end Kolnai has added to the typed text the following: "I did not manage to recite this on New Year's Eve 1924/25. But, Olgi G., I dedicate it to you, since I got to know you then and ..." (the allusive punctuation is in the original). However, there is nothing else to suggest that he had ever been in love with Olga Gémes, whom he thoroughly disliked in later life. "Olgi G" may be the name of the German girl.

The person who probably knew most about the circumstances surrounding the love-affair with Irma is the aforementioned Róbert Vámbéry, who lodged with Irma for a year or so before leaving for Berlin in late 1926 or 1927, where he became assistant director to Joseph Aufricht at the Volksbühne theatre ("the best assistant I ever had", Aufricht wrote in his Memoirs). Vámbéry actually met Kolnai for the first time in Irma's flat, where he lodged, possibly after Mr Gémes had "disappeared".[47] They soon became firm friends, spending many evenings in cafés and in wandering about the inner city. Vámbéry recalls that the affair began after Kolnai's religious conversion, but that he never discussed any aspect of it with him. As Irma was divorced from her husband in 1927 (Vámbéry said he had been "somewhat shadowy", and as "rather an impossible person"), it may be that the affair proper began then. But another fact to be noted is this. In 1970 Kolnai wrote a long, rambling, letter, full of reminiscences, to his wife's cousin, György Lányi, and his wife, Susi, in Oberlin, Ohio. There is much about Irma in this letter, including the significant statement: "she was very good for me as a device to escape from my parents, who were terribly persecuting me".[48] If, as seems likely, his parents required his residence in Budapest again after he had taken his degree, since he had no proper job, then, as her lover (or very close friend), he may well have been in a position to accept an offer of financial assistance from Irma, and his parents have resigned themselves to their steady relationship, from the autumn of 1926. On the other hand it seems unlikely that a man of Kolnai's character could have gone forward to baptism, involving detailed confession of sins to a priest, while "living in sin". It is more likely that the friendship between the two began in 1924,[49] and developed into an affair in the summer of 1925, and was in fact over - as a "love affair" in the sense of a properly sexual relationship - before the summer of 1926. This would account for the delay in his baptism, and possibly also be one reason why he went to Berlin in November 1926 to seek his literary or journalistic fortune, leaving Irma "feeling sad" in Vienna.[50] But this is speculation. What is clear is that, whenever the "affair"[51] did come to an end, the ex-lovers remained for a long time on excellent terms. Vámbéry says that without this relationship Kolnai would never have married Elisabeth.

What did the two see in each other? In so far as one can answer this sort of question at all, the answer might go like this: Kolnai always remained somewhat timid and impractical; he was unsure of himself, longed for "tenderness", "needed" and responded to mothering and associated admiration. Some of these facts are reflected in his later often expressed preference for "fat women"; in similar vein he tells Füst in a letter of April 28th 1948: "I used to think that a woman only began to be attractive around 40 to 50." As for Irma, she greatly admired Kolnai's intellect and sense of humour, and no doubt valued the stimulus of a young man after the collapse of her marriage. By all accounts she was an easy-going, very friendly and jolly person, with a great gift of cheering people up, and no doubt felt sorry for him, and enjoyed her power to revive his spirits during his frequent bouts of depression. Susi Lányi, her niece, called her a "free spirit, often delightfully mischievous and funny and irresponsible", though her own mother, Mrs Polya, disapproved of Irma's way of life. Kolnai, writing in 1970, adds that she lived largely through the lives of other people, which would, of course, have suited a rather self-centred young man like himself. He also refers (in the letter to the Lányis just referred to) to "a certain imposing established objectivity" in Irma's flat in Aichholzgasse, implying the influence of her father, Herr Löwenherz, who had been Jewish cantor in Hungarian Temesvár (now Rumanian Timişoara), and who "was possibly an extremely interesting man"; certainly Irma knew many intellectuals and other people Kolnai was glad to get to know. Their needs in 1925 or 1926 were, in fact, complementary to a considerable degree.

***

Kolnai's book on sexual ethics is an extraordinarily interesting work.[52] It was commissioned by a Catholic press in Westphalia on the basis of his dissertation, no doubt also because he had published an article on sexual ethics in 1924 in the Catholic daily *Die Reichspost*, and won much acclaim for it even among his "progressive" friends in Vienna and Budapest.[53] The book is, as we should expect, far from being a straightforward version of Catholic ethical teaching on sex, yet it is, in its general tendency, in conformity with the Catholic tradition. If we except the matter of artificial contraception, here condemned but in later life defended, we can say that he kept to this for the rest of his life. What made some people wonder about his attitude was that he combined his strong "personalist" line with a deep fascination with sex,[54] which found expression in risqué jokes and scatological verses, and a very flirtatious approach to the women who attracted him.

The work, which one reviewer called the "Prolegomena to any future sexual ethics",[55] contains nearly four hundred and fifty pages of text, and forms a practical application of the dissertation. In the introduction he tells us that his purpose is

> to take a really close look at the most important problems of sexual ethics in order to lay bare their "meaning" and the possibility of solving them. I shall try to establish "what is really at issue" in all these questions, what is the general "logic" of judgements in sexual morality and why they are necessary.[56]

He describes his method as phenomenological, but is careful to add that he has

> no interest in "racial purity" where method is concerned ... Any unduly strict attention to method draws the researcher's attention to himself and distracts him from ... the object of investigation ... [57]

Like the dissertation, the *Sexualethik* presupposes the idea of "spiritual personality" (limited and graded within the compass of the human being) as the central bearer of moral value. Ultimately, he believes this to be anchored in religion, but claims that other, secular, ethical approaches have also started from it, such as the "ethics of obligations on the basis of metaphysical freedom", "ethics of the unfolding of the natural potential of a rational being", and the ethic of Christian socialism. He also points to the formal aspects of his ultimate base: "the divine origin of the person, his ties with God, his inner stratification, the 'Good in him'". These ideas help the moral philosopher not to forget "the reference back to a 'highest good', and the absolute importance of the moral Good". By putting the person at the centre of things, instead of some abstract principle, the thinker is less inclined to ignore the demands of actual reality, and is more continually alerted to "the different shades of moral value".

The first part of the book is entitled "Justification of sexual ethics" - that is, as a distinct department of ethics, rather than as a sphere of application of general moral principles. In the first chapter, after noting that sexual ethics claims to be ethics par excellence, yet is very unsure of its ground and frequently attacked as such, he emphasises that "the movement of the spiritual self" expressed in sexual condemnation is a resolution "to sweep away a certain 'material'", to cleanse life from something experienced as a contamination.[58] Moral "dirt", which is quite absent from, say, murder and lying, is unique to this sphere. Sexual sin may share formal characteristics with other kinds of immorality; but it is its "material" aspects that really count. These point to the act, rather than the agent, as in lying or corruption. Hence sexual sin is sin par excellence: we experience it directly, unmediated by any awareness of logical relations. This is why it is so frequently denied or reinterpreted.[59]

Ethical justification of this special attitude must involve appeal to consensus. All societies have rules about sex, and take them very seriously, interweaving them with social institutions. This cannot be an accident. Indeed sexual morality is always considered alongside other, more transparent, moral rules. Chastity is part of the moral Good; sexual sin leads easily to "other kinds".[60] Sexual morality also has an obvious "naturalness" about it, because of the close connection of sex with spiritual matters, its "separateness" in life as a whole despite this fact, the many possibilities in life of asexuality and the need to make radical choices within the sexual sphere.[61] Kolnai also reminds us of the many degrees of sexual emphasis, the great range of gradation in sexual condemnation and the many moral values it reveals. Sexual ethics is therefore not likely to be entirely negative.[62]

Chapter two deals with relativism and immoralism. His approach to the former is summed up as follows:

> In so far as positive rules are really relative, they do not prove the relativity of good and evil, but only the relativity of all concrete "instructions" relating to good and evil.[63]

Among generally acknowledged aspects of sexual good are chastity and "giving my sexuality a place in the well-ordered totality of my life".[64] There follows an analysis of various "types of immoralism", here understood as the denial of specifically sexual morality, whilst subordinating sexual rules and recommendations to other moral values or non-moral interests. Kolnai argues that, where the "sexual ethical experience" is not quietly presupposed, it is vehemently attacked in a way that shows its deep-rootedness in human experience. His main point is that there is no relevant counter-experience which could justify immoralism; this is shown, for example, by the fact that when the immoralist has to condemn such evil practices as child molestation in terms of his theory, the arguments produced are always much more remote and flimsy than the "material" requires. The basic experience of sexual morality will not be denied, and is just as striking as the "value-plenitude of the erotic experience" itself.[65]

The first part of the book ends with a survey of "what sexual ethics can provide". Kolnai warns us that if sexual ethics is given up as too problematic and difficult, all real moral understanding, which is based on moral experience, goes too, and morality is reduced to something else.[66] There follows a discussion of "ideal and reality" in the sexual ethical sphere. The ascetic ideal, an intelligible response to the life-disruptive aspects of sex, must be taken seriously; yet sex is the source of much good, the sex-drive is powerful, and can seem to make a mockery of the most elaborate precautions. All this underlines the need to understand sexual phenomena, and in particular the possibilities of an ethic that sticks closely to reality.[67]

The second part of the book is about general principles of sexual ethics. Kolnai first turns to the three most basic and essential aspects of sex: sexual pleasure, the relation to the "opposite sex" and the goal of reproduction. He first provides a phenomenological account of sexual pleasure, with its culmination in orgasm, and then drily adds: "In general sexual pleasure evokes a special kind of misgiving", firstly, because the personality is "submerged" in orgasm, and, secondly, because sexual pleasure is very often an occasion for sin.[68] He then argues that, despite appearances, sexual activity always contains a reference to "the opposite" sex. This desire for intimate union is another aspect of the "depersonalising" power of sex, an attack on the separation of persons. The "common submersion in a non-personal, 'material', stream of life" may be the occasion of personal intensification, and receptivity to many spiritual values, but, as such, it is still questionable.[69] The chapter ends as follows:

> The amazing natural fact that the informed life of a spirit-endowed human being reproduces itself through formless life, through actual loss of form, including what it contains of the spiritual (recall simultaneous ecstasy, merging, anti-logic, the handing on of life through the stuff of generation, the blindness of impulse, etc), cannot and must not be itself morally condemned, but prepares the ground for serious and weighty problems of immorality and ethical decision.[70]

Under "special characteristics of sexuality" Kolnai analyses its "detachedness" from the rest of life, and yet its "interwovenness" with it. The latter may amount to a kind of shadow-life of its own. It also has colossal "pretensions" to dominate our lives, made easier by its "protean nature". "The interweaving of body and spirit", more marked than in other departments of life, brings with it the special danger of spirit's being engulfed by the body. Even its "power to create inter-personal relationships", so important and fruitful in marriage and family life, may degenerate into the destruction of independent personality, and undermining of spiritual attachments. Sexual relations, though in a vital sense private, are of great "social relevance", yet they are fundamentally "irrational", indeed hostile to reason.[71] He then passes to consider "the sexes", under the following headings: "separation of Man into male and female", "the striving of the sexes towards one another", "male and female", where he analyses the differences between male and female in a way much closer to Scheler than Weininger;[72] finally he sums up the sexual ethical implications of this differentiation.[73]

The second part of the book ends with an important chapter entitled "Outlines of sexual ethics". Sex is a danger to personal life, and consequently sexual ethics must be largely constituted by prohibitions. But it is also good in itself, as essential to life, and also good, in quite another sense, when "well ordered".[74] He then suggests three fundamental principles of sexual morality. Firstly, an attitude of "withholding oneself" from certain sexual possibilities. Secondly, "completeness": where sex is permissible there should be no stopping short of normal fulfilment. Thirdly, "compatibility": sex should harmonise with the goals and values of personal life.[75]

The third part of the book discusses more detailed problems in the light of these principles, relating especially to monogamy, normality and perversion. But he still has one or two general questions to discuss. It follows from his position that general moral approval and condemnation of types of sexuality should be self-evident to anyone who really contemplates these things as they are, but that there are more general principles which may help where direct apprehension is weak. So, assuming that abstinence for the sake of spiritual goals, and monogamy within the bounds of normality, are the only two approvable "policies", why, if one rejects abstinence, should anything less than "monogamy and normal congress" be wrong, rather than less good? His answer is that it "destroys the possibility of satisfactory sexual relations of a normal kind":[76]

> In this sphere even a single action can bring about serious "disorder"; ... for every sexual act includes an "intensification" of some particular tendency of life, and constitutes something self-contained, discrete, a "unique occurrence" in the full sense, which stands out from the rest of life, and thus, as it were, draws life on ... in a particular path.[77]

As a special test case of his principles Kolnai considers incest, whose rejection often appears so arbitrary to moral theorists. He argues that incest is not merely disordered (something normal "in the wrong place", as it were), but perverse (a deliberate defiance of the norm, which evokes a kind of "mystical horror"). A man who desires his sister will do so not despite her blood-kinship but because of it, and the piquancy this will add to his pleasure. But members of one family should look outward to society at large. Incestuous relations thus challenge both restraint and compatibility. He takes them as a paradigm of promiscuity.[78]

In the last part of the book Kolnai discusses social aspects of sexual morality. He begins with a section on the relation between the individual and the social in the moral life.[79] Although pure ethical value attaches to individual persons, and there is a vital place for the moral genius or "prophet", society nevertheless standardises and concretises the Good, and thus to a large extent also makes it real. Such is our dependence on society for our power to do good that morality largely becomes a matter of maintaining one's honour, self-respect, even reputation, and also their special adaptations to one's social and occupational groups. Because of the admixture of non-moral values in any social ethic, there is always a risk of sanctioned immorality. Hence the need to put up with much imperfection and inconsistency (which does not rule out criticism):

> It is senseless to try and devalue the absolutely necessary organs of mediation and bodies of gradation between value and reality because they are not pure reflections of value itself. The proper task is to ensure that value keeps shining through them in its purity![80]

Kolnai also tries to redeem the idea of "respectability". To pay only minimal attention to moral values must be better than outright immorality, and can be a sign of humility and awareness of human frailty. Where moral questions are concerned, the state must usually be content to remain on the surface, but occasionally, as with the sexual lives of teachers, it must dig deeper. "There is nothing essentially private as such"; all conduct affects others, but in graded fashion, according to its type, and the persons affected. Spheres of privacy must be relative. On the family he argues that its enemies must be fought not just from the point of view of pure morality, but of the continuance of civilised society as such. He singles out for special mention those who regard society as a "Ganzheit", a "whole", of which the individual is primarily a "part", as we find not only in Bolshevism but also in the "Corporativism" which was beginning to dominate Austrian political thought.[81] The family must be maintained as a bulwark of individual personhood against all regimentation. But Kolnai is too honest not to put the other side, the "suffocating" effect of the "cult" of the family, especially among Jews and the bourgeois world in general.[82]

It goes without saying that I have had to omit much from this exposition which is of great interest. Kolnai's analyses are always subtle, and almost never one-sided or obviously biased, though of course he writes as a man of his time. The amount of detail the book contains is astonishing. It should be added that the German of *Sexualethik* is of luminous clarity compared to that of the dissertation, and that - especially in the footnotes - it is enlivened by many delightfully ironical or playful summaries of his opponents' positions. For example, he takes Schopenhauer to task for summarising sexual immorality as "Seeking to satisfy my lusts at the cost of the life-happiness of female individuals": "Sexual ethics", says Kolnai, "is here confined to an appeal to the humanitarian conscience of loose-living, Don-Juanesque, young lords!"

***

Kolnai's only other publication in this area is an extremely long and drily factual survey of contemporary books and articles dealing with sex education and marriage, published in a "non-clerical, westernized, 'objective' and 'progressive'" cultural digest, which took a great interest in feminism.[83] This hardly adds much to our picture of Kolnai. More interesting, perhaps, is his own later pencilled comment on one of the footnotes to *Sexualethik*, where, to counter the generalisation of a particular writer, he appeals to the evidence of "a completely dissipated and lecherous woman known to the author". He also reveals, in his (much later) marginal comments on a Catholic handbook on purity, where the author discusses the corrupting effect of pornographic magazines, that he himself did not always avert his eyes from such magazines, because they liberated him from lewd thoughts.[84] Róbert Vámbéry, who knew Kolnai very well, opined that sex, for Kolnai, was probably to a large extent "in the mind". The depth of insight into the "meaning" of sex shown by the *Sexualethik* is almost certainly due to a relatively confined first-hand experience coupled with an extraordinarily powerful imagination, and to unusual sensitivities.

Chapter Seven

Political Journalism or Philosophy?
(1920-1930)

Although Austria had set itself from the first to provide a haven for all kinds and colours of political refugees from Hungary and other countries, its own transition to normality after the collapse of the Empire had been more gradual and less cataclysmic than that of its eastern neighbour. For one thing, there were very few large estates, and hence no "land problem" in rural areas; for another, there was a very strong and well-led Social Democratic party, many of whose leaders had had considerable political experience. The Austrian SDP was a definitely Marxist party, standing to the left of its counterpart in Germany, but it sounded more revolutionary than it actually was, and was therefore able to contain much of the extreme left without encouraging real revolution. Its chief rival was the Christian Social Party (CSP), mostly Catholic, petit bourgeois and rural, embracing a wide spectrum of rightist positions, from moderate or centralist conservatives to monarchists and embryo Fascists. There were also the liberal and bourgeois "Nationalist" parties, the "Grossdeutschen" and the less influential Landbund, whose importance in the Republic stemmed from the fact that one or both of them was usually needed to make up a governing coalition.

The emergence of the new state coincided with a double process of "falling away"; firstly, of the old predominantly non-German territories of the Austrian part of the Habsburg empire, and secondly, of the Imperial House itself and most of the old ruling classes closely associated with it. This left behind a number of fiercely chauvinist provinces and a vast ex-imperial cosmopolitan city, whose population amounted to nearly a third of that of the new "rump" state. There was hardly any national consciousness at all, since - very different from Hungary - there had never been an Austrian nation. For some years the capital suffered acutely from shortages of food and fuel, exacerbated by a growing feeling of "Vienna versus the rest", the uncooperativeness and sometimes hostility of the former subject territories, including Hungary, the new frontiers consequent on their secession and the obstruction of some of the Entente, particularly France.

Some of the provinces found themselves having to take up arms again against Slovenes, Czechs, Italians, even Hungarians, anxious to establish claims to territory, and the bogey of inflation became for some years a serious threat to stability. Out of this turmoil emerged a small nation-state with certain serious and, in the event, insoluble problems, which led eventually to its forcible "incorporation" into Nazi Germany.

The first republican regime was an SDP-CSP coalition, in which the socialists were the stronger party. During this early period the constitution was thrashed out, and its form reflected the relative strengths of the parties at the time. Consequently, parliament under its chancellor had virtually all the power, whilst the president himself was little more than a figure-head. In 1920, when the CSP became the stronger party, the SDP decided not to cooperate in any further coalition, and from this time forth concentrated its positive efforts in building the socialist state in the new province of Vienna, where their political position was unchallenged. Apart from the constitution, the key issue in the early days was that of *Anschluß*.[1] It seemed, to nearly everyone except monarchists or "legitimists", the obvious answer to the weakness of the new state to join up with their German brothers to the West and North. Kolnai himself was no exception, believing that Weimar democracy could only be strengthened by the admixture of more Catholic southerners, as an additional counterweight to the militarist and authoritarian tendencies of Prussia. But the Entente forbade this, and, when the Austrian Chancellor Seipel came to the League of Nations to beg for financial help in 1922, thus effectively solving the crisis of inflation, he was made to promise that the issue would not be raised again for five years. Another lasting problem was that of the "paramilitaries" - firstly provincial, and then party-sponsored, bands of irregular troops set up to defend the frontiers or keep the peace as events seemed to require, but increasingly used and formed for purely political ends. These were perfectly legal under the constitution, but once the existence of left-wing and opposed right-wing forces became established, it proved impossible to eliminate this element from Austrian political life, thus opening a wide passage for the introduction of Nazi terror into the country.

Among the many political exiles from Hungary to take refuge in Vienna was Karl Polányi, founder of the Galilei Circle. He had been wounded in the war, and did not play a very active part either in the October Revolution in Hungary, or in the Bolshevist regime which followed. Although he had publicly opposed Bolshevism, the brutality used in arresting Béla Kun evoked in him a sympathy for Communism that never really left him. As a non-Marxist revolutionary socialist he was given some official employment in Kun's regime, but left, disenchanted, for Vienna in June 1919. Here he joined the circle around Eugenia Schwarzwald's pension and political centre for refugees at Hinterbrühl in the Wienerwald, where in due course he met Ilona (Helen) Duczynska. Helen Polányi, as she soon became, was, as Kolnai later wrote, "the most impressive and inexorable revolutionary fanatic I have ever met". She was also "a person of high intelligence and culture, of Hungarian and Polish noble extraction, and in private life by no means devoid of straight principles".[2] She was one of the Galileists whose activities had led to the closing of the Circle in early 1918. After her release from prison at the beginning of the October Revolution, she helped to found the Hungarian Communist Party. After training in Moscow she was despatched to Vienna in September 1920 to work with the Hungarian Communists in their schemes for a new revolution. When she and Karl fell in love she was expelled from the party because of Karl's unorthodox leftism, and, after their marriage in 1922, and their move to live with Helen's mother in the Leopold district, they both turned away from Hungarian affairs and settled down as Viennese citizens and members of the SDP.

Kolnai soon found his way to their home, where he found not only the intellectual stimulation he needed, but complete tolerance of his eccentricities against a background of moral incorruptibility, inner strength and personal warmth. The Polányis helped him in countless ways, right up to their final departure for England in the mid-thirties. It was they who coined the name "Grossväterchen" (little grandfather) for Kolnai. Felix Schaffer, an economics student of Polányi's, who also spent much time with the family, recalls his "shy and inward turned manners" and his "pale, expressive face", which made him look older than he was, and recalled many conversations he had had with him at the Polányis'.[3] Kolnai would discuss art, philosophy and religion with them, as well as politics. There are at least seven references to Karl in the notes to Kolnai's dissertation, nearly all ascribing some important point to conversations with him. Kolnai and Schaffer were not the only people who resorted to the Polányis' flat. Trude Kurz, a revolutionary friend of Helen's, who was imprisoned for a time after the Austrian civil war of 1934, recalled that all possible political trends appeared there: mainly the left, but sometimes the extreme left as well.[4] Kolnai himself later introduced some of his monarchist friends at the house.

In 1923 Polányi became chief editorial writer for the *Oesterreichische Volkswirt*. Kolnai says this was a liberal-democratic weekly, which "maintained a respectable standard of non-partisan liberal 'objectivity'" until the mid-thirties.[5] Before that Karl had worked for *Bécsi Magyar Ujság*, being, like Kolnai, a follower of Jászi and in need of a source of income. But his special responsibility for foreign affairs on the *Oesterreichische Volkswirt* allowed him to cultivate his interest in British politics; as Kolnai says, with deep satisfaction, he "lived in a prevalently English mental universe",[6] being especially interested in the British Labour Party. It was no doubt with Polányi's help and encouragement that Kolnai placed an article there while still at university, and then, later in 1926, won for himself a "permanent connection" with the periodical for the next ten or so years, entitling him to attend the stimulating and protracted editorial board meetings, where Polányi, "full of ideas, warm, generous, with a smile that could light up a winter's night",[7] was one of the leading figures. At these meetings Kolnai would from time to time be assigned topics, with suggestive newspaper cuttings, on which to base "glosses", or editorial notes, on religious or cultural matters, but sometimes also on politics. The fact that Kolnai's contributions to the editorial pages were signed allowed him to include specimens of his own brand of humour (on the Pope's approach to Fascism: "The gist of the Pope's position is: I will love you, o wolf, if only you are willing to become a vegetarian - which would also conduce greatly to your health").[8] In addition, he wrote about thirty articles for the journal between 1926 and 1937, about half of them in 1933 and 1934. He was, of course, paid for all this work, but he describes his *Oesterreichische Volkswirt* takings as "pocket-money". I shall say something about the content of these articles below.

During the ten and a half years of his post-university Vienna period Kolnai wrote three books, two of which were published. One was the *Sexual Ethics*, already described, and one was *The War Against the West*, which we shall consider in chapter nine. The third book was commissioned on the strength of the *Sexualethik*, and constitutes the greatest loss from Kolnai's oeuvre. It was a "textbook of phenomenological ethics", written during 1932. The publishers, Dümmler, of Bonn, paid 200 Reichsmarks for the manuscript. Their plan to publish it in 1933 was shelved when Hitler came to power, and the work is thought to have been lost during the war. In addition Kolnai published nine articles for German academic journals, about seventy-five articles for substantial weeklies or monthlies, many articles in dailies and a large number of book reviews. He also engaged in a certain amount of political activity, and read numerous papers to learned societies and discussion groups. Considering that Kolnai almost never repeats himself, and took great trouble over the composition of his writings, this is an impressive achievement.

However, these years later seemed to Kolnai to have been a largely barren period. There was, first, a perpetual conflict between his philosophical-contemplative and his political-activist self. As we have seen, he had eagerly embraced an untechnical phenomenology as the fulfilment of his own natural inclinations; but this, above all approaches, requires peace and quiet and a calm "distance" from the active business of life. But he had to earn money, and the times themselves, especially the thirties, were in any case unpropitious for such a life; he felt imperiously drawn to use his own gifts as thinker and writer to ward off the anti-rationalist barbarism presented by Fascism and its much more virulent associate, Nazism. There was also the fact that, under the pressure of events, and perhaps the influence of some of his closest friends, he never had the space to develop far along his naturally conservative line, but was always being drawn leftwards.

Immediately after his promotion to doctor of philosophy, Kolnai took a ten-day holiday in Germany, during which he spoke to various philosophers who - it seems likely - he felt might be able to advise him in the matter of a philosophical career in that country. These included Max Scheler and Nicolai Hartmann in Cologne, and Hans Driesch in Leipzig. These visits seem to have brought him little but characteristic memories:

> Scheler's marvellous - justly renowned - deep blue eyes, with the half hidden play of pale grey glints in their blueness which enhanced their expression of a gigantic, heaving, life of thought;[9]

as a contrast, Hartmann's "quite different but still most impressive sea-blue 'Baltic' eyes"; Driesch, however, left an impression with his "small, fine frame, his wrinkled face and his short chin-beard", which gave him the appearance of "a French or Swiss watch-maker".[10] Scheler, moreover, had not read the copy of *Der ethische Wert* Kolnai had sent him, and both he and Hartmann expressed rather disappointing philosophical opinions. But at least he saw his Jewish Hungarian university friend, Pál Bíró, now studying with Driesch, in Leipzig. Bíró clearly meant a great deal to Kolnai, and he recalled him in three letters to George Lányi around 1950. The two spent at least one holiday together in Baden. He came nearest to representing Kolnai's idea of "absolute intelligence", and in his memoirs he recalls his "coruscating purity of character". When Bíró moved to Trieste the two began to drift apart. He was eventually murdered by the Nazis in Budapest towards the end of the war, after refusing to go into hiding.

Later that year Kolnai moved to Berlin, driven this time by the journalistic impulse. Whatever personal reasons also played a part in this resolve, Kolnai intended to settle there if possible. The far less bipolar political atmosphere of Weimar Germany was more congenial to him than that of Austria, and he felt that *Germania*, "the daily organ of the (Catholic) Centre Party", would be a natural outlet for his talent. He had just had an article accepted by the *Deutsche Volkswirt* (German Economist)[11] and had at least three contacts in the city, Father Karl Sonnenschein, "leader of 'Catholic social action' in Berlin", and, on the more personal side, his friend

Róbert Vámbéry, and his cousin György Széll (the younger), who was now directing one of the Berlin operas. He went in early November, but had no luck at all, and soon felt he had no chance of becoming a regular journalist there. In fact he found Berlin to be "hell on earth". In his memoirs Kolnai empasises the architecture, which compelled him "always to walk in the street with downcast eyes",[12] but he can hardly have been unaffected by the social and moral atmosphere, where sexual liaisons were lightly entered on and lightly abandoned, and where the essential thing was to prove oneself strikingly original. He was back in Vienna by Christmas, and had a celebratory walk with Róbert Vámbéry (who was passing through), during which he showed him his beloved mediaeval church, "Maria am Gestade", in the old city. He was also in time to say goodbye to Jászi, who was leaving to take up his chair at Oberlin, Ohio. Kolnai later reminded his mentor how he gave him, "young and spoiled" as he was, "a good telling off" over tea.[13]

Early in 1927 Kolnai resumed his occasional work for *Der Oesterreichische Volkswirt*, and very nearly secured the post of sub-editor on a Catholic weekly, *Das Neue Reich*. From now on it commissioned various book reviews from him, including a longish one on Chesterton's *The Everlasting Man*. Meanwhile he had not been neglecting his philosophy, as the previous chapter has shown. Amongst other things, he embarked on a series of papers about the negative emotions, in what looks like a conscious attempt to supplement and correct Scheler's work in the emotional field. The first of these was his analysis of Disgust ("Der Ekel"), which Husserl accepted for his phenomenological yearbook in 1928.[14] Clearly it also revived in Kolnai hopes of a philosophical career, and he took himself off to Freiburg, where Husserl was just about to retire, for the summer term. Nothing much came of this visit:

> The phenomenological circle - teachers and students - disappointed me ... The place was altogether overlain by Heidegger's shadow. That ingenious but wilfully obscure, stilted, tortured and to me most unpalatable thinker was to succeed Husserl after his retirement, and everybody seemed already to pipe the Heideggerian tune ... I learned next to nothing, and contributed less to the discussions.[15]

Kolnai passed some of his time with the French Philosopher Emanuel Levinas ("no genius", but, he implies, very knowledgeable),[16] and also consorted with a "young Manxman", later identified as William Kneale.[17] The main result of this sojourn in Freiburg was that it finally convinced him that he could not live in Germany; he gained relief by periodical excursions to Switzerland, where, despite a pervasive air of "peasant gruffness", he felt at home "in a world of temperate sanity and stable liberal order".[18] But he did make an excursion to Heidelberg to see Karl Mannheim, where he appalled his old acquaintance with his views on the possible physical efficacy of extreme unction.

Kolnai made several other attempts to find a salaried post in political journalism. In 1928 he had published two papers for *Schönere Zukunft* (A Better Future), a Catholic weekly "of markedly rightist and ostensibly 'anti-capitalist' tendencies". The papers are respectively about Scheler's idea of Capitalism - a very useful summarising article - and about the Distributivism of Hilaire Belloc.[19] In the Spring of 1929 he succeeded in obtaining an editorial appointment on the paper. This meant "a daily five hours' drudgery" compiling glosses to order on "ecclesiastical and 'cultural' events in Western countries, from England to Brazil", at "two hundred shillings" a month - the sum he was paid for his two articles. When the political stance of the paper tended even more to the right in 1930, he resigned.[20]

The year 1930 was, in fact, a watershed for Kolnai in his capacity of political journalist, since in November of that year he joined the SDP, an action for which he later bitterly reproached himself. To understand his joining, it will be necessary to say something about the political situation of the late twenties, and the stance of most Catholics to the problems of the day. As I have implied, the politics of Austria between the wars was "dualist", concentrated around the confrontation of the two big blocks, the Marxist SDP and the rightist and Catholic CSP, which - each in its own way - battled for the human soul. During the twenties, and - Kolnai later said - even beyond, this proved a recipe for stability, since it prevented Austria from sliding too far towards either of the political extremes, Bolshevism on the one hand and Nazism on the other.

With a few exceptions, then, Catholics identified with the CSP. But there were big disagreements within the party over what sort of policy would most appropriately meet the social problems of the day. Broadly speaking there was again a "dualism" here - one group, the "Solidarists", favouring a series of gradual reforms within the capitalist framework, another group, sometimes known as "Social Romantics", pinning its faith on a restoration of the kind of "organic" social order that they thought capitalism and liberal democracy had destroyed. They argued that capitalism was inherently divisive and inhuman, and that it could not be reformed piecemeal. They therefore favoured a "corporativist" political and social system based on vocational groups. This would both acknowledge the importance of economics in modern society and also do away with the class system, promoting social harmony and cooperation.

But, after a period of growing "normalisation", even incipient prosperity, in Austria in the early and middle twenties, the balance of these two positions in the church began to tilt to the right in response to two significant events. The first was the SDP conference at Linz, which reaffirmed on November 3rd 1926 that its ultimate aim was the complete transformation of society on socialist and secular lines, and that a violent response could not be ruled out if the Right ever tried to go outside the law. This was followed on July 15th 1927 by the burning of the Palace of Justice in Vienna by an angry mob of workers, as a response to the "not guilty" verdict on the men accused of unlawful killing in the notorious "Schattendorf" case. The occasion of this was a clash between groups of paramilitaries; men of the socialist Volksbund marching through Schattendorf had been fired on from a pub in the village by Austro-Fascist Heimwehr men, and two of them (a war invalid and his small son) had been killed. From that time forth it was clear to many, including Kolnai, that the strong man of the CSP, the priest-Chancellor Seipel, began to abandon the "Solidarist" course and to favour the Heimwehr (a corporativist political group), and to say that only they represented "true democracy". The limit for Kolnai was reached when there was another change of government on September 30th 1930, and the Heimwehr leader was made Minister of the Interior. He now thought there was little hope for democracy in Austria - and hence for any genuine political power for workers - unless it came from the left. Accordingly, Kolnai joined the SDP, urging all Christian workers to do the same, and the press carried announcements of the fact. Both Karl Polányi and Heinrich Gomperz, his former teacher, expressed their concern.

Kolnai's action had much more than personal significance at the time. The "lonely and finally tragic struggle against the errors of his day" on the part of this "Cassandra" - G. Silberbauer here refers to Kolnai's articles in *Volkswohl*, which forthwith refused any further contributions from him - represented the last significant public outcry from the "Solidarists" against corporativism. In May of the following year the proclamation of the Papal encyclical *Quadragesimo Anno*, with its corporativist proposals, meant the collapse of Solidarism and the almost universal adherence of Austrian Catholics to the Austro-Fascist, or semi-Fascist, course.[21] Kolnai came himself to see that his later journalistic activity "had a deadening atmosphere of unreality". As a catholic writing for *Volkswohl* he was sure of an audience, some of whom might be influenced by him to remain faithful to Solidarism; once the pages of Catholic papers were closed to him he could, for the most part, only reach a liberal-agnostic or socialist readership, on whom his articles would have much less effect.[22]

But Kolnai was primarily a philosopher, a thinker writing for mankind in defence of his democratic personalism wherever he could find an audience. Most of his articles in Austrian publications are in fact in some way "occasional", but always thought out in terms of general principles. He likes to analyse slogans and popular ideas, to separate out the various elements of, say, democracy, liberalism, parliamentarism and corporativism (not to mention socialism, Fascism, and so on), so as to display the essential features and their interrelations, sometimes with additional historical explanations. His aim is always to raise the consciousness of his readers about the great issues underlying day to day social and political events and decisions. The *Oesterreichische Volkswirt* articles contain much anti-corporativist material; the two earliest ones are precursors of the "anti-Spann campaign" he waged between 1928 and 1935 in various periodicals. Othmar Spann was a university professor, an "idealist formalist of Totalitarian Hierarchy and a prophet of the Fascist State", though never a genuine Nazi. As a student Kolnai went to some of his lectures, and was "amazed at the colossal impression this vulgar little bounder ... made on Austrian Catholics in particular".[23] On one occasion in 1928 Kolnai was invited to tea with his poetess wife, after he had written complimenting her on her sensible comments at a public meeting. At tea he had to confess that he did not agree with the Professor:

> Whereupon she advised me urgently to try his books and lectures. But when I rejoined that I had already done so she looked altogether bewildered. "'I don't understand you", she gasped. "Weren't you telling me that you did not share his views?"[24]

Two of Kolnai's major points against corporativism are that it reduces politics to economics and that, although it was defended as a remedy for the evils of capitalism, its effect must be to make capitalism invulnerable to non-economic criticism, and to make the workers defenceless before their bosses. He also objects to it as a rationalist blueprint, a predetermined solution like Marxism, and says that, in the last analysis, its appeal is aesthetic. There was also a fundamental vagueness about its positive proposals, and Kolnai had no difficulty in exposing the crudity of the formalist arguments proposed by Spann. From 1933 he usually attacked the greater evil, Nazism; of his five anti-Nazi articles in *Der Oesterreichische Volkswirt* two concentrate on totality and race respectively. Several of them are specific defences of democracy, with special attention to parties and votes, and a good many defend the Christian and personalist basis of liberalism. There are also review articles of works by Mannheim, Felix Kaufmann and Voegelin, and, finally, two interesting historical analyses of the failure of democracy in Austria and the political system of Chancellor Dollfuß.

The eight papers he published in *Der Deutsche Volkswirt*, mostly in 1927 and 1928, are much more uninhibitedly analytic and philosophical. The first is an analysis of Bolshevism and Fascism, emphasising that only the latter is "counter-revolutionary", the former extending the line of liberal revolutions.[25] His paper on Left and Right in politics is an anticipation of his later work on this topic.[26] The two papers on the Ideology and the Critique of Social Progress[27] relate both to the anti-Utopian parts of his dissertation, and also to his late writings on this topic. In his analysis he concentrates especially on postwar disillusion with the idea (the war itself had displayed "progress" in weaponry; the Russian Revolution was "progress"), and on its inevitable association with welfare and other values lending themselves to quantification, and with leftist rather than rightist regimes. Its critique must start from the impoverished conception of the Good underlying it. Is it not bound to divert our attention from the goods we actually have, to postpone "goodness" to an indefinite future? And does it not actually prevent our working towards any specific goals, since anything we attain must be abandoned forthwith for something better? Does not this entail a loss of energy in political life? On the other hand, surely mere preservation is also lifeless. All social realities need reform, but the content of such reform does not follow automatically; it requires discussion. Kolnai ends this interesting paper by analysing reforms which we might rightly think of as "progress". Two other *Deutsche Volkswirt* papers are on a non-utopian concept of democracy,[28] and on the reasons why youth is so vulnerable to Fascism - despite its spiritual emptiness.[29] There is also an exposition and critique of Chesterton's social ideas and a valuable analysis of Scheler's social philosophy, with special attention to The Sociology of Knowledge.[30]

We have already spoken of the general significance within Austrian Catholicism of Kolnai's *Volkswohl* (Commonweal) papers. This monthly was read not only in Catholic Trade Union circles but also by university people. Two of his contributions have already been mentioned in the chapter on psychoanalysis. The other six papers, all written in 1929 and 1930 (the last two were printed with anxious editorial disclaimers), are closely argued treatments of his main concerns, the case for democracy and against Spann and the corporative state. Some definite conservative elements of these papers show how "centrist" his thought at this time still was. This can be illustrated from "The Christian Trade Unions in their fight against Capitalism".[31] There is, for example, the claim that it is the Christian's task to further the existing points of "unity, life-community, just regulation and acknowledgement of objective values" in society, and the insistence that, though social conflict as such is "a normal component of a created and fallen world", it is the task of politics to contain and divert it, to incorporate it in a wider unity, not artificially exclude it by a false promise of managed harmony. Both here and elsewhere he makes it clear that, in vigorously defending democracy, he holds no brief for rigorously Rousseauan (*vox populi vox dei*) democracy, or the absolute sovereignty of parliament. He thinks rather that the existence of a supreme Head of State with genuine power, and of various independent powers in society, "will actually prove to be more of a completion and consolidation than an impairment of democracy". The essentials, on the other hand, are "political equality of citizens, competing policies of political parties and the dependence of the rulers on the clearly established confidence of the ruled".[32] In the second half of this long paper he argues that a Christian worker-movement must be based on a moral personalism. But again, the workers must have power, if they are to bring about needful reforms, and this will not be forthcoming in corporativism. Nor is the solution of the Christian Socialists - to stay in the Marxist SPD - a genuine one, since Christian and Marxist value-positions, for example in relation to the bourgeoisie, or to society as a whole, must be different. A year later, Kolnai himself took the way of the Christian Socialists. At a time when Catholics were streaming like lemmings towards corporativism, he could think of no better response.

***

However analytic his occasional journalism was, it must have been a relief to Kolnai to turn sometimes to the pure structural analysis he loved. Three such papers on social and political philosophy appeared during the years covered by this chapter.

The first two are about social power. One, "An Attempt to Classify the General Social Ideas of Power", was published in a Berlin monthly.[33] Here Kolnai puts forward a new classificatory scheme for political ideologies based on their implicit answers to the question "what should be done about power?" He uses the scheme to argue that certain ideologies cannot be realised, and to defend his idea of personalism. His five main types of social power relations are supposed to be exhaustive - though there are mixed or "nuanced" types. His classification is therefore a "natural", or "essential" one. He calls the first type Oligarchy; there must be in society both *Herren* (those with much) and *Knechte* (those with little or no social power). The other types are Liberalism (only *Herren*), Communism (only *Knechte*), Anarchism (neither *Herren* nor *Knechte*), and Personalism (the *Herren-Knechte* relation depending on context). As regards Oligarchy, despite "liberalistic and class-war theories" to the contrary, there is undoubtedly an experienced "drive to subordination" - even in the lower levels of society; but it is hardly an ideal, and tends to find rather shame-faced expression, as in "but, ... surely, there must be some sort of authority!" Liberalism is only realisable if there is an unenfranchised class of *Knechte* to provide the essential conditions for social life; Communism's "no *Herren*" ideal founders on the problem of who is to represent (and how) the impersonal *Herr*, the State; Anarchism, where the social power relation as such is simply abolished, either tends towards Liberalism, or, in its Communist form, is unable to show how fleeting and ad hoc power relations could ever support complex social life. Personalism has to reckon with the fact that contexts or spheres of power tend to be differently ranked, and natural inequalities tend to frustrate attempts to balance out power relations.[34] Nevertheless, it remains the most possible of the ideals, and is already partially realised in advanced Western societies. Elsewhere Kolnai, in a reference to this paper, describes Personalism as "Society as a complex of mutually balancing hierarchical, counter-hierarchical and straightly egalitarian relationships", contrasting it with Oligarchy, which is "Hierarchism proper, *tending to* a *monistic* conception of vertical splitness".[35]

The paper then goes on to survey various actual examples of mixed types (e.g. Oligarchy and Communism = State Socialism). At the end he emphasises that only the first main type is rightist; all the rest are leftist because only the left is interested in working out "ideals" of power, the right regarding power rather as a necessity sanctioned by existing values. But Personalism is least leftist; it has found a way to come to terms with anti-egalitarian arguments while providing a surer guarantee of wide-ranging freedom than Liberalism and Communism, and, as against Anarchism, affirming the complexities of modern society. It also has the merit of incorporating in itself some of the content of the other types.

"The Social Classes' Ideas of Power", published in a leading journal,[36] may seem at first a more sociological, or empirical, work, but it is primarily inspired by a philosophical concern. It is a long paper, with a great many footnotes referring to, and sometimes criticising, the leading thinkers of German sociology and social philosophy. In an introductory section, Kolnai analyses social power into seven elements (examples are "influence on government" and "superior welfare"). His last element is *Vorbildlichkeit*: those in positions of power tend to set the tone for their inferiors, though the latter may also react antagonistically to them, since power and value never completely coincide. Anarchists, both theoretical and psychological, try to dissociate the elements of power, but are never completely successful, since there is a "natural affinity" between them. He then points to the different kinds of power of different groups; to each group there is a (justificatory) power-idea, but again this by no means always coincides with the idea of its value (as with artists, or small farmers). He then takes up the theme of class power, which is hereditary, and possessed by groups irrespective of any power function or achievement, yet more than any other type of power provides the "fabric" of a society. Since there is contingency or arbitrariness about classes themselves, their "power ideas" can never be "indispensable", or have any value-content, and yet, is it not correct that preference for a person of a "higher" class does "in the last analysis" benefit society? Does not history also show that attempts to abolish classes are always frustrated? In our own society, Kolnai goes on, we have the three classes of Nobility, Bourgeoisie and Proletariat, whose members experience themselves as humanly equal and as belonging to one life-community, within which groups tend to be class-related. But social class is not confined to Western culture, even if it is most strongly developed there.

The main part of the paper, in which the power- and value-ideas of the three classes are analysed and compared, will have to be summarised more briefly. The idea that the Nobility should have social power seems irresistible; in Kolnai's phrase, the power of the Nobility is "directly intended" - it is part of the very essence of the Nobility to cultivate certain personal value-qualities. The power-idea of the Nobility is thus that social power should be founded on the foundational values of different groups, and these values should be general human values with a social reference. Clearly this is an ideal very difficult, if not impossible, to realise. The Bourgeoisie emphasises skill, and also property and finance (capitalism), which are not part of personal being. Their power idea is therefore that those should have power who are closest to the goods and achievement values associated with the world of things; power is, therefore, in principle open to all. For the Bourgeoisie, power-idea and value-idea have come apart, and they may even be indifferent to higher values. The obvious contingencies attaching to Bourgeois power make it "class power" par excellence, and more vulnerable to attack. Lastly, the Proletariat stand for the power of those furthest from and poorest in value, who are supposed to represent the equal value of every person. By taking Bourgeois ideas further the Proletariat's values become more material, and yet at the same time return towards those of the Nobility in the idea of society as a "qualitatively definable totality", in which all have their "place-value". The new feature is the Proletarian idea of a fully human life (conceived "from the ground upwards"). The power-idea of the Proletariat is either identical with its value-idea (the true value of Man is to be realised by class power) or completely dissociated from it (since no values are presupposed in its bearers). Kolnai then goes on to enlarge on the dialectical, the revolutionary and the collective features of Proletarian thought about value, and to relate it further to its power-idea. In a final section he discusses the mutual relations of the three classes and their power ideas, and the limits of class-power as such.

In 1931 his "Counter-revolution" was published in two parts in another sociological periodical.[37] This paper also has many substantial footnotes, and even a bibliography at the end. Its purpose is to exhibit the "logic" or inner "meaning" of counter-revolution, as manifested in various ways in postwar Hungary, Italy, Germany, Austria, and other European countries, and also in the prewar history of Europe, especially France. After an introductory section he examines the distinction between ordinary rightist, or conservative, regimes, and counter-revolutionary ones. The latter always in fact bear a rightist sign, since the social tensions required for a real revolution, as opposed to a putsch, cannot be directed to less freedom, rights, and so on, for all. Even the German Fascists, he writes, promise "freedom and bread". In the course of this analysis he alludes to the utopian temptation of counter-revolutionary regimes - a theme he was later to analyse more deeply. This is partly due to the fact that post-revolutionary conservatives find themselves in a completely new situation. Whereas pre-revolutionary rightism is at first "obvious" or "natural", an appeal to the existing value of particular rulers, ways of life or traditions, it now requires the support of a party doctrine worked out in terms of general principles, which means that the "political" theme becomes much more emphatic. Counter-revolutionary rightists have thus to make themselves into a "movement", a profoundly unconservative thing. Their need to crush their opponents, while retaining the sympathy of the people, also makes them dictatorial. They find themselves falling back on the "leader" principle, to disguise the fact that their positive doctrines are bound to seem rather insubstantial. These facts make them lose touch with the old ruling classes, and turn to the military or to irregular forces for support, and to rely on the still disaffected strata of the people.

In the second main part of the paper, Kolnai compares counter-revolution with revolution, and asks first how there can be general support for a return to pre-revolutionary power relations (to *Herrschaft*)? There are, firstly, various ways in which the leftist revolution can fail to be completed; it can fail to establish a new order, or to do away with enough elements of the old order. Besides, there are always some revolutionary features of counter-revolution, for example, appeals to freedom from new restrictions. But counter-revolution is undeniably more "artificial" than revolution, exploiting rather than expressing the mood of society; even its ideology and internal "wings" have an arbitrary and ad hoc feel about them. Certainly, both revolution and counter-revolution want something "new", somehow connected to the old, but the former has a much more "logical", or developmental, ideal. Revolution has a number of "classic" tendencies, according to which leftist or liberal principle is most stressed - freedom, equality, mutual responsibility, etc. But counter-revolution, apart from its appeal to authority and order, has to fasten on something historically particular, as National Socialism exploits the anti-capitalism of certain circles, and "Corporativism" borrowed from Guild Socialism, to conceal its anti-proletarian and nationalist tendency. Both revolution and counter-revolution need to make use of the masses in order to defeat the powers that be, but revolution has a far easier job of it; the rightists have to set about deliberately selecting and organising their "forces" in order to further their own goals. Hence the inevitable counter-revolutionary stress on power and struggle. If Bolshevists worship power, it is for what it can bring about; Fascists cultivate it for its own sake. Counter-revolution's real aim is thus to "depoliticise" the people, whereas revolution means a more politicised life.

The most successful of these inter-war papers was "Der Ekel" (Disgust), which Kolnai sent to the phenemenological annual founded by Husserl.[38] When he arrived at Freiburg in the summer of 1928, Husserl's comment had been: "This is a strange theme you have chosen for yourself, Dr Kolnai!" Strange or not, José Ortega y Gasset, the Spanish philosopher of civilisation, best known for his *The Revolt of the Masses*, quickly had the paper translated for his journal, *Revista de Occidente*, where it was read with profit by Salvador Dalí,[39] and the translation was reprinted in a memorial edition of selected papers in 1950. Had the phenomenological movement not made its disastrous Heideggerian and Sartrian turns, beginning in Husserl's last years at Freiburg, Kolnai might also have had his "Pride" and "Hatred" published in the phenomenological year-book, and become better known as a result.[40] But his Freiburg experience had clearly inoculated him against the movement as it had developed. When the American Phenomenological Association invited him to become a member on his arrival in New York in December 1940, he seems to have made no effort to keep in touch with it, and, although he had some contact with the British Society for Phenomenology in the sixties, he treated it with great reserve. In any case, it was not in Kolnai's character to become too closely identified with any school or tendency.

The theme of "disgust", especially in view of the ambivalence signalled by it (he apologises for having to use the psychoanalytical term), is highly characteristic of Kolnai, and the attentive reader will not often be allowed to forget his fascination with sex. After a brief introduction, he first attempts a conceptual definition of disgust from seven points of view: the range of its appropriate objects, the kind and degree of its actual object-directedness, the extent to which it is also a mental state, the directness of its grasp of objects, its relation to other defensive emotional reactions, its body-relatedness and the extent to which it is a response as opposed to a mere reaction. These dry categories of investigation yield an extremely subtle initial understanding, helped by frequent comparisons with fear, hate, rage, disquiet, contempt and other defensive or negative emotions. He then goes on to pay special attention to the comparison with fear (*Angst*), the other "basic" type of antipathy (later he was to add "hate" to this list). At the end of the section Kolnai briefly discusses the fact that his comparisons are all with negative emotions. He points out that, except at a relatively "abstract" level, there is no neat correlation between negative and positive emotions. It appears to be the case that affirmation is "a more undifferentiated, a directer expression of the whole life of the person", whose various forms only "secondarily" correspond to particular functions and objects; rejection, by contrast, is from the first bound up with an expression of the precise kind of "injury" the person is exposed to.[41] This is one aspect of Kolnai's later stress on "the thematic primacy of the negative". To return to the analysis, fear intends its object as a "*Daseins-Einheit*", as "something there", which is (usually) "dangerous" to the subject and must be avoided. There is an obvious emphasis on a state of affairs. Disgust also intends its object as something "foreign" which in some way "disturbs" the subject's own being, but it is far more concerned with the object itself than its effects, and "penetrates" it cognitively. Sheer "proximity" plays an important role here. The object at the same time "allures" us, our shudders testifying to the possibility of actual intimate contact, and repels. Here, the "state of affairs" (proximity, pointing to *Dasein*) is far less important; the emphasis is on the nature (*Sosein*) of the object.

Kolnai now goes on to analyse "the Disgusting", that is, the things that provoke disgust. He begins with a highly interesting discussion of disgust and the senses, including the degree to which particular senses are involved (smell most and hearing least) and the particular kind of disgustingness revealed to individual senses ("*Sehekel*" - what looks disgusting - is a sui generis quality of the disgusting). The two great "contact" points with the disgusting, he notes, are eating and sex. He then discusses and carefully delimits different types of the (physically) disgusting: putrefaction, excrement, bodily secretions, dirt, creeping things, kinds of food, meaningless bodily proximity of others, fecund life as such, certain bodily deformities. He then turns to types of the morally, or "spiritually", disgusting. There is first the phenomenon of surfeit, where what once pleased has become disgusting though endless sterile repetition. Then come forms of misplaced vitality, usually with a trace of decay, in one's proximity. He instances body-building, riotous exuberance, certain kinds of disordered sexuality. Misplaced "spirituality", as when absolutely everything has to be "thought out", and journalistic softness and flabbiness also belong here. The most thematically moral varieties are mendacity, the indifference to truth and falsity, on the one hand, and disloyalty and faithlessness on the other. This "decay of moral substance" often connotes a kind of "*Lebensplus*", as many picaresque novels have shown. Lastly, he instances "moral formlessness" and sentimentality, especially of a "Russian" variety, where a kind of "life" swamps firm moral endeavour. This part ends with a general discussion of the relation of disgust to life and death. "Poorly organised life", with its lack of order, measure and boundaries, is one thing which especially provokes disgust. But the related "appeal" of the disgusting is not that of any kind of "love", as many have been tempted to think; it is rather "a mocking grin at our irrevocable affinity with the disgusting objects". But the end of this descent is total indifference and death. As for those types which manifest "*Lebensplus*", or "super-vitality", and display a concentrated but impoverished life, possibly "interesting" in itself, this must also be deadly for the human person. The fact is that what really attracts us in disgust is our own secret desire for death, for decomposition into our material elements.

The paper ends with a short discussion of the ethics of disgust. Its ethical function is clearly to "signal(s) the presence of a particular quality of the immoral", that is, the morally "unclean". In this it differs from contempt, which is, in Meinong's term, an "*Urteilsgefühl*", the feeling side of a judgement. But disgust cannot by itself found a "final moral judgement", since it's too closely bound up with extra-moral taste. As for the moral "uncleanness" revealed by disgust, it characterises those who allow themselves to be overcome by evil after putting up merely a token struggle. It thus points to the decay of personal substance, like decaying food. Such people often have something "attractive" about them. On the other hand, a person's inability to feel physical disgust may also indicate "an atrophy of the ethical 'exclusion-experience', an inadequately developed feeling for boundaries and distance". Finally, there is the question of overcoming disgust, which is often required. One obvious issue concerns the intention. Does the overcoming include the desire to destroy the object, or is it an aspect of love, in the sense of making the object better or affirming its positive values? Overcoming for the sake of love must be good. But if disgust is overcome for the sake of destruction, and especially if the attempt is made to eliminate it altogether, we are faced with an evil. Love should be stronger than disgust; but to eliminate disgust entirely is self-mutilation, the destruction of something of biological, metaphysical and ethical importance.[42]

The other two phenomenological analyses of moral or morally significant affects were published in the philosophical annual of the the Görres society in Germany. This was a Catholic intellectual group named after the great nineteenth-century defender of Catholic thought against protestant Prussia.

"Der Hochmut" was published in 1931.[43] In keeping with the nature of the journal it appeared in, its approach, and certainly its last section, is, in one sense, "religious"; yet, given the underlying phenomenological approach to mental contents, it is undoubtedly philosophical, and forms an interesting counterpart to Max Scheler's papers on Humility and Reverence. The title is naturally translated "pride", but it soon becomes clear that Kolnai is talking about "spiritual pride", or the kind of pride which one might occasionally call "Satanic". This is a very different thing from what is sometimes called in English "proper pride (in oneself)", or pride in one's achievements, family, school, or other aspects of one's "own" value. The latter can be a form of *Hochmut*, but it needn't be. Nor are we talking here about what Kolnai often celebrates as "a proper distance" (or reserve). Kolnai himself was sometimes accused of *Hochmut*. As this paper ends with a section on overcoming pride, it looks as though the paper was written out of his own awareness of his spiritual tendencies, and the desire to be free of them. But he is also anxious to establish a sphere of "proper pride", where moral reproach is mistaken. The main difference between Hochmut and "pride in" things, he says, is that the former puts the prime emphasis on the self whose values "pride in" (*Stolz*) relate to. The *hochmütig* man does not respond to his qualities, possessions, and so on, as such, but as tokens of "the lofty value of his self", since this is for him the real measure of value. On the other hand, *Hochmut* is not necessarily an individual's vice. There can be collective pride of a nation or political party, where one's own group is the standard of value, or intellectual pride, where difference of opinion about the world (including its inhabitants) is "an irrelevance". The point about *Hochmut* being its own source of value can be put in this way: there is "an apriorism of pride". The proud man cannot feel himself a creature among others. In this he is distinct from the vain man; vanity may tend towards an "abstract, qualityless superiority", yet it is still dependent on a "public". *Hochmut*, therefore, though it may start as just a feeling or an emotion, in the sense of a response, becomes a spiritual or psychological posture, or stance, something one "adopts". All moral evil has a touch of it, qua refusal to conform to the order of values, but not all sins manifest it in the full sense. As a form of intellectual pride Kolnai mentions the interpretation of the ego as an exclusively thinking subject (that is, as wholly active, not affected by the world). Philosophical formalists and idealists are always, therefore, liable to pride.

Kolnai then turns to particular varieties of *Hochmut*. There is first the pride of exclusion, in which the whole of the rest of reality apart from the self - and certain persons and things that "represent" the self - pales into insignificance. Then there are forms of pride linked to the desires for power and achievement, including the pride of the tyrant, for whom all subjects are merely instruments, and that of the "careerist" or "striver" who will adapt himself to anything in the effort to "get on". One special form of "intellectual" pride is a kind of Pantheism, which he sees in the Stoics and in Spinoza rather than in Plotinus and Bruno. If everything is God, then I am exempted from any special submission or dedication to any particular objects. But if my experience teaches me that I am not after all lost in the world-substance, I may surreptitiously make an exception of myself and hold myself in proud apartness from the world. Kolnai then discusses the complicated relations between *Hochmut* and feelings of security and insecurity, and goes on to compare "outer" pride, whose occasion or object is, say, physical strength, or "moralistic Pharisaism", with its "inner" counterpart, such as that of the "isolated, world-despising cynic", or the nihilist. "Inner" varieties more easily approach the "ideal" of pride, since they can more easily "represent" the subject. Yet the apparently complete absence of inner spiritual tensions, effort, dividedness, and so on, may also be an indicator of pride. Again, whereas "power emphasises more the 'visible' raised position over others' heads, money emphasises more the denial of the world's intrinsic qualities and the subject's abstract omni-validity". Kolnai sums up his discussion of types of power with the claim that, in the end, all *Hochmut* is a rejection of God, as "the conjunction of concrete value and reality". In the final section of the paper, Kolnai briefly discusses the overcoming of *Hochmut* (rather than the culture of *Demut*, humility, its proper counterpart). All subject-object relations, for example cognitive ones, require the subject to view things from a (metaphorically) raised position; this only becomes pride when the other necessary element of conformity to the object (with its positive or negative value) is omitted. So the overcoming of pride can't be either self-abasement alone or relating oneself to objects alone. He sums it up as follows: "Be aware of your own 'littleness', but yet your own finite measure of 'greatness'; your 'world' is a wonderful manifold, open to you in principle, even waiting for you; but you must approach it with reverence and care, with countless acts of self-mastery."

The last of the three "moral phenomenological" papers is his essay on hatred.[44] It was not published until 1935, well into the period of complete Nazi power in Germany. It is hard to imagine Kolnai spontaneously submitting the paper under these circumstances. But it is part of a Festschrift to mark the 80th birthday of the President of the Görres Society, and was probably commissioned some time before publication. In any case, the theme itself (and its unspoken application to the Nazis) was very near to Kolnai's heart. Though well aware of the superiority of love, he was not only a "good hater" by nature, but convinced that hate had an indispensable part to play in the morally most urgent task - the elimination of evils.

Hate is, then, his analysis begins, a fundamental tone of opposition. Is it only properly applicable to persons, as is often held? Kolnai thinks not. His hatred for, say, conurbations is far more like his hatred for an evil opponent than even his strong dislike of a particular food. Hate is a feeling in which the whole person is involved; it has both "depth" and "centrality", though the former is more prominent. In contrast to passing states, it is a "*Haltung*" or stance which "represents" and partly constitutes the person. Its object must be fully given as objectively powerful or important, not removable without trouble. It must involve some kind of struggle or encounter. Although one can impotently hate "upwards", one cannot hate "downwards" (weaker, less significant objects). Hate is directed towards the essence of its object in its effects on the subject, and ideally ends in its annihilation. Kolnai then passes to the grounds of hatred. There is always, at least potentially, a double intention: its objects are both the object's nature, and its dynamic role, though the emphasis may vary. The hater always somehow "seeks out" his object, though something also "suggests" it. Occasions include vengeance, moral indignation, "objective hostility" (as in serious rivalry), the clash of opposed ways or views of life, possibly "over-compensation" for a love which has to be given up, or self-hate in consequence of failure. In the next part there is a comparison with love. Here we find a much greater range of objects, and of intentions, corresponding to the manifoldness of being and the limitations of non-being. There is in fact no parallel to absolute annihilation. This is no mere accident of language. Love's diversity reflects the variety of functional relations to objects; "getting rid of" is simple. It can be put like this: the *Ordo Amoris* (order of love) structures our lives, whereas hate has a "point-like" existence wherever effective and powerful "antagonists" come on the scene. Hate is in fact "a narrower and more specific phenomenon than love"; almost anything can be loved, but, for hate, there must be at least a suggestion of enmity. Hence the latter tends essentially to be reciprocal, whereas animals can be loved without even knowing it (let alone inanimate objects). Love is an immanent part of life, hatred marks some kind of interference. Love brings a background of other things loved; hatred isolates its object and makes its nature more prominent. Kolnai then discusses combinations of love and hate. It is no accident that love for an object may be succeeded by hate for it, since both imply close attention; but love and hate at the same time (ambivalence) is only possible if we mentally split the object in two. Hate has a metaphysical aspect; in it we seem to struggle with an evil power for the possession of our world. Hence all hate has a religious element ("for God and against the Devil"). This accounts for the many hints of Manichaeism one comes across among unsophisticated people. All hate somehow ascribes world-importance to its object. This occurs with love too, of course, but less immediately, because of the essentially "fighting" element of hate. But it is the "demonising" tendency of hate that makes it morally questionable, since the greater hater is often the worse man. It can so easily happen that the hater, directing himself against "evil", imputes non-evil and valuable elements to this "evil" as a result of the antagonism, and thus himself does evil. Thus hatred has an inescapably destructive element; but there could be no energetic reform or criticism without it. Despite this, hatred can be overcome; we may respect, even love, the man in the hated opponent. There must be some personal representative of evil principles if we are to make our opposition really effective; yet we can strive to put the stress on the impersonal side of things.

It is worth noting once more the personal involvement Kolnai had with the topic of this paper. Both Ferenc Fejtő and Jászi, to take just two examples, accused Kolnai in their letters of unjustly "diabolising" his opponents, but he normally resisted such charges, and justified his fulminations. One of his later correspondents, the Spaniard Vicente Marrero, told him that he knew that, deep down, Kolnai's hate-campaigns against individuals were really directed against the state of the world and the decline of civilisation, rather than the representative figures that attracted his attention. Perhaps this was wishful thinking. If it was, we have at least this paper, with its indication that, for all his protestations, Kolnai was deep down able to accept the bad side of this very prominent and "essential" character trait of his.

Chapter Eight

Fighting for the West in Vienna
(1930-1937)

During the early thirties the Heimwehr group in Austria grew stronger and stronger. The Styrian branch actually staged an unsuccessful coup in 1931, but nothing was done to control the movement as a whole. The elections of April 1932 saw the first marked "democratic" success of the Austrian Nazi party. Parliamentary sessions, never very productive after 1920, were becoming a farce, as the two main power blocs simply "confronted" each other over the burning issues of the day. In May the new chancellor, Engelbert Dollfuß, began his first term of office, and set about trying to awaken a national consciousness, in place of the provincial, party, and religious loyalties which had hitherto dominated Austrian politics. But as bourgeois society began to disintegrate there was a pervading atmosphere of crisis.

The early thirties were also bad for Kolnai personally. He was strongly affected by the increasing deterioration of Austrian social and political life, and later wrote:

> I suffered then more acutely than in later years from my digestive ailment - deserving or not the dignified name of a 'sluggish liver': I used to call it morbus fascisticus.[1]

However, it is noteworthy that the poetry he preserved from his Vienna period is much less subjective than his youthful Hungarian verse. The collection of often swashbuckling "Vienna District Wars" poems is objective in tone, and even the "mood" poems, such as "The Accursed Café" have a universality about them. The most successful is, perhaps, the undated "Song of the Dog", which symbolises the refusal to surrender to barbarism. He pictures the dog in its kennel still occasionally hearing the call of the wild, but resolutely "out-barking" it. He remains faithful to the ancestral covenant with man, and gladly submits to the order and measure of civil society in a human world.

Kolnai was also gradually cementing his ties with Irma Gémes's daughter Elisabeth, whom he had known since about 1924 or 1925. She had first been trained as a gardener at Schönbrunn Palace in Vienna,[2] but then turned to art and design, living a Bohemian life in Paris, then Berlin (where Róbert Vámbéry knew her), then again in Paris, and, for a time, in London. She and Kolnai used to meet in Vienna when she came home on visits to her mother, and began to write to each other - Kolnai calls their correspondence "preposterously bulky" - in 1930. Only two complete letters from Kolnai to her survive; on the other hand Elisabeth kept many extracts from these letters, which are often of great interest, as she encouraged him to write on philosophical and other serious themes. By the mid-thirties they were clearly strongly attracted to each other.

But his letters to Irene Grant provide a much completer picture of Kolnai in his last Austrian years, when, as he later put it, he had "appointed (himself) a spiritual agent of the West on a special mission in Vienna".[3] She and her husband Donald originally came to Vienna in 1921 to administer charitable relief for the Society of Friends. There was no contact on that occasion, but, in the 1930s, they began to visit Vienna as officials of the International Fellowship of Reconciliation, and got to know the Polányis well. They were also important figures in the Christian Socialist revival in England. Kolnai did not meet either of them till early in 1932. Donald was working in Geneva at the time, so he only met Irene, but the two became firm friends. The Grant children gave him the name of Knöpflmacher, after one of his generals in the "Vienna District Wars". Kolnai wrote regularly to Irene until the war took him to America. The passionate feel of some of the letters prompted her to assure me that their relationship was, in fact, always perfectly proper.

When Kolnai entered the SDP at the end of 1930, he also joined the League of Religious Socialists (BRS), which had been a distinct group within the main party since 1926. The slogan of their paper, for which Kolnai wrote at least two articles, was "Struggle for a new Humanity", and its logo was the Red Flag with a large cross on it. The BRS was also inter-denominational and, as such, attracted the interest of Karl Polányi, a religious agnostic, and Christian Socialist friends of his from abroad, such as the Grants, though it was mistrusted by most Austrian Catholics and SDP members. It was a primarily activist group, trying to convert Christian trade unionists to socialism, and to show that socialists did not have to be atheists. Father Bichlmair was a member, and acted as middleman between the BRS and the Catholic hierarchy. When the papal encyclical *Quadragesimo Anno* appeared in May 1931 it was clear that the Pope would not recognise it, since he reaffirmed the incompatibility of Socialism and Catholicism. The BRS took no notice, arguing that, as their view of man and society was Catholic, the rejection was based on a misunderstanding.

Towards the end of 1931, Kolnai was persuaded by his friend Richard Redler to leave the BRS and join him in setting up a new organisation, the Christian Democratic Union (CDV). His membership of the SDP might be useful if the party took exception to Redler's move. Kolnai was not personally inclined to help him, but he did have strong reservations about the BRS. Its leader, Otto Bauer (no relation to the SDP leader), presided over the League in a distinctly autocratic style. Besides that, Kolnai thought that left-wing Catholicism should not be represented by a predominantly pastoral group, but by a proper political association, seeing the political task of the day not so much in social terms (as the Church itself tended to do) as in the attempt to preserve the essential "formal" aspects of democracy, which would alone allow the full development and flourishing of persons. Accordingly, he felt morally obliged to help Redler, and the CDV was inaugurated early in 1932, with Kolnai as its "second vice-chairman".[4] The new organisation announced the appearance of four pamphlets, the third of which, "Christliche Demokratie", was to be by Kolnai. But it was never published, probably because the CDV collapsed soon after he left it towards the end of 1932. Again, the main problem seems to have been the style of leadership. Redler's too much resembled that of the successful Heimwehr and Nazi movements.

But his leaving the CDV clearly had something to do with his having "suffered (him)self to fall rather badly in love with Isolde", Redler's secretary and the former leader of the Catholic Girl Students' Association. Kolnai refers to "Isolde" in his memoirs,[5] but it seems likely that he chose this name (hinting at a certain Wagnerian romantic streak in her) to preserve the anonymity of Ilse von Scholey, who was still living when he wrote. But, as he says himself, the relationship was really an infatuation, although they were "informally" engaged for two years from the autumn of 1932, and he was still deeply affected in September 1934. In the memoirs he says that she was not only beautiful but also intelligent and ambitious, "and capable of fervent devotion to her work and her co-workers"; elsewhere he calls her "poor stupid Ilse",[6] and even writes that he "all but married a worthless Austrian girl for a little wart under her left eye (which she forbade me to eat)"![7] She was also a writer, and in October 1932 they "pondered the plan of editing a Catholic-democratic and pro-Western review, to be financed by the 'Little Entente' governments".[8] But this came to nothing. Kolnai surmises that his attraction to her had something to do with her being the daughter of a cavalry officer; and that she, for her part, was counting on his becoming rich and famous. "In the spring of 1935", he says, "our ways parted definitively". She herself escaped to England after Austria's fall, and taught German in a girls' school.

From at least 1930 Kolnai regularly attended and spoke at what was known as the "Fleischerkreis". Dr Georg Fleischer, a shy and rather silent man, and a little younger than Kolnai, was a wealthy jurist. His *Kreis*, or circle, met at his house on Mondays to hear and discuss lectures or papers on problems of public law, jurisprudence, sociology and Austrian History. Lisbeth Gombrich, sister of Ernst, the well-known writer on art, who was also a member, recalled a rather small group of about ten people accommodated round Fleischer's dining-table. Kolnai didn't contribute much to the discussions, but when he did he spoke slowly, with a pronounced Hungarian accent, and was always worth hearing. His status in the group was second only to that of Erich Voegelin, whose book on the Authoritarian State he reviewed favourably, without wholly agreeing with it, in 1936.[9] Kolnai later felt that he had done him less than justice in *The War Against the West*, and, in his memoirs, expressed great admiration for his particular intellectual gifts, especially his ability to "interpret(ing) tangible single facts in a wide philosophical perspective".[10] The "most attractive" member of the group, however, was Lisbeth Gombrich, "a young lady of superior intelligence, radiant integrity and an unconventionally charming presence". She had wide interests, and would allow Kolnai to escort her home after the meetings.[11] Perhaps Kolnai's flirtatious manner was here directed at an inappropriate target; much later he wrote to George Lányi: "I think she thinks badly of me *both* because I (catholic, plebeian, without money or prospects) was secretly rather in love with her *and* because I never 'declared myself'. I believe she has become a confirmed old maid".[12] Another member, Rudolph Brendel, seems to have impressed Kolnai as a slightly raffish person, but "his dry, rationalistic, juridical turn of mind - by no means indifferent to the spiritual or essential aspects of politics, that is to say - positively enchanted me".[13] Kolnai tried to get Béla Menczer to have his "superb analysis" of the Austrian political situation translated and published in England. Of Gregor Sebba, and of Dr Falk, a female psychoanalyst, who knew Kolnai well and told Miss Gombrich about his phobia for "wood-bugs", he says nothing.

Kolnai does not seem to have played a very active role in either of the two outstanding Catholic intellectual groups in Vienna at this time, the Leo Society ("a kind of Austrian Catholic Academy") and the university Logos Verein, which organised small, intense, discussion groups. Despite his interest in the topics raised there, and the close links between the Logos Verein and the BRS, he probably found them too much coloured by the prevailing clericalist rightism of Catholic circles. However, in October 1929 he addressed the sociological section of the Leo Society on

"Authority and Democracy", and is at least once recorded in a list of "members and guests" of Logos, along with Richard Redler and Ilse von Scholey. An extensive summary of a paper he gave to the "political-sociological" section of some society in late 1932 has survived, without the name of the sponsoring group. Its title is "Outlines of a personalist concept of the state and society". Under the main headings of "the person", "community", "society", "the state", "equality" and "democracy in state and society" it brings together many of the themes more or less briefly touched on in this and the previous chapter. The typed summary of the notes seems to have been kept by Karl Polányi.[14]

Kolnai's preferred colleagues and friends were by no means all on the left or centre. Among his rightist colleagues in the editorial offices of *Schönere Zukunft* was Alfred Missong, who became a close friend and companion, fully appreciating his brand of humour; in 1929, through Missong and the Leo Society he met Ernst Karl Winter, his senior by five years, who made an immense impression on him:

> Winter was not only what might at least be called a genius but also a character of imposing sovereignty; yet at the same time somewhat of the sectarian dictatorial type, prone to overestimate himself - which is by no means incompatible with extraordinary powers - and, though always at pains to overarch and reconcile opposites on a higher plane (the "transcendent" vantage-point of Plato's politikos: that is, his own), indubitably tinged with a slight degree of unbalance; moreover, however widely read and intensely intellectual, he was wanting in polish and urbanity.[15]

Towards 1925, Winter, who had never accepted the legitimacy of Chancellor Seipel's acquiescence in the Republic, founded "Austrian Action", a political movement in imitation of Action Francaise, espousing monarchism, legitimism and traditionalism. Winter's critique of the government was thus at first made "from the right", but, when the government began to move rightwards from the late twenties, he shifted his ground towards the left, with the idea of the "social monarchy": "a Catholic and monarchical State in close alliance with the Social Democratic Party and Trade Unions".[16] This realisation of the need for discussion and compromise with the Marxist SDP led to his re-evaluation of liberal democracy, which he had originally rejected. This, in turn, led his thoughts to its nearest representative, Czechoslovakia, with its quasi-imperial president, Masaryk, and thus to the idea of "The Emperor returning via Prague".[17] These mental gymnastics must have been immensely stimulating (usually *a contrario*) to Kolnai, and he derived enormous pleasure and profit from pitting Winter ("an even more remarkable personality") against Polányi (whose political judgements were more likely to be correct). Winter himself had "Wednesday evening discussions" in his own home, and they also met at the flat of Irma Gémes.

But Winter was by no means just an ingenious dialectical thinker and debater, and his influence on Kolnai also derives from his role in Austrian public life in the mid-thirties. As has been pointed out above, when Dollfuß became chancellor parliamentary government had become all but impossible, though the need to take measures to stave off the Nazi threat was becoming acute. Two months after Hitler became German chancellor, after a bitterly conducted "debate" in the Austrian parliament the house divided equally, and there were loud accusations of malpractice. One by one, beginning with Renner, the three presidents of the house stepped down to vote with their parties, making further procedure legally impossible. Dollfuß at once seized his chance and closed the session. Next day, the members found themselves locked out, and, for the next fourteen months, government was carried on under Habsburg Emergency Powers designed for use in the war to deal with food supplies and never repealed. A series of decrees followed, strengthening the Church and the Nationalist Right - the Nazi party was banned in June - and weakening the powers of the Left. Winter, an old army and university friend of Dollfuß, now protested in public on behalf of the workers, indignantly denouncing the dismantling of Parliament as both unconstitutional and un-conservative, and calling for a new Right-Left coalition to deal with the Nazi threat. The Socialist leader Renner might have been prepared to accept this, but, as Kolnai found out by experience in January 1934, Otto Bauer was not. In company with "little" Otto Bauer, of the BRS, he visited the "great" Bauer in his office and put it to him that the only way of saving Austria from totalitarian rule from the right was for the SDP to cooperate with the CSP in this exceptional crisis. "Sadly and firmly", says Kolnai, he rejected this course, which he said would be tantamount to the "moral suicide" of the party.[18] A month later came the civil war, with a rapid victory for the regime; several hundreds were killed and the SDP, together with all socialist institutions, including the BRS, were abolished. Winter, whose recent efforts on behalf of the workers were widely known - though he now condemned the SDP leaders - was now asked by Dollfuß to try and build up once more a new kind of pro-government and anti-Nazi Workers' Movement within the coming Corporative State. He accepted, on condition that various other things were done on behalf of the workers, and was given the post of third vice-Mayor of Vienna. Winter now approached Kolnai with the offer of a job, to assist him in what had become known - and widely mistrusted - as "Aktion Winter".[19] Kolnai thought for some time, and then wrote a long letter of refusal, part of which survives. The gist of this fragment is that Winter's "Action", for all its encouragement of workers' "discussions", amounts in the end to buying them off in exchange for welfare. It completely ignores the more important thing: that the workers should be treated as persons. Only a democratic constitution can ensure that. For this reason he, Kolnai, will not do anything to identify himself with the Dollfuß dictatorship, though he will continue to support their stand against Nazism. The letter, Kolnai says, was never answered, and their friendship considerably cooled, though was revived later, in the USA. Aktion Winter was shut down by Dollfuß's successor, Schuschnigg, in 1936 under Axis pressure. A small example of Kolnai's indirect support for Dollfuß took place when Róbert Vámbéry was visiting his friend in Vienna, shortly after the rebellion had been crushed. The two of them were in the Café Muzeum with Irma Gémes and Klára Erdélyi, Vámbéry's future wife. Karl Kraus entered. Many young left-wingers had just deserted him because of his support for Dollfuß. Vámbéry, a rightist, stood up, as did Kolnai, "although he had reservations about Kraus's position".[20]

In July 1934 Dollfuß was brutally assassinated in an attempted Nazi coup, and there was a relative lull in Austrian politics as support for the Nazis and even the Heimwehr temporarily abated. But, since the West now did little to help in the struggle for Austrian independence, far too much depended on Mussolini's support. This situation was exacerbated when Schuschnigg, the new chancellor, refused to condemn the Italian invasion of Abyssinia in October 1935. But German pressure on Austria was steadily growing, and when the Rome-Berlin axis came into being in 1936 it was only a matter of time before Germany would enforce the *Anschluß*. After a great deal of dithering, Kolnai left the country in March 1937. A year later the Nazi tanks rolled over the Austrian border. Having put up a plucky fight against the arm-twisting "diplomacy" and other terrorist tactics of Hitler during the three and a half years of his chancellorship, Schuschnigg, resolved that no "German" blood should be spilt in Austria, surrendered his country without a shot being fired in self-defence.

***

Towards the end of 1933 Dollfuß inaugurated a new weekly, *Der Christliche Ständestaat* (The Christian Corporative State). Its purpose was to fight Nazism, and incidentally attract readers away from the increasingly Nazi-tainted *Schönere Zukunft*. Dietrich von Hildebrand, critical disciple and friend of Scheler, was appointed editor. Dollfuß also found him a university chair in philosophy at the expense of Heinrich Gomperz, who was forced to retire early because his leftist sympathies would not allow him to join Dollfuß's new patriotic "Fatherland Front". Dollfuß made the university accept Hildebrand against the will of the faculty, who did not share his (and Kolnai's) assessment of Hildebrand's stature as a philosopher. His lectures could at first only be given under police protection. The sacrifice of Gomperz and the title of the weekly gave Kolnai two good reasons for not wanting to contribute to it. He also loathed Hildebrand's widely shared partiality for the Italian Fascists - only the absence of racism, he thought, distinguished them from the Nazis - and the unctuous clericalism he frequently displayed: "Hildebrand", he wrote, "so great a philosopher, and no character, no backbone at all. Clericalism educates people to dispense with honour".[21] Nevertheless, he was prepared "to combat the central Foe of Humanity, without ever ... approving of any other Fascist element in the world"[22] under the pseudonym of Abraham van Helsing, who, in Bram Stoker's *Dracula*, fights the spiritual power of demonic evil with intelligence and ordinary material means - in Kolnai's case, pen and ink. Kolnai wrote nine articles and a short gloss for it between June 24th 1934 and June 28th 1936, all but two of them in 1934 and early 1935. After that he may have begun to find the political atmosphere insupportable, as he certainly did in the matter of editorial meetings at *Der Oesterreichischer Volkswirt*, and was in any case now deeply involved in *The War against the West*.

In the first of his "Van Helsing" articles, "Marxist and Liberal Elements in National Socialism",[23] he develops the theme that leftist thinking derives from a fall away from Christianity; Nazi thinking takes this much further. In "Heidegger and National Socialism",[24] he compares Heidegger's analysis of human being (*Dasein*) with characteristic themes of Nazi writers; there is an unmistakable kinship between them, he says.[25] "The Idea and the Form of the State"[26] explores the limits suggested by Christianity on the central question of politics, with special reference to totalitarianism. The most philosophically interesting of these papers is "The Misuse of the 'Vital'",[27] an excellent discussion of vital values (with special reference to Scheler) and of vitalism in political and social life (as in the Catholic youth movements). Kolnai's analyses cast doubt on Scheler's claim that there is a stratum of vital values superior to and clearly distinct from utility and hedonic values. Why, for example, cannot sexual pleasure itself be a vital, instead of a lower hedonic value, and are not the values of good biological functioning themselves useful in relation to preserving life? There is surely also a close relation between vital and aesthetic values, for example "good breeding" and beauty. These and many other instances show that things are more complicated than Scheler thought. He then shows that the typical values of Nazis are not "vital" ones, as Hans Eibl argued in their favour; nor is liberal utilitarianism in fact exclusively tied to the lower values of utility and pleasure and cut off from spiritual values, as its concern for the person alone shows. In late 1934 he wrote two more hard-hitting analytical articles on Spann's theory of *Ganzheit* (Totality);[28] he shows that Spann's formal analysis of wholes and parts will not stand up as a general thesis; it is merely tailored to the task of showing that the individual has no real being at all except as a member of state and society, and that the sole issue is: is he making his contribution to the whole or not? This, says Kolnai, has nothing whatsoever to do with the community of human persons, and is totally anti-Christian. In the second paper Kolnai sets out his own social philosophy whilst attacking further elements of Spann's shaky conception.[29] The following articles, on the spiritual foundations of Catholic Nationalism, and on Julius Langbehn, author of the notorious *Rembrandt als Erzieher*, are of less interest.

Kolnai also contributed regularly to the Budapest periodical *Századunk* (Our Century), the true successor (from 1926) of Jászi's *Huszadik Század*. It was run by Róbert Vámbéry's father, Rusztem, a clever lawyer, who knew how to evade some of the more severe censorship regulations of the Horthy regime, and continue almost in the pre-revolutionary tradition. Of Kolnai's articles (excluding notes, answers to questions, reviews, etc), three are longish factual-historical surveys of recent events, and one is a very long joint obituary article on Chesterton and Karl Kraus[30] ("two utterly different and unconnected but in some respects strikingly analogous champions of Common Sense and haters of Commercialism").[31] The two most important philosophical papers are entitled "On Human Equality" and "Democracy and Reality".

The heart of the Equality paper[32] is the "The five bases of Equality". There is, firstly, personhood, and the (graded) moral disvalue of persons or institutions that ignore or deny this. The second support is objectivity in human relationships, including treating one's fellows as the persons they are, and the sense of standing with others over against an objective reality. Then there is the unity of mankind; some kind of mutual understanding is always possible among human beings. But there is also a vital "element of partial inequalities"; human beings are not just abstract "persons", but members of groups, for example, national groups, which are not equal. Lastly, there is the principle of variations, as in the idea of "equality among unequals"; value-differences between persons are important, the crucial equalities are "despite" these, and must not lead to their complete removal. In the final section of the paper Kolnai makes four brief points about social equality. Firstly, it is indispensable as a "measure of social progress". Secondly, there is no one organizational principle here; the important thing is to reduce selected inequalities. Thirdly, equality is only a value against a background of mutually compensating inequalities. This requires social stability, rather than totality. But, lastly, there are irremovable limits to this; inequalities will always tend to coincide."[33]

The paper entitled "Democracy and Reality"[34] reflects, inter alia, on the self-destruction of democracy in Germany and Austria. Kolnai's conception of democracy is of a political universal of great value, that "ought" not to be rejected, except as a temporary expedient which will not kill its spirit, but only some of its manifestations. He then turns to the question, much canvassed at the time, whether a democracy may legitimately defend itself by force. He accepts a strong affinity between democracy and the renunciation of force, but argues that peace is not the highest value, and that, if we accept that the police must sometimes use force against law-breakers, then we must logically accept its use against a Fascist putsch. It is a test of the soundness of moral judgement and the wholeheartedness of political will. He goes on to attack the contemporary mistrust of democracy as "formal", and the claim that "material" democracy, as in welfare provision, is the only true democracy. Democracy, he replies, is essentially formal, and concerns the structure of human relations. Democratic "formalism" is quite another matter. In a last section he defends the conception of human rights (e.g. freedom of speech) as limited and graded, as well as the need to keep alive the sense of limitations being exceptional.

Towards the end of his life Kolnai looked back on "Der Inhalt der Politik" (What politics is about) as his best work in political philosophy, writing "eine gediegene Arbeit" ("a sound", or "well-fashioned, piece of work") on the cover of his copy.[35] Here, in his analysis of politics, and especially his treatment of its "irrationality", we find an anticipation of his later thought about "practice". In the first part he strongly attacks the conceptions of the State and of politics put forward by Carl Schmitt in his very influential book, *Der Begriff des Politischen*; in the second he puts forward his own view of what politics is about.

Kolnai first briefly identifies Schmitt as one of a group of "irrationalists of life and power", alongside Nietzsche, Klages, Sorel, Pareto, Spengler and Heidegger. These thinkers tend to hold that "life" and "existence", and their (vital) values, are self-sufficient and not in need of any guidance by reason. Indeed, the attempt to give it, as in liberalism and democracy, simply weakens them. Since life in the social sphere is power, its only test is conflict with other powers. Accordingly, Schmitt holds that the Political is founded on enmity, and the state on war and preparedness for war. The central value categories of politics are thus Friend and Foe. Although Schmitt's book had a special attraction for the German Right, it also reflected the widespread disillusion with rationality characteristic of Europe as a whole at this time. Democracy and liberal values had taken a serious battering in the parliaments and the press of Europe; almost everywhere opinion tended towards the two irrational poles of Fascism and Bolshevism. Kolnai therefore saw in Schmitt's book a serious and impressive attempt to defend the kind of views which made support for National Socialism possible among German academics and other thinkers. He also saw that Karl Schmitt had some right on his side. So the book had to be carefully answered. Underlying the difference between Schmitt and Kolnai about politics there was, of course, a fundamental difference of world-view. Kolnai does not make any systematic attempt to meet Schmitt at this level, but concentrates his fire on the interpretation of politics. His strategy is to show, by an appeal to ordinary experience and common sense, that, though Schmitt makes some valid points about politics, he wildly exaggerates their significance, and produces a very distorted picture. He also hints that this distortion is itself politically motivated.

Schmitt's position is based on the fact that there comes a point in many practical debates when reasoned discussion can take the parties no further; principle collides with principle, and there is no higher principle to appeal to. This, says Schmitt, is where, say, an economic conflict would cease to be just economic and become political. Kolnai agrees that there is a difference between political and non-political antagonisms. But experience shows that the economic dispute would only become a political one if it was something one could argue and discuss about in terms of shared value-categories, since debate is universal in politics. Behind Kolnai's critique of Schmitt is a disagreement about what counts as reason. Schmitt's view appears to be that, where there is no "algorithmic" procedure for settling a dispute, it cannot be settled by reason, but must be settled by political means (i.e., in his opinion, war). Kolnai assumes that reason is not exhausted by logical procedures, but includes concentrating oneself in one's personal being, responding sensitively to all relevant values and their demands, treating one's fellow disputants as fellow persons, and so on. He is aware that this will not always avert war, or violent conflict. But it often does. Even if it doesn't, war is not just an irrational collision of powers, but can be "bound up with the value and dignity of persons and communities". Underlying his position is the assumption of a common humanity, which must include shared values, a common ground on which to meet, as opposed to the view of the "irrationalists of life and power", for whom different social groups could amount to different species.

Kolnai also points out that Schmitt's definitions, especially the emphasis on war and readiness for war, implausibly suggest that politics is almost entirely a matter of external relations. On the contrary, he argues, politics is primarily a matter of internal relations: "the detailed structure of the 'order' of the State, the question of how it is ruled and ought to be ruled". Even though politics cannot be confined to internal matters, "the question of who is to prevail over whom is necessarily subordinate to the question how the communal life of mankind is to be structured". Politics is precisely an alternative to physical annihilation. Not friend versus foe but "the co-existence of opponents on the basis of a social unit of reference" - something the parties have in common. Kolnai again and again concedes the irrational element of politics. Even discussion is fundamentally ambiguous, and the element of power-struggle is never absent from it. But this is "spiritual irrationality", inevitably to some extent conditioned by instinct. Without some conception of a common good, however vague, argument would not make sense. Political rationality is, he agrees, manifold and in many ways elusive; its elements, even its ground, is not fixed; compromise is essential to it; it is, he implies, hardly ever a matter of simple linear argument from a set of premises. All this may give the appearance of total irrationality. But there is always some common ground upon which fellow persons may stand. We see here again the scope of Kolnai's personalism. It hovers in the background of this paper, though it is not as such appealed to.[36]

***

Several facts about Kolnai's life during the thirties suggest the idea that it was a kind of prelude to his emigration to the West. But the most decisive factor was of course his work on *The War Against the West*,[37] the book which made him, for a time, well known in certain circles in England and the USA. He was always exceptionally vulnerable to stimuli from his environment, and never found it very easy to decide what to write. So, after sending off his "lost" textbook of phenomenological ethics in 1932, he was casting about for another major topic. He was seriously considering a book on Spann, and also one on Equality - especially after Irene Grant sent him R.H. Tawney's book on the subject. But then E.K. Winter suggested that he write a book on "the National Socialist mind". This was an excellent idea, and its first fruits seem to have been a lecture in Budapest, given on January 5th 1933 to an audience of bankers and treasury officials on the political programme of National Socialism. The *Pester Lloyd*, which briefly summarised it, also recorded the "loud applause" which followed his "luminous" presentation. This was quickly followed by his first published paper in English, "Will German Catholics Go Left?". Donald Grant helped him to place this in an American "Protestant-progressive" weekly, *The World Tomorrow*.[38] Kolnai describes it as:

definitely Catholic in spirit; it emphasised rather originally the nexus between Catholic dogmatism and the quest of "objective truth" - seen in extreme opposition to Nazi and similar "collective subjectivism".[39]

Work on the book itself - so far confined to the accumulation of material - began to make him think seriously of emigrating, first to Zürich, with its excellent German libraries, which he visited over Easter 1933, then, at the prompting of Irene Grant in the summer, to England. He went home to Budapest for a fortnight in the autumn to discuss the matter there. By March 1934 he told Elisabeth Gémes, who was then living in Paris, that he was giving her address to the publishers of his articles and books as a forwarding address for the future.

The following extracts from Kolnai's letters will serve to shed more light on Kolnai's life during these last Austrian years.

April 11th 1932. To Irene Grant
This first, very long, letter is in poor English compared to what he will be writing in a few years' time. He writes of books lent or recommended, makes a joke about the split infinitive. He's in hospital, hoping for a visit from the Polányis. Then: "I never was an adherent of Knöpflmacher" (the "Vienna District Wars" general), but could never help admiring him. "I am not a pacifist." There follows a long defence of his position. We can see this as a series of sketches for his unpublished book on pacifism (finished in 1938). It is followed by another five-page section about Richard Redler and the CDV, with which she is familiar. He passes to an analysis of the "Youth Movement" mentality, which slightly affected even non-Fascists like "Isolde". "Its irrationalist naturalism is a more extreme one than the rationalist naturalism of the old freethinkers":

> One of the main symptoms of this disease of the mind is a general hatred of logics, the love of a stilted kind of 'inwardness', the impurity and imprecision of the language, and a nebulous way of exhibiting the warm underwaves of your soul rather than to tell simply what you mean.

October 9th 1932. To Irene Grant

> I am altogether anti-naturalist, but not anti-materialist, for I love matter, vividly feeling its clumsiness and humorous imperfection. For me, the acceptance of imperfection also hangs together with democracy, for I rather incline to the aristocratical views of the inferiority of the popular masses. Only, a dictatorial clique will never be really the pick of good

men, and I believe far more in the goodness of men ruling themselves than in their being ruled by the good.

October 27th 1933. To Irene Grant
She has been making enquiries in connection with his coming to England:

> Now you see the matter is enormously difficult. I should be very glad to be put up at your friends'. On the other hand, I have very great fears from health disturbances and errors in everyday behaviour, which is governed by strange and intricate laws in your country. At any rate, if there can be any question of a visit to England, surely not before the spring! I dread the fog, and lack of heating. Dyspepsia does not altogether place me above weather and infectious influences.

The main problem was economic. He might get his parents to finance his travel and, say, a six months' stay, but no more unless he is earning money by then:

> By the way, what of the "aliens" on British soil who are unable to give a bail of £1,000? Do the police not track them very hard?
>
> Now, dear Irene, look here: do not imagine that I try to heave up sham difficulties, only to gratify my laziness and my conservatism (though I do not dream of denying either) ... Let us stick at first to that book affair. What is to be expected? I shall write the book (a beast of a work, if you will excuse the term) or 2/3 of it, for the last 1/3 I could even better concoct in the English atmosphere itself; then I shall call on half a dozen of publishers, who, each in their turn, will answer after a month's delay that they find it very remarkable and sincerely hope that another publisher would print it.

So it goes on, a mixture of timorous objections and shrewd analysis of probabilities, charmingly expressed in his still deficient English:

> You see, the publisher you consulted prophesied, it is true, a general interest for a book of this kind; but he did not say, for instance, that he himself was likely to publish it ...

In 1933 it became apparent that Karl Polányi could not stay much longer in Vienna doing the kind of work he believed in. So he went to England in the autumn, where his contacts helped him find work as an evening-class lecturer for the WEA and the Universities of Oxford and London. A few months later *Der Oesterreichiche Volkswirt* (for which he still wrote from

England) became subject to censorship before publication. Polányi's removal to England was an enormous loss to Kolnai. He sorely missed both his intellectual vitality and also his advice in his own "petty political manipulations with the Religious Socialists and Christian Democrats". But Karl's departure seems to have brought him closer to the noble "Communist fanatic", Helen, who remained based in Vienna to carry on her Austrian political activity, under cover of a study of Physics; she eventually joined Karl in England with her daughter in 1936 when she had to drop this illegal work on health grounds.

December 12th 1933. To Irene Grant

> I long to see you. You are one of those cases of "classical" friendship in my net of relations which are beyond being substituted by any other type.

Polányi was back on a visit, and he and Macmurray[40] had been discussing an early draft chapter of "War". There had been some discouragements, but Kolnai was now determined to go ahead, and wouldn't blame her or anyone else if it was a failure. Meanwhile, he'd been "eviscerating" Stapel's *Christian Statesman* - frequently mentioned in the published work:

> By the way, Irene, as to Stapel and Gogarten: Supreme evilness and immoralism is only possible on a Christian basis. The said fellows: Lutheran. Stefan George, the ingenious poet and true prophet of an artistic reign of Blood and Lust, the father of all such beasts as Klages, Blüher, Spengler, down to Göbbels and Röhm, is a Rhenish Catholic, and though a Pantheist, somehow Roman ... It is not only difficult to digest all that foul stuff, but even more difficult to get it. (In this country it is forbidden to criticize Hitler, but equally forbidden to read him. Deeply Austrian ...)

May 8th 1934. To Irene Grant
On the *Oesterreichische Volkswirt* editorial team now Polányi has left:

> Hopeless burghesses. I tower above them at least as high as Karli surpasses me, but he was at the same time a ruthless tyrant, while I am an uninfluential weakling laughed at by everybody ("for you *are* ridiculous, Großvater"), though they know themselves (dimly) that I am more intelligent than they.
>
> Strategical plans are under discussion to deprive me of my appendix or of my Gall Bladder or both.

Undated, probably November 1934. To Irene Grant

I have thoroughly revised the plan of *The War against the West*, and completely refashioned the syllabus. So the question is whether you like it more in its present shape, and think it worth to "tempt" a publisher (Gollancz?) with ...

As this is a business letter, I won't load upon you further communications, - especially my habitual moanings. Life is bad as it is, - that's all. If but I could be in England. Old England muddling through this mire of an age. Lovely, plump old England. Big old London, home of the homeless ...

Placid and majestic Cats of London, I know of your existence, but you (happily) are unaware of mine.

November 30th 1934. To Irene Grant
She had showed the preceding letter to Gollancz, and it seems to have done the trick. What he needed before producing a contract was "(say) Chapter I". There is much on "Karli" and Ilona and mutual friends:

How can you ask how is Irma? She is always well. A little buffalo cow, nice as she is. Her younger daughter Bözsi (Elisabeth) now lives in London; perhaps she will come across you. I certainly do not hate her. Nor do I like her ...

Two predominant aspects of Fascism whose connection I've not yet fully succeeded to bring out; the MarxoPolányians only seeing one, and their antipodes, Clericals, Literary Culture Historians, specialized Nazi-Eaters etc., only the other. "Capitalism re-arranged for fight" - and "Mystical relapse into tribal Barbarism". I cannot make up my mind to consider the one as a mere mask or implement for the other. Karli's great visions of the "unendurableness of moral claims" provide, of course, the most important key for the solution.

December 11th 1934. To Irene Grant

Well, well - things begin to don an alarming feature: Mr Gollancz replied to my reply and is looking forward to the specimen chapter - so I am compelled to work - darn it. Let it be told to all Liberals and Socialists: men won't work except under strict compulsion.

January 16th 1935. To Irene Grant

Believe it or no, - I have risen to the rank of a British Taxpayer.

Do you know any English person In Vienna who would help me to revise my manuscript, for which I could, of course, pay?

(Marguerite Kay was recommended and her services obtained.)

September 3rd 1935. To Irene Grant
He asks her to help his friend Ruth von Schulze-Gävernitz, who is going to London (she became a close friend of Béla Menczer):

She does not dream of my intervention, as I am afraid she very seldom dreams of me at all, since most women don't ... It is Miss Elisabeth Gémes, a lovely though slightly cumbersome little creature, whom I do love indeed (at the same time wishing her to hell) who told me about (her).

This letter contains an unusual amount of nonsense. For example, on the Italian invasion of Ethiopia:

What about Abyssinia? If I were in England's shoes I should simply fight Italy. Thus England could assert herself as the hegemonic power of Islam. Perhaps communicate with the Foreign Office and call their attention to this point of view ...

Shut up - I am telling myself ... Life is unbridgeably more horrible than anything that could be expressed in so many sensible words. "No rational life at all". Apply it to me.

Irma sends you her kindest and most affectionate greetings. And I, - well I, to avoid effusions that might justly anger you, I will simply call myself

Yours sincerely, Aurel.

October 5th 1935. To Elisabeth Gémes
He describes one of Dietrich von Hildebrand's "Metaphysical Exercises", which he attended at the university; "Most of what he says is superb":

It was a great moment when he suddenly called out: "Ladies and Gentlemen, you must not think that an object is not so certainly given to you as real because it is not absolutely 'simple', not an elementary sense-datum, but requires of your intellect more appropriate understanding and compliance, more 'conspiring' with its essence!" - H's phenomenology, however, is a philosophy from the point of view of Everyman, directed against the pseudo-world of constructivisms, snobisms, philosophies of ressentiment and of power-seeking spiritual supermen - intended to overcome the professional feeble-mindedness of thinking in formulae ... What a shame that he's a toady of Austrofascism. Next time I'll ask him tactfully (he was very pleased to see me there - yes, it does happen) whether he realises that his philosophy (as opposed to his philosophising on political matters) is absolutely anti-Fascist ... There is no philosophical thinker whose thought I am so close to (I've known that for years!) - and yet I shudder to shake hands with him when I think of his vomit-making Regime-salon Thursday evenings and his apotheosis of Dollfuß!

January 4th 1936. To Béla Menczer

You cannot imagine the torture and agony of being condemned to live here. The very feeling of almost undisturbed personal security contributes to it. It is a Mire rather than a glaring Hell ... No comfort is provided by the sign of nobleness and tragedy on the faces of the persecuted ... Nobody takes anything very seriously here, you see ... This is a unique thing: a non-national Fascism ... chauvinist, nationalist, and nationally treasonous at the same time ... And one is very much ashamed of oneself! Bözsi knows it. Because one cannot help finding the town charming, great, mystical, homely, etc. in spite of all ... O! my dilapidated life, irretrievably past ... spent away into nothingness by the narcotic forces of this cursed place! ... I haven't lived entirely in vain, ... the small pleasures I had do not count, but I think I have just understood the meaning of Liberty, that's all!

I have little hope as to the prospects of my book, but I should not exclude beforehand all possibility of a medium success. (America is stirring too! Roosevelt's Message is a great thing, in some ways it renews the Wilsonian gesture, - though of course I hate the "neutrality" matrix. What we need is not neutrality but an iron determination to fight, to shake their damned souls out of all the earth's Fascists.)

He also refers here to Elisabeth as "our glamorous little monster".

October 5th 1936. To Elisabeth Gémes
There is quite a lot in this letter on philosophical method:

In thinking about phenomena one should never stray very far from what gave one the initial stimulus, i.e. think back to it from time to time, and above all reject mood-like generalisations. If you become aware of purely abstract formulae dancing about inside you for any length of time and yourself encourage this dance, in the end ... you'll find everything dissolving in a fog and feel properly disgusted with it all ... But if you think back to a single easily graspable yet at once spiritually suggestive effective concrete phenomenon, you'll at once feel yourself on solid ground.

He gives three typical criteria for the assessment of philosophical thinking:

1) Honesty (intended and achieved) as against false pretensions.
2) ... Object-directedness as against subjectivist self-reference. Thus, when we're dealing with something real: increased knowledge of the thing as against producing a more aesthetically pleasing or contradiction-free picture of it. We also need a sense of proportion for this ...
3) ... Proper correspondence between the necessary "intuitive activity" of the "educated" ... mind and the finished, authoritative, informative account.

He goes on to discuss certain problems of social philosophy, but the material is too dense for easy selection or summary.

March 20th 1936. To Elisabeth Gémes
He is so glad she likes Larousse:

He who despises dictionaries is a priori a damned soul in my eyes. It is a rather frequent, and a cheap and repellent, form of snobbism. Lexical knowledge is "un-organic"! "Spurious"! Grouped in alphabetical order! Absolutely un-literary! (because of its being literal). Why, it's one of the most valuable forms of conveyable knowledge at all! Absolutely pertinent to intellectual dignity and sobriety! The right thing is to avail oneself of it even as reading-stuff, not merely as an occasional source of information! And you, have grasped that. Certainly there is a lot of Scheinwissen [pseudo-knowledge] in lexical knowledge; but even then it is the most innocuous, the most chaste (as it were) form of Scheinwissen. Unpretentious, and at the same time very dainty for the true intellectual gourmet, who must be humble before all!

May 15th 1936. To Béla Menczer
He is appalled that the West does not see:

the iron necessity to fight both evils [Germany and Italy] together. England and France are fallen to the deepest depths of humiliation, and we must continue to cling to them with fanatical love, faith and hope.

June 26th 1936. To Elisabeth Gémes

I'm all to pieces, overworked, distracted by secondary tasks. Chesterton's death is like a permanent eclipse of the sun. I couldn't refuse that rag, *Der Christliche Ständestaat*, an obituary. And I'm tied up in a long Kraus-Chesterton essay for *Századunk*.

July 13th 1936. To Elisabeth Gémes
(Written two days after the Austro-German agreement, which amounted to a virtual capitulation to Hitler):

The situation here is growing dangerous for me. Hungary will not be an absolutely safe place for me, and will finally shut off my chance of escape towards the West. I should like to go to London, but I dread slow - and still more, rapid - starvation, which is my prospect there. I cannot even know whether my parents would send me money there in the proportion they could. I cannot go to London without a prospect and a firm will to earn money. Even today I got a charming little letter from dear Helen Polányi, who almost desperately calls for my coming ... I might live at her little boarding house ... She even promises to cook for me.

But if the book doesn't appear "the danger here is less and the 'prospects' are nullified". But I have lost touch with Gollancz, and don't know what is going on.

August 17th 1936. To Elisabeth Gémes

You will probably remember it is my ingrained conviction that all men must be poor in the sense of "*paupertas honesta*" (poverty with honour); a socialist or democratic society, in a word, a society of serious grown-up men, is inconceivable except on that supposition, because in fact man is poor (his supplies are limited and infinitely inferior to his needs ...), and the illusion of "richness" in the minds of a ruling or inactive minority cannot mean anything other than a general deficiency in consciousness; indeed, an infantile stage of mankind as such ... But all children should be rich. Children must not have any contact with practical cares and worries. Because man must have an aristocratic substance of inner freedom in him, something like the traces of an original virginity and ethereal playfulness; and surely you know that he can acquire that in childhood alone.

November 21st 1936. To Róbert Vámbéry
Entirely about Karl Kraus, whom Kolnai had always admired, but with certain reservations (for example about his sexual ethical views). There are strong similarities between them, for example the moral passion for honesty and accuracy in the use of language. He had certainly met Kraus at least once, and was a keen reader of *Fackel* (Kraus's self-composed periodical) rather than a rapt auditor at Kraus's public readings. Vámbéry had written to him about his long Chesterton-Kraus article, and, in Kolnai's eyes, showed himself little better than a Kraus-"groupie". In this long, doggedly-magisterial letter, Kolnai answers Vámbéry's criticisms of his article.

December 2nd 1936. To Elisabeth Gémes

I am still sorry to see the Church so firmly entrenched on Hell's side. I am sorry - for, as you know, I can never cut all wires finally, and do not conceive "Heaven" pure and simple as the embodiment of politico-social democracy. In fighting Fascism I am in perfect harmony with myself; in fighting the Church I cannot escape a sense of tragedy.

December 3rd 1936. To Béla Menczer

The problem of democracy itself [is] to create the optimal preconditions in society for the development of noble mankind.

In contraposition to totalitarian Communism (or indeed 'Leftism') I believe that all society must needs be oppressive, barbarous and ultimately reactionary without the presence of supra-social standards, the faith in meta-social powers.

But what I think matters most is this: The natural corresponding complement to a person's nobility is not the vulgarity of others but the nobility of others.

December 19th 1936. To Elisabeth Gémes

D. Grant has been here, a charming Highlander, and has brought me good news. No need to worry about my book. It has come a bit late and it has grown a bit too longish, but it has been found good and the year of grace 1937 will see it printed (provided that Britain will live so long). The likelihood is not small that I should haunt you with my portly personal appearance in April or May next - whether or no you will believe it.

January 25th 1937. To Elisabeth Gémes
Written from his parents' home in Budapest (extracts from one of the two complete surviving letters to her):

My kind Child,
Life is a big horror, apart from any sort of doubt ... I hear that Gollancz ... has entrusted his cooperant Dr. Lewis with some overhaulings he thinks necessary, and I am not a little inclined to assist and control the good Dr. Lewis lest he should make nonsense of my precious ms. On the other hand, I must own to you I loathe to leave Vienna! A month spent here (o! here!) has taught me again what a heaven Vienna is (Fascist Vienna! fie!). Vienna! its placid nobleness, its distinguished vacuum, its paradisiacal coffee-houses! And London - with all the horrors of an extremely new and strange milieu! This is a double-faced attitude: I both long to see London, including some of its present inhabitants, and dread it more than I can say. Then - the horror of dissolving my 'household' in Vienna - to take with me my necessary belongings - to spend a week in Zürich and another in Paris; which would be inevitable on account of German and French-speaking publishers. Perhaps I'll do it; perhaps not. Heaven knows if I could extort another advance payment from old Jewish Golly. He is enthusiastic and furious at the same time. (On the whole I think I have had more luck than understanding.) ...
Irene and Ilona have written me so sweet letters. It is a comfort to feel the tender rays of cool loves in the desert of sorrow. Polányis have got a cat whose name is Dunya. And Spain is lost; there is no hope left. And redemption will come some day, but it will have a dreadful look. America and Russia are the poles of salvation: the Pillars of Bounteous Might. England and France will be forlorn hopes: outposts to be razed away by the first impact of the Hosts of Hell ...
Nice huggings. Your Aurel.

January 28th 1937. To Irene Grant

Dearest Celtic Irene,
Thank you very humbly for your kind and mirthful letter... This is fine news indeed ... Under these circumstances, I very seriously contemplate a trip to London. A trip, that is to say, a sojourn from the end of March up to the publication of my book (which, I still hope, will

not be later than September): particularly, in case I should succeed in extorting a little advance payment ... As for later, I believe there are no chances for me in the world, if there are any, except in the British (or American) climate. [But ... difficulties of the move.] I have no courage at all except a very limited one which is tied to inexorable moral insight ...

To wile away the hours, I am working on the rudiments of a pretty booklet termed "Democracy and Value", its real theme being my favourite one, - "Spiritual height and the Average Man." Mainly and essentially, Karli has taught me the fundaments; but I have also drawn on Chesterton, Veblen, Santayana and others.

Dear beloved Irene

I am yours as ever, Aurel.

Kolnai's hesitations and ditherings had, of course, led to many arguments with friends in Vienna. Irma had tried hard to make him leave the previous summer, when the completed "War" had finally been sent off. Over Christmas in Budapest he had once more raised the matter with his parents, who realised that they would probably never see him again, and might not be able to send him any money:

They understood that I could not remain in Austria for long; but nursed the illusion that I would be safe in Hungary. I got them round, however, by a skilful manoeuvre. Overemphatically though by no means insincerely, I bemoaned the necessity of having to live in London, a city that had no lucid plan of districts but was a welter of boroughs fusing into one another imperceptibly and at random; I added how frightened I was at the idea of having to address the porter in French when passing through Paris and Boulogne. My parents, who had always deplored and resented my being "quaint", now said with grim satisfaction, "Serves you right - it won't kill you - if you don't rid yourself of these neurotic whims you'll never make your way in life"; and so to London I went.[41]

He left Vienna on March 6th 1937:

At Buchs ... the Austrian customs official asked what my destination was, and on learning that it was London, wished me a pleasant journey in strangely sentimental tones: it was as if Austria, "my country" for sixteen years and in some sense very much mine, had bidden me a solemn farewell.[42]

In the event he made no provision for visiting libraries en route, so, apart from a brief nocturnal break of journey in Basle, he travelled without a break. Late in the evening of the 8th, he writes:

> I found myself, trembling with fear, on board the English steamer for passenger traffic between Boulogne and Folkestone. My dismay turned out to be all too justified. The sea was exceedingly choppy, and no sooner did we move than I fell a prey to sea-sickness, its reality far surpassing the wildest of my anxious imaginations.[43]

The next hurdle was the Immigration Officer. Kolnai knew that the government of the day was strongly anti-Communist, so he made a point of dissociating himself from the leftism of the Gollancz publishing house. Polányi "severely reprimanded" him for this in London, saying that it was "a tactless thing to say". At all events, he was only allowed to enter the country for two months, provided he abstained from any kind of political activity. Reflecting later on the "forbidding", yet "grumbling friendliness" perceptible behind this conditional welcome, Kolnai ascribed it to "the 'feudal' trait of English life: a closer interpenetration, as compared with Continental society, of the private and the public spheres". After the customs officers had thoroughly ransacked his luggage, and he had repacked, he found he had missed the boat train. He eventually arrived in London at Cannon Street Station towards three o'clock in the morning, and took a taxi to Elisabeth's lodgings in Chelsea. After "comforting" him with strong tea she escorted him to a boarding-house at Manson Place, where she had booked a room for him. No doubt he slept well, but it was a very long time before the after-effects of his sea-sickness wore off.

Chapter Nine

Peripatetic
(1937-1940)

"Something choked me in England", Kolnai wrote to Irene Grant on June 17th 1937, to explain his "bolting" to Paris while she was abroad. It seems likely that both he and his friends assumed that his visa was renewable, and that he would stay, perhaps permanently. His immediate reason for coming to London was, of course, to see *The War against the West* through the press. This was not to be the triumphal progress that some of his friends, at least, imagined it would be. For one thing Dr Lewis, Gollancz's right-hand man, told him that Gollancz was too busy to see him. But it had now also been decided to give the manuscript another overhaul with a native English speaker (at Kolnai's expense). Although he found Miss Lowe "intelligent and pleasant to work with", he decided to put an end to their "verbal arguments", and to carry on the business by post. This was one reason for his departure.[1] But it is clear that - despite certain aesthetic and gustatory delights - London itself, especially as a social reality, disappointed him. In a letter to Jászi he mentions "snobbery, their absurd state church, London's chaotic jumble of houses",[2] and elsewhere "restraint of expression and emotion; the 'Greek' cult of a fine soul in a fine body; the [London] Squares, ... the absence of genuine bourgeois pride".[3]

There were compensations, however, in reunions with old friends and in the making of useful contacts. Béla Menczer, now working as a writer and journalist in London, recalls meetings in Bogey's Bar in the old Royal Hotel, Bloomsbury, along with Róbert Vámbéry and his fiancée, Klara Erdélyi, and a first cousin of Elisabeth Gémes, George Lányi, who was studying at the London School of Economics. This group, which also met in the Witley Court Bar over the street, might also include other Hungarians, such as Arthur Koestler.[4] There were also meetings with Irene Grant and the Polányis, though these were clouded by elements of the socialist Grants' class-conscious milieu and Polányi's now embarrassingly pro-Russian stance. Menczer introduced him to Wickham Steed, editor of *The Times*, who agreed to write a preface to *The War against the West*, and also to R.W. Seton-Watson, the historian of Central Europe, who tried to dissuade him from publishing his book on the grounds that the changing political situation was making it obsolete. Kolnai felt that "appeasement" motives had underlain this advice.[5] He had, in fact, been appalled at the "peace at any price" atmosphere of England, and decided to write an anti-pacifist book. "Democracy and Value", which he had begun earlier in the year in Budapest, was accordingly abandoned.[6]

Kolnai "bolted" to Paris in May, where, he later wrote, though "I had nothing to look for or to do, ... the French climate, cheapness and wine attracted me, and there was a pale substitute for café life".[7] He took up residence in the Hôtel de Tours, where he stayed, with longer or shorter absences, until 1940. This good bourgeois hotel, a cut above the accommodation to which most of the many Hungarians in Paris had to accustom themselves, was in the Rue Jacob, a narrow mediaeval street on the Left Bank - a very different atmosphere from that of the "cold" architecture of French classicism he disliked so much. Yet, in his somewhat muted letter of June 17th to Irene Grant, in which he explains his move, he admits that "something ... chokes me even here". "I am just a shade too *krank* [ill] for France, to say it in German, and to say it in English: well ... I am just a shade too cranky." Although there was much around him to admire and much to delight the senses, "I am not really up to them, or in other words they lack something for me: a sort of *lourdeur*, a suggestion of formlessness, an aura of mystique". However:

For the moment it seems as though I were slowly getting on with my "Case against False Pacifism"; and Dr Lewis tells me it is not impossible that Gollancz might take an interest in it.

In August he applied for a French identity card and went to Zürich, where there were decent libraries. For some of this time he was joined by Elisabeth, and the two of them sent a card to Béla Menczer: "Come here at once, it's nicer than in the criminal [i.e. pacifist] West".[8] The first month of his stay was "one of the finest of my life ... Wonderful nights alone in Zürich, in the shabby little Rämi Café-Konditorei ... What have I to do with France's classical 'beauty' and 'perfection'?".[9] But on his way back from a trip to Fribourg he "fell a slave to the magic of Bern". In December he moved there, staying for nearly a month in the Hotel Gotthard, while he roamed the boarding-houses of the city (Elisabeth came for a few days to assist) trying to find less expensive quarters for a longer stay. He also attended philosophy lectures at the university. Kolnai was not over-impressed, but singled out Professor Herbertz (formerly of Bonn) as the best. Though "he only just attains the stature of the intellectually 'significant'" and is not "exercised by spiritual passion", he is "really

penetrating" and "genuine(ly) interest(ed) in the subject-matter". Kolnai
also attended a lecture by Karl Barth, whose "voice and language" might
have been those of "an Austrian country priest of middling education".[10] At
the beginning of March he was "in a way expelled" from Switzerland by
the police; he had for some reason been "persistently suspected [of]
peddling cigars or engaging in some other kind of remunerative 'work'".[11]
Accordingly, he left for Dijon, arriving at 11 p.m. on March 8th, thinking
that it would be easier for him to write in this provincial town. But, as it
was now clear that Hitler would invade Austria, he went on to Paris to
renounce his nationality, but by the time he arrived it was too late. He was
now, to his utter disgust, technically a citizen of the Third Reich.

Kolnai's three months in Bern (December 1937 to March 1938), which
he called "The City of Lords", made a very deep impression on him. In
later years, especially after he had fallen in love with Madrid, and then its
Northern surrogate, Brussels, his love for the city tended to become
subsumed in his enthusiasm for Swiss democracy. But for some years after
his stay the city is mentioned again and again in his letters. As we might
expect by now from Kolnai, this love for Bern had had to contend with
some considerable obstacles. For example: "Bern is the only town I have
ever seen which is actually reeking with malignant xenophobia". Then,
more generally:

> Swiss food is uneatable, or rather indigestible, save for breakfast. Swiss
> air is good, but harsh and sterile. While the English, probably the most
> acuminous race of the world, take the most elaborate pains to achieve to
> appear stupid, the Swiss are stupendously stupid in actual and aboriginal
> fact. Cretinous mountain peasants.[12]

In another letter he writes of their "queer little cantons! What a world of
cosy boorishness is there! You feel as though you were yourself a 23rd
canton with a single inhabitant!"[13] Kolnai clearly throve on this isolation,
which stimulated his receptive faculties. The result was the poem sequence
"The Songs of Bern", and a number of remarkable analyses of the Swiss
atmosphere, especially in contraposition to the French and the English
respectively:

> How delightful it is to be noticed as a foreigner with a faint trace of
> disdain by the English. It is so utterly different from the feral mistrust of
> the Bernese or the cold but full acknowledgement of one's "humanity"
> (though definitely not their kind) by the French with their much-
> trumpeted and much-disparaged "logic", which seems to me more like
> "logical aesthetics".[14]

Writing later to Irene Grant from Paris, he tries to explain why he finds living there so unproductive; the main problem is that he has "no feel of Reality, of Things". This is "not because of the inane condition of my vital self but because Things, in the qualified sense of the term, are not (t)here". This is connected with "a smooth superficialness, a mere functionalism, a 'lack of dimension'":

> A French house is not a house in the sense as [sic] a Swiss house is a house; culture is more perfect (final) and yet primitive, "linear" at bottom; there are no backgrounds; intelligence lacks the balance of stolidity; distinction is pale, academic, classic ... Here one doesn't feel the "resistance", the "pressure" of extra-human things; the French are the "nation humaniste par excellence", and by monopolizing existence too easily and completely, mankind is in fact very much poorer.[15]

Many of these and similar ideas find expression in the "Songs of Bern". The original German sequence was followed in 1941 by a much longer English one. These unpublished poems (technically rather crude) are full of passion, that of a lover for ever shut out from his beloved. Some of them are historical, recalling Bern's aristocratic and war-like role in "forging" Switzerland into a power, which he likens to that of the Castilians in Spain and the Prussians in Germany.[16] Others recall those physical aspects of the city that he loved most, and in one "prose poem" he runs through all the strange and exotic people he saw in boarding-houses and cafés during his stay, with one or more telling details about each. These experiences could not but affect his political convictions:

> Berne by subjecting me to a novel experience of dense, solid and irremovable Reality helped me draw nearer to Conservatism; again by its strong and all-pervasive aristocratic coinage, it taught me to some extent the dependence of democracy on the values, absorbed by the plain people, of aristocracy.[17]

Once back in Paris he renounced his Austrian (now technically German) nationality and had his identity card altered accordingly. He was now "ex-Autrichien", which, of course, meant "stateless". In April or May Dr Lewis wrote from Gollancz to say that both he and Mr Gollancz were "delighted" with his Pacifism book and considered it "an honour" to publish it, though it would need some stylistic revision. This virtual guarantee of publication galvanised him into activity, and he finished it in June. But the ensuing relaxation of tension meant that the rest of 1938 was almost totally unproductive.[18] Sometime in the summer he began an extended stay in Dijon.

***

The War against the West at last appeared in July. This "war" is, in the words of Wickham Steed's preface, Kolnai's term for the "conscious, deliberate revolt of Germanism against the freedom of the human personality alike in its religious, social and political forms".[19] The vast bulk of the book is an exhaustive documentation of this apostasy, and the representative authors are, for the most part, allowed to speak for themselves under the chapter-headings of "The Central Meaning of the National Socialist Attitude", "Community", "State", "Human Nature and Civilization", "Faith and Thought", "Morals, Law and Culture", "Society and Economics", "Nation and Race", "The German Claim" and "Nazi Germany and the Western World". Most of the written material cited was published after 1930, and it is this fact, together with the relentless thoroughness of the approach, that gives the book its enduring value. Kolnai does also frequently cite older authors, such as Nietzsche and Stefan George (whom he calls the two "fathers" of Nazi thinking), as well as Luther, Spengler and Klages, but his book is not so much a history of Nazi thought as an attempt to place the developed product before the reader as a fact, which he must first accept just as it is, the good as well as the bad. He must see it as a "serious attempt to 'solve' the socio-political problems of the present age". Only if this is done can it be effectively fought. Many reviewers complained about the book's length,[20] but Kolnai, writing to Béla Menczer (whose "Charter of the West" appears in the Introduction) dismisses their complaint as follows: "It had got to be 'monumental' to the point of forbidding monstrousness; it is the Kunstform appropriate to its subject".[21]

Apart from quoting at great length from Nazi writers, says Wickham Steed,

> M. Kolnai ... now and again pauses to take breath and to reflect awhile. Rarely, if ever, are his reflections wide of the mark. If they have a quaint flavour of their own, his readers will soon learn to appreciate it.[22]

But many reviewers of the book reacted against Kolnai's mild line on Communism. H.A.L. Fisher, for example, was clearly unable to stomach his obvious approval of a war against the enemies of mankind "in which the Dictator of the Kremlin joins hands with the Western Democracies".[23] In his letter to Jászi of December 26th 1938 Kolnai accepted his charge that he had been temporarily blinded to the Soviet menace, and later wrote that he was "not altogether happy to have brought out the Nazi book".[24] His interspersed comments are, in fact, those of his unmodified liberal self. It is significant that no less a leftist than Helen Polányi should have told him in person that:

> She found in the book too much of yesterday's trite and vapid liberal-progressive phraseology; she would have hoped for a more original, more pondered and more politically relevant "conservative" critique of National Socialism.[25]

Although the work was cited in the House of Lords by the Bishop of Durham, and praised by Lloyd George, the American reviews were much more favourable than the English ones.

Kolnai tells us that the process of writing the book was very instructive for him. Without for a moment reconsidering his own fundamental allegiances, he came to see that some of his Nazi writers defended their own false doctrines with "arguments more vivid, better balanced, and more firmly rooted in actual human experience" than those of their liberal, socialist and humanitarian opponents.[26] This led him to hold that the West was partly to blame for the rise of National Socialism, not because Germany had been treated too harshly after the First World War, but because the foundations of democracy had not been sufficiently elaborated and publicised, and because:

> Democratic theory had been too much concerned with the 'postulates' and the 'architecture' of democracy, and too little with the consolidation of power in the hands of a group destined to serve and administer [it].[27]

It would be pointless to summarise here the way Kolnai sets out the thought of Nazi and allied thinkers. Rather, I shall simply quote from Kolnai's own "reflections" to try and convey the flavour of this monumental work. Here is part of his opposition to the Nazi claim that there can be no productive social relations without complete self-surrender to the one all-embracing Community:

> We hold that the increasing *souplesse* and differentiation of social ties does not mean futility but rather a precondition alike for personal liberty, for intimacy between individuals, and disinterested solidarity; we argue that for civilization a certain splitting up of the social surrounding of man is essential.[28]

On the National Socialist attack on Liberalism:

> Whatever the shortcomings and blunders of the liberal civilian world may be (and I would be the last to deny them), it is still incomparably closer to the Christian axioms of spiritual personality, or to a world-embracing community in God, or to the Socialist vision of a workers' society dwelling in sober modesty, equality and justice, than is the world of a new Paganism, Daemonism and pan-social Militarism.[29]

Here is Kolnai on varying attitudes to the human body (*Leib*):

> The Christian may be either severe or indulgent towards the body, or even honour it with a kind of chivalrous tenderness; the Rationalist, dry and narrow-minded, may be hard on the body; the Utilitarian may allow it too large a place in his consideration; and the Materialist may sink so low as to become a slave to it. But the Nazi ... philosophers of the Body do something entirely different: their allegedly "Greek", or rather "Doric", creed implies a *worship* of the Body ...[30]

Here he is on common sense:

> Seeing that "society" is always but an uneven mirror of "humanity", commonsense is necessarily variable and imperfect; nevertheless, it forms the intellectual and emotional organ of men in their social existence by means of which they strive to keep in touch with objective Truth and absolute Right, with spiritual eternity and perfection.[31]

On humanity and science, respectively:

> "Man" as such begins, not with "spiritual" existence in the sense of mental as well as merely corporeal capacities, but with his awareness of objective data, his voluntary recognition of laws, his readiness to dissociate his will from "positive", "plastic", "tangible" interests and attractions either private or tribal.[32]
>
> ... It may safely be maintained that modern science is the instrument of an exaggerated endeavour to imprison in a net of "exact" constructions the objects presented by nature, life and mind, in order to render them "calculable" and "previsible" at will; a strategy of knowledge which forcibly induces a loss of contact with the heart of things, and deadens the sense of a humble unprejudiced search for the inmost reality of the world without and within.[33]

Kolnai sums up his moral objections to eugenics in four points as follows: (1) "[They] carry in them a sort of temptation to skip the ineluctable spiritual problems of our existence, supplanting a real effort to grapple with them by a pretension to produce new and better-equipped bearers of existence". (2) (On Eugenics' pretensions to prevent things.) "The more the scope of prevention is enlarged, the more its very idea becomes spurious and futile. We can only deal with the future inasmuch as it is still an organic part of the present". (3) "Eugenic rationality is a typical instance of alien rationality. It seems to submit the lives of men to regulation by human thought; but it is essentially the thought of other people, not their own". Thus men may cease to "behav(e) on the basis of thinking" at all. (4) "... the danger of fundamental inequality inherent in the "planning" of men by men. The dogmas of personality and equality are inseparable from an ultimate "*givenness*" of *human existences* claiming absolute respect and unquestioned recognition." The dangerous idea of human "material" must be severely limited. Breeding men must lead to breeding varieties of men.[34] On anti-Semitism he says: "Anti-Judaism ... entails hostility to Xianity". And yet:

> Our judgement of the new Nazi Germany must be determined above all by its negation of mankind and its intrinsic enmity to Western democratic society, and not by its special ill-will against Jews.[35]

And on Prussianism:

> It is precisely the dry and *sachlich* [objective] aspect of Prussiandom, its quality of emotional thrift and barren sobriety (it has, I confess, some appeal to me), which seems ruthlessly to have been thrown overboard by Nazi fascist neo-Prussianism.[36]

As an example of characteristic Kolnaian humour, here is a passage from his chapter on "The German Claim". When Houston Stewart Chamberlain praises the Germans "what is really meant is that they incarnate human value and could as little be evaluated by any universal criteria as God could be held to account by an assembly of curates".[37]

As in his article for *Der Christliche Ständestaat*, Kolnai has nothing good to say about Heidegger in this book. But he does not flinch from saying hard things about Scheler:

> one of the most subtle and powerful thinkers in history, perhaps the greatest of his time. In many important respects, Scheler stood for truths and methods diametrically opposed to Naziism in all its varieties.[38]

Yet there is a strongly Nietzschean vitalism in him, and the Nazis were not mistaken in appealing to his arguments. Despite Kolnai's misgivings about his book he sent many copies to people of influence, as this passage from a letter to Irene Grant shows:

> My character, as you know, is essentially servile. Sending my book to the Czech and American envoys in Paris, to the Paris Cardinal and the French Cabinet Minister Reynaud, while writing the address I was continually bowing and smiling respectfully in my lonely room, - like subaltern officials telephoning with their superiors on the stage.[39]

***

In September Kolnai was bewildered to receive from Dr Lewis the news that his pacifism book had now been definitely rejected by Gollancz. He gave as the reason that, despite more than one trial, no one could be found to put it into acceptable English. At the same time he mentioned that he was writing a book of his own on the subject, and asked Kolnai if he could quote some of his "good points" in his own work. Kolnai consented, without asking him to be more specific. In January 1941 he saw a review of Lewis's *The Case against Pacifism* in New York, and sent for a copy. He soon saw "that Dr Lewis had used (his) 'good points' very liberally and often very literally indeed"[40] - although he had inserted two acknowledgements of Kolnai's help. Kolnai and Elisabeth, now married, were incensed at this, and though the old lawyer Rusztem Vámbéry doubted it could do any good in war-time, Kolnai sent off a registered letter of complaint to Victor Gollancz himself. Lewis's act was made much worse in his eyes by the fact that his own semi-conservative attack on pacifism had been transformed into a pro-Communist one, which included a "justification" of the Nazi-Soviet pact of August 1939. Kolnai thus saw himself associated in print with an attempt to "whitewash the base accomplice of the Nazis while, having subjugated France, they were battering the gates of England".[41] As for Kolnai's book, which Jászi tried to recommend to the Viking Press, Kolnai later wrote that he was "not altogether unhappy to have failed to bring (it) out".[42] The original title - 'The Case against False Pacifism' - implies the author's allegiance to something called "true pacifism", by which he meant the "pacifism" of "militant humanitarianism", and "a rational and workable creed of International Community and Morality", as promoted by the League of Nations. But very shortly after Gollancz's rejection of his book, the Munich pact, signalling the West's abandonment of Czechoslovakia, was signed, and he came to suspect that Democracy would always tend to prefer the soft option of welfare to the rigours of ensuring the country's ultimate survival.[43] Accordingly, he "revamped parts of the book" and changed the title to "The Fallacies of Pacifism". Apart from this, he later felt that he had opposed the policy of Appeasement too stridently. While never prepared to agree that its supporters were right, he was later able to regard their point of view with much more sympathy.

The main points of Kolnai's manuscript are summarised in a section of the introduction called "The author submits to an interrogatory". After explaining the sense in which he calls himself a pacifist, he summarises its difference from pacifism in the usual sense:

1) ... The ideal of peace has a valid meaning only in relation to a more comprehensive conception of humanity and society, wherefore "to preserve peace" cannot be an absolute and self-sufficient principle of policy.

2) War, though a great evil which necessarily involves moral evil, is not the supreme evil.

3) No rational and legal system of peaceful cooperation among nations ... can work on the assumption that the elimination of war (or of coercion by force) is taken for granted.

4) The idea of Non-Violence precludes the idea of Responsibility.

5) Collective security depends on individual readiness to fight the aggressor.

6) Superior civilisation implies a predominant but not exclusive position [that is, "positing"] of the superior spiritual elements in human nature.

7) The usual Pacifist slogans affirming the indifference of power, the futility of decision by war, the general superiority of a yielding attitude etc., are materially false and morally pernicious.

8) The principle of impartiality and neutrality is incompatible with moral objectivity.

9) The reality of evil powers in history cannot be explained away by "psychological" and other pseudo-scientific or pseudo-"generous" platitudes.

10) Instead of the system of self-reproaches, concessions and surrender, civilised humanity has the right and the duty to deal with such evil powers, according to necessity, adequately and integrally.[44]

War, then, must never be absolutely ruled out. In accord with his stated purpose to "clarify preliminary questions of principle" he shows that the claim, often repeated at the time, that "war is never inevitable" can really mean no more than "peace at any price". Much of the book continues this work of "unmasking" and usually showing the absurdity of radical pacifist doctrines and slogans. But, underlying all this, there was a manifest disagreement on the relative weight to be attached to the various principles that would have to be appealed to in deciding whether to wage war or not. For example, Kolnai puts more stress on "national self-preservation and the ultimate standards for the life of mankind", attaching less importance to physical welfare and comfort, than his opponents, as the following exchange makes clear:

> Q. Do you not think that war would mean universal and irreparable destruction, to which even the worst kind of peace would be preferable?
> A. No. If civilized society accepts blackmail as the fundamental law of its existence it commits a suicide that means extinction far more complete than even a prolonged modern war could entail.[45]

Again, even if opposition to Fascism entails a kind of "Iron Age" for ourselves, it would still be possible for us not to let it overwhelm us but to keep alive "the soul and the basic institutions of liberty and rational society". Appeasement, on the other hand, means that we should "abandon ... moral, political and social standards, ... resign ... national dignity and independence, ... break with all traditions and institutions of international solidarity and justice".[46] There was also a disagreement about human nature. For example, he assumes that Man's vital nature (the condition of any form of physical action, including violence, etc.) is important as a "substructure for man spiritual". Pacifists, on the other hand, vainly believe that, in place of the "severe rational control and rich emotional counterbalancing of aggressive instincts", one may substitute a "peaceful nature".[47] Those who think violence barbarous as such, "depreciate physical reality", and "dream of the soul being everything, and the body nothing".[48] Some of the essential points of the book were set out in his article "Pacifism Means Suicide", the first in a three-cornered "debate".[49] Reinhold Niebuhr's contribution is very similar to Kolnai's, but Bertrand Russell sets out to defend the Munich pact, not by an appeal to absolute pacifist principles, but as the least damaging policy available to the West at the time. During the course of his exposition he rather unfairly accuses Kolnai of meeting a point "with anger rather than with argument". Certainly Kolnai's paper betrays some moral indignation. But why not? Writing a few years later to Jászi he mentions the incident and mocks "the supreme Anglo-Saxon tabu on 'anger'".[50]

***

Kolnai and Elizabeth seem to have lived together from about October 1938, possibly for a time in Dijon in November, but certainly in the Hôtel de Tours in Paris. Surprisingly, he more than once writes that he had no friends in Paris, and gives the impression of an essentially solitary life there. However, he met various expatriate Hungarians, including his cousin Pál Winkler, who was now a rich man. At some time Kolnai sought his help in Paris, and describes his response in the Memoirs:

> He explained to me that in order to escape from the condition of a failure, I ought to renounce writing "formal" books or articles, with "architecture" in them, and try to write "spontaneously" instead: to write "letters" for publication, as it were. This idea of making one's "spontaneity" as such serve the purpose of one's commercial adaptation to consumers' demands struck me as abjectly diabolical ...[51]

Light is shed on the extraordinary severity of this judgement by Kolnai's posthumously published paper, "Dignity". He clearly felt that Winkler was urging him to do something "meretricious", that is, to earn his bread by entering a world "from which all reference to dignity *and the missing of it* has been crowded out"; in other words again, to surrender a distinctively *personal* value.[52] And yet Winkler not only helped other people with his money (for example, Ferenc Fejtő), but gave Kolnai much occasional financial help during these years, and even a regular monthly allowance during the last nine years of his life. But this never seems to be counted to Winkler's credit.

Kolnai was also lent money by the writer László Dormándi while he was staying in Dijon. The three or more months he spent in the Hôtel de la Cloche were part of his almost completely unproductive period, though one or two of his American articles were probably written there. A letter written to an unknown recipient contains an enthusiastic response to the idea of meeting in Switzerland over Christmas, but ... "money, and Elisabeth's passport, are lacking". In another letter fragment he bewails the statse of France, predicting imminent capitulation to Germany, and linking this to previous breakdowns, instancing the Popular Front, Empire Classicism, the Revolution itself, and surrender of India and America:

> You're always wanting to know about "me" [he continues], but I no longer "exist". I don't know whether I'll manage to get safely to America, and whether things will be better there. At least one cannot live in the Anglo-Saxon world in such total isolation as I experience here and in Paris.[53]

Kolnai was certainly back in the capital by Boxing Day and soon after wrote a "stocktaking" letter to Irene Grant, asking her advice about his future.[54] It starts with a preamble, in which his human desire to get out of his increasingly desperate situation strives against the impersonal elements of his character:

> There is no reason why I should escape starvation, particularly today when, owing to historical causes, it has become a mass phenomenon among people of my description ...

His special handicaps are his inability to earn his bread "by honest work", his "chronic illness (gravely worsened by now)", and his "not belonging to any definite social camp or group". However, he has published *The War against the West*, and has, for a foreigner, above average French and English:

> Taken all in all, - should you try to help me towards any sort of activity (facilitating my survival), your generous friendship would not strike me as a surprise. And again, if you throw away this letter unanswered, no one will understand it more heartily than I.

He then proceeds to a survey of his financial circumstances. His parents have not been able to get any money to him for some time, and may not be able to in the future. His cousin won't help him. As for his book, Gollancz paid him £77 net in 1935, and there is another £63 (net) owing to him. It is very unlikely that he will get any more.[55] Nor have his efforts to get the pacifism book published achieved any kind of success. Since July, he goes on, I've done almost nothing, except perhaps brood on my project for a book on democracy - "its meaning, its relation to an aristocratic conception of life and the problem of Value, its suicidal aspects and the spiritual conditions of its regeneration". He would love above all things to get out of France ("politically ... a decaying heap, utterly rotten"):

> Doctrinal Pacifism may be less rampant here than in the English-speaking countries, but there is a predominant pacifist psychology incomparably more despicable.

On the "technical" side, a move to London is fraught with problems. He could perhaps "'survive' for two months longer" in France. But his position

> is partly alleviated, but partly (financially) aggravated by the presence of Miss (Elisabeth) Gémes.[56] To her presence I have to thank, apart

from things more psychological, that I can have some warm food in the proper sense and do not live merely on coffee and ham with rusks. On the other hand, her financial problem is completely unsolved in spite of her immensely rich uncle (Irma's brother)[57] in Buda-Pesth. In England, I think, she could do some work on her carpet designs, perhaps in collaboration with Olga ...

In a postscript he asks for her reactions to another book project of his, to be entitled "Hitler's God", on the relation between "Nazi religion" and Christianity. Also: "do you think a publisher could be found for this [six-page] letter, and on what terms? I should concede some abbreviations".

Irene Grant, backed by Donald, wrote a very friendly and understanding reply on January 30th. She had discussed his predicament at length with John Macmurray, Karl Polányi, and others, and gave him the following advice. On balance, she thought it probably wouldn't be much use pressing Gollancz about the pacifism book, but recommended him to send it at once (together with outlines of "Hitler's God" and the book on democracy) to Macmurray, who would strongly commend them to Faber & Faber. She also advised him to get to the USA, and to take up the offer of another friend, Elinor Ulman, to introduce him to Max Lerner, who was an ex-editor of *The Nation*. She and Donald could easily find friends to give him hospitality when he arrived, and visitors' visas were extendable, if one knew the right people, which she would arrange. Kolnai replied in a letter of February 23rd. It gives a much more optimistic impression than the previous one. He hoped to have a French travel permit in his hands very soon, valid either for England or for Switzerland. Thanks to a Swiss dentist in Bern he might even get permission for a six-month stay in the City of Lords. He had written to John Macmurray, whom he had seen the previous August; Macmurray would be offering Faber & Faber some of his "scribbling". In addition, he had got some more money, $45 from *The Nation*, £59 from Gollancz,

> as well as 2,500 units of the French monetary system from my sires, anxiously watching over my dark destinies on the borders of the majestic Danube, in the fair Kingdom of Hungary.

He is now projecting a book on Swiss Democracy, "inspired ... by love instead of hatred". But he has been diagnosed as suffering from "'perivisceritic adherences' in his abdominal cavity"; diathermy and injections have been prescribed. "Thrive and put some flesh on, Very much yours, Großvater."[58]

These dreams of another journey to Switzerland or England gave place to a feverish revision of the pacifism book after Macmurray's approach to Faber & Faber. In April, Elisabeth, who had to spend at least half the day attending to Kolnai's dietary and other needs, reported her amazement that he had the strength for it, since

> now he only gets up for his work, and is completely exhausted after a few hours. Even a half-hour walk makes him quite unfit for it ... I think he can only manage it because he is absolutely convinced of the urgency of bringing out this book; only his passionate hatred[59] gives him the strength to do it.[60]

Apart from that, she herself had managed to sell two designs for carpets through her sister, Olga, in England, who had built up contacts with various textile firms. And, thanks to Professor Lerner, Aurel had been sent Lewis Mumford's *Men Must Act*, which led to a very fruitful, if short-lived, relationship with the author.

In May, Germany formed the "Pact of Steel" with Italy, and the many foreign refugees and emigrants in Paris felt increasingly anxious about their position. During the first half of 1939 Kolnai became friendly with Ferenc Fejtő, the distinguished Hungarian historian, whom he had briefly met in Budapest.[61] They met first at the Dormándis' and quarelled at once over their interpretations of Marxism. Next time, however, Kolnai brought Fejtő a copy of "War" which he promised to review.[62] Fejtő recalls the strange and ugly, slightly hunched, look of one careless of his appearance, a conspicuous sight in this upper middle-class milieu. But his eyes radiated intelligence. He had an excitable manner, spoke and gesticulated with passion, and loved being provocative. Most remarkable of all was the intensity of his entire being, whose predominant quality, Fejtő goes on, was not so much intellectual as religious. He was a believer, and yet an anarchical heretic - "the most contradictory character I've ever met". His sense of humour was grotesque, sarcastic, ironical. He had an extremely combative way of arguing. When he had won a victory, he was utterly scornful of all those who didn't agree. He hated being contradicted or accused of one-sidedness, and would react heatedly. "We had a lot of arguments," Fejtő recalls, "and began to see each other often, and I became attached to him, fads, paradoxes and all." They often met in the Café Bonaparte, a favourite haunt of Hungarian artists and intellectuals, including Otto Indig, the dramatist and Andor Németh, the writer. Despite Kolnai's meetings with Hungarians - never looked for as such - he took no part in the Paris Hungarian Association, and refused to meet Count Károlyi.[63] Kolnai also had French contacts, usually Catholics opposed to the Munich pact. Fejtő himself used to visit Jacques Maritain, the Thomist political theorist and philosopher. But Kolnai strongly disapproved of his socialistic Catholicism, and normally refused to accompany him. But he had an argumentative friendship with Marc Sangnier, who founded the Catholic modernist socialist group, "Le Sillon", a precursor of the French Christian Democratic Party. Fejtő sometimes visited Kolnai in the Hôtel de Tours, where he often found him in bed, and arguing with Elisabeth. They had two rooms, one of them full of home-made electrical-mechanical gadgets with which he amused himself.

Fejtő knew Kolnai best when his political beliefs were changing. During their many discussions Kolnai kept returning to the idea that the roots of totalitarianism lay in illiberal democracy. Hence, despite his growing rightist sympathies,[64] he remained a militant believer in liberalism. His leftist sympathies had gone down with the socialist capitulations in Germany and Austria. He now believed socialism too weak to stand up against totalitarianism. Fejtő also says that when they corresponded after the war Kolnai regularly sent him Ulászló bulletins, which were composed with great seriousness. They were, says Fejtő, the sort of records that "a good, reliable native informant" might have written. Their frequent disagreements were usually the result of their different starting-points. Whereas Fejtő discussed politics as a historian, Kolnai's point of view was consistently moral, and often open to the charge of abstraction. However, "I considered him a very great thinker, who, alas, never expressed himself in a magnum opus".

In September 1938 the Left Book Club commissioned a second edition of *The War against the West*. One result of this was an invitation to lecture to the club's summer school in August 1939. Kolnai entered England on the 10th, and made his way to Digswell Park, a country house in Hertfordshire. During his short stay he gave two lectures, one entitled "The Pivotal Principles of National Socialist Ideology" and another on Pacifism. This time he saw more of the good side of England. "In some way", he writes, "it was at Digswell that I learned what civilization meant", and singles out the quality of the discussions, the tactful way in which he was treated, the excellent food. Among nearly two hundred assorted leftists at Digswell, he says, "there were no more than two whom I found personally repulsive". He recalls with pleasure the communal singing of "revolutionary anthems" and the impeccable moral tone of the participants (no "ritual jibes at 'Victorian' morals" here).[65] After the conference he spent a day with the Grants at Finchley, and then a few days in Central London, returning on the 20th, three days before the Nazi-Soviet pact was signed and a fortnight before Britain and France declared war on Germany.

Kolnai had in fact wanted to stay longer in England, and Elisabeth says that he returned to Paris "to extend his passport".[66] His longing for England had previously had to compete with his love of Switzerland and the urgency of his literary tasks. Now, galvanised by the flattering Digswell Park visit and the declaration of war, he began to take more vigorous steps in this direction. He had already applied for a job in the BBC. In a letter to Béla Menczer he says he has written to Rennie Smith, of "The Friends of Europe", offering his ability "to read the Enemy's mind", the fruit of his long experience of dissecting and summarising Nazi books.[67] This letter was soon followed by one to Irene Grant from Elisabeth, asking her to canvass her friends for some kind of authoritative recommendation or provisional job, to enable Kolnai to come to England. Six days later, however, she wrote with the bad news that Kolnai had already been summoned as a German national to the *Stade de Colombe*, and asking her again to "do something". Elisabeth's chief worry was for Kolnai's health, since at the stadium they had to sleep in the open on concrete benches. It was very hot during the day and cold at night, and, after a few days the stench from the latrines became almost intolerable.[68] However, the soldiers in charge had "most remarkable faces", which greatly cheered them both as they were parted.[69] After a week or so the ex-Austrians were taken to an internment camp at Méslay, in the departement of Mayenne. As Kolnai was officially classified ill, he did not have to work, and records that the internees were, on the whole, well treated. However, they had to sleep in tents, and the frequent rain eventually made conditions extremely uncomfortable. He could only eat a small part of the food provided, though Elisabeth was able to send him parcels. He alleviated the inevitable boredom by writing to her, "reading Count Witte's huge Memoirs in French, and doing mathematics".[70] Other compensations were his conversations with a young Communist in his tent, and above all his walks about the camp in the early hours of darkness, with the wonderful autumnal moon and stars of an unpolluted countryside, faint glimpses of the chateau and the hilly landscape beyond, and the glowing embers beneath the camp cooking pots.

He was released on November 11th, and returned, bearded and almost unwashed, to Paris. Elisabeth had meanwhile written a further ten letters (often very lengthy) to the long-suffering Irene Grant, many of them almost hysterical (poor Béla Menczer was continually attacked), and endlessly going over and over the same ground, while Irene had in her turn been acting chiefly through her uncle, Basil Mathews, who was Deputy Director of the American Section of the Ministry of Information. On November 14th (when Kolnai was already out) she wrote to Rennie Smith (Head of "The Friends of Europe") listing the interventions she had been concerned with.

Apart from Rennie Smith himself, there had been the Archbishop of York (William Temple), Wickham Steed (possibly twice) and Basil Mathews. Two more were still needed, one from a government department and one from an organisation offering Kolnai a definite job. She therefore asked Rennie Smith to send him an official invitation to "whatever small position you can offer him".[71] There had certainly been other interventions, for example from Jacques Maritain and Stanislas Fumet, a prominent Catholic journalist, in France, from members of the Paris Hungarian group, and even - so Kolnai was later told - from the Austrian ex-Heimwehr leader Count Rüdiger von Starhemberg. The French Commandant at Méslay had also written very favourably about him, as Elisabeth wrote to Irene Grant, adding: "Aurel will be very proud of this document from a French military! It will be for him worth his internment!".[72] On November 15th Kolnai got a letter from Noble Hall, of the British Embassy, telling him that he was now free to come to England. But to the astonishment of many, he was still there in May 1940. His own explanation is encapsulated in this extract from a letter to Jászi:

> Idiotically, I hadn't bothered about a visa, but went running around after a French exit visa and married Elisabeth. A long time passed, and in the end after the Norwegian invasion the British authorities refused my request for a visa. Why? I don't know; perhaps there was a general tightening-up then and the validity of the permission of November 1939 had lapsed; but I think that intrigues of Central Europeans living in UK also played some part.[73]

The real explanation is more prosaic. Kolnai had been released from Méslay at the request of the British Foreign Office, on the understanding that he would be allowed to leave for England. But permission to come to England was a Home Office matter. They had to be assured above all that there would be a permanent post (of "National Importance") waiting for him, so that he would not become a financial burden on the State. But neither the Ministry of Information nor anyone else was prepared to offer him anything more than a three-month job. It may be that, had Kolnai taken energetic steps to secure his visa at once, it might have been granted; again, even as late as April 5th 1940, the possibility of "grant(ing) facilities for them both to help the FO out of an awkward situation" was noted in his Home Office file; but in refusing permission they were in fact sticking to the rules. Kolnai would have been the last person to challenge them.

Meanwhile Kolnai himself, recovering slowly from a bad bout of flu contracted in Méslay, was looking forward to reaching England, probably early in the New Year (1940). It is clear from his letter to Béla Menczer that he had only the vaguest idea of the kind of conditions a technically German citizen in his situation would have to meet to be admitted. The bulk of the letter discusses "after-victory reconstruction" of Germany, and the vital question of "the meaning we give to victory", and he looks forward to a "durable union between the British and the French Empires", and "a politically, spiritually and economically united Europe" on this basis.[74] There is nothing about his approaching marriage here, but, on November 21st, his mother wrote a brief note to her "dear little Auli" expressing her joy at his release: "now you really must look after yourself and your health!" They were so pleased to hear about dear Elisabeth; the engagement had delighted Papa. They wished him many happy returns of his (approaching) birthday. As for the civil marriage, which involved much time-consuming form-filling and visits to offices, neither Kolnai nor Elisabeth seems to have been under any great illusions about the other. During Kolnai's time at Méslay Elisabeth wrote about it to Irene Grant:

> I don't like to let him alone any longer ... because of his lefthandedness and idiotic timidity and modesty. I will marry him because of his idiocy and he will do it because I am just the contrary of his dreams for I am (just now!) the thinnest woman upon earth and unable to learn something of algebra or orthography, which is the worst in his eyes, besides I am lacking intelligence in a high degree.[75]

She also confided to her cousin George that they were not planning to have children, partly because she was too thin, and added that she thought Aurel's decision to marry her dated from the previous August when he had spent a few days in London. On this occasion he had stayed at the same hotel as the one he had used in March 1937, when the "landlady", Mrs Evans, had seen quite a lot of Elisabeth. Finding no alteration in their official relations after so long a gap, Mrs Evans had "reproached" him. This, says Elisabeth, "made a great impression on him". Kolnai's own accounting is given in an undated letter to Irene Grant of the beginning of 1940. The absence of fatness receives its due, but there is something to balance it:

> The good side of espousing Elisabeth lies in the fact of an uncommonly strong identity as regards some of our important instincts, preferences and aversions. There will be a long and laborious ecclesiastical sequel ...

At all events, they were married on February 19th 1940 at the Mairie of the St. Sulpice district (Elisabeth thereby forfeiting her Hungarian nationality and her permission to come on her own to England). Apart from the civil wedding, the first few months of 1940 were largely wasted because of their ignorance of the true situation regarding the visa. Elisabeth tried to get Irene Grant to prod him into forwarding his own case more effectively, especially by enlisting the help of Pál Winkler and other influential people, whom he was reluctant to "disturb". In March, having at last obtained the requisite French documents, his visa application at the Paris passport office was refused, so he wrote to Wickham Steed to ask for help, mentioning that he had not yet given up hope of publishing "The Fallacies of Pacifism", which Faber & Faber had clearly by then turned down. Elisabeth then wrote to her sister Olga asking her to win back Irene Grant's support; it seems that she had got one of her friends (Dr Douglas Jolly, a volunteer surgeon in the Spanish Civil War) to visit him in Paris, and that Kolnai had written her a letter purporting to be from Jolly, which expressed distaste (involving a chamber-pot) at the Kolnais' domestic arrangements. But when it began to be clear that they were not going to get a visa, Kolnai wrote a very sad letter to Irene Grant. All he had been able to achieve in the last few months was a contact with the London fortnightly, *Free Europe*, edited by Mr Smogorzewski for The Friends of Europe; they at least would be publishing articles of his.[76] But he felt like "unusable scrap-iron", though Elisabeth, despite having "no flesh to lean on, as it were", was "a support to (him) in several ways":

But if after all I should happen to enter: how would Karli and Ilona receive me? Mystery. I am desirous but afraid of seeing them. Especially, because I long for nothing more than for the return of a petty world, which I know they despise.[77]

On May 10th the German offensive though Belgium began, thus ending the eight months of "phoney war". All German subjects in the widest sense of the word were ordered to report for reinternment, since spies were flooding into the country among the great crowds of refugees. Kolnai was ordered to report to the *Stade de Buffalo* on the 14th. He at once wrote a letter to Irene to inform her of the extreme seriousness of his position ("this looks like death, very soon" - because no food parcels were allowed), and also of the fact that women were not being excluded from internment this time. Could some sort of "service" or "function" be offered from England? "Perhaps now, under Mr Duff Cooper, the Ministry of Information could use me?" He also wrote in similar terms to Wickham Steed and Rennie Smith. Then the Austrians were reprieved, and Kolnai was able to reply on the 22nd to Elisabeth's cousin, Yvonne Lányi, who was now working in the Franciscan Convent in Toulouse, and was encouraging them to join her. Once again, their coming depended on some sort of proof that he would have something to do there. But, as he had just had some more money from his father, the journey would be possible. It would be wonderful to work again, in the quiet of Toulouse. He was still dreaming of a book on the philosophy of "nobility" values and their relation to democracy. The following day he was "arrested" in the early morning by a "detective", and taken to Buffalo. Mercifully, the Austrian women were not interned. Kolnai says that the French were "a little ruder in their manners" this time. It was not their fault that the stadium was actually bombed. Kolnai's detention naturally sparked off another round of letters from Elisabeth to Irene Grant, and then from her to people she knew, but it seems that none of them really understood the reason for the refusal of Kolnai's visa. Elisabeth meanwhile prepared for a possible meeting in Toulouse, and sent clothes, papers, and so on in advance. In England Harold Nicolson was drawn into the business of a possible "rescue", but the situation was then so chaotic, that no one could see any possibility of anything being done "until the situation at the front has stabilised".[78] Kolnai and his fellow internees were taken this time to a camp at La Braconne, south-east of Angoulême. This was a proper camp, with accommodation in wooden huts, but it was run by a "former Prussian officer whom the French had installed in almost complete authority", a man called Schwab. This man took every chance to bully his fellow prisoners. No letters were allowed in or out, no smoking was permitted. There was a roll-call three times a day, at which he would shout at his "inferiors". The food was uneatable to anyone with a normal digestion; Kolnai himself practically starved, though, "contrary to the opinion of many doctors, I found that prolonged fasting improved rather than impaired my health".[79] Joseph Aufricht, however, records that the latrines were cleaned out every morning. But again, the quality of the inmates was, Kolnai says, inferior to that at Méslay. Most of the internees at La Braconne were "German Aryans", rather than "Austrians, Christian or Jewish"; consequently theft and personal violence were much more frequent. Here he spent much of his time with "the Hungarian Trotskyist G.", who had been a fellow member of the Galilei Circle in Budapest; he was much cheered by G's "ghoulish and inventive humour" (as no doubt G. was with Kolnai's).[80] Meanwhile, the French army collapsed before the German onslaught, and Paris was occupied. On June 22nd the Pétain government signed an armistice, with the Germans already pressing south towards Bordeaux. La Braconne was in the line of their advance, and the camp was full of people (Kolnai, of course, included) whom the Gestapo would be only too pleased to find. Some of the internees began to discover that they had perhaps been over-hasty in rejecting Nazism. At last one brave and resolute man, Erich Noth, prevailed on the French commandant to dissolve the camp. Kolnai, with two companions – one of them, Egon

Biel, was an Austrian Catholic artist, designer and writer - set out on foot in the general direction of Toulouse, through a country "swarming with French soldiery ... and innumerable tanks", about two hours before the Germans reached the camp. The three made a good team (Kolnai providing the money), and eventually reached Dignac. The armistice had partitioned the country, but Dignac was still within the German sector. They were beginning to despair of eluding the Germans when they found a lorry just about to depart for Perigueux and still able to take on three more passengers. So they reached relative safety in the "French" zone, and, in a few more days, arrived in Toulouse, already crammed with refugees, but where the Franciscan friary still amazingly found room for them. Kolnai at once hurried to the nuns' convent, to be told by Yvonne that Elisabeth had already left for England.

Elisabeth had stayed in Paris until just before the Germans entered. "I never will remember on Paris [sic, passim]", she wrote to her sister four months later,

it was all the surrender in air at this time, it looked so shameful - everything en déroute - everything on the way to Limoges, the great army in flight, but still I couldn't believe it to be true - only when the Armistice was announced.[81]

She went first to La Braconne, but was not allowed to see Kolnai. So she pressed on to Toulouse as agreed, and then, when he didn't turn up, went to Bordeaux and Bayonne to make enquiries, not knowing but that he might already be in the hands of the Gestapo. She returned to Toulouse, then went back again to Bayonne, to be told that the Germans would be there next day. So she took a taxi with some Polish soldiers to St Jean de Luz where the last British ships would be leaving for England, prepared to take on any refugees without formalities. Public order was in these last days being maintained by the Polish troops, "untouched by the plague of disintegration".[82] But, her foot already on the gangplank, she turned back in the sudden conviction that he was still in France. Overnight she travelled somehow to Pau, and from there to Cauterets, a village high in the Pyrenees. Here she halted for a while, sent a telegram to her cousin, and received the news that Aurel had reached Toulouse after all. They were soon reunited.

For a month or so the couple had to live apart, Elisabeth with the nuns and Aurel with the monks, while the former was prepared for reception into the Catholic Church by the monks' superior, Fr Castaing. In August, she was baptised, and the couple forthwith blessed in the nuns' chapel. Kolnai was disappointed that the little cats - "tutelary deities of our union" - which had entered the building, were driven out. The Kolnais were now able to move into a small flat nearby. Meanwhile, Yvonne Lányi had wired to her cousin George in Cambridge, Massachusetts, on July 6th, telling him of their situation. This was, in fact, still very bad. Not only were they now penniless again, but in constant danger of arrest by plain-clothes officials, since the Vichy government had undertaken to hand over certain named refugees to the Gestapo, and later, of course, Jews began to be rounded up indiscriminately. Kolnai later referred to his "three month hell of dread in the South of France",[83] and even began to feel relieved that "War" had not, after all, been quite such a success as he had hoped. Lányi at once began to write around for funds for their eventual journey to the USA, and quickly despatched $50. Jászi, faced with many similar requests, had only been able to manage $10, but Mumford sent $50. Then, following a nomination by the American Federation of Labor, the American State Department wired to their consul in Marseilles instructing him to issue the Kolnais, as non-Communist refugees in danger of death, with "emergency" visitors' visas. On August 19th, therefore, the Kolnais presented themselves in his office, where they were given visitors' visas intended to serve instead of passports. But there were problems over the other documents they needed, so they returned to Toulouse for a while. In September they returned to Marseilles, and agreed with the American Rescue Committee that they would try to reach Portugal despite their inadequate documentation. So towards the end of the month they travelled to Cérbère on the Spanish frontier, where they were to cross over on foot. They called on the priest, who prayed with them in church and sent his nephew to keep an eye on them from a discreet distance as they trudged up the mountain, "disguised" as anglers, to avoid French scrutiny at the official crossing point. At last they were beyond the watershed and beginning to descend. Kolnai was at once ravished by the magic of Spain, but first they had to be accepted by the Spanish frontier police. As soon as they had presented their papers they were ordered back to France because they had no passports. All explanations regarding statelessness proving unavailing, Kolnai got out his letter of recommendation from the Spanish priests in Marseilles. "Misled by an ambiguous phrasing in its text", Kolnai writes,

> he asked whether I had been a correspondent of the Madrid Catholic daily *El Debate*; no, I explained truthfully, I had only been charged with translating news from *El Debate* for a Catholic weekly in Vienna. He would not yield; but neither would stubborn Elisabeth, whom once in London her cousin George Lányi had, in spite of her thinness, called a 'bull-dog'. Law-abiding and anxious to be always right with the State, I was determined to turn back and was impatiently tugging at her sleeve,

but she went on expostulating with the poor official all the more violently - in French, for she had no Spanish at all. To my dismay, she told him the true but entirely irrelevant fact that she had once spent a month or two in Mallorca and that that had been the happiest time in her life ... Suddenly, our man jerked his arms above his head with a Gorgon-like grimace, and with grim satisfaction I whispered to Elisabeth in Magyar, "There you are - we're going to gaol". But in fact, the exasperated gesture only meant that he threw up the sponge. In the next instant, our papers were duly stamped and our presence in Spain was legal.[84]

After a leisurely journey across the country, they reached Lisbon at the beginning of October. There they settled down to wait for their boat tickets. Elisabeth also made more than one appeal to George Lányi for money to meet their living expenses, and mentioned that Kolnai was now beginning to get rather cold in his "sports dress", which included knickerbockers and a beret, and "a knapsack on his shoulders",[85] but, as they had had to abandon luggage in various places, they had hardly any clothes other than those they had been wearing when they left France. But they had met Pál Winkler since their arrival, and he had given them $50, and an American Help organisation had also given a little assistance. Kolnai certainly did ponder the idea of visiting the British Consulate about a visa, but refrained, partly because he thought it pointless, but partly because he was still "shaking with fright" at the idea of falling into the hands of the Gestapo, and "felt certain" that the Germans would invade England.[86] Meanwhile, though he enjoyed walking about Lisbon and deepening his knowledge of Portuguese, he was dreading the long sea voyage, and would rather have been in Madrid. Eventually, $225 was paid to the steamship company through the Emergency Resue Committee on November 18th, and about a week later the Kolnais boarded the U.S.S. *Siboney* bound for New York. Elisabeth later reported to George Lányi that the steward had refused to bring Kolnai tea in his cabin when he was not feeling well, but that the doctor had refused to accept the $7 they owed him. After an exciting (though routine) interlude in Bermuda, when British naval officers boarded and questioned some of the passengers (Kolnai, to his chagrin, was ignored), they reached New York - or rather Ellis Island - on December 3rd, where it almost began to seem as though they would be sent back to Portugal. Kolnai was first put in the island hospital for examination; then, on the 6th, they were examined in the "general place of detention". Since they had no passports, and were unable to prove that they would have the means to leave at the end of their month's stay, they were told they would have to leave at once, but advised to appeal. Meanwhile, they would have to remain on Ellis Island, "in the immense common room ... reminiscent of a lunatic asylum", until the appeal had been heard. Kolnai, who at once wrote to Mumford and Lányi to tell them what had happened, told them that the decision in Washington could take weeks, and that, meanwhile, they would have to "remain imprisoned here". "We can see the monument of the Liberty statue from our window," added Elisabeth; "it still stands there, [but] seems to us as for archaeological studies only".[87] Eventually a telegram from Mumford arrived, wheels were made to turn somewhere, and after about a week "Washington ordered us to be released - on some mildly tedious technical conditions".[88] They were free to make their way to the North Manhattan apartment of Klara Erdélyi, who had booked a room for them at some unknown address, and to celebrate the British victory in North Africa.

Chapter Ten

New York and Boston
(1940-1945)

Klára Erdelyi, Róbert Vámbéry's partner, had been hard at work making arrangements for the Kolnais' accommodation and other material needs. In the absence of Vámbéry himself in Cuba (much lamented by Aurel) she had met the S.S. Siboney, but didn't know exactly when they would be released from their detention on Ellis Island. So when she returned home at 1.30 a.m. on December 12th from a visit to friends, she found them "hanging about in the street", as Kolnai reported in a letter to Róbert.[1] Eventually she got them temporarily settled in the Scitovskys' apartment at 401 West 118th Street, a corner house near Columbia University. Tibor, a friend of Róbert's, equipped Kolnai for the rigours of the New York winter by giving him a dark grey suit and an overcoat. Many other items of clothing were awaiting them from the Lányis and other relations of Elisabeth's, including Maurice Schleß, a wealthy New York jeweller. Pál Winkler had sent them money to Ellis Island, and Schleß now contributed $200.

Kolnai's most pressing task was to find a regular source of income. In the first few days he was taken by Róbert's father, Rusztem, to a "Nation-lunch", where he met the editor, Freda Kirchwey. She was in fact far too "pink", politically, for Kolnai, but the meeting did give rise to his placing "Fate or Freedom?" in the May number,[2] where he "lent some aid to the men who were kindling the interventionist mood", and "tore to shreds ... various fallacies of the neutralists and pacifists, then in vogue".[3] Writing this kind of thing was, of course, no substitute for a proper job, and in the New Year he went to see two important members of the Emergency Rescue Committee. Alvin Johnson was President of the New School of Social Research, where so many refugees from the old world both studied and taught. But there were no more professorial vacancies, Johnson explained. He advised Kolnai to go to a cheaper university in the mid-West and study for a doctorate while supporting himself as a tutor or chauffeur, or perhaps from some kind of manual work. After this, his prospects would be much greater. In his letter to Jászi, Kolnai remarked that this was "as Utopian as if I were to begin teaching chemistry in Chinese from tomorrow!"[4] But in his memoirs he stresses the cultural shock at being thus "cast into a world without bearings and standards".[5] George Schuster, President of Hunter College, "a dear, refined, man, of enormous presence", could only advise a - fruitless - visit to Dr Árpád Steiner, a Hungarian historian of literature and art.

During January he also saw Mr Huebsch, of the Viking Press, who had published the American edition of *The War against the West*. He was smoking a large cigar during their interview, without offering Kolnai one, so Kolnai ostentatiously got out his cheap cigarettes and lit one himself. Huebsch made it quite clear that he had no interest in publishing the revised pacifism book. Nor could he even give Kolnai a copy of "War", since all had been sold at a handsome profit. Kolnai also saw his former mentor, Karl Polányi, and his benefactor Lewis Mumford; he also heard from Theodore Koppányi, his Catholic friend from Vienna. All had suggestions to make, but nothing did Kolnai any good. "Obedient to further pressures", he wrote, "I am also going to ask for an interview with Dorothy Thompson, though I really don't think she'll give me one."[6] Whether she did or not, the result was the same. In a letter to Elisabeth, Jászi mentioned a serious "*Schwindelkonkurrenz*" among the refugees;[7] Kolnai had little chance where so many of his competitors were free with the truth. Kolnai himself found this continuing succession of profitless visits exhausting and bewildering.

He was, however, obliged to follow up all possible chances of paid work because he and Elisabeth were now being supported by the Committee for Christian Refugees to the tune of $15 per week. Every so often the committee would ask him to give an account of his efforts. After a time Kolnai even welcomed their suggestion that he train as a radio technician, but, he says, "my wife's opposition brought the project to fall".[8] Apart from their regular allowance they had intermittent help from the Lányis and other relations and friends (including Donald Grant, then in New York), and Kolnai got $150 from the New School of Social Research's voluntary fund. He at once invested $30 on a typewriter, only to be offered one the very next day by Pál Winkler. Fearing that Winkler might think they no longer needed his help, they accepted the second instrument. They also had difficulty in organising their uncertain finances, and after they moved to Boston, Elisabeth was constantly asking Róbert Vámbéry to cash a cheque or lend them something in order to pay the rent (with various excuses such as the cat's hunger and Aurel's dental bills). Another symptom of their precarious existence in New York was the fact that they had to move at least twice during the eighteen months they spent there, and that, in one flat, they only had a bed-sitter of their own, cooking and bathing arrangements being communal. There were also cockroaches in all their apartments. Possibly because of this, Aurel, who hated the idea of living in the country, actually consented to go with Elisabeth and inspect a substantial furnished cottage on a farm about three quarters of an hour from New York city, in which the refugee committee had offered to house them. Even the related possibility of being able to keep cats and a dachshund failed to bring about their acceptance. It is, then, hardly surprising that Jászi told Béla Menczer in February that "[Kolnai] is not in good health, neither in body nor in mind", and then, two weeks later, added that "Kolnai has great difficulties in securing his existence".[9]

Indeed, Kolnai had found reality hard to bear ever since the German occupation of France, and had frequent recourse to his fantasy world, Ulászló. Elisabeth's urgent letters to George from Lisbon about steamer tickets, money or lost baggage have Kolnaian postscripts detailing the results of recent Ulászló elections, or describing the constitution, political parties, or the latest court scandal. On one occasion in New York, Elisabeth read aloud from George's letter his expression of allegiance to the "Personalist Party". Aurel "deeply enjoyed" this; "it has sufficed only to see his radiant face".[10] Once he sent Lányi an article purporting to be an extract from the *Óbudai lapok* (Óbuda News) of December 5th 2021, examining the claim that the obscure Kolnai prepared the way for the Personalist Party. The Ulászló bulletins also mark his own changing political views. Until the Kolnais reached Lisbon, Ulászló was still a palatinate; one of his letters to George announces its transformation into a monarchy. After a year of egalitarian New York, he announces the reintroduction of the peerage. Another amusement, through which he "covered" his own awkwardness in the strange social milieu of New York, was his eager perusal of etiquette books, which enabled him elaborately to "confess" his "misbehaviour" at the houses of Elisabeth's rich relations, and to bewail the absence of social rules about behaviour to superiors, as he had found in Spain and Portugal. He also organised a "Presidential election", and an enquiry into why "we" (the Kolnais) are "disliked", sending out voting papers and a detailed questionnaire to his friends and relations.

Many other refugees were, of course, in a similar, or worse, plight, and Josef Aufricht describes how the gardens below Riverside Drive, which Kolnai would have known well, were full of despairing-looking and sometimes suicidal men. Aufricht, a good friend of Vámbéry's, lived just round the corner from the Kolnais, and got Aurel to coach his son in mathematics. When he once gave him a cigar, Kolnai prostrated himself on the floor in gratitude. Through Aufricht he met the Berliner Herrmann Borchardt, almost totally deaf and with a smashed hand, thanks to a spell in Buchenwald and Dachau before the war. He had a philosophical training, but had composed a 1,700-page film manuscript, which Franz Werfel persuaded him to re-cast as a novel. Kolnai was absolutely bowled over by this Christian-conservative political saga, *The Conspiracy of the Carpenters*. Unfortunately, it was badly translated, and was never a success.[11]

Kolnai fairly quickly reestablished contact with E.K. Winter, who was lecturing at the New School of Social Research. In one letter he compliments Winter on his paper on Christian Personalism, but points to the key difference between them: "the interpretation of consciousness".[12] Whereas Winter stresses the "constructive" and "creative" side (as in German Idealism), he, Kolnai, affirms the "intentional" "subject-object relationship", like the Scholastics and their modern followers, Brentano and Husserl, where the individual subject "confronts" a world of objects which is "given" to him. He would very much like to discuss this with Winter, or, even better, hear Winter discuss it with Maritain or Hildebrand. As Hildebrand, who was now a Professor at Fordham (Jesuit) University in New York, held regular "evenings" in his apartment, this may well have taken place. Kolnai had already been to dinner with Maritain, who, according to Menczer, "had a very high opinion of him".[13] As a social occasion the reunion was rather a failure. Maritain's Catholic leftism, which he had attacked in Paris, was becoming ever more irksome. But the food was good and Kolnai much enjoyed the dismay of Mme Maritain and her sister at his decisively rejecting "belief in" democracy, and professing the strange creed of Conservatism.[14] As for Hildebrand, whom he had met again in Toulouse, Kolnai felt much better disposed to him now that the poisonous Vienna atmosphere of the Dollfuß and Schuschnigg dictatorships was a thing of the past, and describes him to Jászi as a friend and "to a certain degree my master", though one "a little too much involved in politics" for his taste.[15] In his later marginal comments on Hildebrand's ethical books he expresses impatience with his pietism and clericalism, and also his rather Germanic English style, but shows great admiration for his insights. Kolnai in fact translated Hildebrand's German book, *Umgestaltung in Christus* (a work as much ethical as religious), at his request. At another dinner, in the home of Balduin Schwarz, who edited the Hildebrand Festschrift to which Kolnai later contributed, Kolnai kept paying compliments to Mrs Schwarz, and at one point exclaimed: "Ich habe doch dicke Frauen so gern!" (I do so like fat women.) It is not clear whether Elisabeth ("the thinnest living lass") was present or not.

During the Kolnais' first summer in New York, Elisabeth wrote to Jászi to request a letter of recommendation for the "Pre-examination". This was the first step on the slow journey to U.S. citizenship. In his testimonial Jászi wrote: "There are few authors in the present [*sic*] world literature who could analyse the deeper foundations of present-day moral and political problems with a greater competence than he." He also assured the authorities, who might jib at his membership of the Marxist SPD, that "Kolnai, a philosopher, was never in touch with practical daily politics."[16] Their registration certificates were issued in the following February. The previous June, Kolnai asked Jászi for his help in getting Andor Németh, their recent Paris companion - still stuck in Marseilles - to the United States. He also sent, at Elisabeth's insistence, his recent article "The Techniques of Fascism".[17] It is another pro-interventionist piece, but "I think it better than my *Nation* article, since it's not rhetorical but written in a quiet and sober tone and clearly makes for intelligent reading".[18] He was also working on "Personalism, the spiritual basis of democracy", for the *Political Review*. This never appeared, any more than did an article he suggested for *The Thomist*, "Society and the hierarchy of values", or one for the *Journal of Social Philosophy*, "The suicide of political groupings". Elisabeth also told Jászi that Aurel had been invited to lecture by the American Lecture Bureau. His suggested topics were "Psychology and Fascism", "Psychology and Appeasement", "The Ideological War" and "The Common Man and Power".

Kolnai's renewal of regular contact with Oscar Jászi was of great importance to him. Although he says in his Memoirs that he learnt nothing new from Jászi, he still admired him and needed to feel his old mentor's approval, especially now that his own views had diverged so far. It is also significant that, when he began his extended apologia, he wrote in Hungarian again. This was not only the language in which he could express the finest shades of meaning, but also that of the country he had rejected, whose best sides Jászi most fully represented for him. But the correspondence did not really become easy and frequent until 1944. Jászi himself held back because he felt that Kolnai was associating too closely with those Austrian émigrés who wanted a Habsburg restoration.

New York was then teeming with ex-Austrians of almost all political shades. Although the old Social Democrats had declared in favour of Austria's remaining part of a de-Nazified Germany after the war, all the other parties wanted her eventual independence. But there was naturally a great deal of argument about the future constitution. Unlike E.K. Winter, Kolnai refused to get involved in this "politicking" (though the question of who was to stand on this or that committee is often pursued with intense interest in his letters to Winter), and told him that, although he would do what he could for the independence of Austria, he didn't regard himself as a member of any of the rival political groups. The most he was prepared to do was to sit on the "Austrian National Committee",[19] though his reputation was such that he was sometimes elected onto committees without being consulted, and had to repudiate the proceedings later.

But there is guilt by association, and Kolnai had not only "once or twice ... had audience of Otto d'Austria at the Essex Hotel in New York",[20] but had begun to write regularly in *The Voice of Austria*, whose owner and editor, Franz Klein, "was a Habsburg Monarchist in close touch with" the heir to the imperial throne himself. Kolnai and Klein had known each other in Vienna in connection with *Der Oesterreichische Volkswirt*, and it was presumably this fact which induced Klein to hand over the editorship to Kolnai during October 1941, while he went on a lecture-tour in Canada. Kolnai also associated with other monarchists, such as Hildebrand. However that may be, his contributions to the "Voice" are never primarily monarchist, and he wrote there rather than elsewhere because he saw it as the best organ for disseminating his own views. The main concern of his eleven articles is to argue for Austrian independence with constitutional democracy, under either a republican or a monarchist sign. In considering the possibility of a federalist solution to the problem of Central Europe, he argues that this could not work without some power to hold the various elements together, and what could this be if not a reformed Habsburg? It is the same in his longer articles in the *Journal of Central European Affairs*. A Habsburg restoration is possible, even desirable, but only in a "liberal-democratic" version. He is, however, always aware of the extreme unlikelihood of the Czechs and the Jugoslavs consenting to cooperate with Austria and Habsburg in any form, and seems to have dropped the idea during 1943 or 1944. Nor did he ever seriously consider the idea of "little Austria" becoming a constitutional monarchy on its own, even though he now thought highly of constitutional monarchy in some circumstances.

Kolnai, therefore, was far from being unequivocally "legitimist" in his approach to postwar Austria. Yet Jászi could write: "I cannot continue my friendship with a man who is now cooperating with the crowd around the Habsburgs and Mr Eckhardt, the former leader of the Awakening Hungarians", as a seeming corollary of his Catholicism.[21] When Menczer defended his old friend against this very heated attack, Jászi took up the matter again:

> I am not unjust to Kolnai. I never said or thought that he is not honest in his convictions. I esteem his personality as a scholar and a thinker. What I resent is his practical incapacity to evaluate a situation. The case of Otto Habsburg is simply ridiculous. He is surrounded by the old imperial reactionary gang. He has nothing to do with the vital part of Catholicism. Jacques Maritain has openly and forcefully repudiated the whole restorational and legitimistic ideology.[22]

Later in the year we find Jászi complaining to Arnold Dániel (now in Cambridge, England), that "Kolnai continues his agitation for the Habsburgs and a Catholic rebirth".[23] Jászi certainly had more justification in accusing Kolnai of promoting "a Catholic rebirth", since it was axiomatic for him that postwar reconstruction must be based on the reaffirmation of Christendom. But he never "agitated for the Habsburgs". From all this it is not difficult to see the importance Kolnai's changing views held for Jászi at a personal level. If there is still something of the father in Jászi for Kolnai, there is certainly still something of the favourite spiritual son in Kolnai for Jászi. Even his cautious and reasoned advocacy of a possible Habsburg restoration in modernised form felt like a betrayal.

In July 1942, the Kolnais moved to 43 Banks St, Cambridge (a suburb of Boston), partly because George Lányi taught at Harvard, and partly because it seemed a more human and cultivated environment than New York. But prospects of employment seemed even slighter, so for the next year Elisabeth worked in a factory sewing buttons on military uniforms. The totalitarian aspects of American life, which weighed so heavily on them both, were now greatly mitigated by the accession of a cat to their *ménage*. Their apartment also contained "a wonderful Civil War iron stove", mostly tended by Elisabeth, and no cockroaches. In September he almost got a job teaching Hungarian at Harvard, but demand for the course was too small. Meanwhile, Kolnai's request to Jászi for a reference had brought down upon him all the latter's pent-up reproaches. It is worth giving the flavour of his very long and elaborate letter of defence.[24] He begins with a kind of declaration of loyalty to Jászi, who "somehow stand(s) out from the world as regards intellectual stature". He goes on to explain that, in his slow departure from "leftist orthodoxy" from 1922 onwards, he was not a little influenced by Jászi himself. He realised that Jászi was a cut above the other Octobrists, and this drew him on to "an intellectual impartiality fatally transcending the favorite narrow-minded schemas of leftist thought". He then turns to the accusation that "Habsburg propaganda", with which he is supposed to be identified, serves the Nazis. If this were true, and he were a part of this service, one might as well say that Jászi serves the Nazis because of his influence on Kolnai! The only really important thing is that "Habsburg ... embodies a political tradition at the opposite pole from Nazism ... and in practice Nazism must self-evidently wish for its destruction". He then turns to analyse his own political position. The key words of this very long statement are those of the second sentence: "I couldn't say whether I am Left or Right, or between the two, since I ponder the matter too much." He then affirms that, whatever position he takes up - and he admits a desire to counter the fashionable trend - he does so always with "qualification and balance". He is on safest ground when he calls himself a "centrist", directed by a "personalism" which differs from Liberalism and is closely related to Catholic thought. After a long list of leftist policies which he abhors, he returns to his relation to Habsburg legitimism, and his cautious advocacy of a "well devised Federal Danubian Empire", itself "totally subordinate to that [of] allied victory and the survival of Christian civilization". As far as the "Voice" goes, he says that he has had to twist Klein's arm to some extent in order to write as he has done, but feels that, in the last analysis, "Klein is the only one who propagates the liberty of Austria with some kind of vision, intelligence and journalistic skill". But - in case Jászi thinks he writes in it for the money - he is paid nothing for his articles, whereas, if he had kept up his connection with *The Nation* (axiomatically anti-monarchical), he would have had a little money from time to time. But if there were a decent Austrian republican journal, he'd happily write for it. Jászi replied quite soon, and Kolnai wrote again in November, enclosing his first *Journal of Central European Affairs* article.[25] But, as regards Central European reconstruction, he assures his old friend, "the issue is not so much the '*ancien régime*' or 'uninterrupted progress', 'loftier' or massiver Catholicism", but rather the question to be or not to be, "conservation ... in short, our skins".[26]

In the Spring of 1943, Kolnai was summoned to Washington for a hearing in connection with his application for citizenship. Koppányi was also present to vouch for him. He told Jászi that the committee were chiefly interested in whether he was a "Bolshie" or genuine socialist. He goes on:

> On this question I was able to reassure them. At last the chairman said: "We committee members have reached (sic!) the conclusion that socialism is incompatible with a Christian and freedom-based society." Short pause. The chairman went on: "What do you think?" Solemnly, I answered: "That exactly expresses my own opinion." Their faces beamed. "Thank you, you may go. Send in Koppányi".[27]

This trip to Washington, where he "suffered cruelly from the heat", was the furthest south Kolnai went in the United States. Although he found the "cold classicistic pomp" of the "a priori capital" depressing, it nevertheless managed to convey to him a vivid impression of the South. He especially liked the old-fashioned men-only Cosmos Club, where Koppányi lived, and the domestic amenities of the house belonging to a rich female friend of Koppányi's, where he stayed.[28] In his various writings he more than once laments the crushing defeat of the Confederacy in the Civil War. Slavery was certainly "untenable in the long run", and Lincoln was an admirable man, but the civilisation of the United States lost something of permanent value when the Yankees triumphed.

It was around this time that Lewis Mumford sent him a copy of his *chef d'oeuvre*, *The City of Man*, with an earnest request to tell him what he thought of it. Kolnai, who, in his letter from Ellis Island, had written: "I happen to know no other writer or spiritual leader with whose views I agree so wholeheartedly",[29] found the last part of *The City of Man* "execrable". Of course he said so, and even the toned-down version of his letter prompted by "conjugal censorship" caused great offence and brought the relationship to an end.[30]

In the happier, if provincial, surroundings of Cambridge, Kolnai had begun to feel a new access of energy, and had decided to work up the themes of his recent articles into a proper book. Accordingly, with the backing of Hildebrand, he applied to the Catholic Committee for Refugees for help to enable him to write *Liberty and the Heart of Europe*. This was now granted in the form of a "scholarship", to be repaid if the completed product produced any income. Around the same time the Kolnais joined the St Benedict Centre, in Cambridge. Before I say something about this, it may be as well to set out a little more directly the Kolnais' attitude to the country in which they had applied for citizenship.[31] He (in complete accord with Elisabeth) loathed New York, together with a great many other manifestations of the American way of life, including, of course, its very concept. Kolnai was aware that one could live perfectly easily as a detached "dissident" in the USA; he also acknowledged many of the good things about it, especially its unparalleled benevolence. And yet it was "the most successful of Totalitarianisms", endlessly ramming home the central lie that, through hard work and inventiveness, the ideal of happiness was being realised. In any case, Kolnai concluded, this was not the happiness of real persons, of Homo Sapiens at his highest, but of Homo Faber, of man the "button-pushing animal". The most serious defect was the lack of the "appreciative" spirit, of respect and reverence for the good that is given, irrespective of our purposes. A particularly savage aspect of this was the equalitarian attack on differential human qualities as such. All this went with a great number of naive illusions and indifference to truth. Some of this had been present, of course, in Europe, but it had always been tempered by long-established custom, ancient privilege, the virtual omnipresence of what is old and venerable. This kind of background greatly lessened the difference between religious believers and non-believers in the West. But in America, not only was there far less of the "simply given",[32] but much even of its religion largely lacked reverence. Most American believers were in fact deists, having banished God to a remote corner of reality. Only in Catholicism was the true presupposition of religion, that "response" comes before "fiat", to be found. Hence the Kolnais' preference for Catholic circles, and their finding it natural to join the St Benedict Centre in Cambridge. In a letter to Jászi he calls 1941-2 the year of his "second conversion", and links it with the recovery of his conservatism.

The St Benedict Centre was opened in 1940 to provide a counter to the liberal humanism conveyed to its students by Harvard. As part of its mission it put on lectures, philosophical discussions and question-and-answer sessions, and provided a social centre for Catholics wanting to resist liberal trends. By the time the Kolnais arrived, the Centre was chiefly identified with the Irishman Father Leonard Feeney, S.J. Feeney was just the sort of man to attract Kolnai - anti-Thomist, anti-Maritain, "one of the few outstanding writers now living",[33] a forceful and unconventional personality not afraid of saying what he thought to anybody, and a lover of argument and controversy. Kolnai admired his versatile mind, and learnt much from him, both in philosophy - especially Scholasticism - and theology. He was immensely gratified when Feeney said to him once: "Doctor, you've got instinct!", and, on another occasion, called Kolnai "inspiring".[34] He also made friends with Dr Fakhri Maluf, later Brother Francis, SIHM,[35] who, in 1996, still recalled Kolnai as "the most remarkable person I have ever met". Maluf organised the philosophy teaching at the Centre on Tuesday evenings, and his usual practice was to announce a topic the week before and select an introductory speaker and a panel for the evening, who had to be ready to answer the audience's questions. Kolnai was much in demand, but Maluf recalled that whenever the topic concerned Plato (for Kolnai, primarily an apostle of "rightist utopia"), he would refuse to participate, but sit quietly by himself in a corner. But during 1944 things gradually began to go wrong. By April 1945 Kolnai was even expressing to Jászi his longing for non-Catholic society, even that of "bourgeois pinks":

> But then I scuttle back to St Benedict's, gratefully endure the unjust sorties of Fr Feeney ..., his capricious smiles of favour, sugary angelicisms and anti-puritan puritanism. To him I am a manichaean puritan sniffing out immorality, and if I say that music has a "certain immoral aspect", then "I want to prohibit music as sinful"![36]

Then came an occasion when Feeney would no longer tolerate Kolnai's refusal to discuss Plato, and insisted that he join in. He had in fact been warned long before that the Centre was in danger of becoming a sect. The Kolnais now realised the truth of this, and, after their last "Plato" evening, never came back. A few years later Feeney was excommunicated for disobedience to the hierarchy.

In July 1943 the Kolnais received their ID papers from the Commonwealth of Massachusetts, and on October 19th they took the train to Montreal to get their new visas, combining this with an excursion to Quebec. On their return to Boston, they took out their "First Papers", signing in December an additional "Declaration of Intent" to become American citizens. Six weeks before, he wrote a short note to the old liberal leftist, Rusztem Vámbéry, almost entirely confined to a summary of his current views about liberalism.[37] It is worth quoting in full:

> Liberalism is by no means a wholly wicked thing. Certain essential aspects of it are essentially good: such as the emphasis placed on

personality and the basic human rights; the rationalization and humanization of legal justice (to a degree); the conception of the Constitutional State; the affirmation of individual freedom of choice (within the framework of objective morality!); and a certain cult of disinterested knowledge as such. What is definitely wicked is the conception of Popular Sovereignty (identification between the so-called Will of the People and the Good - and Rousseauism in general); the substitution for objective morality of a formal construction of absolute liberties limited merely by one another; the derivation of all authority merely from the arbitrary choice of those subject to it, etc. As we see, Liberalism has ultimately (but rather promptly) led to Mass Rule, the cult of the Common Man, the complete destruction of culture and spiritual life (including its non-religious forms), radical contempt for the very idea of Truth, and a gigantic surge of socialist Totalitarianism in its various forms. Every ideological movement contains certain dialectical germs of its own destruction, but Liberalism is eminently a self-destructive force. In sum, Liberalism is highly valuable as a corrective (an attempt to place moral checks on the authorities that be, both secular and ecclesiastical), but deleterious as a self-subsistent pattern of society. Civilized society can, and should, be made into a soil in which Liberty thrives, but it cannot be constructed primarily out of the principle of Liberty. The Conservative Monarchy will be an incomparably higher and more tolerable thing by the inclusion of spheres of opposition and discussion; but Revolution is the Enemy, for it is bound to result in Barbarism and Tyranny.

This new conservative perspective probably owes something to his activities at the St Benedict Centre, and certainly much to Herrmann Borchardt (especially his novel) and to Kolnai's many discussions with Róbert Vámbéry. Róbert and Klára also lived now at 43 Banks Street, and the two couples spent much time together, though the fiery Elisabeth had frequent feuds with her old friend Róbert, from which Kolnai kept studiously aloof. After the war Klára recalled to Irma Gémes the jokes and games the men had shared, but could recall no details. But Vámbéry remembered the occasion when he and Kolnai went out to buy Sunday papers. Without a word Kolnai extracted the sports section and solemnly presented it to Vámbéry; equally poker-faced Vámbéry handed Kolnai the business section. They turned as one to the nearby trash can.[38]

Meanwhile Kolnai had parted company with Klein, who seems to have sold *The Voice of Austria* to "the capitalist Géza Antal", who continued it under the new title, *Liberation*. He published one article under the new dispensation, in which he strongly attacked "League of Nations" pacifism, and the idea of a world-state,[39] and then refused to have anything more to do with it. In his letter of explanation to Klein he reveals that Klein altered his title from "The Fallacy of Collective Security" to "Collective Insecurity", which, he says, allies him by implication with all the liberal campaigners for "collective security" from whom he has done his utmost to distance himself. In any case the new paper "navigates under false flags and has no substance".[40] His other four American journalistic articles, including two more about Austrian nationhood, and an attack on utopian schemes for postwar international order, were published in *Free Europe*, and seem to confirm a growing loss of interest in any kind of Habsburg revival. Conscious, perhaps, of the effect all this might have on Jászi, he wrote him a gigantic eleven-sided and closely typed letter in February 1944, headed "Mere prating without any topical justification". Here he reports that Elisabeth is now trying to earn money by making designs for children's aprons, and that his *Liberty and the Heart of Europe* is only about a quarter finished, though the grant has expired. He then turns to apologetics again. It seems that Jászi, who still could not accept Kolnai's conservatism, had taxed him with inconsistency in continuing to be such an admirer of the Czech statesman and democrat, Masaryk, who turned against a Central European federation after the First World War. Kolnai first excuses Masaryk's decision in the light of the situation at the time. As for his own "turn":

A man ages, personality integrates, and the deeper, more decisive, psychological motifs more effectively pervade all points of view, whereas the seemingly accidentally developed "pseudomorphoses" can be sacrificed.

But there were also "painful concrete experiences and observations", from which he had learnt

the meaning of Fascism, the deep connection between Communist-Fascist Totalitarianism and democracy and "modernity" as such, the pathetically stupid interpretations and self-delusions of "leftist" critiques of Fascism, the conquest of the "democracies" by the pacifist poison, the gradual decay of culture, the emptiness of human existence and growth of meaninglessness in democratic societies - my observation from within of the rotting of French democracy; the trauma of Munich; last but not least the appalling, choking experience of the desert of the USA.

Towards the end he turns to their social life, much of it provided by Harry Levin, of Harvard. He had "misbehaved himself" towards the "narrow-mindedly intolerant and humourless" Professor Matthiesen, "had a little argument" with the English historian of religion, Professor O.S. Nock (the Philosopher A.N. Whitehead was also present), but very much enjoyed the company of the Karpoviches, the husband coming from an old Russian pre-revolutionary liberal family. There are still men alive on earth, he reflects. But for how long? Your, or rather our, old hatred of "feudalism" was so one-sided and ressentiment-laden![41]

Róbert Vámbéry was now working at the Office of War Information, which was full of Communists and fellow-travellers. He and his immediate superior thought it would be good to procure the services of a fellow-conservative, so in the Spring of 1944 Kolnai was offered a job at the "Hungarian desk". Kolnai turned it down, Vámbéry's explanation being that "he thought I would dominate him".[42] However, at the end of the year he undertook to do some translations for them. The main task was to turn Nevins and Commager's propagandistic history of the United States into Hungarian. Meanwhile his Catholic Committee scholarship was renewed for a further six months, so he remained busy on *Liberty and the Heart of Europe*. But his efforts to win Jászi's full favour had still not been wholly successful, and the business was aggravated by his having published what Jászi calls a "*Harc*-spoof" before parting company with "Klein's circle". *Harc*, "the little Hungarian rag of the [Rusztem] Vámbéry group",[43] had recently published an interview with Helen Polányi, still an ardent Communist. The interview may well have inspired the spoof article, which angered Jászi "as an indiscretion and, worse, a piece of bad taste", since *Harc* was

> the only Hungarian paper in the USA which offers the possibility of an honourable future for Hungary between the silly clerical Habsburg Utopia and Bolshevist devilry.[44]

Jászi pulls no punches in this letter, accusing Kolnai of "swimming ... in a sea of ressentiment, from which the coral islands of holy Catholic dogma stand sharply out", of making a virtue of intolerance, of glorying in the "master-slave relation", of abusing the laws of hospitality, and so on. But he only wishes they could meet, so as to clear up face to face what must be a host of misunderstandings. At the end he expresses the hope that the letter hasn't sounded too cold. No, Kolnai replies almost within the week. It was a bit cold here and there, but "I prefer a slap in the face from you to flattery from the *gens minor intellectualis*". He follows this with some affectionate reminiscences, which will all "come in my memoirs of Jászi, if I ever write them".[45] During the course of the letter, Kolnai defends himself stubbornly against all Jászi's accusations, occasionally giving way on small points, and using the opportunities thus offered to give his views on a great many topics of mutual interest. Jászi in his turn replied fairly soon, expressing his relief that Kolnai was not angry at his letter. He briefly takes up the main points again, but there is far less of indignant accusation here. He ends by asking Kolnai if he would comment on the last chapter of his book on tyrannicide, which he has to revise.[46] Kolnai did this quite quickly - without damaging their relationship - and pointed to various features of Jászi's attitudes which separate him from the run of leftists: he had never denied and simplified "God, essence and object", and had always had a "metaphysical streak".[47] These letters abound in reminiscences of Vienna days and earlier. They keep returning to Hungarian literature and culture, religion, Jewishness; Kolnai says: "I am afraid I am the most pungent possible incarnation of the Jewish mind." Jászi thanks Kolnai for the comments on *Tyrannicide*; he is a wonderful catalyst of new and better trains of thought. He admits to being normally prejudiced against Catholic writers, but, somehow, Christopher Dawson, Maritain, Mounier and Kolnai are so much nearer to him than Laski, J. Huxley and the leaders in *The Nation* and *The New Republic*.[48] Kolnai's next letter, of July 9th, contains one most revealing passage. Jászi had said that Aldous Huxley, though not a deep thinker, was an outstanding writer and "a seeker after truth". Kolnai points out that, in *Ends and Means*, Huxley says that to wage war is morally on a level with the sadistic actions of De Sade. In his own opinion, this kind of talk amounted to "systematically corrupting moral common sense", which was surely much worse than De Sade's conduct. He also renews his attack on Jászi's political concerns; he's still fighting his pre-1918 battles against "feudalism" and "the powers-that-be". The question surely is the very survival of the state and of civilisation. Hence his own concern for the renewal of élites, and "the ethical relativising and balancing of social privilege; I see the 'ruling classes' primarily as society-forming, civilization-creating factors". Besides, Jászi's conciliatory stance towards the USSR (whose rulers he cannot stop seeing as "heirs of the French Revolution") is really a form of appeasement.[49] Jászi's reply is very eirenic in tone, his criticisms relieved by teasing. The great thing is that they will soon be able to meet regularly, as he is shortly coming to Worcester (not far from Cambridge) as Visiting Professor.[50] In October, replying to a lost letter from Jászi, he assures him that he's not easily offended:

> Among my gigantic faults (laziness, selfishness, hedonism, in a certain sense intolerance, too much respect for my own personal fads, a certain authorial conceit, etc, etc) personal over-sensitiveness is hardly represented. I thirst for criticism, preferably of course on the part of those whom I can intellectually and morally respect, especially yourself ...[51]

He then refers to an "angry attack" made on him by the Harvard Professor Friedrich in the *Review of Politics*, and "4 or 5 very sharp critiques published in English papers". These may refer to his last short journalistic paper in *Free Europe*, "The American Mind and the Problem of Europe",[52] in which he defends the American State Department's divergence from public opinion in foreign affairs:

> mass democracy is fundamentally incapable of the direct management of vital policies, and public opinion here is not manufactured from above as it is in the totalitarian systems, nor framed organically by a highly-conscious political élite, as is the case in the old conservative democracies.[53]

The American mind is incapable of grasping "the existence of ingrained evil in the human soul". All this was, of course, part of his growing conviction that the approaching victory of the allies was equally an approaching defeat at the hands of the Russians.

Thanks to Jászi's sojourn at Worcester, the two were now able to meet fairly often. On one occasion Jászi met Elisabeth for the first time. Kolnai was evidently anxious for Jászi's approval of his marital choice, and expressed the hope that, despite her "manifest intellectual inadequacies", he nevertheless detected something positive.[54] It was around this time that Kolnai abandoned *Liberty and the Heart of Europe*, since he could now see that the West would have no say whatsoever in the form of Central European reconstruction. I shall say something about the unpublished text below, but the events that occasioned its abandonment were taking toll of Kolnai's mental state, and Jászi, sensing that something was wrong, had mentioned symptoms of his "touchiness". This was the signal for another long apologetic passage in Kolnai's December letter, concerning the apparently casual way in which he says he would consign certain people to the gallows if he had the power (for example, Helen Polányi). Kolnai says he doesn't mind Jászi thinking him an intolerant fanatic, but he would mind if he thought him capable of "hysterical and evil subjectivism" in the matter. There are also some brief remarks about the Karpoviches (they are Russian Orthodox, and hence we are always "wringing our hands over schism"), and, in a renewal of the theme of his "failure", Kolnai quotes Karpovich as saying that in his character "the 'exasperating' not only wipes out (to a considerable degree) the 'inspiring', but could not exist without the 'inspiring', the two being inseparable". Lastly, he returns to their political discussions, which endlessly revolve round Jászi's "destruction of magyar feudalism" obsession, and his tirades against the "Bethlen combination".[55] All this impresses him "like Dollfuß and his circle in the Spring of 1933, who exultingly celebrated the downfall of liberalism while the Nazi noose tightened round their necks". But their differences are ones of interpretation:

> You find plausible a democracy working in the service of a "cautious" Russian imperialism, or a free order based on "people's power" on the ruins of the Hungarian ruling class; I don't.[56]

And, he adds, he sees a much closer connection than Jászi does between freedom for all and the traditional élite.

In March 1945 Kolnai wrote what amounts to a long political lament when the new Hungarian government set up by the Russians in Debrecen invited Jászi for a visit. It elicited the most affectionate letter yet from Jászi, in which for the first time he calls him Aurel instead of Kolnai. He has been suffering from a very severe depression himself:

> I feel the Russian pressure almost physically. And I see ever less clearly how to safeguard the few, but genuine, values of Magyardom, in the Russian "orbit" which it cannot escape.[57]

In what follows Jászi chides his old disciple, but does it gently, in a supportive fashion. Of all the letters from Jászi, who was now at the centre of liberal hopes for Hungary after the war, and corresponded as intensively with many other people, there is probably none which witnesses so strongly to the esteem he felt for Kolnai. In his reply Kolnai bewails the present appeasement, especially of the disguised kind, that exists in the USA; it's much worse than pre-war European appeasement. And of the only two extensive centres of value today, the British Empire and the Catholic Church, the former is threatened by the USA, which is really a "counter-empire". Our biggest problem then is: how can we protect the Western constitutional tradition from the "self-poison of all progressive democracy"?[58]

Kolnai's poor mental state at the beginning of 1945 was not alleviated by the fact that he was committed to the unpalatable work of translation he had undertaken. He produced it eventually after many delays, and was paid $940 for his pains, but, not surprisingly, his text was never used. However, quite unexpectedly, a new hope of salvation appeared. During the previous August, at a St Benedict Centre Tuesday evening, Elisabeth had heard a couple sitting near them speaking French. They turned out to be Arthur and Pauline Tremblay from Quebec, and had come to Cambridge for a year so that Arthur might do some postgraduate study at Harvard. The two couples quickly struck up a friendship. When the time came for Tremblay to return in the Spring of 1945 Kolnai enquired about the possibility of his getting some work at Tremblay's university, Laval. The latter felt that Kolnai's best plan would be to present himself first at the annual Summer School, and accordingly induced the university to pay him a bursary to enable him to attend in July. Kolnai enormously enjoyed being a student again. The lectures forming the course were virtually all on Thomism, with hardly any reference to other mediaeval philosophers and virtually none but polemical references to modern thinkers. Nevertheless, he gained some valuable new insights into Aquinas' thought, and acquitted himself very well in the concluding exams. Before returning to Cambridge he was interviewed for and informally offered a ten-month appointment from September to teach the History of Modern Philosophy. Once home again, however, his elation was seriously tempered by the long delayed news of his parents' deaths "in internment, under the Nazi terror, during the siege of Budapest".[59] In a fit of coughing he broke a rib, and developed double pneumonia, and, although he had by now been officially offered and had accepted the temporary appointment, had to write for permission to miss the first few weeks of the semester. His illness was alleviated by the prescription of "beefsteaks and port", and a personal visit from Jászi to congratulate him on his appointment. Just before the Kolnais' final departure, the Levins gave them a farewell dinner, at which the well-known American philosopher, R.B. Perry, was present. "A most acrimonious debate" about the Nuremberg Trials arose, says Kolnai, in which he roundly condemned

> our forming a council of judgement in common with the Bolshevists, our adoption of the Nazi principle that you could "punish" a "crime" defined by no law; our return to the practice of the times when the victors executed the losers.

Perry, fuming with anger, "retorted that these were the rough beginnings of a Higher Moral Order of the World". To make matters worse, Levin, who really agreed, failed to back him up properly. The old philosopher "wished us gruffly a very good night" and departed.[60]

***

Liberty and the Heart of Europe, of which only about half was written, is addressed to a particular political task - the rebuilding of Central Europe after the second world war. Despite its "occasional" conception, the manuscript contains much political philosophy and historical analysis of great interest. It shows Kolnai continuing to work out his understanding of conservatism, liberal democracy, nationalism, internationalism, and related ideas, and the gradual emergence into full clarity of his later anti-utopianism. Accordingly, we find many echoes of *Der ethische Wert und die Wirklichkeit.*

The completed part of the book is organised as follows:

Introduction: The Theme of the War
I.1. The Central European Menace to Liberty
I.2. The Failure of Nationalism and Self-Determination
I.3. The Inadequacy of Internationalism and the Pacifist Peril
II.4. The Ambiguous Position of Liberal-Democracy
II.5. The Personalist and Pluralist Conception of Liberty

In the Introduction Kolnai compares the Second with the First World War. There are parallels, but the old principles of progress, democracy and self-determination no longer sound as evident as they did. What remains is the principle of Liberty. What we are really fighting for is the restoration of

Western Civilisation, which is founded on Christianity. But this has not always manifested itself in the same way. The appeal of Liberty is not just to the West; there are essential differences in the Central European political consciousness, where "neither 'bourgeois' leadership ... nor the pattern of the sovereign 'National State', nor ... the trend towards constitutional Democracy" have prevailed as in the West. Chapter one begins with a lengthy discussion of Germany's relation to Central Europe, in which he contrasts the German, or Prussian, style of rule ("domination") with the old Austrian imperial one ("hegemonic federalism"). The German political mentality tends towards totalitarianism, expressed especially in the succession Fichte, Hegel, Marx. National Socialism (and other Central European Fascisms) must be seen as a local reaction to the weaknesses of Western political ideology. It is, above all, Germany's answer "to the challenge of Western ascendency and the crude attempt at a universal Westernization of society". Chapter two starts with a discussion of the totalitarian nisus of nationalism. Rather than developing genuine political thought, which is based on response to "the realities presented by history", it has an "inherent preference for an a priori 'geometry of the state' (composed by a mass of equal individuals)". Through its efforts to eliminate divisions within the unity of the state, via its utopian belief in the possibility of an immanent "perfection" of things human, it tends to absolutise external antagonisms. As for self-determination, its central fallacy "lies in the basic error about the relation between State and citizen". Democratic decisions by vote are essentially changeable, but presuppose something unchanging whose detailed character is being voted on. When the very existence of the state is the subject of vote, all order and stability tends to be subverted. There cannot be any simple or single principle of state-determination; reference must always be made to the variegated data of past history. The "false perfectionism" illustrated in these attempts usurps the place of true, reality-based, ethics, and leads to all kinds of unforeseen evils. The limitations of democracy themselves gave rise to "self-determination"; even the idea of "minorities" implies "the stigma of abnormality". In the end, only non-national states can solve these problems, without either a "melting-pot" ideology or natural assimilation.

Chapter three is designed to show the utopian nature of internationalism as a solution to national antagonisms. The idea is of something "between" the nations, as opposed to something "supposed to transcend and to transform" them, as in the idea of Christendom, and the normal system of political forces. The League of Nations idea is that positive law can replace the latter. But intra-state law works because of state power, together with public consent. The "primary solidarity" this presupposes is absent at the international level. Yet the idea as such has reinforced nationalism and paralysed "intelligent statesmanship". It has also tended to destroy state-transcending but non-universal bonds like Christendom. The "collective security" idea is pure magic, embodying "the great comprehensive heresy of modern Mechanistic Naturalism: the mania of manufacturing 'happiness' for all". In fact the "World-state" will not be the fruit of "good will" but of "one-sided domination and enforced uniformity". "World-wide automatic cooperation would require an unimaginably docile, uniformed, and mechanised mankind, systematically trained for identical (and accordingly, shallow and ungenuine) emotional reactions and mental habits". "The modern claim to 'moralise' secular power really points towards public administration and social organisation 'embodying' or rather swallowing morality". "Mankind must be articulated in distinct units of some kind", so as to be faced with social alterity in some form, but these cannot just be willed into being. "A sound order can be built on force and justice, balance of power and moral community, retaliation and reconciliation, but not on basic hypocrisy". Internationalism is in fact based on pacifism, "the monomaniac over-valuation of 'peace' ... as such", to the neglect of everything else.

The second part of this work begins with some general remarks about the place of liberal-democracy in the Western world and the "crisis" in which it found itself towards the end of the war. This leads to a subtle discussion about "definitions" in general, and to Kolnai's own elucidations of liberal-democracy, liberalism, democracy, "right" and "left", socialism, Communism and National Socialism. A sound political system, he says, must have room for both left and right,

> for they both stress legitimate aspects of human nature in its political implications and requirements. The tension between 'Rightism' and 'Leftism' is in itself a creative agent, an indispensable instrument of public discussion.

He then discusses the good and the bad sides of liberal-democracy. Its weakness is its attempt to ensure a civilised life for all. This is bound to involve a formalisation of civilisation rather than its essential reality. It is at its best when continuing older traditions, and in its achievement of juridical order. "We should view Liberal-Democracy as a grievously diseased patient, but not as the disease itself." There follows a brief section on liberal-democracy as "secularized Christianity", its neglect of evil forces in human nature, and the consequences of this. But its besetting sin is the attempt to build Heaven on Earth. He then surveys some particular defects: the tendency to self-contradiction (subjectivism ends by stifling individuality; tolerance leads to the discounting of divergences; definite authorities succeeded by arbitrary ones); unwarranted optimism (especially about human nature, extended democratisation, survival of civilisation); its "downward trend" (quality yields to equality, humans become machines, all human paradigms are done away). He then passes to matters connected with hierarchy. Hierarchies are important. The "legitimate problem of Equality" is "the preservation of man's personal dignity, selfhood and sphere of sovereignty in spite of his social subordinations and through them". He then goes on to consider the need for other "background" principles of order (moral experience, existing "authorities") if the basic liberal principle is to work, though Liberalism cannot acknowledge this. Rather, it tends to produce a "social monism". Hence we find the "utopia of Identity; the rejection of a world of ordered division, tension and plurality, a cosmos stratified and hierarchical" - indeed, a hatred of Being. The content of the next section, on the Curse of Techno-Barbarism, should by now be familiar enough. In "The Will-o'-the-wisp of Progress" he examines the self-stultifying idea that, if a thing is good, one cannot have too much of it. The last section of this chapter is "The Problem of Restoration", of "a saving return to our moral roots, sources and foundations". Kolnai suggests that our examples should be "the orderly civic and juridical liberalism of yesterday", "the older concept of the legitimate monarchy", together with "noble and patrician élites", the idea of the nation as part of the supra-national Christendom, the good side of leftism, moderate mechanisation, and so on. The last chapter of the unfinished book is itself hardly begun, but one of its keynotes must have been encapsulated in this sentence:

> The value of freedom really stands for the value of what is "free" ... (and) for the values of the unspecified manifold of objects in correlation with the subject of "free" behaviour.

Freedom matters, then, because persons matter. It is given especially in the "peculiar quality of 'concentration' and 'distance' proper to" personal life. So ends this remarkably concentrated and pregnant work. We can be thankful that much of its material was further developed in later publications.

One other work of Kolnai's written during this time, "The Humanitarian versus the Religious Attitude",[61] can be looked at more briefly. It is a fruit of his "second conversion" to Catholicism, and, since it was written for a religious periodical, looks like an attempt to recall American "deists", or perhaps liberal Catholics, back to their primary allegiance in the matter of general moral attitudes. It raises the question whether "humanitarianism" is not liable to condemnation on non-religious grounds, as leading to Barbarism. In the first section, Kolnai attempts to elucidate, uncontentiously, what he means by "the religious attitude". He then does the same with "humanitarian attitude" (centrality of human "need", equality of "needs", subject to rational criticism), and "quasi-religious attitudes", especially Communism and Nazism. He then turns to the question of the difference between the behaviour of many "civilised" people who do their "moral duty" on humanitarian grounds and that of religious people. He argues that the difference is not just one of motivation, but that religious people can attain a much more adequate knowledge of moral content (the humanitarian can never grasp "the full meaning of justice"; "truth" cannot be the same for the humanitarian). A second point is that the humanitarian cannot have a place in his system for "intrinsic moral evil" and "the moral scissure in human nature"; consequently, he will see morality in terms of desire, and substitute prevention and cure for retaliation. As a result he will have a tendency towards both immoralism and hyper-moralism. His morality will tend to be formal and material; the idea of intrinsic and spiritual value will fade away. The centre of reference will be the "physical substratum of human nature". Above all, his understanding of sexual morality will be impoverished, and with this will come the general corruption of moral sense. This will lead to a neglect of procreation and extending the family line, and to a contraction of experience to the present moment, and absence of a sense of duration, which is a prefiguring of eternity. Neglect of the past will in turn lead to a detachment from the future, and from reality in general, to the detriment of general vitality. Lastly, the humanitarian will, in the long run, suffer from comparative poverty of imagination and creative thought. "Humanitarianism suppresses, thwarts, and stultifies too much that is by no means a mere froth upon the surface of 'serious' life but belongs to the very viscera of human constitution".

Although this paper is full of subtle insights and analyses, Kolnai himself felt it needed some revision.[62]

Chapter Eleven

Quebec
(1945-1955)

When Kolnai was well enough to travel to Quebec and take up his post he was, for the first time in his life, in receipt of a regular salary "earned by a fairly estimable activity more or less in keeping with my real interests".[1] This "civic birth", as he called it, was highly gratifying. The actual teaching duties were by no means unusually onerous, and Kolnai was at first regarded as a half-timer. He was primarily employed as an Assistant Professor to teach the history of post-Scholastic philosophy to a mixed group of graduates and final year undergraduates for two hours a week. Since he felt he knew very little of renaissance thought this involved him in a good deal of preparatory reading. He also had to give a one and a half-hour seminar on Saturday afternoons to the same group, and chose the theme "Utopias and the idea of Progress in early modern times". In November, Charles DeKoninck, the Professor and Dean of philosophy, persuaded the authorities to increase his salary from $1,500 to $2,500, since it was obvious that he was giving the whole of his time to his teaching and related studies. The following year he also had to lecture on the same theme to junior undergraduates, making 4 hours in all, and DeKoninck managed to get him paid a further $500. The one-month summer school in July, which Kolnai also taught during the early years, brought in some additional pay. Annual increments would bring the salary up to $4,000.

Unfortunately, Kolnai was not a good teacher. There was, to begin with, his "timidity". During his first year he actually had Elisabeth attend his lectures to give him moral support. And, although he always had a good reputation among his colleagues for his powers of academic judgement, he found oral examining a great trial. This helped the students, since he also tended to feel that their shortcomings were largely the fault of "the 'democratic' ideal of 'education' for everybody and of the university as a 'degree'-stamping apparatus". John Beach also recalls that he never looked directly at the students when lecturing. But there could also be a certain easy-goingness in Kolnai's approach; Beach, who became a firm friend and admirer, and whose doctoral thesis was for a time supervised by him, thought this amounted to laziness. But the most serious defect was Kolnai's inability to adjust his style and delivery to the capacities of his audience. Thomas DeKoninck, a son of Kolnai's superior, recalled his teaching as follows:

> We were a total of four registered for his class the year I heard him - seldom more than one or two actually present, however. Although we loved the man and his eccentricities, and respected what he had to say, he tended to be difficult to follow ... He would start digressing in mid-sentence from the outset, then digress further within that digression, and so on (one could not easily tell if the opening sentence had ever ended), with the result that students complained that they could not follow him.[2]

Kolnai, usually very ready to admit his defects when writing to old friends, never mentions this one, though he does say that his course on the History of Modern Philosophy was not a good one,[3] and found it difficult to plan ahead. But the interesting passage in the Memoirs devoted to his Laval teaching is almost entirely confined to the general problems of objective communication, especially where it concerns "philosophical truth". Certainly he mentions a "faint aura of imposture attached ineluctably to the very act of teaching", and the difficulties of imparting philosophy to a young person who may never have felt the slightest impulse to philosophise.[4] But he never discusses whether there may not be better and worse ways of evoking these impulses, or of nourishing them with appropriate material.

As for the students themselves, Thomas DeKoninck's claim that "we loved the man and his eccentricities" seems to have been generally true. Elisabeth writes about an unexpected "invasion of American students with a bottle of genuine Scotch whisky, which we all emptied together" – imagining them in the same "state of siege" against the Quebec climate as themselves.[5] Kolnai got on especially well with his prettier female students, and the more intelligent male ones, and there was a good deal of open flirtatious banter with the former group, where he also made some firm friendships. Some of the girls would give him little presents reflecting his own eccentricities and tastes (e.g. chocolate dachshunds). At the same time he built up a formidable mental dossier about each of them, which included appearance, origins, character and mental style. In the end, one is left with the impression that his interest in most of his students, where it exists, is predominantly aesthetic: Kolnai appears as a connoisseur of human individuality.

Professor DeKoninck thought highly of Kolnai, and he, in his turn, admired his superior. In a letter to Jászi he calls him a Flemish St Thomas, great thinker and scholar, a great personality too, weighing hardly less than 150 kilos, under whom it's no little honour and pleasure to work.[6]

DeKoninck had been "head-hunted" from Notre Dame University in order to develop the philosophy department, and was the big "star" in Laval when Kolnai arrived. He was one of the four deans who, with the Rector, ran the university. He was eventually the father of eleven children, the last of whom was born in 1952. Elisabeth Kolnai was asked to stand godmother to the ninth, Jean-Marie, born in April 1948. Kolnai commented admiringly to Jászi: "this Fleming must have an amazing quantity of vital force!" After the christening he was introduced to the Austrian Empress Zita, then resident in Quebec, with whom DeKoninck had much to do, as private tutor and then family friend. Kolnai had long wanted to be noticed by her, but the actual "audience" was rather disappointing. Jászi, to whom he related the incident, commented: "I feel that this reaction sheds much light on your whole religious and political structure".[7] He was also fascinated by the "social power" aspect of DeKoninck, and soon realised that he much enjoyed its symbolic forms. "Some of us amuse ourselves", he wrote to Füst, "with our chief's ... mania for titles".[8] He would accordingly address DeKoninck in notes and letters in such terms as "My Most Learned and Powerful Chief", "Euer Spektabilität!"[9] or "Seigneur!", and sign off "in prostration" as "colour-sergeant Kolnai", or "votre obéissant serf". DeKoninck once asked Kolnai to speak at the departmental dinner on "Man as subject in the world university". "But", he told Füst:

I spoke on "myself as subject in the university", and stressed how good it was to have people above us whom we gladly and happily obey, but that in that case we are bound to be always afraid of them, as I tremble before Mgr Parent (who happily and proudly whinnied at this). There was much laughter.[10]

The substantial collection of Kolnai's departmental communications saved by DeKoninck between 1948 and 1953 also show how useful Kolnai was to his chief in assessing books, articles submitted for publication in *Laval Philosophique et Théologique*, applications for research studentships, and so on. On one occasion, Kolnai suggested a detailed practical reform of the oral marking system, and at least one of his trips to New York was a commission to select and buy new library books for the department. He also undertook to translate into English DeKoninck's little study of the Aristotelian-Thomist traditional teaching on "Abstention and Sobriety"; Kolnai's comments are full of both wisdom and fun. He also sent

DeKoninck copies of some of his latest "nonsense", including "A Complete Rhymed Course of Medical Science", consisting of twenty-six pages of couplets and other short verses "based, in parts, on *Wheeler's Handbook of Medicine*, by William R. Jack". The rubric at the beginning, "*Ne convient qu'aux lecteurs formés*" [Adults Only!], might almost have been justified, in view of its "pornosophic" section.

Although residence in Quebec had a great deal to offer that was superior to anything the Kolnais had experienced in the USA, it also had some very serious drawbacks. The place itself was hard to beat as a "townscape". The ancient French city at a bend of the St Lawrence, its citadel perched high above the water, and the ground sloping away down through the first of the city gates to the narrow streets full of old French colonial houses in painted wood and grey stone, past the towering Château Frontenac, adjacent Board Walks below the top of the cliffs, and the old university buildings, and then dropping steeply down to the little fishing-port and narrow-streeted "lower town" - this marvellous ensemble could not fail to win the Kolnais' hearts. But against this was set the terrible Quebec climate:

> The first winter plunged me into a kind of psychotic condition, comparable to an all but total, unchanging and unrelieved, darkness of the mind and obtuseness of the animal spirits.[11]

These "five months or more in the midst of snow and ice, with snow-boots needed all the time" are succeeded by "its second edition, still very depressing but much less oppressive, which is the equivalent of what elsewhere constitutes Spring", which is in turn the harbinger of "the brief summer mixed of humid heat and moist but moderate cold".[12]

On the social and cultural side there was French-English bilingualism, and its accompaniments, which made him feel "more at home than he had felt in either England or France". "All in all", he wrote,

> the situation in Canada, thanks to the obvious absence of a solution to the nationality question, gives me a certain melancholy awareness of imperfection, which I much enjoy.

"Of course", he adds, thinking of the USA,

> it's just as "democratic" here, constitutionally. But there's no religion of the state. A book about coffee-making here would be called "How to Make Good Coffee"; down there it would be: "How to Make Coffee Fit for Democracy".[13]

Certainly, there were no proper libraries in Quebec, and life was more boring than in Cambridge or New York. However,

> one is not here struggling against the very essence of the place. It is very "colonial". Lack and immaturity reign here, whereas in the USA I was assailed by the Positive. It's "exile" here, true; but only exile. One's here in a last "corner" of civilization - but worth preserving![14]

Kolnai was keenly aware of the deeper problems of Quebec Society, and their historical roots. After the English gained power in French Canada, nearly all the nobility returned to France, leaving behind a nation of peasants ruled by the Catholic Church. Only in the nineteenth century did a middle class begin to emerge, and this was still describable mainly in terms of a capitalist stratum of *nouveaux riches*. This produced a period of liberal government in the early twentieth century, but during the war - when there was much support for the French Vichy government - the Union Nationale gained power under Maurice Duplessis. Under Duplessis' rightist authoritarian rule (he was Prime Minister from 1944-1959) health, education and social matters were in the hands of the Church, and anything which might undermine order and tradition was ruthlessly repressed. All this was accompanied by aggressive business expansion with American finance, and the consequent struggles for wealth and power produced an appalling level of corruption, at which all too many church people connived.[15] The result was a small-minded "ghetto" in which almost anyone who was not both Catholic and native French-speaking was made to feel an outsider. Nevertheless, there was an excellent antidote to "Québecisme" in Montreal, where they already had friends, and which, with its large English-speaking minority, was a genuinely bi-cultural city. The relative proximity of this "capital of civilization", and the concessionary railway fares available to academics, made the city an important safety-valve for them during their Quebec years.

But the most serious problem of all involved "Thomism", the systematised expression of Aquinas's doctrines. As a Catholic, Kolnai knew that St Thomas had an "official" status within the Church, especially in Catholic university departments of philosophy and theology. But this privileged position of Thomism - which he was prepared to support within limits - is capable of very different interpretations, and when he accepted DeKoninck's offer of a post he was still in what he later called his "right-wing, even clerical period".[16] Being badly in want of a job, he was ready to give Laval the benefit of the doubt. In the Summer School exam he made no secret of the fact that he approached "the Doctrine" "'from the outside'; acknowledging it as relevant to the philosophical search for truth but in a style entirely alien to its a priori identification with 'the Truth'".[17] This he could do with integrity, and he assumed that he would be allowed to take this general approach in his teaching. Though DeKonick was himself a Thomist, he was ready to consider particular criticisms, and gave Kolnai the impression that he wanted to encourage a less narrowly Thomist atmosphere in the department. For some time, however, Kolnai hardly put these assumptions to the test, since teaching the history of modern philosophy could be done without having to challenge any aspects of Thomism in any very noticeable manner. So this particular difficulty was not fully confronted during the first few years of Kolnai's Canadian period.

Meanwhile, old friendships were revived and new ones made. The Karpoviches came for a visit at the end of January, and brought Kolnai "a lovely winter fur hat". There were regular meetings with the Tremblays, from whom they learnt a great deal about the intricacies of Canadian politics. Arthur was now a Professor of Education, and, after the Union Nationale lost power in the province, began to play a very important part in the redevelopment of the school system in Quebec, and eventually became a senator. Of his colleagues in the Philosophy department - apart from DeKoninck - Kolnai seems to have had most to do at first with Jacques de Monléon, who lived and taught in France, but also came regularly to teach at Laval. Although he too was a dedicated Thomist, one of those who taught "the doctrine" through the seventeenth century works of a great exponent of Aquinas, known to posterity as St John of St Thomas, his personal qualities were such that this was not a barrier to their friendship in the early years. He also got on well with the layman M. Trépanier, Professor of Metaphysics, who was later replaced by a priest, and with the Franciscan Father Gaudron (Greek Philosophy), "gentle, shy, melancholy and unassuming, but ... a true scholar in his own field", and above all "unquebecised".[18] They both also liked another layman, M. Simard, and his wife, enjoying their company as good, straightforward people with no pretence about them. Of his friends outside the department, two should be mentioned here. One was Jeanne Lapointe, a lively and intelligent young Lecturer and later Professor of French, in whom Kolnai found a receptive audience for his more extravagant flights of fancy. The other was the Hungarian Mgr Ibrányi, who arrived in Quebec from Hungary in 1949, after being closely associated with Cardinal Mindszenty. Mlle Lapointe recalls him as a "dark" person, and Léon Dion (see below) saw him as "temperamentally akin" to Kolnai himself. Kolnai was fascinated by his strangeness, and his "radical difference" from his own "epicurean-ascetic petit bourgeois" nature.[19] He seems to have manifested some mildly flirtatious gallantry towards Elisabeth, who, for her part, found him "a remarkable specimen", and not altogether "nice".[20]

Further afield, Kolnai soon reestablished contact with his old Vienna associate, Richard Redler. He was now a businessman in Montreal, where the Kolnais sometimes had the use of his flat, or stayed as his guest. During the following year they met a friend of Füst's, the ex-Transylvanian Reginald Menzer, and his Austrian wife. Menzer, also a businessman, painted in his spare time, and undertook to sell some of Elisabeth's designs.[21] Another Montreal family with whom Kolnai had much to do were the Germains. Thérèse was one of his first students, and she introduced him to her parents and sister, also to her uncle Stanislas and his family, who lived in Quebec. They were unconventional enough to appreciate Kolnai fully. He stayed with Thérèse's family often, especially when visiting Montreal on his own. He had, in fact, discovered in himself a new inclination for the company of younger women. As he wrote to Füst:

I exhibit many traces of senility; thus not only do I usually gladly look about me at the women here (usually very poor, especially the American ones older than 5!), but I've also discovered the charm of young women, even young girls, though I used to think that a woman only began to be attractive around 40 to 50.[22]

This relationship with Thérèse - a "crush" freely proclaimed by Kolnai, and seen as a part of his eccentricity - was one of the first of a number of similar innocent friendships, which would characteristically involve visits to dog- and cat-shows, cafés or tea-shops, cinemas and art galleries.

If Montreal was Kolnai's "real home in exile", he also fell in love with Ottawa and occasionally visited Toronto. But he also went quite often to the USA, where he would stay with the Lányis at Cambridge, and later at Providence, R.I., after George transferred from Harvard to Brown University. In New York he sometimes stayed in George Szell's apartment (Szell had recently taken over the Cleveland Symphony Orchestra), though he also used the Henry Hudson Hotel. When he went in his first Christmas vacation to buy books for the library, he stayed with Balduin Schwarz, and was able to compare notes on teaching with him and Hildebrand. He often visited the flea markets for second-hand electrical equipment. In September 1947 he told Füst:

I have acquired a very nice little (primitive) electricity laboratory ... Besides buzzers and other similar simple pieces of apparatus I mostly collect light-bulbs and neon tubes. I've got about 350 light-bulbs of different types and voltages, of which perhaps 80 are carbon-fibre, bizarre enough even among the others. I'm a great connoisseur of 25-60 volt bulbs.[23]

Nor was his enjoyment of such things confined to his apartment. On one occasion in Quebec Thomas DeKoninck happened to glance in at the door of an Amusement Arcade. Kolnai was intently working one of the machines, complete with flashing lights and buzzers set going by the movement of heavy metal balls, quite oblivious to the wondering crowd of small boys who surrounded him. But all this had its serious side too, since he also performed simple "experiments" with circuits and voltages. During the later Quebec years, when the Kolnais lived by the city wall at the bottom of Rue Ferland, overlooking the harbour, they took over the neighbouring apartment to supplement their own, thus giving Kolnai an entire room in which to indulge his hobby.

At first Elisabeth flourished in their new surroundings. But in early summer she had an appendix operation which went wrong, and was almost continually ill for three years, when she was operated on again and began gradually to improve. It turned out that the first surgeon, a luminary of the University Medical School, had left a swab inside the wound. This piece of extraordinary negligence and its aftermath created very powerful resentment in the Kolnais, and Elisabeth, to her dying day, was convinced that the surgeon "had tried to murder her". This "crime" became for them a potent symbol of the corruption of Quebec society. Thus in 1951 Kolnai discourses in a letter to Lányi about the "underworld" mentality of the Germains' Quebec relations and their evil criminal accomplices, who included several of the leading figures of the public life of Quebec.

Quite distinct from this, however, was Elisabeth's miscarriage in the summer of 1948. The Kolnais spent a few days together in Montreal before parting company for a week or so. Elisabeth went to the Karpovich "dacha" in Vermont, and Kolnai went off on his own to Ottawa and Toronto (to sample the unusual electric current) so as not to "abuse their [friends'] hospitality", but also, Elisabeth added in her letter to Mrs DeKoninck, "to be a bachelor again", and "to flirt with fat ladies".[24] Before they parted, Elisabeth, thinking she was pregnant, consulted a doctor, who assured her that this was definitely not the case. She therefore took no special care of herself and miscarried. This sad event did not arouse much resentment, but is highly significant in itself. Several people who knew the Kolnais thought there was something odd about their marriage, and it may well have begun as a marriage of convenience. On the other hand, others who knew them felt that, despite their incessant squabbling, the extraordinary alternations between near-worship and seeming hatred characteristic of Elisabeth's talk about Kolnai, and the rude and dismissive way in which Kolnai sometimes treated Elisabeth, they were in fact very closely bound together. Although Elisabeth added a post-script to Kolnai's explanatory letter to DeKoninck (in which he asked for leave to return late for term to Quebec), ascribing her pregnancy to the work of a "good Quebecese cabman", she was simply conforming to the usual style of Kolnai-DeKoninck communications. We can hardly doubt that the marriage was consummated.[25]

***

Kolnai's publications during the Quebec period were nearly all devoted to political philosophy. His first anti-leftist articles continue his campaign against leftism in the Church. "Le Mythe des 'Enfants de la Lumière'",[26] which appeared shortly after his arrival, was a critical review of a book by Reinhold Niebuhr, in which the author distinguished political movements according to whether they were exclusive ("children of darkness") or universal ("children of light"). The effect of this was to put Nazis and all Fascists into one group and all liberals, democrats, Marxists, Communists, and Fichte, Hegel, Nietzsche and their followers in the other. "Sober analysis with a bit of invective thrown in", was Kolnai's summing up of his own critique.[27] The other anti-Catholic-leftist article was "Le Culte de l'Homme Commun et la Gloire des Humbles",[28] in which he argues that the Christian-social-democratic view of Maritain, and other leftist thinkers, not only undermines the positive social and political function of the Church as counter-balance to the State by encouraging destructive egalitarian views, but rests on a false understanding of the Gospel. The Christian requirement of humility has nothing to do with "common man democracy". This paper has much in common with the more important one, "The Meaning of the 'Common Man'", described below. Another paper in French was "Les Ambiguités Nationales".[29] Although he does here imply the desirability of Canadian bi-nationalism, the paper is a general discussion of the problems of nationality and nationalism, and was clearly an offshoot of the unpublished book, *Liberty and the Heart of Europe*. Two papers about philosophy also appeared in his first two years at Quebec. One, "Les Débuts du Formalisme dans la Philosophie Moderne",[30] probably arose out of his teaching in the Laval Summer School, for which the theme in 1946 was "Subjectivism and Naturalism in the Renaissance". Kolnai had long been extremely hostile to "formalism" in philosophy, by which he meant a preference for forced precision and "tidiness" (a consequence of pride, or *Hochmut*) over the patient teasing out of meanings and relations, however theoretically or aesthetically "unsatisfactory" the result may appear to be. This short article reveals the penchant of many Renaissance thinkers for this intellectual weakness. The other paper about philosophy, "The Indispensability of Philosophy",[31] was written at the suggestion of one of his earliest students, a Hispanic American called Mendoza, and published in Mexico. Kolnai here argues that philosophy, like any thought, affects the way we live; it is therefore very important that it be cultivated. He analyses the mental and moral qualities needed for its pursuit and the vital relation to common sense. He then sets out to refute various arguments against the "necessity" of philosophy: its confinement to a minority, its dispensability in a religious society, its practical ineffectiveness, its virtual unteachability and its actual subordination to ideology. He ends with a short statement of its place in mental life. Although Kolnai himself writes about his "excessive wallowing in platitudes",[32] the paper is a clear and concise statement of the nature and importance of philosophy, and deserves to be better known. Another short paper about philosophy was published in 1952. In that year he received the first of several invitations to contribute to the annual conference of French-speaking philosophy societies. Illness prevented his personal appearance at Strasbourg, but his short paper, entitled "Le Conditionnement Historique de la Pensée Humaine et la Philosophie de l'Expérience Commune", was published later.[33] Kolnai here explores the issue of philosophical relativism; after surveying various false ways out of the difficulty, he turns to his own frequently explored claim that some kind of recourse to common sense, or consensus, is ultimately indispensable. The paper is related to "The Sovereignty of the Object" (which, though not published until 1960, was written in 1951).

"The Three Riders of Apocalypse: Communism, Naziism and Progressive Democracy",[34] written around 1950 but unpublished in his lifetime, is Kolnai's fullest statement of the thesis that Progressive Democracy essentially tends towards some form of totalitarianism, and represents itself a mild form of it. It helps to explain the virulence with which he attacked the Catholic leftists. The paper investigates the common essence of the three "riders", and discusses their obvious differences. The comparison between Nazism and Communism yields many shared features relating to the "technique of government". In comparison with them, even the "gravest" forms of Progressive Democracy - "Socialist party rule and Americanism" - retain some sense of "normality"; there is compromise; empirical tests of "success and immediate pleasure" still prevail; "massive totality of uncontrolled power" is impossible. But Nazism and Communism fill up the increasing "emptiness " of Progressive Democracy with a new meaning of life. Nazism and Progressive Democracy share the property of "incomplete totalitarianism". The latter may not even seem totalitarian, but may even be so to a higher degree than the other two,

> assimilating as it does (under the deceptive verbal cloak of liberalism and tolerance) the thinking, moods and wills of everybody to a wholesome standard of the "socialized" mind more organically and perhaps more durably.

Nevertheless,

> neither our horror of Nazi perversity, cruelty and vulgarity nor our disgust at the mediocrity and duplicity, the inner unfreedom, the deadening quack rationality and the sickening pseudo-culture of Progressive Democracy

should disguise from us the infinitely more totalitarian nature of Communist society.[35] Totalitarian traits of Progressive Democracy lacking under Communism include the endorsing of all up-to-date thought and "a medical and psychiatric dictatorship", though its categories of value are still not defined, as in the other two, in terms of government will.

Neverthless Progressive Democracy and Communism both cherish the "selfsame basic concept of social revolution", whereas Nazism, carefully distinguished here from various forms of Fascism, is counter-revolutionary "on a cosmic scale" and has nothing to do with Socialism. The superiority over the other two of Progressive Democracy comes from the fact that it still

> represents in a backwater fashion the obscured, silenced, disfigured and disinherited remains of true Christian civilization, with its timeless standards of right, honour and wisdom.[36]

But both Nazism and Communism have shown us where it is heading, for they have

> exploded the lying prophecies and fond hopes clustered round the dogma of progress and the myths of "social science" about an approaching golden age of sweet silliness and meaningless abundance.[37]

Nazism has also shown that the developmental line from Progressive Democracy to Communism can be resisted, though it took too much from Communism itself. Whereas Leftism means

> the ... endeavour to abolish contingency and man's dependence on an order of things he cannot fathom and an order of right and wrong he can discern but not decree or improve upon,[38]

Nazism made "brute contingency itself" the law of the universe.

In the last section of the paper, on Conservatism, Kolnai stresses that conservatives must be wary of Progressive Democracy. Otherwise Communism cannot be fought effectively. But the "unconditional

Rightism" of the twenties and thirties was also a colossal mistake. There must be cooperation with Progressive Democracy, and no flirting with "universal solutions", which are marks of the subversive and totalitarian mentality. The existing good, including that in Progressive Democracy, must be conserved and improved, not "created", and that means support for

> the genuinely traditionalist centres of power and types of society - such as, for instance, Spain - which are likely to play an invaluable part both in bolstering the anti-Communist front and in counterbalancing the world supremacy of Progressive Democracy, circumscribing its range of influence and breaking its Totalitarian monopoly after the downfall of Communism.[39]

When F.A. Hayek later wrote to Kolnai asking what he had written on liberty, he sent him "Privilege and Liberty" and "The Meaning of the 'Common Man'", explaining that they "exhibit ... some arbitrary clerical and rightist exaggerations, but in essence they express my outlook of Conservatism with a specific emphasis on Liberty".[40]

"The Meaning of the 'Common Man'" appeared in 1949.[41] In an explanatory commentary on this paper,[42] Kolnai points out that the term became popular with left-wingers in the USA in the early thirties in a definitely polemical context, but became rather less so after the war. In the paper Kolnai points out that the continuing use of the term, especially in connection with the future "rule" of the Common Man, is bound to hinder the general resistance to Communism. But he hopes that his warnings will help the reader to

> displace the spiritual stress from the "common man" aspect of Democracy to its aspect of constitutionalism and of moral continuity with the high traditions of Antiquity, Christendom and the half-surviving liberal cultures of yesterday.[43]

The concept of the "Common Man", he goes on, is essentially "privative". The being whose political power the left wants to extend is man conceived as deprived of any kind of social distinction, especially any kind of privilege or hereditary power - man in his nakedness. What is more, this being without intrinsic distinction is also regarded as an ideal. But the Common Man does not represent an identifiable type of man in reality (such as a social class). It must be, then, that the reason for this "Total Equalitarianism" is that any particular determination would imply man's "creaturely limitation".

In the next section, "The Dialectics of Equality", Kolnai shows how the equalitarian unintelligibly extends "a certain marginal type of situation between two individuals or two groups" (where strict formal equality of treatment is required) "into a general conception of social relationships".[44] In doing so he ignores the real problem of Equality: who is to give the Common Man what he is "entitled to" if there are only Common Men to do it? He then goes on to consider the contrast between the equality of opportunity (here "equal footing") and the levelling variants of egalitarianism, and the unconvincing argument that all actual inequalities must be traceable back to inequalities of opportunity. However, the leveller does appreciate the all-important fact that social (or artificial) and natural inequalities cannot in the end be kept apart, since they reinforce each other. But once people abandon

> the wholesome and Christian principle of a limited equality, formal and material, as implied by Man's basic dignity and rational nature as well as by the radical transcendence of the person's ultimate value before God above his [other] distinctions and shortcomings,[45]

the slide down to material equality and uniformity is irresistible.

Kolnai then turns to the axiological consequences of egalitarianism, the reduction of all values to quantities of some standard unit of measure and the "functional" interpretation of cultural achievements. These fly in the face of experience. The fact is that egalitarians cannot bear to admit that "every intrinsic difference between man and man contains the seeds of a hierarchical tension and distance". Of course:

> Social nobility is not and never was - except in the imagination of imbecile snobs - an equivalent of human and personal, or moral or intellectual nobility; nevertheless, its existence is indispensable for the existence of such nobility: indispensable as a stimulus and a gross, provisional measure of value. It serves as a pattern of orientation for society's groping attempts towards experiencing, appreciating and fostering intrinsic distinction.[46]

Kolnai then goes on to examine the idea that egalitarian measures can be justified because they raise the average level of value and therefore the total measure. This cannot be so, because it treats human values as a finite store of goods, and ignores the fact that the high peaks are needed for the good average to form. Society needs exemplars. Whatever egalitarians think about that, they find in practice that room has to be made for some kind of "functional" and "natural" inequality. What then do they really object to in

Inequality? It is clearly privilege and nobility, the antithesis of the Common Man. But nobility stands for "value intrinsic, distinctively 'qualitative', pervading the essence of its bearer" and hence claiming social eminence, not because nobility means "supreme value", but because it is conspicuous and therefore exemplary. Where the idea of nobility is alive in society,

> it expresses the submission of Society, on the natural plane - in its vital organization and government - to what is higher and better than its own "thesis", "volition" or "appointment" may be.[47]

Thus nobility stands for moral authority, something that liberal societies cannot bear to accept; they lack the necessary humility, being wedded to the myth of collective "Reason". Nobility is, therefore, an aspect of "a social order pervaded with natural bases of authority" independent of the state. Hence it is a "pawn in the game" of "metaphysical rebellion" against "man's bondage to an objective order of natural being".

Kolnai goes on to contrast the Common Man with the "Plain Man". Opposition to the Common Man is often represented as a kind of misanthropy, or support for a tiny minority of exploiters. But the Plain Man is not the same as the Common Man because he "is not his own theme"; however much he may grumble at the aristocracy he is a traditionalist at heart, having "a semi-potential balance, sanity and universality". In fact the Common Man (a creature of ideology) is a plain man "gone mad, who, by exaggerating and puffing up his plainness, aspires to embody the fulness of human perfection".[48] Indeed, the Plain Man "presupposes Distinction", to which he is "complementary". The paper ends with some consideration of anarchism (refusal to accept given reality or value) as the "soul of totalitarianism", individualistic and collectivistic aspects of the Common Man, and the consequences of "the subversion of human nature": "the self-enslavement of man". These are matters more fully dealt with in other papers.

"Privilege and Liberty"[49] begins by taking up again important themes from the two previous papers. The cult of the Common Man and hatred of privilege - two sides of the same coin - constitute the classic bridge from Progressive Democracy to Communism, a surrender experienced as a "dialectical self-fulfilment". One reason why the "Common man" is sometimes equated with, say "the majority" is because the Common Good is interpreted in terms of "a sameness of reference, use, enjoyment and immediacy". The "subversive mind" believes that "the curse of division and of being 'set against one another'", which is the normal human condition, cannot be surmounted except by a "fusion into one"; an intellectual identification of consciousness, of qualities and of interest. Individualism (tending towards equalitarianism) prefigures collectivism from the outset, and again, collectivism is only individualism raised to the higher power of an absolute monism centred in "all and every one".[50]

The Common Man, then,

> means Man aspiring to "have" all goods and to "be" all that is good ...: any one man attaining, through the oneness of Society actualized into a common Subject, all that any other men attain, according to the mode of *Identity.*

Privilege, on the other hand,

> means the social projection, the institutional recognition, the traditional embodiment of the essentially insurmountable dividedness, imperfection and subjectivity (in the face of a transcendent Object and Good) of Man, and by the same token, the really existent ... remedy or correction of that metaphysical smallness, failure and fallenness of Man: the fact that a few, or rather, very many men in different ways transcend the "common level" of mankind, as though that in man which points beyond man took shape in them, in this or that limited respect, so that through their instrumentality others reach out beyond their own immediate possibilities or proper nature, and enrich themselves by a contact with higher values primarily alien from them and not properly theirs, according to the mode of *Participation.*[51]

Kolnai's aim is, then, to interpret Privilege "in terms of the Common Good as attained by Participation", and, in view of its representative importance, to concentrate on that aspect of the Common Good we call political Liberty.

The ideal of Identity, he continues,

> means the exclusion of participation in whatever presents itself as "transcendent" ... in the sense of qualitative otherness, and in particular, superiority, to the private self.[52]

This means that the Common Man refuses to include as part of the Common Good whatever "he cannot immediately and unequivocally 'place' in the scheme of his pursuits or 'subsume' under the categories of value with which he is fully familiar". An example of such "subsumption", or "expropriation", is the Common Man's purely functional or instrumental approach to hierarchy. As with Nobility in "The Meaning of the 'Common Man'", so with hierarchy. In neither case would any sensible person claim it as a perfect projection of real value. But it is a vehicle of such:

> Hierarchy means that a certain personnel, by virtue of its very constitution and in a sense penetrating its very "being" as it were, is primarily ordained to actualize and to cultivate a certain set of higher values; to attend to, and serve, certain aspects of the common Good.

The great contrast here is at the level of value. "Identity" interprets every value "as an immanent function of the unfolding of my [anyone's] volitions, needs or capacities"; only "Participation" can acknowledge that high, or transcendent, values are part of the Common Good,

> not only in the sense of benefiting me as a recipient of its causal effects but of perfecting me through an appreciative response on my part, - in the sense, that is, of contributing to inform my conscious behaviour.[53]

Far from expressing the intrinsic superiority of some men over others, then, hierarchy "expresses Man's bondage to what is above Man yet forms the object of Man's striving", and can only properly contribute to the Common Good "if we relate to it not just as to something functional but as subordinates":

> Hierarchy stands for the submission of man to what is highest in man and higher than man but claiming his attention ... "Emancipation" stands for the subjection of man to man, and his bondage to what is lowest in him.[54]

Without Privilege, then, "that 'exemplary' ... participation of 'the person' in the common good", a phenomenon that recognises that the individual is not identical with the community, but yet raises him up, is impossible; an individual may now be "divinized" by the community he is a part of, since it is now sole author of value, but he is, by the same token, annihilated by it.

Kolnai now passes to the idea of political liberty. The totalitarian concept, which goes with Identity, is absolute, since Totality knows no restraints whatever. Since the individual is now identical with the state, whatever it chooses to do must express his will. This heady experience of absolute freedom has often been noted in fact. He then points to the totalitarian aspects of liberal democracy, as manifested in its idea of freedom as "freedom from want":

> In the Common Man's mind ... the straight Liberal emphasis of freedom no longer occupies a central place. What he craves for is comfort, security and the bliss of never being denied the gratification of a need.[55]

The change of value-priorities is camouflaged by the new phrase. Liberty no longer means "the Constitutional State", "implying certain checks placed on public power, be it state-power as such or class oligarchy", but the "Welfare State" - now including "psychic welfare", pointing to the possibility of conditioning. If liberty is still desirable, it seems to be liberty through government, not from it. This is, of course, still a long way from the totalitarian conception of liberty, but it is a big step towards it. The fact is that liberal democracy's two "'lines' of self-assertion", "popular sovereignty" and the "rights of the individual" are only prevented from collapsing into Communism because of the survival within society of pre-liberal traditions - a situation indicated in the phrase "liberty under God", the idea of an "intrinsically limited freedom" inherent in man's rational nature as created by God. But these conservative "liberties" are continually eaten away by the logic of liberal-democracy as such:

> The logic of the Liberal principle of "absolute freedom for the individual, not limited by anything except the equally absolute freedom of others" is ineluctably suicidal, and conducive to the Communist principle of an absolute freedom of the individual in the sense of an actually identical absolute power of "all".[56]

The only way of preventing the ultimate surrender is a return to the conservative principle of "an equilibrium among finite, limited and unequal weights" (Aristotle's "mixed form of government"), as in Constitutional Democracy. This is no mere *pis aller* but an ideal, founded on "the ideas of division, limitation, and cooperation on a basis of distinctness". As against the ideas of Identity, this view will stress the rule of law, respect for customs and statutes, the postulate of "responsible" government, "checks and balances", the promotion of "independent ownership", municipal self-government, government by consent, etc. - all these principles being meant to "curb all arbitrary rule of man by man",

> not by equating freedom to arbitrary power on a supreme plane of monistic human self-worship but by protecting freedom, on a diversity of planes, against the temptation to an arbitrary use of power.[57]

In the last section of the paper Kolnai works out more fully the idea of Privilege as an expression and support of liberty:

> "Privilege" is nothing but an "established" positional value in Society which - unlike "rank" in the hierarchy of State officialdom - is relatively independent of the "unique" actual "will" of Society, yet fundamentally "in tune" with the political constitution of Society, with the "habitual will" of state-power itself.[58]
>
> It is only because some people, in different manners and different respects, "weigh" something in the scale as against state-power that the "individual" as such, the "plain man" who is not in any sense a "master", may also "count for something" and make an active contribution to the life of the State.[59]

The alternative is to make the "entire order of society the function of One all-determining central consciousness, the object of One omnipotent arbitrary human will". "It is ... essential to Privilege to have centred round it a zone of 'abuses'"; to try and make them impossible is to root out privilege itself. (There follows quite a long passage in which Capitalism and wealth are also defended as, within limits, a bulwark of liberty.) Privilege, of course, is not the only safeguard of liberty, since "the principle of objective value and moral obligation over and above human desires", and above all "man's submission to God and his Holy Will" are also indispensable, but it is, for all that, essential.

***

During the Kolnais' first Spring he had begun to feel reasonably certain that his position would be renewed for at least another year, and had set in motion the slow official machinery which made possible his proud oath of allegiance to King George in 1951, and their joint relief from long "statelessness". Summer 1948 saw his promotion to "Professeur Agrégé", with a starting salary of $4,000. He was now used only for senior undergraduates and graduates. But during his stay in Montreal, where he heard the news, his thank-you letter to Füst on receiving his friend's *Aesthetics* effectively brought another correspondence to an end. Füst's work, he begins, takes him back to the "timeless world" his poems revealed to him as a young man, but then he bursts out in horror at the unforgiveable and deliberately shocking use of the words of the Black Mass in the epilogue.[60] He also wrote to E.K. Winter: "Soon I must return to Quebec to tell the stolid youths about Descartes' evil deeds",[61] and then, a few months later, in the light of Winter's repeated claim that the world needed a powerful USSR as a counterweight to the USA, clarified his own position as follows:

> All that would follow the uprooting of the Soviet Plague is not a golden age, but "a little peace"; the Western democracies are only slightly preferable to the red louse-colony, in some ways more disgusting, but at least our rulers rule less totally and monothematically than theirs.[62]

Kolnai's reactions to world events were regularly publicised in letters to the editor of the *Montreal Gazette*, just as in Boston he had frequently appeared in *The Globe*. They are often exhortations to take the threat of Communism more seriously, and to be prepared for war with the Soviet Union. Despite his loathing for Duplessis, he was even prepared to vote for him to keep out the main, pinkish, liberal opposition (the CCF).[63] In January 1950 he was one of several speakers asked to address the first full-scale meeting of the new Canadian Anti-Communist League. Focusing on the fate of Cardinal Mindszenty, he showed what Communism meant in practice in one of the countries where it had been imposed. Characteristically, he told Lányi that his own speech had been the second poorest given on the occasion.[64]

John Beach was a Ph.D. student at Laval from 1948 to 1951. Soon after his arrival he and Kolnai became firm friends, taking regular walks together. For most of that time Kolnai was full of praise for DeKoninck. But he was beginning to get more uneasy about Thomism in general, as a "Report submitted to Dean Charles DeKoninck", dated June 29th 1949, shows. Its occasion was clearly a desire to do something for his friend Hermann Borchardt, but it begins with a "general remark about our attitude to modern thought":

> I am at the same time both anti-modernist and radically pro-modernist. (a) I reject, with the utmost rigour, ... every attempt to 'catholicise' naturalism, idealism, pragmatism, Marxism, vitalism, relativism, voluntarism, existentialism, etc. The more "alive" an evil is, the more pitilessly it should be combatted ... (b) I am in favour of ... forming alliances ... with whatever bears an ... essentially anti-modern accent in the tissue of modern thought (in the chronological ... sense) ... E.g. Reid's Scottish school, the Aristotelian Trendelenburg-Stumpf-Brentano line, Meinong's object theory (with reservations), Husserl's phenomenology in the *Logical Investigations* (Pfänder-Geiger-Reinach-V.Hildebrand); the Aristotelianism of Hans Driesch ... and Rehmke ... (c) I therefore reject the very alternative which all catholic philosophy (with a few exceptions, such as Bochenski) seems to accept as

unavoidable: either to 'understand' and be nice to Satan, to "baptise" him and "interpret" him as a fellow-worker with Christ, or to enclose oneself in "textual geography" and to "dispose of" all thought emanating from a different tradition by affirming that it shows such and such a contradiction with Thomism, and "solving the problem" by means of such and such a formal "'proof" or "refutation".

The "report" then goes on to say something about Borchardt's teacher, the realist Rehmke,[65] and about Borchardt himself - neither of them Thomists, though very much on "our side". He admits his own "difficulties" with Thomism. But surely the important thing is "to be a 'living' thinker in the fight against the essential foe of what St Thomas represents". In a further report in November, Kolnai outlines Borchardt's "Treatise on Immortality", or "The Roots of Modern Scepticism". He is not scant with his praise, and ends with a kind of challenge to his colleagues: would it not be a "calamity and disgrace" if the author of such a work were not to receive our encouragement? (It is not clear what, if anything, was done about Borchardt and his work.)

During 1950, the reactionary course of the provincial government was intensified, and this strengthened the position of the fanatical Thomists in the university. The former easy relations between the Kolnais and DeKonincks began to deteriorate, and, at a fiftieth birthday party for Kolnai put on by the Beaches in December, it was obvious that relations were very tense. By a strange coincidence he had recently composed an amusing poem, prompted by a speech of the Rector in which the students were told that sport was part of their education, and that the university "will not tolerate mediocrity". In his "Chant D'Adieux" Kolnai bows to the inevitable; since he is both a mediocrity and knows nothing of sport he will have to leave. George Lányi's poem for the occasion, however, stresses the combative and self-assertive aspects of his character, which were more in evidence after the following October when, at his own request, he was transferred from the relative "safety" of History of Philosophy to Political Philosophy. At first he felt this would ensure his position, since the largely Aristotelian subject-matter would not produce any great conflict with Thomism.[66] But when he was later informed that he would only be teaching higher degree politics students, and that for only two hours a week,[67] he thought this was probably "the writing on the wall", and dreaded the idea of having to go on publishing whether he wanted to or not. His hopes of avoiding serious conflict were also frustrated. However, it is clear that, from the beginning of 1951, Kolnai had at least been putting out feelers for a job elsewhere, since he knew now that he could not seriously hope to survive at Laval until the retirement age of 70, and he had just finished his commissioned paper "The Sovereignty of the Object", which he describes as his accounting with ideological Thomism, and for which he felt his "head would roll".[68] Other letters to Lányi refer to a new Catholic university in New South Wales, and he also mentions London (Ontario), Toronto, McGill, and the Jesuit Loyola College. He later wrote that he was actually offered a "Chair" in Philosophy of Religion at a "first-rate university in the mid-West". Much later he recognised that his rejection of this offer (and perhaps the transfer to Politics) had been at least partly motivated by the excitement of unrestrained conflict.[69]

During 1951 he published a review article of a new book by Jacques Maritain, *Man and the State*. Kolnai called it "A synthesis of Christ and Anti-Christ".[70] Underlying his quarrel with Maritain ("... a clever poseur and charlatan, an industrious mediocrity"[71]) is his very different assessment of the French Revolution. Maritain, like Niebuhr, regarded this positively, and argued that a Christianity which accepted its main political and social results without distorting them would be better, because more in keeping with the "law of progress", than one which remained wedded to monarchism, or regarded democracy and equality with suspicion. For Kolnai, the source of the Revolution was pride and rebellion against God. The Revd John M. Oesterreicher, an opponent of Kolnai's in Austria under Chancellor Dollfuß, wrote a strong letter to the editors, protesting at its intemperate and unchristian language, inquisitorial tone and base insinuations. When the editors of *Integrity* refused to publish his letter, Oesterreicher had it published in another Christian periodical, *Commonweal*.[72] All this was manna from Heaven to Kolnai, and he gleefully had the letter reproduced and circulated to his colleagues, expressing the hope that it would "hilariously widen their perspective in regard to this matter", though later he admitted to Lányi that he had come to think his own review had been "too personal". Kolnai's act amounted to another challenge to the department.

The years 1951 and 1952, wrote Kolnai later, marked a notable deterioration in the atmosphere at Laval. But certain rays of hope were beginning to gleam from Europe. During the autumn of 1949 and later years, Leopoldo Palacios, Professor of Philosophy at Madrid, was a visitor in the Laval department. The first year he was accompanied by his wife, Carmen, and the Kolnais and Palacioses found they had much in common. Kolnai had at once engaged Sra Palacios to extend his knowledge of Castilian. In a letter to Palacios of April 8th 1951 he praised the lectures of another visitor, the German Professor Goetz Briefs, with whom he also spent much time, and wondered whether a translation of his own "Quelques Erreurs Courantes sur le Communisme" would interest Spanish readers.[73] Palacios soon found a publisher for Kolnai's essay, and, what is more, got the Madrid Ateneo, a well-established cultural institution, to invite him to give a lecture-tour in the summer of 1952. After much discussion with Elisabeth, he wrote to accept. Another glad sign from Europe was his contact with Douglas Woodruff, editor of the English Catholic weekly, *The Tablet*. He gladly accepted Kolnai's suggestion to write a review article of Erik Kuehnelt-Leddhin's *Liberty or Equality: the challenge of our time.*[74] It was followed in 1954 by three letters to the Editor, on Husserl, Scholasticism and philosophy in general.[75] The Spanish tour, which Elisabeth undertook as well, extended to France and England, where Kolnai renewed old contacts and made some new ones, and lasted for nearly five months.

They returned to Quebec on October 1st just in time for the new teaching year. In December Kolnai's old friend E.K. Winter submitted what seems to be a research proposal to DeKoninck, who handed it on to Kolnai for his comments. It was accompanied by Winter's Curriculum Vitae, which Kolnai annotated in great detail for DeKoninck's guidance, implicitly showing the esteem in which he once held him. But his verdict on the application was negative:

> As far as I able to judge it, this is scarcely more than weak verbiage; confused, ill-arranged, meagre and trivial in its results, flameless and exhaling deadly boredom - though the author seems to think a lot of himself.[76]

Kolnai had at this time begun to work on his memoirs. The original text contained about a dozen pages on Winter, most of which were eventually cut out but never thrown away. Winter, like Karl Polányi, Jászi, Feeney and DeKoninck, was clearly a highly significant person in Kolnai's life. And yet, faced with this application from his old friend, he was not prepared to support it. Is this simply an example of supreme objectivity, or is some more powerful subjective mechanism responsible for this? It is impossible to say. At all events, Winter seems to fade out of Kolnai's life at this point, but, because of some of his writings and his political activity during the Dollfuß regime and among the American émigrés, he is today regarded in certain circles as a kind of Founding Father of the Second Austrian Republic.

Meanwhile, John Beach was trying to find a post for Kolnai at Dartmouth College. Although he and DeKoninck had still been occasionally writing notes in the old jocular manner Kolnai says that by 1953 the gap between him and the Laval authorities was "unbridgeable", and that by the end of this year "personal relations" between him and his Professor had ceased. In May he issued another of his mocking challenges, a closely typed four-page "non-confidential" document entitled: "The Ultra-Thomist Faculty in the Service of the Worst Pseudo-Catholic Modernism and Philo-Bolshevism? - or - I Protest". This time he sent copies to the Rector and Vice-Rector of the university, as well as his philosophy colleagues. He begins with a significant concession. Granted that man's task in life is to serve the Good and to fight Evil, which, in the departmental context, means "the Americanist religion of progress and democracy, atheist 'existentialism' and above all Marxism", the "ultra-Thomist" course may be defended - misguidedly, but still in good faith - as the best available means of fighting this intellectual fight. It was not "naive optimism" that led him to accept this, but the highly meritorious example of DeKoninck. But, he goes on, it seems that I was mistaken. The university has recently been visited by one Béguin, "director of the para-Bolshevist review *Esprit*", to give an expository lecture on Emmanuel Mounier's "Personalism". But, he explains elsewhere, in its proclamation of the "infinite" value of the human personality and "infinite" dignity of man *qua* man, these "personalists" deny the division and splitness in man, like the Communists. Well, that is life in a liberal democracy! But not only were the students encouraged to attend the lecture; no one in the department was deputed to challenge it in the name of Thomism! This, he implies, was a serious dereliction of duty. Why have these things been allowed to happen? Could it be that "Ultra-Thomism" and "unbridled Modernism" are two names for the same thing?[77]

At the beginning of 1954, wrote Kolnai,

I made it clear that I laid no stress on keeping my post, and in the autumn the Rector informed me (this being the entire text of his letter) that "my services would no longer be required from 1st June 1955 on"; which fitted in with my own intentions.[78]

Whatever his intentions actually were at this time, his bitter resentment at the "Thomist skunks at Laval" (one could fill a page with similar descriptions) ate like a canker into his soul, and, though his attitude softened to some extent after visiting Quebec in 1968, he never really forgave them. What for? Sometimes it is the dismissal, at others the circumstances of the dismissal, at others the atmosphere which gave rise to it. But the chief target of his resentment was Charles DeKoninck, and one may be pardoned for thinking that DeKoninck himself had got rid of him because he would not accept the local doctrine of "intellectual *mores*", which (Kolnai said) made it incumbent on lecturers to toe the Thomist line. Yet DeKoninck, who had done a great deal to tailor Kolnai's working conditions to his particular abilities, later gave him an excellent testimonial, and wrote privately on January 3rd 1955 to Goetz Briefs to ask if he knew of any suitable opening for this "valuable man". There seems little doubt that DeKoninck continued to appreciate Kolnai, and that he never demanded from him absolute allegiance to Thomism. Indeed, soon after Kolnai's departure he himself was deprived of his deanship. The reasons for Kolnai's hostility against him, and also the meek and inoffensive Archbishop Roy, nominally head of the university, and the uncomprehending administrator, Mgr Parent, its Rector, must be largely sought in his own unresolved ambivalence towards authority figures.

Interesting light is shed on Kolnai's last years at Laval by the memories of Professor Léon Dion, who first met Kolnai as a student investigating National Socialism in 1953. Kolnai himself wrote in very laudatory terms both about his thesis and also about his "self-evident honesty of mind" and his "unpragmatical, sovereign interest in the Object".[79] The first time they met, Kolnai put his hands round Dion's skull to feel its contours. "You are a genius", he said. This informal master-teacher relationship soon developed into friendship, partly, Dion surmised, because he had lost so many of his friends among the university staff. He found Kolnai to be completely obsessed with DeKoninck. The only relief he could find was to unburden himself to Dion (and a few others), and by writing sarcastic and ironical notes to his superior. At this time his Christian faith seemed almost obliterated by his hatred of Quebec Catholicism. "Even the potatoes are Catholic here", was a characteristic outburst, followed by an antagonistic fantasy about a special French Catholic way of growing them. He also loved to assert himself against Quebec society. On one occasion he asked a friend if he could give a talk in his house entitled "The Phenomenology of Cats". The guests were at first fascinated at the way Kolnai explored the feline nature, so dear to his heart. But he would not stop, and eventually spoke for three hours, while expressions of impatience and irritation were freely voiced in the audience. All in all, Kolnai struck him as a kind of anarchist. As for his teaching, his great gift was to create a kind of "atmosphere" around his topic (of little use, obviously, to most students). He mentioned an instance of his approach. The subject was Hegel's idea of the "absolute" State. Kolnai embarked on a long digression about the meaning of "absolute", illustrating it with the supposition of the absoluteness of cats.

After Kolnai left Quebec he asked Dion to sell his books for him. They were mostly detective stories and infested with mites. Indeed, he said, the Kolnais' flat was very dirty. This last point was strongly confirmed by Jeanne Lapointe, who also stressed the Kolnais' shabby appearance. Kolnai described himself to her as a "black sheep", and she also said that many people in Quebec disliked him intensely, some of them probably because of his letters in the *Montreal Gazette* ridiculing Quebec nationalism. Mme Tremblay said that she once took Elisabeth with her when visiting a large but poor family in the "lower town" in the course of her social work. The latter was much impressed with this family of thirteen children, and was well received. For some time afterwards she would belligerently proclaim that "real personality" was only to be found in the lower town. Kolnai's assertion in the memoirs that, in Quebec, charity is "all too prone to stop at home" was decisively rejected by the Tremblays and Mlle Lapointe. There can be little doubt that both the Kolnais had a strongly paranoiac streak in them, as implied by Kolnai's writing of the Tremblays that "we would never have the feeling of being let down by them".[80]

The rest is soon told. In November 1954 Kolnai wrote to various friends to ask if they would support his application for a Nuffield Foundation Travel Grant for one year beginning in July 1955, to enable him to develop his "Critique of Utopia". By the New Year he had collected a superb set of testimonials, from John Macmurray, Karl Popper, Goetz Briefs, Wilhelm Röpke, Leopoldo Palacios, Arthur Tremblay and Francis Ibrányi, and sent in his application on January 5th. The grant was approved. So on June 29th they departed down the St Lawrence in S.S.Scythia, arriving in England on July 7th. What sort of send-off they had is not recorded. But they were heartily glad to see the last of Quebec.

***

In November, the liberal quarterly, *Cité Libre*, of Montreal, published Kolnai's "Notes sur l'Utopie Réactionnaire".[81] This was the first of his papers on the theme of Utopia, and also constitutes a kind of philosophical accounting with the Quebec regime. He begins by analysing tradition as "an organic body" of established values, mingled with some defects. But one cannot live by tradition alone, since the world is changing, and life necessarily brings renewal. The essence of Reactionary Utopia is a rejection of the ineluctable changes of reality, which make reform necessary, and the belief that some particular example of present or past human social reality, described in "local" or particular terms, is perfect and can be preserved or recreated intact. The imposition of this belief in the impossible brings profound moral corruption. Kolnai goes on to distinguish this form of utopianism from a respectable traditionalism. Firstly, the traditions to be preserved have to be twisted and their values inflated. Secondly, reactionary utopia tends to grow in vehemence and rigidity, which is disguised as "false progress". Again, to cover its unreality, it has recourse to certain extrinsic aspects of modernity, such as a brutal technological "realism". But the chief mark of reactionary utopia is its false attitude to tradition. In the normal case, tradition makes for a kind of humility, tolerance and awareness of limitations; in the Utopian case, it becomes a schema of perfection already achieved. Lastly, we find a set of fundamental contradictions - philosophy appealing to reason but more "papal" in content than the Pope himself, an unchristian church supposed to be a shining example of Catholicism, an education which discourages all criticism of commercialism. In all this we may see a successful regime which cannot bear to change in response to new conditions, and relying on the intellectual sloth of the ruled. The only remedy is a rebirth of the critical intelligence.

But when the Duplessis regime in Quebec Province finally gave place to a liberal government, Kolnai began to feel that the reaction might go too far. In "Société 'Unanime' ou Société 'Neutre'", published in 1961,[82] he warns the liberals not to turn the "Integrist" policy of the *Union Nationale* on its head, and try to make the state completely neutral in religious matters. For one thing, conscience is not an organ of "occult origin", but depends to a large extent on the religious tone of society, and needs the protection of the Church if it is not to succumb to the interests of the State. They should therefore abjure both "unanimity" and "neutrality", and favour an autonomous and non-clerical state "with a Catholic sign", a pledge of which would be a second, Catholic, university as counterpoise to the newly secularised ones.

Chapter Twelve

England or Spain?
(1952-1961)

When the Kolnais left Quebec at the end of June 1955, they hoped that Aurel would find employment in England, so that they could settle there. On the other hand, they now had plenty of contacts in Canada ouside Quebec Province, and it might be easier to get a job in a Canadian university than in the United Kingdom. But what they probably had not seriously reckoned with was the possibility of settling in Spain.

In the sixties Kolnai used to tell people that he had a "guilty conscience" about Spain, which, for many years after its Civil War (1936-39), had been treated as a pariah by the Western democracies. Even though he had really known that there was an enormous moral difference between Franco and Mussolini, let alone Hitler, he was still taken in by the leftist view of the Spanish "Counter-revolution", and would have laughed at anybody who had foretold that Franco would cheat Hitler after using him to defeat the Reds.[1] When he and Elisabeth passed through the country in 1940 on their way to Lisbon and the United States, he had realised the falsity of this interpretation, though he says that he did witness a certain amount of official brutality. After his lecture-tour in the summer of 1952 he wrote to George Lanyi recording his impressions. He admits that his contacts were almost all with the conservative "restorationists", who pinned their hopes on the fact that Franco had declared Spain a monarchy in 1947; he had no contact with the Fascist Falange (whose power began to diminish almost as soon as it was clear who was going to win the war). He accepted that Franco's dictatorship was justified as a temporary expedient - though disliked Franco personally - and also hoped to see the regime develop towards constitutional monarchy. But he felt it had reached an impasse, because he could not see how leftist parties and organisations could be made legal again without another revolution. On the other hand, the state was far less genuinely fascist than Austria had been under Dollfuß and Schuschnigg; it was less clerical, more sincere and realistic. His friends spoke of "the victory of one Spain over the other Spain" rather than of Spain's defeat of Jews or Reds. Kolnai felt that the traditional Right was the nation's sole classic "reality", since its anti-conservative regimes had never succeeded in creating solid leftist institutions. Thus, he concludes, the regime has something of "normality" and legitimacy about it. Besides, he says, the country's morale is good, there is confidence and enterprise. In addition, Spain presents an aspect of "reality" which, in the West, only its "intrinsic antithesis", the USA, could equal - namely, its acknowledgement of "Communist world-conquest as the central political reality today". What is more, Spain, unlike the USA, is "unburdened by sentimentalities and by feelings of essential sympathy with the enemy". Hence the feeling that everywhere else people move in a "world of shadows".[2]

Kolnai's account of this lecture-tour begins with his almost "total immersion" in the language for two months or so before writing out his lecture in Castilian. Then comes the long sea-voyage, and his admiration for a party of "Galician sailormen on leave" who "constituted, as it were, a grave and dignified aristocracy" amongst the other, predominantly Italian, passengers. The details of arrival in the crowded port of Barcelona ("everything packed with living mankind overshadowing the machine") are lovingly described, and then at last the paradisiacal train journey through the "vigorous and meaningful landscape", with its "man-made structures of stone grown of that landscape, the occasional figures and faces marked with the accent of personality". So it goes on, with an excursus on the "expressive and plastic" nature of Spanish as instantiated even in the "solemn inscription" in the railway carriage (a comprehensive exhortation to considerate behaviour); it is all a long paean of praise of Spain:

> Catholic in its bones and marrow, unblighted and unregenerated by Calvin's breath, but with an undergrowth of authentic and ancient paganism never cleared away and on the other hand, with a proverbial aspect of Islam and a less often signalized yet unmistakable Old Testament background in its landscape and "inscape".[3]

Elisabeth used to say that Kolnai liked Spain so much because of its Jewishness, and he himself pointed more than once to the similarity with the Hungary of his childhood. That there was a very strong affinity between Kolnai and Spain there is no doubt. His Spanish friends were amazed at his increasingly profound knowledge of their language, and a newspaper in Valladolid, where he had just lectured, delighted him by calling him "as thin and lean as a Castilian peasant".

In Madrid they were eventually lodged in the Residence of the National Research Institute - a predominantly Conservative and monarchist institution at the time, whose aim, and that of its periodical, *Arbor*, was to "Re-christianize culture" - where they found no trace of totalitarian-mindedness or party-line fanaticism, but much open-minded discussion, humour and mutual leg-pulling. Though Kolnai emphasises here his hearty preference for "a constitutional monarchy with publicly recognised parties" over a "military dictatorship with its scramble of informal factions" (Franco skilfully playing these off against each other), he pays tribute to the regime for having preserved

> the paramountcy of the State, with its meaning of objective dignity and its liberating effect on the mind, as opposed to the totalitarian degradation of the State to a mere administrative machinery in the service of a "Party" inspired and ruled by sullen sectarian ideologists.[4]

Amongst the "Catholics" in the residence where the Kolnais stayed there were also people who, had political parties been allowed, would have voted social democrat, or even supported parties further to the left. Hence the political discussions he refers to were wide-ranging. Kolnai's lecture was delivered in four different cities, Madrid, Burgos, Barcelona and Valladolid; a mere 18 to 20 attended in Madrid, among them, to his amazement, a stout, red-haired journalist cousin of his, Ilia Stux; by contrast, "some hundreds" were present in conservative Burgos, though the local paper felt the turn-out had been on the small side.

***

The unshortened text of "*La Divinización y la suma Esclavitud del Hombre*" was published in paperback form the same year.[5] The title is explained in one sentence: "Communism means the absolute subjection of man for an idea whose main content is the absolute sovereignty of man." Its five parts explore five major aspects of Communism, which are related to aspects of liberalism, to make it clearer what anti-Communism really involves. The first part is "Emancipation versus Liberty". The emancipation Communism offers is from anything which restricts man's will; it is achieved by subordination to a single system of power which represents humanity. This did not begin with Marx: Communism is merely the consummation of the Liberal dream. Liberalism has already begun to trade liberty for "security, abundance and equality" guaranteed by a governmental plan. Hence the paradox that emancipation and elevation bring degradation: on the one hand man as "sovereign personification of scientific reason" and on the other as wholly determinable by scientific laws and hence open to "conditioning". Under the heading "The Man God" Kolnai claims that the kind of knowledge Communism seeks to attain is God-like and quite unlike ordinary human knowledge of things and rational governance of life. This is shown by the close analogy between the reciprocal implication of God's omnipotence and omniscience, and the Communist "destiny" of omni-domination through knowledge, and knowledge of things acquired through their control, which is the well-known correlation of theory and practice. Other parallels between God and the Communist man are also noted, among them between proletarianised man, stripped of all distinction, and God who contains in himself all distinctions; God as master of history, to whom nothing is contingent and man as disposer of history who eliminates all that does not fit its scheme of development. The topic of the following section is "Total alienation" - that is, from all "objectivations" (laws, conventions, values, etc), including aspects of his own nature, which man has not himself chosen. In Kolnai's view the guarantee of liberty is precisely the "multiple objectivations and interlinked hierarchies of civil society", though the feeling of alienation is apt to become oppressive when they become atrophied, and lose all personal meaning. But for Communists all these represent subjection (ultimately to God), and must be replaced by a new world, and by a new human nature undivided and identical with itself. Enslavement to the absolute power dedicated to producing these things gives the illusion that they will be attained. In "The Necessity of Tyranny" Kolnai shows that terror is a necessity for Communist states in order to prevent human normality reestablishing itself, which would mean the collapse of the system. In the last section Kolnai considers the difficulties involved in persuading someone of the errors of Communism. The best way in the end is always to attack the ideals (or ends) themselves, never the "means" being employed and the contradictions in actual systems. So we must continually attack the ideas of man's divinity and emancipation. This can really only be done fully effectively from a Catholic position, untainted by "modernism" - yet, it should be added here, the features of the human condition he mentions are all accessible to the secular "phenomenologist", and often mentioned in this book.

The same year saw the publication of *Errores del Anticomunismo*,[6] the Spanish edition, in paperback form, of the essay "Quelques Erreurs Courantes sur le Communisme" mentioned in the previous chapter. Its exposure of common misconceptions about Communism was so painstaking that some prominent Quebec citizens complained to the university authorities, accusing them of harbouring at least a fellow-traveller. Kolnai begins with the observation that it is our attraction by Communism which makes us fight it so half-heartedly. Pure pacifism plays very little part in our "appeasement". He then starts his survey of various types of error, beginning with "pragmatical" ones, such as the idea that Communism and Capitalism, being two economic systems, can learn to live alongside each other, that Communism is really a form of "Oriental Despotism" suited to Asians but posing no essential threat to us Westerners, that it is irresistible, so we might as well allow it to take its temporary course, and that it is no real threat because the Russians have so many problems to solve at home. All these errors stem from failure to understand that Communism is a "real, spiritual and material, sui generis and extraordinary, force". He then turns to "the Progressivist Critique" of Communism as "Red counter-revolution", and the idea that the USSR has failed to live up to the Communist ideal. It is an illusion to think that an absolutely totalitarian system based on the assertion of man's will "in defiance of God" could "develop" into something better, or that a "real dictatorship of the proletariat might be preferable". Finally, he suggests that all utopian thought must end in totalitarian barbarism.

Under "Naturalist and pseudo-scientific interpretations of Communism" he considers the ideas that it may be the most suitable regime for industrial society, that it is the product of "want and anarchy" and that it is the result of "social injustice". He attacks the historical and sociological basis of the first and the feeble determinism of the second. With regard to the third he asks what social justice is, and how we recognise it. These are very hard questions to answer. But particular reforms are possible without falling into Communism. As for the assumption that "Communism can only be overcome by opposing it with an ideal of equal psychological power", this fails to grasp that, in this respect, Communism is incomparable. Real life and faith are fragmentary and only half comprehensible. Communism must be beaten in a much more material way.

Finally, there are the "pseudo-religious" misconceptions, including the idea that Communism, despite being atheist, does establish social justice; wouldn't opposition therefore brand us as "reactionaries"? Kolnai's answer to this is to remind the reader what atheism really implies - man in God's place; the whole Communist programme is in fact inspired by it - it's not just "tacked on". But it ought to be fought not just in the name of Catholicism but of humanity. Nor will it do to oppose it with a non-materialist picture of man, since the West is itself strongly infected by Materialism. In any case, certain things are far more essential to Communism, for example denial of eternal moral laws and absolute truth, monism of the collective will, terror as State-constitutive, an infallible science of history as source of norms for conduct, progress of humanity towards omniscience and material omnipotence, class struggle, etc. Nor is it any good restating the old principles of Liberalism, since these gave rise to Communism in the first place. As for the "good end, bad means" argument, its real end is "*non serviam*"; if we don't fight it, it will fight us. And when did Communists ever find *our* ends good, and merely the means lacking? But in any case the argument presupposes a very simplistic idea of the relation of ends and means. As for the idea that in defeating Communism we will merely replace it with something worse, this ignores the moral principle of urgency. Our society remains "sick Christianity" in mortal danger. The most important thing is to save it from destruction. It is also part of the human condition to be again and again faced with having to choose the lesser evil. Our moral task is clear and unambiguous. Communism must be destroyed.

***

From Spain they moved on to France, revisiting the Franciscans in Toulouse, who had given them hospitality in 1940, and spending some time in Compiègne, where the family house of Jacques de Monléon, of Laval, was situated. They spent two weeks in Paris, where they breathed once again "the mild, thin, neutral and free - not by any means empty or scentless - air of Paris", which seemed a "relief" after the supercharged atmosphere of Spain.[7] But Aurel also had another attack of flu there, which prevented him from reading his paper at Strasbourg,[8] and denied him the chance to revisit Bern. When they crossed the channel from Dieppe to Newhaven, Kolnai felt a twinge of conscience because, as a Canadian citizen, he was now free to join the "British" passport queue without having had to suffer the German bombardment. But they could now absorb again

> the sweet old-fashioned artificiality of England, the maiden-auntly comfort of the English railway carriage, the English landscape even more thoroughly yet more discreetly civilized than the French, and then the purring and mazy luxury of the London tube, the enchantment of the streets and the human countenances in London, the archaic charm of English money ...[9]

so that at times "the vision of Spain would fade into unreality". The resulting personal dilemma is nicely summed up in the postcard of the horse-guardsman he sent DeKoninck:

> General,
>   discounting exceptions, provisos, qualifications, here is a résumé of my travel impressions: To see Man, - go to England. To see women, - to Spain. To see cats, - to France. Paris is pleasant, agreeable, likeable. Neither Spain nor England are. But how am I to choose between my Love splendorous, triumphal, redundant with sweet laughter, which is

Spain, and my Love dolorous, tearful, deeper and more passionate which is England?[10]

In London he spent much time walking, and "lost [his] heart most especially to the bewitching railway landscape of Chalk Farm", where Bela Menczer was now living. It was presumably his old Hungarian friend who got him to give a talk to the London Catholic "Logos" Circle. Kolnai spoke on Progress and Reaction - a defence of Conservatism against the "self-evident" rationality of Progressivism - and provoked a good discussion.[11] Menczer also took Kolnai to see Douglas Woodruff, editor of the *Tablet*, who also had an interest in the publishers Hollis & Carter. Here the conversation turned to memoirs, and Kolnai (with no ulterior motive) let it be known that he was thinking of writing his own. Before they left, Menczer had ensured that Hollis and Carter would be at least favourably disposed to consider them, on the basis of a synopsis and single chapter. There is no record of a visit by the Kolnais to Olga, Elisabeth's sister, and her husband Elemer; there was always tension between the two couples, since the sisters invariably quarrelled when they met, and Kolnai and Forbát (anglicised to Ford) could not stand each other. But they certainly visited Irma in Oxford, where her friend Lisbeth Gombrich also lived. Through her and Miss Gombrich's brother, Ernst, he made contact with Karl Popper. George Lanyi had encouraged Kolnai to write to him the previous year, but various characteristic inhibitions had prevented him from doing so.

During his short time in London, Kolnai and Popper met several times. Writing to George Lanyi in December he records an occasion when he, Popper and the Gombriches lunched together in the refectory at LSE. They had a violent argument about democracy in America, of which Popper expressed his approval, "even though, as Harvard guest Professor, he was shocked at the low level of the PhD candidates he had to pass".[12] He accused Kolnai of aestheticism, and ascribed his desire "to raise barricades and bastions" to simple fear. Gombrich later put much of this down to his deafness,

which [writes Kolnai] is worse than mine, but I think it is connected with his basic nature: that of the engineer who is impatient with descriptive and intuitional data and would like to formulate everything immediately in "arguments" and "theses".

Kolnai summed up his intellectual relation to Popper as follows: what they had in common was "radical rejection of totalitarianism", and the theory of piecemeal social reform "on the basis of logic of action and antihistoricism" (which Kolnai felt he had anticipated in his doctoral thesis); but what most attracted him to Popper was that he saw in him "the final incarnation of the anti-charlatan", something perhaps even rarer than "real genius". But he could not stomach his enthusiastic humanism, which made him "capable of saying seriously that he 'believed in man'". What Popper really liked in America was what repelled Kolnai so violently, "namely 'that men feel there they possess the earth'".[13] Popper also admired Kolnai, and wrote to him after his return to Canada, telling him that he had learnt a lot from "Privilege and Liberty", and hoping to have a chance of discussing it with him one day.[14] He wrote Kolnai a glowing testimonial when he was applying for his Nuffield grant, and in 1957 sent a long and very laudatory reference about him to the Society for the Protection of Science and Learning, which includes the following passage:

> I have the highest opinion of him both as a thinker and as a person of the highest integrity. He has also great personal charm - for me, at least ... My main point is that I personally think I could learn more from Kolnai, by way of stimulation, than from any other thinker in the field of political philosophy alive.[15]

Once back in Quebec, Kolnai lost no time in composing a paper "Revolution and Restoration", in which he develops some of the themes of "Liberty and the Heart of Europe" and applies them to the new political situation, especially that in Spain.[16] It appeared next year in *Arbor*. Kolnai makes one or two references to Rafael Calvo Serer's recent book, *Teoría de la Restauración*, with which he is generally in agreement, though his own more liberal and less traditionalist approach is clearly apparent. He begins with a statement of fundamental political principles. "Restoration" cannot be just a matter of keeping Communism out, since Communism is the entelechy of any leftist-liberalism. In fact it means the West's "return to itself, its principles, its faith, its values and its structural and distinctive roots". The lesson of history is that the higher the civilisation, the greater the danger of its overreaching itself. Restoration therefore means vigilance and moderation, a concern not to develop indiscriminately along society's natural line. In the next part he summarises the essential features of Western civilisation thus: (i) an independent and limited state power inserted into a divine moral order to which all are subject, and hence obliged to consult the people and respect established rights and usages, (ii) cooperation between Church and State, (iii) government from above but with participation of the people, (iv) multiple and varied social hierarchies, with some reference to a transcendent order of values, (v) social justice, protecting, excluding, etc, especially the possibility of an exploited under-class. All these elements require to be carefully weighed; the price of evading this task is surrender to the one revolutionary principle: the omnipotent rule of the human will above all objective value. Kolnai then turns to address the Spanish situation more specifically. It must not be forgotten that there are different forms of the Western pre-revolutionary tradition. To fasten on any one as a "reactionary Utopia" would be to turn one's back on reality, which always implies division and finitude in human affairs. Nor should they talk of a "restorative revolution", since thereby they can only play the enemy's game. Such talk also suggests that attack is everything, whereas restoration may involve phases of alliance with liberal democracy; it also encourages blindness to the fact that some aspects of Christian civilisation still live on in it.

***

Kolnai was invited to lecture in Spain again in 1953 or 1954, but this time felt he could not afford it. During his remaining years at Laval he still had occasional contact with Palacios, but his energies were increasingly absorbed by his feud with "Québecisme" and the university Thomists, and with the writing of his memoirs and preliminary anti-utopian studies. After the removal to England in June 1955, the Kolnais intended to stay for a time with "London friends".[17] Eventually they took possession of their first flat, 71 Clifton Hill, NW8, on October 1st. Kolnai now had to write his book, but he also had to try and establish himself in English academic life. One achievement was the rapid acceptance of his paper "The Thematic Primacy of Moral Evil", begun in Quebec in 1953 and published early in 1956 with very little alteration.[18] But he also visited the philosophers he already knew. Foremost among them was Popper, with whom he wanted to discuss his ideas about Utopia. But many people now wanted to consult Popper, and his wife was protecting him from disturbance so that he could get on with his work. Kolnai did see him, "but", he wrote - all too characteristically - in 1958, "(he) has ever since 1955-56 evinced a conspicuous absence of interest without giving the slightest hint as to his motives".[19] He also went to see Macmurray, who had been a referee for his Nuffield Foundation grant, travelling up to Edinburgh at the end of September to see both him and his wife, and also the city that had so much in common with Quebec. But the most important task, obviously, was to work at the book, which involved a great deal of reading. However, early in 1956 he was invited to lecture on his new topic to the Madrid Ateneo. Although he had only completed part I, he accepted, and proposed a second lecture, "a kind of philosophy of Canada - its national structure and the tone of its civilization"; this formed a section of his memoirs,[20] which had been accepted for publication by Hollis & Carter, and were now being shortened and overhauled. So he and Elisabeth travelled to Madrid in the middle of May, where his lecture was entitled "A Critique of Political Utopias".[21] At the beginning of June they went to Tortosa, where Kolnai spoke on "The problem of the Canadian nation" in the Arts Club.

Before leaving for Spain he had written to the Director of the Nuffield Foundation with a copy of part I of "A critique of Utopia" and asking him if his travel grant would be renewable after August 31st. He explains in this letter that the essay "embodies the gist of ten or more years of speculation, see-saw attempts at provisional formulations and strenuous self-criticism", adding that the award of his grant had been the main factor in his having at last completed it. He adds that, if no further help is forthcoming, he wonders whether he will be "technically able" to take the book any further.[22] But the foundation, reaffirming what they had said the previous year, were not prepared to extend his grant. At this point it seems that Kolnai was unable to begin concentrated work on part II of the book. His head was full of more specific political reflections which he badly wanted to pass on to his Spanish friends, and there was also the other matter of how they were eventually to live. The Nuffield money would support them for the period up to August 31st, and possibly beyond, and after that they would be able to draw on their Quebec savings, but sooner or later he would have to earn some more money. It was around this time that he approached J.N. Findlay,[23] who invited him "for a chat", and subsequently got him elected to the Aristotelian Society. As regards his political ideas about Spain, he had at first intended to write an article, but his thoughts were primarily conceived as the answer to a personal request from Salvador Pons in a Madrid café, so he decided to put them down within the framework of a letter for circulation among friends. This he did, and sent it off on August 8th, craving Pons' indulgence for any offence he might give:

> But I feel imperiously commanded to express as much as I can, as intelligibly as possible. This even outweighs my desire to please - despite the fact that I know I would lose a treasure if I forfeited the sympathies I seemed to enjoy in Madrid.[24]

"Carta-Memoria" extends the views about restoration expressed in the 1952 article, and applies them with some detailed suggestions to the situation in Spain in 1956. The Franco regime had now run about half its course, but had reached a period of crisis, largely due to the economic policy of "autarchy", or self-sufficiency, which the government, ostracised by the victors, had had to adopt after the war. Politically speaking, the Catholics and monarchists had gained ground at the expense of the Falange, but the universities had been rediscovering socialism, and there were students' riots and other disturbances, as well as a great deal of grinding poverty. When Kolnai wrote, a new political grouping was just beginning to form, the so-called "technocrats". This faction, one of whose main spokesmen was Rafael Calvo Serer, consisted of rightists chiefly interested in economic matters, who were members of the lay Catholic organisation, Opus Dei. They believed that a mature state would rise above the quarrelling of factions and parties and apply itself to the most important task in the modern world - economic and industrial development. (They gained several seats in the new cabinet of 1957, and continually increased their power for many years after.) Kolnai ignores economics in his paper but outlines the possible constitution of a monarchical Spain based on the ideas of a "responsible citizenry" and a monarch with genuine but limited authority, suggested by his political hero, Antonio Maura.[25] The key idea is that the relation of state and people should be that of "compenetration". Liberal constitutional monarchies inevitably produced a situation of "confrontation": the people gradually gaining the "infinite" freedom to which they are supposed to be entitled at the expense of a once "absolute" monarch who inevitably becomes redundant. For in liberal (Rousseauan) democracy the people and the state are thought to be one, a doctrine which is bound to end in totalitarian tyranny. In Kolnai's scheme the state (conceived as having a lasting, though slowly changing, identity) is embodied in the Crown, and is conceived of as rigorously separate from the people. The relation of compenetration works out as follows: the people have a part to play in government in that they are enabled to make genuinely free political choices. The Crown in its turn makes this possible by protecting the nation's institutions, and influencing the formation of public opinion. In this way it is the source of real authority but also political liberty. The underlying conception of man is of a being who is both formed by institutions and exercises a formative influence upon them. Two of the suggested "institutional forms" are especially worth noting. One is the "active citizenry", themselves elected for life, who would be responsible for electing parliament, and might number about one sixth of the population. This electoral body would itself be socially representative (with a preponderance of various élites), politically diversified, would exclude elements hostile to the state and be subject to special obligations. It would be a forum for responsible political debate, and go far to eliminate some of the least satisfactory features of direct universal suffrage. The other special institution is the "National Institute", an educational body partly dependent on the Crown, though not on the government, whose task it would be to inform, orientate, moderate and rectify public opinion. Among its special responsibilities would be watching over the life of the political parties and exercising some strictly delimited censorship. It would be above all concerned to raise the level of political discussion, and keep the citizens' minds on the general good and permanent substance of the state.

Having composed and despatched this "memorandum", Kolnai turned to more immediate practical tasks. He had already applied unsuccessfully for a lectureship in the Cambridge Moral Science Faculty.[26] Now he wrote out a new general letter of application for university posts, at the suggestion of Brigadier Huxley, Fellowships Adviser to the Nuffield Foundation. The bulk of this is an explanation of why he accepted a job at Laval in the first place, and why he left it. But, although this is a fairly objective account, he could not keep out every trace of the burning sense of injustice he felt over the sequence of events he describes. In early September his applications to the Universities of British Columbia and Toronto were turned down, and, as in New York sixteen years before, well-meaning suggestions about other kinds of employment began to be made to him, but nothing came of them. But after the Hungarian uprising in late 1956, the Society for the Protection of Science and Learning, originally set up before the war to deal with academic refugees from Nazi Germany, received a large number of requests for help from Hungarians. Someone had the idea of getting Kolnai, a "refugee" from "Thomist-totalitarian" Quebec, on their books, and Esther Simpson, who found many places for refugee academics in England during her long service as its secretary, became actively engaged on Kolnai's behalf. She had in fact briefly met Kolnai in Vienna in the early twenties, and was therefore able to tell John Macmurray that she had been "asked to help our old friend Aurel Kolnai find a position".

The society's archive in the Bodleian Library reveals Kolnai's ambivalent attitude towards advertising his Catholicism. On the one hand he was consorting with some of his fellow-Catholics in the London "Logos", and regularly speaking at meetings (topics include "The advantages and disadvantages of proportional representation", "On intellectual pride in Thomism", "The Christian idea of moral philosophy"); he also sent Miss Simpson a separate list of Catholic referees. On the other hand we find her bewailing the fact to Popper that "Dr Kolnai is most reluctant to work with Roman Catholic colleagues".[27] Elisabeth had also told her cousin George the previous August that Aurel was in no hurry to see his memoirs in print, since their pronouncedly Catholic slant might hinder him from getting an ordinary philosophical appointment. However that may have been, neither Miss Simpson's numerous enquiries nor his own applications achieved anything in early 1957, and in July Macmurray had to tell Kolnai that the Edinburgh post he had been encouraged to apply for had been designed for recent undergraduates "in the Oxford tradition".[28]

When Elisabeth wrote impatiently back to him about this, he wrote again pointing out that Aurel's "interests and aptitudes" were very different from those normal in English philosophy departments. This really limited his chances to research posts, whose terms of reference often excluded him (though Kolnai had been runner-up at Bedford College). Then again, his philosophical line was not only unusual in Great Britain, but even discouraged; the idea that Miss Simpson was not interested in helping him was utterly false; he just was very difficult to help. "He is not good at compromise - and England, at least, lives by compromise".[29] Earlier in the year, Popper had blamed the English university system: "He is a very original thinker, and an extremely unusual one, and for this reason also an unusual person." But British universities don't "offer a platform for an original thinker", their main concern being "to get the prescribed stuff across to the students".[30] All this discouragement had lately been compounded by the financial difficulties of Hollis & Carter. It now seemed probable that the Memoirs, much abbreviated at their request, would not be published at all - though some small compensation would in that case be paid.[31] Both Gollancz and Routledge & Kegan Paul looked at and rejected the manuscript, and Kolnai, fearful that his work would go for almost nothing, had asked the Society of Authors whether he should try and seek redress, though they had advised him to let the matter lie for the time being. Although he seems to have written one or two protesting or "warning" letters to Tom Burns during the winter about this repudiation of his contract,[32] and put out some feelers in Spain, he eventually accepted that he would never see his book in print.

Kolnai had already been encouraged to think of further work in Spain by Pons and Palacios when he was in Madrid in 1956. Of all his Spanish friends, Kolnai liked Pons the best. It was he with whom he had worked on the Spanish text of his lecture and on the translation of "Quelques Erreurs" in 1952, which had enabled Pons to write a very perceptive article about Kolnai.[33] Being full of fun himself, he thoroughly appreciated Kolnai's unconventional humour, and was flattered by his attention. Although he belonged to the circle around *Arbor* and the National Research Institute, he was more open to the liberal elements of Kolnai's position. Such a modification of an otherwise rightist posture was a refreshing novelty to him, but rather disturbing to most of the others; hence Pons was his most unconditional admirer. His reply to the Carta-Memoria letter had contained another, and more definite, reference to work in Spain, which, Kolnai admitted, both elated and alarmed him. The prospect must certainly have been very alluring. He was something of a celebrity in Spain, a person who could command a respectful, even an enthusiastic hearing in the highest intellectual circles, whereas in England he was a relative nobody. Then again, in Spain he was surrounded by militantly anti-Communist fellow-Catholics, whereas England was mainly Protestant and seemed largely unconcerned about the growth of Russian power and influence. There was more intelligent political discussion in Spain, with its café life, and the publication of his ideas would be easier. The tempo of Spanish life was more to his taste, and the more aggressive elements of modernity were hardly to be seen. All in all, the social environment was much more "human". He had also been attending lectures and courses at the Spanish Institute in London, and thus in a sense further preparing himself for a possible extended stay.

Pons replied on November 28th with the news that he had been promoted Secretary General of the Office of Information - hence the delay in replying. But he enclosed receipts and authorisations relative to a "short course" that Kolnai could give. If he signed and returned them, he would have the money as soon as he reached Spain. He assumed that Elisabeth would be coming too. Once they were on the spot, the title, place and audience could be properly fixed. What was more, the memoirs could easily be published; he could raise enough subscribers to warrant their publication by February at the latest. Nor would there be any problem about publishing his Utopia book. Apart from that, he could count on being paid for various lectures in Madrid and "some other civilized place, where you won't be obliged to make an exhibition of yourself, in the way you so dislike". The long and short of it was that he could guarantee Kolnai an income for a stay in Madrid of at least a year. "You can even take the train tomorrow and leave other, stronger, beings to endure this winter's London fogs, which are even now piling up overhead." We need you here, he went on, with your constructive criticism of our doings.[34]

Kolnai wrote back on December 12th, definitely accepting the small course, but uncertain whether to make this a separate trip and return later with Elisabeth or to take the plunge and come with her for a year. He had been gradually making new contacts in England, and had been very impressed by the Aristotelian Society - the like of which he had never experienced before. And he realised that, though his Catholicism was mistrusted in England, the fact that he combined this with a strongly rational-secular streak would hardly be to his advantage in Spain. He also recalled Gonzalo Fernández de la Mora y Mon's lecture at the Spanish Institute; it had indeed been a fine lecture, but it assumed a black and white division between "orthodox" and "heterodox" which was completely alien to him, yet all too characteristic of Spanish thinking. His "constructive criticism" might stimulate them, coming from a passing visitor; if he were a more permanent part of the scene, was it not probable that Madrid would become another Laval? Kolnai closed his letter with an expression of confidence in him (Pons) and Vicente Marrero; but he was by no means sure about the others. Apart from Fernández de la Mora there was Calvo Serer, whose thinking had considerably impressed him in 1952, and who seemed to have a political future. Would he continue to accept him?[35] (Kolnai continued to be very concerned about this question, and, although Calvo, whose political career was extremely eccentric, visited him later more than once in London, he brought out all Kolnai's latent paranoia.) But it was Kolnai's need for a special diet that really decided the issue of an extended stay. They would have to find an apartment so that Elisabeth could cook for him. Pons eventually declared that no flat was to be found, so he had better come by himself in the first instance. He reminded Kolnai that their circle had contained at least two who were to his political left, but added the unreassuring caveat that longer plans were dependent on his and his friends retaining their present posts. In the event, Kolnai travelled out by himself at the end of February, and gave four lectures on the meaning of the Hungarian Uprising. After regularly spending

> sixteen hours out of twenty four on the go, in the street, in the open air, in the sun, in the wind, watching the women, absorbed in men's faces, rapidly alternating between cafés, the Ateneo, the Office of Information and bed, wearing out shoes and devouring Vergara biscuits ...[36]

he returned in the middle of March. A condensed version of the lectures was eventually published as "Reflections on the Hungarian Uprising".[37] Kolnai here emphasises the non-ideological nature of the rising. What underlay it was an aristocratic trait in the Hungarian nation, thanks to which all classes were able to unite to throw off the Russian-Communist-Utopian yoke. It thus shattered the Communist myth that the enemies of Communism must be "bourgeois", and that its leaders represent the proletariat, and showed that, however much people are indoctrinated, human "normality" will always reassert itself in the end.

On Easter Sunday he wrote to Pons about his journey home, with "tonsillitic fever" beginning in Madrid (maximum temperature 103°F)[38] and treated also in Barcelona, and a stay with his friend Professor Rambaud (who had lectured at Laval) in Lyon. There are the inevitable travel impressions, and an example of his oft-repeated complaint that Pons and his friends don't appreciate the rightist treasures of the writer Pio Baroja, one of the "Generation of '98", and hence mistrusted as a liberal. They can't see that real conservative thought has a disinterested, anti-pragmatic and reserved character. The complete lack of references to future work in Spain (as opposed to occasional lectures) make it clear that the scheme had been, at least for the time being, abandoned. Kolnai's correspondence with Pons became very occasional after this, and eventually dried up altogether, though it is clear that there was no "breach" or unbridgeable difference of opinion in this case. Rather, Pons's new career left him no time to keep up the relationship.

However, Vicente Marrero showed more determination to foster Kolnai's interest and activity in Spain. When they first met in Madrid in 1956 Marrero was thirty-four, already a well-known figure in Spanish literary and intellectual life, one who enjoyed the patronage of the regime. His prolific output includes six books on art, seven studies of philosophers and five political works, as well as several volumes of poetry and numerous publications about his native Canary Islands, not to mention a great many articles, reviews, prefaces, and other minor works. He had lived six years in Germany, and travelled widely in Western Europe, especially Italy and France, and several of his works had been translated. He was also physically and psychologically imposing, well aware of his own intellectual worth; he and Kolnai were obviously very interested in each other from the first. When they met he had just launched the periodical *Punta Europa*, a general review of politics, art and culture, and he began to send Kolnai copies regularly, astonishing him by including in the number for October 1956 a Spanish translation of his paper on Reactionary Utopia.[39] During his short visit in early 1957 Kolnai agreed to contribute a pair of articles on personal and political liberty respectively, and another on Chesterton and Belloc. He also attended an editorial board meeting, and strongly approved of Marrero's aim to make the periodical as open as possible to different points of view, provided it remained Catholic, national and restorative. Kolnai's article "The Positive Conception of Liberty" appeared in the summer.[40] It is clearly related to "Privilege and Liberty", and takes issue both with the liberal over-emphasis on negative freedom (freedom as "freedom-from"), with its consequent tendency to reduce man to his desires, and also with conservative positive conceptions which identify liberty ("freedom-to") with acting rightly. Kolnai argues that the relation between liberty and the objective good is one of consonance. The mere absence of compulsions of various kinds (the liberal conception) is self-stultifying unless choices are made within a framework of objective values, instantiated in institutions, persons, authorities, and the like; but choice of the good is not liberty unless it is made "in a mode of liberty", that is, deliberately, and against a background of possible error or failure. The political sequel to this paper was never written, any more than the article on Chesterton and Belloc. In response to Marrero's often-repeated assurances that he would publish anything Kolnai sent him, he suggested "Conservatism with open horizons" (never written), and Marrero anounced his desire (again, unrealised) to print "Carta-Memoria" - or as much as the censor would allow. However, apart from the text of an Ateneo lecture he delivered in 1959, to which we shall return, nothing else of Kolnai's was ever published in the magazine. One reason was his continuing preoccupation with Utopia, and with his employment chances in England. But he also had a change of heart about the periodical over the years, as I will show below. However, two other matters connected with *Punta Europa* are worth mentioning here. Kolnai persuaded Marrero that it would be a great thing if he could publish a translation of the English philosopher Elizabeth Anscombe's well-known paper "Modern Moral Philosophy". He himself went to a great deal of trouble to help arrange this, but for some reason it never happened. The same fate befell Marrero's long-cherished scheme to publish a feature on Kolnai himself.

Kolnai's later attitude to *Punta Europa*, and to Marrero himself, is expressed in the last surviving communication from Kolnai to Pons - in the form of a paper, like Carta-Memoria, entitled (in Spanish) "Your Three Questions".[41] Pons's third question was "What do you think of Vicente Marrero's articles on the Spanish Civil War?" The summary answer was: "(they are) readable and, to me, very interesting ...; but in essential respects deplorable and absolutely unforgivable". He adds that, to mitigate his disloyalty, he's also sending Marrero a copy of what follows. The gist of Kolnai's reply is that there has been a disastrous deterioration in *Punta Europa*. Between 1952 and 1957, he says, the "monarchical neo-traditionalists" seemed genuinely concerned to find a way out of the blind alley into which their brand of politics had brought them. But all they had done, he goes on, was to promote the worst (Falangist) elements of the regime, and to attack the better (liberal) elements. That there is a way out is shown by Gonzalo Fernández, who had reached a "civilized, reasonable, juridical, humanist and even more 'Christian democratic' way of thinking" (he became a cabinet minister in the seventies), and there are aspects of this in Calvo Serer, who, for all his clericalism, believes in constitutional order. This deterioration, Kolnai adds, is typified by the periodical's intellectual style, which has reduced philosophy to the level of "party-line ideology as such".

This "change" - which seems to have been largely a projection of Kolnai's - is reflected in his letters to Marrero, which are at first very positive. However, after Marrero had read "Carta-Memoria", Kolnai evidently felt a need to reinforce his message, since he sent him an even longer political paper, "Eight Theses about the Restoration".[42] His first concern is to emphasise that a restored monarchy must be a modification of the non-Carlist line (whose last representative, Alfonso XIII, abdicated in 1931); any attempt to go back to the monarchy of pre-liberal times, or to the line of Carlist pretenders, would make no sense at all.[43] "The King is essentially ... the real head of the nation, not the tool of fanatics ..." He then has to insist that the divisions in the nation do not constitute "two Spains" except where Spaniards are really loyal not to the Crown, or the State, but to some external power (as in Communism or ultramontanism). The attempt to substitute some "third way" of "unity" for "Left" and "Right" is Utopian. He then turns to the lessons of history. Traditionalists like Marrero believed that the Alfonsine line could not succeed because of its past failures; Kolnai says this is to misread the past, and appeals to the example of Adenauer's Germany, which had completely confounded the prophets of doom. He then expands a little on his thesis of "compenetration", drawing out a little more the implications of conceiving the state, in Aristotelian fashion, as a form of shared life (*convivencia*) amidst recognised divergences; this has not only personalist and anti-fascist aspects, but also anti-liberal ones, since it "points to the need of a 'substantial', not just formal, social order over and above the 'rights' of every individual". He emphasises that this is a very different conception from the Platonic one of the state as "organism", or "work of art".

As the ordinary - and prolific - correspondence with Marrero proceeds Kolnai begins openly to voice his misgivings, and castigates him with an increasingly bitter choice of insults and comparisons. By 1961 he is capable of bracketing him with Goebbels and Mussolini; in his 1963 paper, "Existence and Ethics", which he sent to Marrero, he is simply a "Spanish fascist". But the extraordinary thing is that Marrero never seems to take offence, and that Kolnai, even in his latest letters, having piled insult upon insult, takes his leave (with his usual exaggeratedly florid Spanish courtesies to Marrero's wife) as though nothing had changed. What must have increased his frustration and disappointment is that Marrero more than once says how much he has profited from Kolnai's political papers. When he was "about to change his own political position", they were like "manna from Heaven", translating him into a world of "purity and rigour". At Marrero's earnest request, Kolnai also commented at length on the manuscripts of some of his books, confining himself at first to the undisciplined manner of writing, but increasingly finding fault with the content. He makes it clear that he regards Marrero as a thinker endowed with exceptional philosophical talents but reared in a very unhelpful intellectual atmosphere. Marrero always expresses gratitude to his "inquisitor and friend", pointing out that ruthlessly honest detailed criticism like Kolnai's is hardly ever found in Spanish intellectual life. He even dedicated his book on Ortega y Gasset to him in 1961. On at least one occasion he invited Kolnai to stay in his Madrid flat, and on another gave him the use of it, complete with domestic help, while he was away. Marrero also invited him to lecture at a university summer school in Santander in

1961, and the year before apologised for not having been able to fix anything up at the Ateneo. In 1962 Kolnai all but calls him a liar before saying that it is his possession of great intellectual virtues (so often concealed by his clericalism, and other time-serving vices) which

> has for so long prevented a complete rupture between him and me, which I for my part absolutely want to avoid. One could put this another way by saying that I seldom find Marrero completely boring, and quite often find him very interesting.[44]

Kolnai follows this passage to his friend with a list of the eight "most significant Spaniards of the last hundred years". Most of them are men Marrero probably had serious reservations about, so the list is another barb in Marrero's side. About a month later, he wrote again to Marrero with another version of the same material, telling him that he had written to Pons about the "eight greatest Spaniards", and wondering whether Pons had told him. It is hard not to see in these events a faint echo of his obsessive conduct vis à vis DeKoninck in his last years in Quebec.

One of the men Kolnai includes in his list is the philosopher Ortega y Gasset. Around this time attitudes to Ortega's philosophy provided in Spain a serviceable touchstone of a person's general intellectual-political stance. Liberals usually rated him highly, as their predecessors did in the thirties, whereas traditionalists, who tended to be Thomists in philosophy, mostly thought little of him. The periodical *Arbor* had provided the occasion for a heated controversy over whether Ortega could be considered a genuine Catholic or not. This was later taken up in *Punta Europa*, where the anti-Ortegan position was especially represented, with Marrero's full support, by his friend Fr Santiago Ramírez. José Luis Arangúren, on the other hand, who had passed from enthusiastic support of Franco to progressive Catholicism with some admiration for Marxism, took the other side, and also valued Ortega highly as a moral philosopher. Kolnai thought Ramírez to be an intellectual nullity. On the other hand he called Arangúren "the biggest name in Spanish Catholicism this century", because of his comprehensive *Ethics*,[45] yet also thought that he absurdly overrated Ortega as a moral philosopher. Though he himself was, in general, "no Ortegan", he had high praise for Ortega's attack on the Thomist identification of the Christian God with Aristotle's "Prime Mover". He also thought that Marrero had gone much too far in attacking Ortega in his own book, and that, despite the very fine passages of criticism it contained, he had in fact succeeded in revealing Ortega's greatness, which, he says, exceeds that of Heidegger. Despite this, Kolnai admitted that, at bottom, Ortega "bored" him, though he had to confess to a sneaking sympathy for his "ratio-vitalism", which, in another letter, he equates with "common sense". A very fundamental issue is involved here, though, to some extent, it is a matter of terminology. Ortega's "ratio-vitalism" is related to the claim that some cognition has affective foundations. Despite his own emphasis on the cognitive function of, for example, hatred, Kolnai seems to shy away from the implications of this. As he puts it in the letter of June 25th 1957: all his sympathies are with "civilization", order and rules; the often anarchic nature of feeling and emotion, and hence the philosophical affirmation of these, which was so common in the early part of this century, always aroused his deep suspicion. This is in fact one of the main complaints he had against Marrero's own philosophy - despite the latter's poor opinion of Ortega: that he inclined to moody existentialism as against sober phenomenology, appreciated figures like Kierkegaard and the "hyperemotive" Unamuno, who had no proper content to convey, and so on. And yet he himself is drawn to the "vital" side of things, as this passage from another letter makes clear:

> Like you I accept that effective state power needs more "visceral" foundations than the representatives of bourgeois civilization have ever dreamed of ... Well, but I stand for the contrary. All my sympathies are for civilization as such, for the Rechtsstaat, for "society"; it's just that I know how fragile it is, and see the liberal imbecility of thinking that normative postulates are enough ... to construct and maintain a solid instrument of civilization.[46]

It is almost as though Kolnai felt that to explore a metaphysic, or even a conceptual scheme, to fix these insights (as Marrero did in his early political book *El Poder Entrañable* (Visceral Power)) would amount to accepting, even wallowing in, them, and thus to destroy the will to control the underlying realities.

It is, perhaps, significant that Kolnai's paper "Political and Non-political Interests", first delivered as the Wright Memorial Lecture at the Royal Institute of Philosophy in November 1960, was not translated for *Punta Europa* but for *Atlantida*, in the Spring of 1965.[47] This was a new periodical committed to dialogue between conservatives and technocrats. "Political and Non-Political Interests" suggests Kolnai's concern at the technocrats' increasing influence, which encouraged the view that political issues were really technical, implying the search for the best means to the end of national prosperity. Kolnai argues that it is inadequate to see them as simple means-ends issues of any kind. Nor can they be identified with moral questions, which are inseparably bound up with human conduct and the quality of intention, whereas politics involves choice between practical programmes of certain kinds. Thus, political interests always presuppose other interests, which, because of man's varying pre-political nature, makes conflict inevitable. Consequently there will always be a combination of rational and non-rational, cooperative and antagonistic factors in political discussion. The year 1965, by which time the Spanish economy was bringing increased prosperity to the country, also saw the long-delayed publication of his "Objetividad y Tecnicismo", delivered originally at the 1961 University of Santander Summer School; it came out as a "Selected Text" in *In*, the bi-monthly review of the National Industrial Institute.[48] This paper explores the moral and spiritual effects of increasing technologism, the unfettered pursuit and use of technologies to satisfy human desires, which increasingly produces a sense of emptiness and meaninglessness, as control over the environment cuts us off from living contact with it. It is again not difficult to see this essay as a warning against the "technocratic" attempt to make political debate redundant (though it also relates to his anti-Utopian writings). It was in fact the last lecture Kolnai delivered in Spain. Apart from 1952, he had lectured in 1956 and 1957, and then again in 1959 and 1961; he also visited the country in 1960, thanks to a grant from the Rockefeller foundation, when he made contact with Aangúren, and later tried unsuccessfully to persuade certain English publishers to pay him a decent fee for a translation of the latter's *Ética*, whose "completeness of perspective" he especially commends. Some of the friends who had originally invited him or got him invited, such as Pons, were no longer in the appropriate posts to secure this any more; others, like Marrero, were being politically stranded (in the end, uninfluenced by Kolnai) as the current of change slowly began to drive Spain towards the mainstream of Western political culture, and other acquaintances, like Calvo Serer, were evolving too far to his left to have any sympathy for Kolnai's own monarchical centrism. By 1970 he could say, in a letter to Klaus Hartmann, that he would still really rather live in Spain than anywhere else, but, apart from his own conservative opposition to the present regime, recent years had seen there a crop of "to my taste much too leftist philosophical and political writings".[49] Nevertheless, in the last year of his life he undertook to deliver a conference paper in Madrid, but did not live long enough to make the journey. The paper, "The Morally Improving Function of Law", which he was to have presented at the conference of the National Institute of Legal Studies, was, however, published in the institute's annual.[50] In this short essay Kolnai enquires into the question how the law can raise the moral tone of society. After a brief examination of the similarities and differences between law and morality, he passes to moral "legalism", criticising especially the "pharisaical" form of this, according to which everything pertaining to morality has a legal form, as though it were a part of justice, and the even more pernicious "anti-legalism" - the attempt to exclude the quasi-legal form of "obligation" from morality altogether. The main "moralising" function of law is located in its attempt to compensate for the weakness of purely moral sanctions; the law maintains the ideal (the moral law) in the real world, and strengthens the tension between values and reality.

Some account must finally be given of the two papers Kolnai delivered in Spain in 1959. The first, "Pluralismo y Correlación de las Finalidades" (Pluralism and the correlation of ends) was a "communication" to the fifth Spanish Philosophical "Week" at Madrid, organised by the Luis Vives Institute of Philosophy and the Spanish Philosophical Society. The proceedings of the conference were never published. Kolnai's paper - many of his audience would have been Thomist in philosophy - has much in common with the slightly later "Deliberation is of Ends"; it investigates the extreme ambiguity and provisionality inherent in the ideas of "means" and "end" in human practice, and shows the superiority of the idea of more or less permanent, and continually competing, "concerns" and preferences. The idea of "happiness" only makes sense in relation to a multiplicity of "ends". Kolnai had almost certainly been invited to this conference by Professor Palacios, who was then President of the Spanish Philosophical Society. Relations remained good with his old Laval colleague, and they continued to correspond very sporadically until at least 1970 - though in the mid-sixties there are Kolnaian complaints at Palacios's preference for writing postcards. Palacios, who dedicated his essay "De Balmes a Husserl" to Kolnai, and introduced into his brief remarks about Kolnai's *Errores del Anticomunismo* an account of his first visit to Kolnai's flat in Quebec,[51] remained to the end an extreme conservative and traditionalist, in politics as well as religion. In his letter of Easter 1961 Kolnai tries to persuade his friend that his total rejection of democracy, expressed in his recent book, is based on false premises; democracy is legitimately founded not on the doctrine of popular sovereignty, which he also rejects himself, but on "the relativity of all human sovereignties and social authorities". He also gives it as his opinion that modernity also connotes an advance, "the discovery of subjectivity (conscience, 'I', the 'person'), and the intuitive experience of values". "For this reason doctrinal positions defined in historical terms cannot be sustained." Returns to the past are good if they mean attending to it; but "integral returns" cannot be good.

The other 1959 paper was originally a lecture delivered in both Madrid and Barcelona, and then published in *Punta Europa*. It is entitled "Contemporary British Philosophy and its Political Implications".[52] Kolnai's Spanish friends tended at this time to be wary of all things from England because of its traditional liberalism and Protestantism, and to assume that its philosophy must be positivist and leftist. The paper sets out to persuade them that, on the whole, Linguistic Analysis lacks the "nihilistic and subversive prejudices of recent neo-positivism", is much more phenomenological and Aristotelian than the latter, and is strongly conservative in its political implications. In these respects it compares very favourably with American philosophy, as their different approaches to language reveal, the Americans being still intent on the search for a totally clear and unambiguous "perfect language", the English regarding ordinary language as a source of valuable "pre-philosophical knowledge and thought". This means that, despite its programme of "therapy" towards ordinary language, it is in fact returning discretely towards metaphysics. There follows an interesting comparison between the linguistic analytic and the phenomenological attitudes to language. He then passes to ethics, or "logic of moral discourse", a formalism far more sensible than Kant's, but a bit sterile and meagre - even morally dangerous; but consensus and common sense still prevail for the most part. Despite its obvious defects, he concludes, linguistic analysis is "an admirable achievement of intellectual honesty and authenticity". Like any genuine philosophy, it is bound to be conservative in its effects, since conservatism essentially means "primordial and fundamental assent to the world as work of God".

In January 1961 Kolnai wrote a letter to *Cité Libre*, in Montreal,[53] to correct the "disheartening picture" of the Spanish regime presented by one of the paper's directors, M.Pelletier, and to show that Spain had far more liberty than the genuine fascisms of the past. He made three points. Firstly, Arangúren, an Ortegan Catholic and "well-known leftist", held a philosophy chair at Madrid; secondly, the danger presented by Communism was real, and therefore some at least of the persecutions of Communists were justified; thirdly, the fact (if Pelletier's sources of information were correct) that four hundred trade-unionists had been imprisoned before the recent trade-union elections showed that the elections themselves were not just rigged, but had some real substance; however little effect on the government they might have, they contained an element of "education for democracy", and an admission of the principle that government must listen to the people. This did not justify the "falango-traditionalist" regime; but we had to be clear about the limits of its justified criticism. If we compare this with the letter to George Lanyi quoted at the beginning of this chapter, it seems that Kolnai's early hopes for the regime had by now been moderated - a disillusion which may partly account for his increasingly bitter frustration with Marrero. Despite his intention to visit Spain again in the year of his death, he never in fact returned after 1961, and his desire to live there never seems to have become more than an idle fancy after the winter of 1956 to 1957. The lecture on British philosophy shows clearly enough why. The English philosophical scene suited him; and, having once again tried in vain to influence the course of political events, he hoped to be able to devote himself - with what remained of his strength - to "pure" philosophy.

Chapter Thirteen

England - Early Difficulties
(1958-1964)

Kolnai's English life between 1958 and about 1964 is dominated by two things - the struggle to obtain an adequate income and, in close connection with this, failure to complete *The Utopian Mind*. Accordingly, much of this chapter will be about these two things, beginning with the financial question.

Kolnai, we must remember, was brought up in a prosperous bourgeois household where almost everything was done for him. Although his situation was very different when he left home, he continued to receive financial support from his father until 1940. The uncertainty of his sojourn in France was continued in the United States, but here he could enjoy the fruits of a recognised status, that of learned catholic refugee, and could rely on Elisabeth's regular support and the help of her relations to supplement his own exiguous earnings. There followed the time at Laval, where he had a monthly salary which provided them both with a modest living - even though during this time Elisabeth's bungled operation largely deprived her of the means of contributing much to their income. Meanwhile, his parents had been killed by the Nazis or their sympathisers near the end of the war, and any hopes of an inheritance been dashed by the turbulent events of Nazi rule in Hungary, the Russian siege of Budapest, the chaos that followed the German retreat and the ensuing political struggle, which ended in the Communist take-over. So when the Kolnais came to England they had no source of regular income to look forward to beyond that which Aurel could secure by his own efforts. After his Nuffield Foundation grant ran out and he had been disappointed in various applications for teaching and other posts in England and Canada, and after finally giving up hope of being able to settle satisfactorily in Spain, it was imperative that Kolnai should find some permanent position in England sooner or later. His cousin George Szell did help him during this time, and it may well also have been in late 1957 that Léon Dion raised about two hundred Canadian dollars for him from his Laval colleagues, but Kolnai could hardly expect to go on living entirely on grants or occasional handouts.

This knowledge weighed heavily on him, and is one reason why he never finished his critique of Utopia. As we have seen, having completed the first introductory part, he found it very difficult to get himself into the right frame of mind for writing the second chapter. It doubtless seemed easier to concentrate on getting better known in the British philosophical community, though these efforts were not always very encouraging. When, for example, he re-submitted a short piece to *Mind*, and wrote to enquire about it after waiting for over two months without receiving any acknowledgement, the editor, Gilbert Ryle, briefly apologised and, almost in the same breath, continued: "It seems to me quite publishable, but I haven't got room to publish it".[1] This is the kind of thing that no doubt prompted him to tell Vicente Marrero:

> My position is very doubtful. I have much love and respect for England, and would like to live here - if that were possible for me. But England's attitude is: "I don't see why that's necessary."[2]

"The Universality of Loyalty Rules" seems never to have been submitted anywhere else, though the essential points appeared in "Erroneous Conscience".

Although Professors J.N. Findlay, H.B. Acton and possibly others at London could by now be numbered among Kolnai's new supporters, he was also trying to make contacts elsewhere. A short-lived correspondence with Elizabeth Anscombe, a fellow-Catholic, is instructive in this regard. It seems to have begun with Elisabeth Kolnai's letter to her in the autumn of 1957 about possible jobs for Aurel. Anscombe was naturally rather pessimistic, pointing to the strong influence of philosophical fashions in England, and wondering if he had considered librarianship. However, she agreed to meet Kolnai when he was next in Oxford, and they subsequently argued by post on ethical matters, he discussing points in Anscombe's "Modern Moral Philosophy",[3] and she criticising Kolnai's "Erroneous Conscience", which he delivered to the Aristotelian Society on February 24th 1958.[4] But, despite the willingness of both parties to say exactly what they thought, and even hammer away at a particular point over two or more letters, the exchange is not as fruitful as one might hope, and the two fail to make real contact with each other, especially about "rationality" in ethics. Anscombe implies that Kolnai is not rational enough because he relies too much on his Judaeo-Christian background; he needs to take up some more purely rational position. For Kolnai, this abandonment of the actual moral roots of Western culture, in which they are both steeped, would itself be irrational; Anscombe's demand - though he does not say so here - is virtually utopian. Anscombe was also unable (like many before) to match the sheer volume of Kolnai's letters, and the correspondence seems to have come to a fairly abrupt end not very long after its beginning. However, George Lanyi (who was spending the summer doing research in London) thought that "Erroneous Conscience" had been very favourably received when it was read. He was present on the occasion, and, in his letter to George Szell of October 18th 1959, presents it as evidence of Aurel's having "attained a certain standing among English academic philosophers", mentioning "several appreciative letters" received from important thinkers. Although Lanyi was trying to put the best possible face on Kolnai's professional prospects so as to to convince Szell that he was taking active steps to secure his future, he was not wrong about the favourable impression Kolnai was making in some quarters; Stuart Hampshire wrote to Kolnai in July 1958 warmly thanking him for his contribution to the Joint Session meeting on "Pretending". Both he and others, he says, thought it was the best that was made.[5]

During the autumn of 1957 Kolnai's Canadian friends had alerted him to the new scholarships being made available to Canadian citizens by the Canada Council, and he had applied accordingly. In early 1958 he had heard of his success, and it was agreed that the *Bourse Spéciale* he had been awarded would start on October 1st. Meanwhile Acton, Professor at Bedford College, suggested that he apply for a post at Sydney; Kolnai, alarmed by the implications of "another New World", was thankful to be able to remind Acton of his obligation - now backed with the promise of material means - to continue with his critique of Utopia. The date of October 1st was fixed because Kolnai felt he would need until then to translate Brugger's *Dictionary of Philosophy* for the Herder Press, which offered the handsome sum of £800. Unfortunately, he hesitated so long about accepting the commission that it went elsewhere. This loss was partially offset by Esther Simpson's holding out the hope of a British Academy grant, for which he applied successfully, taking it up a few years later. The promises of money to come also spurred him into producing "Right and Left in Political Division", which he submitted to Acton, as editor of *Philosophy*. It was partially designed as a chapter of the Utopia book, but appeared first as "The Moral Theme in Political Division".[6] By the summer of 1958 his savings began to run out, and he tried unsuccessfully to bring forward the starting date of his *Bourse*. Kolnai thought that this grant of about £1,450 might be enough for perhaps two years' living - though Elizabeth Anscombe wrote that she thought it "little to live on for two years".[7] But it could hardly be expected to support them much beyond early 1960, so he applied for a lectureship at Glasgow in February 1959, with Acton, De Koninck and Popper as referees, but again without success. After his lecture and some research in Spain in the early

Spring, he completed chapter two of the Utopia book, and also "La Mentalité Utopienne", in response to a general invitation of the previous December from the French journal, *La Table Ronde*,[8] before applying on May 12th to Nuffield College for a research fellowship, with the help of which he hoped to finish the book. He was optimistic enough to calculate that, by the autumn, when it would begin, he would have completed two more chapters, but was not even placed on the short list (in a letter to Marrero he comments that, at least, he wouldn't have to live round the corner from his mother-in-law, Irma).[9] There followed an unsuccessful application to Birmingham for an assistant lectureship. Austin Duncan-Jones, Professor and Head of Department, wrote to Acton, again a referee, expressing the obvious objections to appointing a man of 58 to a post intended for those at the beginning of a university career. There was, however, a slight possibility of "a special ungraded lectureship at a modest salary" if he really was worth it. But hadn't *The War against the West* been "a bit journalistic and propagandistic"? However, he had been impressed by his contribution to a Joint Session meeting. Unfortunately, "so often these clever middle-aged refugees who have not struck roots anywhere are rather difficult people".[10] In his reply, Acton left no doubt of his own favourable opinion, adding, diplomatically, "I suspect that his wanderings are partly due to the fact that he is both a Catholic and a liberal". He thought Kolnai eminently suited to a university post, and was full of praise for "Erroneous Conscience".[11] Duncan-Jones wrote in due course to say that, as he had expected, they had had to appoint a younger man, but added: "It seems a discredit to the academic world that he should be at a loose end", and mentioned his hope that a research fellowship might fall vacant in the near future. If so, he went on, "I shall run him for it as hard as I can".[12] In spite of this, Kolnai was again unsuccessful when the post was advertised in July. Two further disappointments followed. Professor Findlay had hoped to be able to offer him a temporary research post at King's, London, but the existing incumbent decided to change his mind about leaving. Then, contrary to his Canadian friends' assurances, he was told in October that the *Bourse* could not be renewed. But Acton had at least acted on his own account, and secured Kolnai a very modest contract to deliver a weekly lecture on ethics at Bedford College at 5 guineas a session. When George Lanyi reported the financial situation to George Szell in late October, he felt that their savings would probably last until the end of the year.[13] Szell sent off another cheque.

Obviously £157/10/- per annum (the Bedford College fees) was not going to provide for the Kolnais in London, however much Aurel was becoming known as a speaker at philosophy meetings ("Moral Consensus" at Birmingham on November 21st, and "The Concept of Practical Error" at

King's College, London, in February). But Lanyi - who did so much at this time to look after his cousins' interests - had already set in train the mechanism which brought Kolnai a Rockefeller grant (about £1,430) from the beginning of 1960. (This enabled Kolnai to do a lot more reading for the Utopia book, but only about twenty pages of chapter three were ever completed.) The Bedford College lecturing continued for the next academic year, and some lectures at King's College were definitely fixed (though at the pitiable rate of £2/10/- an hour, rising later to £3) for the Lent term of 1961. What is more, Duncan-Jones, of Birmingham, was now able to help him substantially by his part in getting Kolnai the Lloyd-Muirhead Fellowship in Political Philosophy for the year 1961-2 at £90 a month. George Lanyi estimated, in a later letter to Szell, that this, together with the Bedford College lecture fees, "was adequate for a very modest living". Kolnai kept his expenses down by staying as little as he could in Birmingham. 1962 must have been a relatively prosperous year, since the fellowship continued until the summer and Kolnai took up his £200 grant from the British Academy to begin work on "Morality and Practice". Bedford College also began to pay him a salary (£400 p.a.) from October, and, in addition, he stood in for Findlay at King's, earning now at least £12 a week for two one-hour classes, one two-hour class and a seminar, work which "absorbed most of (his) energies".[14] Findlay, ashamed at how little Kolnai was being paid for doing his job while he was being "overpaid" at the University of Texas, sent him $150 as a Christmas bonus.[15]

But Kolnai had still only completed about half (possibly less) of his projected book on Utopia, and only two chapters of "Morality and Practice". Whether or not he applied for any more grants, no more grant money ever came his way, and 1963 and 1964 proved to be the most difficult years. In 1963 he had the extra King's money until the summer, but then he would only have the small Bedford College "salary", which, in April 1964, Kolnai wrote to Arangúren, "hardly constitutes a third of a lecturer's remuneration".[16] Accordingly, Lanyi wrote again to Szell in August to let him know how things stood. He laid stress on the fact that Elisabeth, now suffering from a liver complaint, was very frail; his son, who had visited the Kolnais the previous year, had reported that she now looked older than Irma, her mother. All she could manage, apart from looking after the flat, was to sort mail for the Post Office every Christmas ("Poor people do, you know", Kolnai once said in explanation), and sell the occasional design to handicraft shops. Lanyi's own ability to help them financially was severely restricted by the fact that he had been giving a lot of help to his sister and her son, who left Hungary in 1956, and that he was still helping his own son, now married, to complete his graduate studies at Berkeley. Szell, at all events (childless and now a wealthy international celebrity), sent £50, and mentioned that he thought Paul Winkler had also helped them.

A difficult situation was now developing. It is clear that, for Kolnai, "the urgent pressure of material cares", as he put it, was a major cause of his inability to complete his larger undertakings - though he seems to have found no difficulty in writing papers. Had he been able to secure a full-time research post, and to look forward confidently to several years free from financial and other worries, the difficulty might possibly have been overcome. But it was by now clear (a conclusion reinforced by more failed applications around the end of 1963) that, despite his growing - if still very "patchy" - reputation in British philosophy, he was unlikely to get one. On the other hand, his two chief private benefactors, Szell and Winkler, wanted some assurance that the couple would "pull their weight", and keep trying to raise money on their own account. Winkler in particular seems to have felt that Elisabeth's "artistic" line was too self-indulgent, and that, though Kolnai himself was not exactly shirking, he ought to make greater efforts to write things that would sell, such as short and pithy articles in, say, *Encounter*. Lanyi accordingly advised Kolnai to follow his mother-in-law's example, and try to get some financial compensation for his two spells of internment in France, and perhaps for the murder of his parents in Budapest and the consequent loss of his inheritance. In October, when it was absolutely clear that the Bedford College money was all they could count on, Elisabeth wrote to Szell asking for further help, and Szell in his turn wrote to Lanyi asking him what he should do. Lanyi knew that the only real solution was a regular allowance, and suggested that he and Winkler jointly gave them £50 per month until Kolnai got something better than the small post at Bedford College. In fact, they decided to send a lump sum, so Lanyi wrote again in April 1964. He sent Szell an amusing article by Kolnai[17] and expressed his regret "that a person of this talent cannot earn enough for even a modest livelihood". He had heard that the Kolnais were in a bad way, and, after all, "how can one live on £400 a year?" Attempts to earn decent fees for translating (including the Arangúren scheme mentioned in the previous chapter) had foundered and the "German restitution case is also dragging on". He ends by saying that he will be in England in the summer and will send a full report of their situation.[18] Meanwhile, Szell had himself received "a rather pitiful letter" from Kolnai and sent another cheque. He looked forward to hearing Lanyi's report. Before that, Professor Daiches Raphael, then of Glasgow, wrote to Acton asking for his frank opinion as to whether Kolnai might do for a Lectureship in Social and Political Theory. He mentioned that he knew the committee would ask awkward questions about his age and why he had not yet found a full-time post. Acton's reply stresses his diffidence, and says that Kolnai got on best with postgraduates and "honours students after their first year". He was convinced that he would "give very good value". He himself had found him an excellent colleague. "His trouble is that he is too self-effacing and has been very unlucky".[19] It is not clear whether Kolnai applied for this post; he certainly didn't get it. Two months later Lanyi was in a position to give his report on the Kolnais' situation. Although Acton had been trying to get Kolnai some more teaching, it was now clear that he would not get anything for what happened during the war. The Bedford salary, their only source of regular income, covered less than half of what they needed (£900) for rent, food, fuel and rates. He and his own sister, Vera, had themselves been looking after the Kolnais' clothing needs for the last few years. He therefore suggested that Szell and Winkler pay a regular allowance of £40 per month between them, to be reduced pro rata if Kolnai got a better post. He mentioned that he also needed £50 to enable him to attend a conference in Belgium, where he was giving a paper.[20] This time Lanyi's suggestion was followed, and the joint monthly allowance (possibly raised at some time) was continued until 1970, when Szell died, and then carried on, slightly reduced, at least until Kolnai's own death and possibly beyond, by Winkler alone.[21] Shortly after the allowance was settled, Acton, about to leave for a chair in Edinburgh, succeeded in extending Kolnai's teaching responsibilities. He was thus paid £700 from the beginning of the 1964-5 academic year, and, since his salary was now made proportionate to a full-time lecturer's salary, it gradually rose to £1122 by the year of his death.[22] Although attempts were made within the college to bring Kolnai's teaching to an end (he was still taken on in his seventies after his first heart-attack), the two successive professorial Heads of Department concerned, Bernard Williams and David Wiggins, supported by Mrs Sally Chilver, the Principal, strongly resisted them, and he was left in peace - though in his later years he never ceased to be haunted by the fear that his deteriorating health would soon bring his teaching to an end. Nevertheless, though never well off (except for one short period when Kolnai went to the USA in 1968), they were never in serious financial difficulties again. It is worth noting that, quite early in his time in England, Kolnai secured the services of a Viennese accountant, Rudolph Weiss, with whom he seems to have maintained friendly relations (perhaps he was a friend or acquaintance of his youth); through his help he was even able to set up a little pension fund, from which Elisabeth benefited when he died. This money was supplemented by a small pension which Professor Wiggins got the college to pay until her death in 1982.

***

We must now return to Kolnai's unfinished critique of Utopia, which had clearly seemed to three grant-giving committees to be a reasonable research project. It is, however, significant that nearly all his philosophy bore some relation to it, and that he found it very difficult to divide it up into subordinate themes. He also needed some powerful stimulus to make him stick at a task. Kolnai could usually be productive when he had a grant specifically obliging him to write something, or had a real chance of publishing a paper on a clearly defined topic. After his grants had been used up, he responded for a time in 1964 to Acton's suggestion that he write a short book about politics; then, in 1966, he met D.Z. Phillips at a Joint Meeting, and Phillips encouraged him to publish some of his material in a series he was editing for Routledge & Kegan Paul. The new problem here was that Phillips could not guarantee publication unless he had seen completed sections of the work, whereas Kolnai needed some sort of guarantee to keep his mind on the project long enough to produce them. He also felt unable to do justice to his theme unless he had digested almost everything bearing on it written by other people. Kolnai's work on Utopia, as sometimes conceived, was to have included an account not only of what others had said about it, but of its historical roots, and all its major social as well as political manifestations. A letter to Phillips shows his anxiety about the recent emergence of "the Althusser sect in Paris", which - as far as he was concerned - meant more essential interpretative work on his part.[23]

But the greatest difficulty probably lay on the thematic side. Kolnai always needed something to combat. As I have tried to show, this need is the well-spring of a great deal of his philosophical *oeuvre* (a fact which, since he always preferred to make his attack from an unexpected quarter, by no means detracts from its compelling interest). To a man who felt almost continually battered by the evils and the errors of the modern world, the general theme which attracted his fighting instincts was almost bound to absorb into itself everything he felt was wrong with modernity. "Why single out, and fasten upon, Utopia?", he asks himself in what he calls his "Final Notes" of October 1958. "Because Utopia is the seductive falsehood that occupies the focal point of political (practico-historical) aberrations", he suggests. "The distinctive preeminent features of 'Modernity' ... are certainly Utopian", he tells himself, yet, just as one cannot "do without the concept of Utopian aspects", so one cannot "interpret modern history as the unfolding of Utopia pure and simple". The centrifugal tendencies of his project were also strengthened by the penchant for exploring the dialectical logic of ideologies or beliefs, an offshoot of his respect for human reason. So we can see his efforts to concentrate on one particular theme, which crops up again and again in the notes and papers he left behind, as continually renewed attempts to keep a garden free of weeds. On the inside cover of the second of his Utopia notebooks this is poignantly expressed: "One point - salient point - to be chosen for treatment ... Which?", and, among the numerous re-castings of his "synopsis" he adds to a sober self-reminder that he was merely writing a list of themes in no particular order the words "this is a chaos".

The uncompleted manuscript of *The Utopian Mind* begins with a chapter entitled "Critique of Utopia". Here Kolnai argues that Utopian thought is intrinsically wrong and must lead, if given its head, to Totalitarian tyranny. Its essence is the striving for a perfect state of things, where no evil (lack, want, painful tension, division, discrepancy) of any kind exists; Utopia is thus not a modification of reality, which is the point of institutional reform, but a radical alternative to it. Such a state of affairs logically cannot be held before the mind. The next chapter, "The Utopian idol of perfection and the non-utopian pursuit of the good", develops the sub-theme that Kolnai most often puts at the centre of his sketches and synopses. Utopian thinking is a perennial temptation for human beings precisely because it is closely associated with the sometimes laudable pursuit of perfection. Kolnai first shows that the approval of utopian thinking which this association seems to suggest is not justified, and then proceeds to an analysis of perfection itself. What is perfect is the best of its kind, as measured by a rule of correctness; unlike the majority of axiological terms, which are about qualities an object may or may not have, "perfection" points to a completeness of being. These facts show why there is a strong connection between the perfect and the artificial, implying an existence controlled by human purposes, and why an emphasis on perfection values, including "compelling logical evidence" and formal completeness excludes "a properly estimative response" (that is, an informally rational choice requiring the weighting of different value-qualities). The next section, "Perfectionism", is most important. It begins with a contrast between the "perfectionist" and "common-sense" outlooks. The latter assumes a distinction and tension between value and being, and the many different ways in which the former may "claim" us. Though common sense is "inter-subjective", and may always yield mutual understanding, it remains uneasily aware of division, imperfection and limitation. What is more, there are spheres of life such as logic, science, religion, and dedication to a task where common-sense itself cannot be content with its own pluralism and perspective, and has to yield before expertise. Hence arises the temptation of perfectionism, including "perfection-models of practical thought", which delude us into believing in "perfect solutions", and losing our grip on "the mundane manifoldness of limited, uncertain and foreshortened goods, values, aims, and concerns". In the next sub-section Kolnai describes the non-Utopian and possibly over-scrupulous perfectionist, who is "not fundamentally at war with reality", and the ordinary enthusiast for "correctness", who does not necessarily hold that there is always one correct way of doing things; they can be set against the various types of monist perfectionist, such as the "naturalist" (Value is the fullness of being) and "idealist" (Being is the self-realisation of value). Kolnai then goes on to enlarge on the "perfectionist attitude", issuing in the attempt to remodel the world in accordance with certain common-sense standards of evaluation quite divorced from the appropriate value-experience, which is always more subtle and less clear-cut than the perfectionist thinks. Such "rationalist" ways of evading the uncertainties of ordinary practice through "all-determining self-evidences" seduce us because they are emotionally satisfying. In the last section of this chapter, Kolnai shows how perfectionism all too easily passes over into Utopianism, and in itself often constitutes "departmental utopianism" (belief in a single kind of solution to all the problems of a particular sphere). Then, after a discussion of practical contradictions in general, he passes to the fundamental Utopian contradiction: the perfectionist concept of good, which "implies at the same time an abstractive negation of reality and a full identification of itself with reality", and the desire to make this world into a "non-worldly world". The Utopian "wants to create the country he might love if it existed", although "the concept of getting what we want is empty except by reference to the things we do want". Kolnai then passes to "the incongruities of ordinary practice", such as our need to act as though we and what we do were really important, to decide arbitrarily sometimes and to bear the contradiction of feeling now that we are our bodies, now that "it is only the spiritual that matters". On the other hand, many of these are only contradictions on perfectionist presuppositions. "Utopianism rejects the common-sense submission to the human condition and pursuit of the good on its terms", and replaces it with non-human submission to an abstraction. Instead, we have to accept imperfection of ourselves and our aims, and put up with our limitations and the ineliminable varieties of value. The third, uncompleted, chapter, entitled "The Utopian 'Godhead of Man'", begins with a discussion of the differences between imperfection and moral evil, and the Utopian refusal to accept this commonsensical distinction, its "rebellion against Reality as beset with non-moral evils and condemnation of the moral evil which pervades its structure", because "imperfection brings out the 'merely human' stature of man". Of course, it is sometimes right to try to deal with imperfections; but the Utopian thinker cannot tolerate "matters of degree". Indeed, rather than fight specific evils themselves, he prefers to fight the conditions that make them possible. In doing so he distorts the crucial factor of "moral emphasis" - which does not bid me create a "moral world", except in a very indirect and attenuated sense - harnessing it to the removal of structural imperfections. In fact, he confuses morality with practice, a confusion characteristic of Utopianism because of morality's continual reminder of human splitness, its "deep, background emphasis ... on our not being, ultimately, lords over our own lives".

This summary of the completed parts of the Utopia book[24] also hints at two other related inhibitions which Kolnai suffered from in his attempts to finish the work. These have their source, firstly, in the fundamentally religious or at least spiritual issues underlying it, and, secondly - though in close consonance with the foregoing - in the apparent feebleness of the "common-sense", or conservative, answer to Utopianism. In his "pre-final" notes of September 1958 he writes: "The way back to God, Humanity and Personality [goes] through the recognition of, and piety towards, Things. [What is] needed [is] a new cult of Smallness, Limits, Irreplaceable Given Goods: as it were, This Grain of Wheat." But how could he recommend "Love, Appreciation, Affirmation of Thisness, Identity, Concrete Reality, Loyalty, Limitation, Ownership" - acceptable enough maybe in Catholic Quebec - in virtually post-Christian Britain? The weaknesses of the common-sense attitude are frankly admitted and analysed, but again we find him reminding himself that to unmask and analyse the prideful sin of Utopianism needs a special kind of "spiritual courage", precisely because of Utopia's entwinement with "rational and moral demands 'obviously justified'"; if Utopia is "the subversion of Reason from anxiety to escape the Irrational", Common-sense means "acceptance of the Irrationality of existence and at this price penetration thereof by elements of Reason". In some notes probably connected with his renewed study of Utopia in 1960, he asks again: why prefer the irrationalities and imperfections of Common-Sense to those of Utopia? In his answer, he first stresses the limits of "experiential knowledge, thought, belief, wishing, valuing and planning", which result from our "constitutively imperfect cognitive and evaluative equipment". He goes on:

> This will be expressed in such necessities as having to take arbitrary decisions, acting on arbitrarily preferred suppositions, substituting "conscience" for plainly arguable justifications, avowals of ignorance and withdrawal from some practical themes.[25]

"Life is full of mysteries and opacities", he continues. It makes sense only if we rely at times on mere "belief", if "we include in our experience an awareness of trans-experiential meaning". If this were not so, "the very concept of 'Common Sense' would never have emerged". But the utopian mind, in a way strikingly reminiscent of paranoiac "logic", "places its perfection-schema above experienced reality, including 'ordinary' pluralistic value-experience," and replaces the "inadequacy of life lived on common-sense presuppositions" with "a fundamental rupture of continuity with the commonsensical universe". This attitude is also expressed in the anti-Utopian resistance to the tendency of "science" to take over the human sphere (and of the "common man" to acquiesce in the take-over), which prompts Kolnai to remind himself "not to sacrifice what I do know to what might seem more worth knowing".[26] Kolnai's fundamental problem with these insights, which can all too easily be dismissed as "obscurantism", was to find a way of putting them both honestly and convincingly. His natural timidity was here, perhaps, compounded by a feeling, in which his paranoiac tendencies were also present, that he had very few philosophical allies. On one occasion, before reading a revised version of "Moral Consensus" to the Aristotelian Society, he notes with apprehension that the session will probably be chaired by Strawson or Winch. Strawson, he writes, would make

> acid remarks to the effect that my train of thought be simply obsolete nonsense, whereas Winch's criticism would be possibly more caustic and devastating, but certainly more relevant, and at the same time more vulnerable to counter-attack.[27]

One irony of this, of course, is that Kolnai himself was not really a pedlar of obsolete certainties, for all his support of common-sense and a "moral consensus of mankind". "Ethics cannot aspire to certitudes", he notes in private, and, in a letter reproached Elizabeth Anscombe with being too keen to press on to the sphere of detailed moral rules.[28]

***

As I have already pointed out, nearly all Kolnai's writings during this time relate in some way to his attack on the Utopian Mind. The self-contained section of his utopia notebook "Copybook I", "The Utopian Negation of Fundamental and Ineliminable Distinctions", can be read as a comprehensive introduction to these distinct yet related papers.[29] One of them, "A Note on the Meaning of Right and Wrong", was commissioned by the Hungarian Academy of Science and Arts in Rome while Kolnai was still at Quebec, though it did not appear until 1958.[30] Its anti-Utopian thrust, as so often, consists in the demolition of over-simple views of morality (involving the "negation of distinctions"), and the defence of something much more open-ended, less uniformly rule-bound, with room for individual judgement and insight. He shows here that neither the "high-principled" duty-performer of Kant nor the "virtuous" prudent man of Aristotle can be made to yield an adequate picture of the good man. This leads on to the important distinction between "thematic" and "implicit" morality; in the former the "good intention" is "doing the right thing", in the latter it is doing something in which the agent is interested apart from the moral theme but which he knows to be a right thing. Though moral value has to be interpreted in terms of natural concerns (without being deducible from them), implicit morality cannot by itself exhaust the meaning of moral Right, since "a general readiness to self-restraint, self-detachment, self-criticism & self-abnegation" - that is, a practical receptiveness to the moral "theme" - are part of its meaning. Nevertheless, the "immanent" conduct of life is "a moral performance", morally valuable in various ways. Implicit morality is thus also an essential mode of the moral life. "The Thematic Primacy of Moral Evil"[31] extends the division of morality into "thematic" and "implicit" by showing that, though there is a "primacy of Good on the level of reality", moral experience is chiefly an experience of Evil. Thus, since duty-fulfilment in life is basically assumed, the primary note of moral emphasis is obligation, in the face of natural concerns which threaten the moral order. Though the ills of practice also have a note of urgency about them, they are often barterable against natural goods, whereas there is an "absolute" urgency about moral evil, since it is a mortal threat to the Good, as implied in the concepts of dishonour or spiritual death. Kolnai then shows the non-uniform way in which his claim is true of various departments of moral value. In the last section of the paper he shows how moral themes are "superimposed" on practice; there is no domain of "moral activities proper", and we can only make morality into a practical theme in a secondary sense, since moral performance is primarily implicit.

"Erroneous Conscience",[32] the third member of this trio of "early" ethical papers in English, attacks the formalist view that "conscientious" action is always right. It begins with the thesis that genuine conscience expresses and presupposes knowledge of and assent to "the valid intrinsic principles of morality as we know them". So what do we say when we come across a dissentient view, conscientiously held? It must first be recalled that conscience is not so much "about" itself as about the duties, and so on, which constitute it. We are responsible not only before (our own) conscience, but also for it. There follows an analysis of different kinds of erroneous conscience, which demand respect where the agent's allegiance is still to moral Right. It is otherwise with "Overlain Conscience", where "the agent subjects and adapts his conscience to some non-moral 'absolute'", usually a concrete human entity to which he has attached himself "as a natural fact" (e.g. The Party or The Cause). The test of genuine (if perhaps erroneous) conscience is "the agent's ... recognition as a moral basis & standard of the open consensus of mankind", which can include an appeal to a moral authority. The paper also includes a fine analysis of "moral fanaticism", and thus links up directly to the Utopia theme.

"The Sovereignty of the Object: Notes on Truth and Intellectual Humility" was contributed to a Festschrift for his old friend, the Catholic phenomenologist and defender of orthodoxy, Dietrich von Hildebrand.[33] It is not surprising, then, that Kolnai should return here to the problem of Thomism in Catholic intellectual life, especially since, in his eyes, much Neo-Thomism, and even some aspects of Aquinas' own thought, especially in the relations between reason and faith, amounted to Utopian thinking in the sphere of religion. Nevertheless, the anti-Utopian message he directs towards thinkers in general is clear from the introductory sentences:

> Thought, in the sense of thinking, is always somebody's thought. But again, by its very nature, it aims at Truth as such, and not at somebody's truth. This ineluctable paradox - this dialectical tension inherent in the finiteness and the embodied condition of Man's mind - lies at the root of huge difficulties and grave aberrations in our thought-life, and particularly, in that more explicit and elaborate (but virtually all-pervading) form of it which we commonly call Philosophy.

Kolnai's idea of philosophy is familiar enough to us now to make a summary of the paper unnecessary, but it is worth noting the important principle that we can only interpret another's thought in the light of our own understanding of its object. To this I will add two anti-utopian points about Husserl which occur in footnotes. The first runs as follows:

> A widespread "rationalistic" or pseudo-scientific error will have it that impressions are all "merely subjective", while an elaborate formal construction of concepts and "demonstrations" is a pledge of "objectivity". Husserl's phenomenology has greatly contributed to dislodging this gross equivocation.

Another footnote concerns Husserl's *Erfahrung und Urteil*. In comparison with this book, there is no "more convincing restatement of the Aristotelian position that the only possible basis of our 'scientific' knowledge of objects is the confused and virtual world-knowledge implicit in our 'common experience'".

The anti-Utopian aspects of "The Moral Theme in Political Division"[34] are again largely implicit, but clearly indicated in Kolnai's introductory paragraph:

> In this paper, I try to show that antithetic political positions appear to imply different moral attitudes not only accidentally but essentially, yet in a peculiar, limited and ambiguous fashion; and that political relativism or pluralism is far from implying moral relativism or pluralism in a corresponding and coextensive sense ... Political positions are not as such derived from moral demands, nor consequent upon moral errors; nor do they, as such, determine the moral convictions of those who hold them; but they tend to be associated with distinct kinds of dominant moral emphases rather than simply to respect or to disregard morality.

It may be added here, to avoid confusion, that "moral emphasis" in the above quotation is not the experienced emphasis or urgency of "emphatic morality", but the practical "weighting" among moral principles of roughly equal importance brought about by inevitable difference of perspective.

Several of Kolnai's implicitly anti-Utopian papers are about Practice, or the management of inevitably conflicting human concerns. In the first of these, "Deliberation is of Ends",[35] he discusses Aristotle's conception of practice, especially the (utopian) idea that, since the ultimate end for any person is happiness, deliberation can really only be about means.[36] Kolnai shows that no rigid division of pieces of conduct into means and ends is adequate to the way we have to choose, given our human nature and condition. As so often, he detects a "paradoxy" in practice, since it is neither a matter of technical (rule-bound) skill, nor of "straightforward preferences", nor of "random hits" (however arbitrary it may sometimes be). To grasp this paradoxy is to choose better; to refuse to accept it and act as if "wise choices" were either totally illusory, or completely rational, would be to choose worse. Aristotle, whose follower Kolnai so often professes himself to be, comes in for much criticism here (as elsewhere) for his "all too confident and short-circuited rationalism", and his resort to a mysterious and uncheckable virtue of "prudence", to make up for his (commonsensical) rejection of "general criteria of wise choosing"; nevertheless, Kolnai pays tribute to this "great pioneer of the theory of practice" for having bequeathed us the problem.

The two completed chapters of Kolnai's projected book "Morality and Practice", are entitled "The Ambiguity of Good" and "The Moral Emphasis".[37] The first begins with the familiar question "What shall I do?", and shows that it need not be a moral one, despite being often taken as such. He then goes on to analyse the different senses of "good", especially the difference between a person's good and his goodness, the idea of the "good thief", and "The Good" (meaning "Value") and the various types of the same. Section four consists of an analysis and critique of Aristotle's metaphysics of Good, and certain themes from his ethical theory. Section five is an illuminating account of "Bad and Evil", in which the idea of moral evil as an attack on a previously existing and somehow "normal" good state of things is carefully expounded in such a way as to resist the pitfalls of naturalism (what is good = what is); by contrast, the "deficit" theory of evil is shown to be quite inadequate, though it fits the clearly distinct idea of "badness". In the next section he deals further with the question of metaphysical naturalism, in particular the question of the connection between moral goodness and human concerns, with special reference to Plato and Kant. Surely, he argues, the moral demand would be powerless unless it somehow related to life. And yet, he ends characteristically, a sterile intuitionism is still vastly preferable to any form of Naturalism. This leads to a subtle examination of the genuine question: "why should I be moral?" Chapter two, "The Moral Emphasis", begins with a sketch of ways in which man's being and goodness are not merely contingently connected. So much may be conceded to Naturalism. But it ignores the "Moral emphasis" (here in the sense of "emphatic morality"), which attaches to conduct very unequally. The question whether every single action must be good or bad is first approached via the arguments of Aquinas and Scotus. Kolnai finds neither of them wholly satisfactory but comes down on Scotus's "indifferentist" side because not all actions "carry a moral emphasis" - "a tone of warning, urgency, vetoing and commanding" in an "ultimate" sense. This, he says, is the major subject of ethical enquiry. The next sections, "Negative and Positive Morality" and "Thematic and Implicit Morality", coincide to a great extent with some of the papers analysed above. He then goes on to stress the importance of the fact of the "intrinsic relevancy of rules and their content" for human life, and to discuss the "intelligibility" of moral rules, and the question how far belief in obligation is tenable without reference to "transcendent authority". His answer is that, like all other elements of morality, it is not derived from any "religious framework", but from moral experience. There follows a discussion of the Ten Commandments in terms of thematic and implicit morality. In the last section, Kolnai examines "The Dimensions of Moral Emphasis", asking what holds them all together. Something surely does, but no attempt to derive them all from a single principle seems plausible. It seems that a "residual opacity" is part of the essence of moral emphasis. Nor is there any neat correlation between aspects of emphasis and departments of practice, though there is some connection. His highly anti-utopian conclusion is that the plurality of moral points of view does depend on the manifoldness of practice but neither merely reflects nor expresses it.

Another paper about "the logic of multiple purposes which in diversified forms underlies the whole fabric of ... practice" is "Games and Aims".[38] Playing games is a natural human concern. Yet, in order to do so successfully, one has to pursue a quite different aim, namely whatever constitutes winning in the chosen game. Kolnai calls the relation between the two aims a "paratelic" one, and uses his analysis to reveal paratelic elements of "serious" practice in education, the law, and other spheres. There follows an analysis of the "game" of politics, where a concern with party policies is paratelic to pursuit of the common good. It is, he says, "an attempt to seize the intimate irrationality of human willing and force or entice it into a rationally acceptable mould; whereas morals and law are concerned with the criteria of that acceptability and the devising of by-laws for their application". His additional (unpublished) notes reveal the fact that he toyed with the idea of writing a short book on connections between the Serious and the Lusory in human life. They also reveal once more the fundamentally religious basis of his anti-utopianism:

Paratelic consciousness is one facet of the fundamental law of human existence - that we "cooperate with God's design" on a level not coincident with his level, our autonomy being inseparable from our imperfection.

He also writes, in notes on "Game-likeness and Utopianism":

The lusory aspect of Practice is antithetic to Utopianism ... in that it manifests competition as an integral part of human relations (the intrinsic dividedness of will-centres) and, at a deeper level, the inherent split-tendency of all human willing and teleology.

Another practice-related paper, "The Concept of Practical Error", was read to an audience at King's College, London, but never published. Kolnai starts by emphasising the strangeness of the concept, since "error" is a theoretical term, but its centrality in Aristotle's Ethics and its pointing to the widely recognised defects of "foolishness", or "folly", seem to justify attention to it. The extensive discussion emphasises the need to know oneself, to distinguish short- from long-term concerns, especially in the light of personal change, and considers eccentricity and habit, rigidity and indecision. Kolnai concludes that practical error is extremely hard to test - Aristotle's test of prudence is of little help. He approves the idea that the agent is the best judge of his own practice, and points to the test of "real willing", the degree to which the agent puts his whole self into the actions he has chosen - a question that only the agent can really be sure about. But, he concludes, practical error is probably not as common as we like to think. He ends with a brief glance at the partial convergence between moral inadequacy and practical error. This typescript is also accompanied by a set of related sketches and notes.

There are, finally, some papers which bear directly on Utopia, not just by implication. In the previous chapter, mention was made of the Spanish booklet, *Crítica de las Utopías Políticas*, which is a condensed version of Chapter I of "The Utopian Mind".[39] "La Mentalité Utopienne",[40] translated as "The Utopian Mentality",[41] was written after the completion of chapter II of Kolnai's book, and is therefore of wider scope. It forms a useful summary of the basic ideas. An unpublished paper in English, also bearing the title "The Utopian Mind", is another version of chapter I, but further shortened for presentation within the compass of an hour's reading. But the two papers on Utopia and alienation are a kind of anthropological concentration of the theme. One, in French, "Éloge d'aliénation", has not been published, but the other, "Utopia and Alienation", has also been included in *The Utopian Mind and other papers*.[42] Kolnai accepts, by and large, the analyses of alienation from Rousseau to Marx, and down into the twentieth century. He also accepts that the conditions of the modern world have greatly increased alienation, to the extent that certain measures to reduce it are right and proper. His fundamental point is that alienation is part of the human, especially the "personal", condition, and that to try to abolish it is, firstly, wrong, since morality itself is alienation (one is confronted by one's conscience as by something alien), and, secondly, doomed to failure, since the "new humanity" of utopian reformers is something so utterly alien to our existing human nature, that we could not but experience it as "super-alienation". In any case, alienation is by no means always painful even today, since it is a source of pleasure, happiness, vitality, and a sense of "being in the world". The theme of alienation is also prominent in Kolnai's contribution to a Joint Session symposium on Existentialism with A.R. Manser, where his own paper was entitled "Existence and Ethics".[43] Here he emphasises that "reification and alienation" are inherent "in the human, and more particularly the civilized, mode of being". Personal freedom is not independence but "ability to balance, revise and modulate limitations, ties and obligations" (which all constitute alienations). Heidegger's attack on the thoughtless conventionalities of "*Das Man*" seems to be aiming at "sovereign and unlimited selfhood" for everyone, but in reality it must end in the Identity of all. Sartre, too, Kolnai goes on, produces a caricature of bourgeois social life. Free choice is not possible except in relation "to given desires (including appreciative beliefs, the attraction of 'dignities' and the desire to comply with obligations)". That is, it is inseparable from reification and alienation; it is "limited, i.e., 'impure', or nothing". In a final summing up he looks at the common assumption that Existentialist ethics is non-naturalist because there is no appeal to an "a priori hall-marked moral authority". On the other hand it rejects "diversified intrinsic qualities of good and evil", and reduces the moral problem to being "genuinely existent". It is therefore a "metaphysical naturalism", underlain, what is more, by "value-experience [which is] unmistakably aesthetical", and with a tendency "to value intensity at the cost of direction".

The last paper written during this period I shall mention here is "The Ghost of the Naturalistic Fallacy", first read to the Muirhead Society at Birmingham University in 1962, but only published in 1980, through the agency of David Wiggins.[44] This is not really an anti-utopian paper (though it touches on anti-utopian themes), but a reinterpretation of G.E. Moore's ethics, with special attention to the "Naturalistic Fallacy". Its special excellence derives from Kolnai's ability to take a really fresh look at a topic which has been endlessly discussed in modern "Anglo-Saxon" ethics. Briefly, Kolnai argues that what Moore really meant by the "Naturalistic Fallacy" (not really a logical "fallacy" at all) was the "identification of Good with reality as such", not with some aspect of reality, such as "pleasure". The paper is by no means confined to discussion of Moore but contains some illuminating passages on the place of "good" in ethics, the doubtfulness of an absolute separation between questions about the meaning of good, and about what things are good, the moral status of pleasure, and the meaning of "Naturalism".

Chapter Fourteen

The Last Fifteen Years
(1958-1973)

On March 14th 1958 the Kolnais moved to their final home at 24 Hilltop Road, West Hampstead. Although the Clifton Hill flat had been a little nearer to central London, Hilltop Road was much more convenient, since it was nearer to a variety of shops and to various forms of public transport. The Kolnais' flat occupied the top floor of a three-storey corner house, part of which had been bombed in the war and later rebuilt. It was spacious enough for their needs, with a large living room (where Aurel slept), a bedroom, kitchen and bathroom and a small hall or landing. But the huge areas of Victorian speculative housing and often dingy shops that surrounded them probably contributed greatly to Kolnai's sense of the squalid ugliness of London, which greatly depressed him. Even the close proximity of three different railway lines could not make up for that.

There were other things about England that seriously grated on him. More than once he mentions "the deep moral perversion" - most characteristic of the middle classes - of despising any determined effort to eat well, and found the badness of "English institutional food (to be) without parallel".[1] Another serious irritation was English "discretion" and reticence, and the class system. This probably explains his attitude to Jane Austen. Kolnai found this "Philistine totalized into a genius" unreadable, and was repelled by the suffocating world of "absolute self-contained snobbery" portrayed in her novels".[2] One consequence was that the Kolnais' social contacts tended to be with fellow Hungarians, or else with younger people not yet wholly absorbed into "polite society". It seems that, though Kolnai was fairly good at "playing the Englishman" occasionally, if only to avoid being seen as an exotic "specimen" of the Austro-Hungarian Empire, he could not relax into the role, and yearned to express his peculiarities in anarchical ways. The first time he met his Hungarian doctor's wife he took his leave with the words: "Madam, I hope you will forgive my saying so, but you seem to me like an Apfel Strudel." Mrs de Tószeghi, was, according to her husband, delighted with the compliment.

Kolnai also greatly disliked the National Health Service. In his experience the English GP simply examined the patient and handed out prescriptions, whereas he wanted to *discuss* his complaint and its cure, and to be treated as a knowledgeable amateur. Hence the large number of medical professionals consulted by him (and sometimes befriended), and the fact that virtually all of them have Austro-Hungarian names.[3] It is easy to get the impression from Kolnai's constant references to ill-health that he was a hypochondriac. In fact he was a connoisseur of illness, in himself or others, observing the subtle differences between febrile sensations of different origins, and longing to be able to show his doctor "interesting" symptoms (for example, those of the second stage of syphilis - "without having sinned", of course).[4] The same extreme sensitivity was at work here as in all his phenomenological awareness.

Despite the undoubted drawbacks he saw in England, Kolnai registered as a British citizen in 1962. A strong inducement towards this was the quality of English academic life. Almost as soon as he could, Kolnai joined the Aristotelian Society, regularly attending its meetings and the "Joint Session" weekends with the Mind Association, and the papers read at the Royal Institute of Philosophy. He was also subscribing by 1970 to the *British Journal of Aesthetics* and the *Philosophical Quarterly* - also to Dr Williams' Library - and went to philosophical lectures at the British Academy as well as philosophical meetings in the various London colleges. He continued also to be in demand as a speaker at philosophical society meetings outside London, including, in 1971, the British Society for Phenomenology. He was somewhat scathing of this group, calling it, in a letter to Klaus Hartmann, the *"sich phänomenologisch nennenden Gesellschaft"*[5] (the society that calls itself phenomenological), because of the prevailing interest in existentialism and other aspects of the phenomenological movement he could not approve. Although Kolnai's own papers were sometimes far too long (he once spoke to the Cerberus Club at Balliol College, Oxford, for an hour and forty minutes), his verbal comments from the floor at meetings were often excellent. I have already said something about his attitude to the prevailing fashion of "linguistic Philosophy". Here are some of his brief comments on certain prominent philosophers he heard and met during the years 1956-59. They come from a letter to George Lanyi:

Both [R.M.] Hare's and (even more, though his is I think the finer mind) [P.H.] Nowell-Smith's ethics are much too positivist for my taste.

Bernard Mayo ... is a first-rate moralist, strongly trained (like everyone else) in LA [linguistic analysis] but with views strikingly akin to mine.

John Niemeyer Findlay, who may "easily" be the foremost philosophical mind in the UK, is a Hegelian atheist mystic with a superabundance of Common Sense ...

[Karl] Popper ... For all his wilfulness, waywardness and self-admiring arrogance, a very great genius.

Michael Polanyi (whom I've never met; though an anti-Bolshevist and a strong one, he is on good terms with Karl [Polanyi] and would probably refuse to mix with me), in spite of some tendency to irrationalist obscurantism, is a most original mind (his critique of the critical attitude is more than remarkable in a man of Liberal substance), of course also schooled to some extent by LA as every decent person should be.

H.B. Acton, not a pure, much less a fanatical LA-yst; I should think his centre of gravity was Common Sense with a tint of robust yet flexible Liberalism.

John Austin ... is the *fine fleur*, the filigree subtleties' master, of LA, almost a gourmet of idioms I would say, and although delightful ..., an outstanding example of the danger which many "adherents" fear is overtaking their mental world in the shape of anaemia, sterility, not to say scurrility.[6]

Kolnai also expressed great hostility to Philippa Foot and Iris Murdoch, as moral philosophers actively championing immoralism. Foot, who promoted human "flourishing" as the criterion of right conduct, was an obvious target. But his frequently expressed hostility to Iris Murdoch needs more explanation. A typescript in the *Nachlaß* consists of some very brief notes on Murdoch's paper "Metaphysics and Ethics".[7] From these it emerges that, in Kolnai's eyes, she was guilty of a grossly irresponsible account of the main ethical positions current at the time: "'Natural Law' [was] identified with Naturalism and contrasted with Liberalism", and "The most systematic exposition of modern liberal morality [was said to be] Existentialism". Apart from that, she confused the autonomy of ethics with the ("Kantian or Existentialist") moral autonomy of the individual, promoted the idea that moral cognition relied on "irresponsible, incommunicable, unarguable *vision*", and appeared to deny one of the keystones of Kolnai's ethical position, that, despite absolutely unavoidable differences of "perspective" between individuals and groups, all mankind inhabits the same moral universe. In another very brief paper Kolnai sets out what he takes to be the really crucial division of ethical theories, that between "'Universalizability' and 'Totality' Types of Ethics". The former is basically "commonsensical", with "intuitional, deontic, axiological, etc." variants, and is primarily characterised by its refusal to speculate about the "nature and destiny of the world".[8] The latter include "Marxist, Utilitarian, Scientistic-Evolutionist, Religious and Occultist" theories, which all assume that "the world is moving towards a goal", and that furthering or identifying with that goal "is the standard of morality". Existentialism actually repudiates this, but, says Kolnai, latently postulates it, as Sartre perhaps reluctantly accepted when he turned Communist. Kolnai's hatred of Murdoch, then, was strongly linked with his abhorrence of "gnostic" totality-type ethics and the essential kinship between these and Existentialism.[9]

It is clear, then, that Kolnai was anything but uninvolved in the professional concerns of British philosophers. But, in spite of this, he remained on the periphery of things. What is more, his manner and often unusual way of approaching a topic was such that even thinkers fundamentally in sympathy with him would fail to realise the fact, and thus overlook him. For example, when challenged over some point he had made, he would all too often avoid a direct confrontation by returning to his topic from some new and totally unexpected direction, thus all too often disarming his critic. Even when engaging in linguistic analysis he might confound his opponents by instancing usages from foreign languages they were not familiar with. In short, most of his colleagues found it very difficult to penetrate beyond his peculiarities so as to have a genuine dialogue with him. One wonders, for instance, what the bulk of his audience really made of a paper called "The Logic of Sex", which he read in 1963 to a group of philosophers at London University. In 1969 Kolnai himself called it

a highly original paper (completely free from ethical points of view) except for one important stimulus received from Scheler's *Wesen und Formen der Sympathie*. It definitely interested [David] Pole, who was my Chairman, and even more so, Findlay and Prof. Silber, but nobody else.[10]

One report mentions that Professor Findlay "nearly fell off the bench laughing"; another records that it contained an elaborate vision of "goats coupling on the slopes of the Carpathians". Professor Silber, Kolnai tells us elsewhere, encouraged him to submit it to the *Philosophical Review*, but he decided not to, "mainly, to be frank, from laziness".[11] There was certainly some element of self-protection in these eccentricities. I have already mentioned his fear of Strawson's "sarcasm". He also tells Lanyi (completely mistakenly) that he has won Bernard Mayo's "lasting antipathy" for criticising some of his views, and in some private jottings written on the occasion of the Joint Meeting at Cambridge in 1961 he records with satisfaction that, having "strongly attacked" Philippa Foot two years before at the Aristotelian Society, he has now made peace by "address[ing] some friendly words to her".

Things were not always greatly different among his immediate teaching colleagues. At Birmingham in the academic year 1961-2 Kolnai undertook to give a weekly two-hour class on Social Contract theories, and to engage in some more informal teaching, such as graduate supervisions. He was also expected to contribute to the Muirhead Society and the Metaphysical Circle, where he tried out early versions of his papers. But he spent very little time in the department, and his colleagues' reactions conform to the general feeling about him. Professor Duncan-Jones called him "a very able man". Bernard Mayo agreed with this, adding that Kolnai was "unusual", "rather an austere personality", with "an incisive manner in discussion".[12] Margaret Boden, then a young lecturer, recalled him to Mayo as "a *very* weird and cadaverous person, with old-world politeness but a very off-putting air". Alec Fisher, studying for a higher degree, could not recall the content of Kolnai's teaching but recalled his lecturing seated and bowed in on himself almost "in the foetal position", his legs preternaturally entwined. His habit of chain-smoking hand-rolled and evil-smelling cigarettes seemed disagreeable even in the early 1960s.

Reactions were certainly more favourable on Kolnai's home ground. As I have already recorded, both of Acton's successors in the Bedford College Chair valued and ensured his continued presence on the teaching staff. In general, colleagues appreciated his humour and charm, his inexhaustible fund of reminiscences and fantastic sallies, and they were also aware of the learning and wisdom underlying them. Nevertheless, there was a subtle atmosphere in the department of Kolnai as a kind of mascot or "institution" - certainly full of wisdom and fun, but too exotic for complete assimilation. This may remind us of Kolnai's own defects as a teacher. He does not seem to have changed in this respect. "Kolnai's appeal as a teacher was far from universal", we read in Williams and Wiggins' introduction to *Ethics, Value and Reality*:

> He spoke in his lectures without regard for the limits of time, timetable or the philosophical or historical incompetence of his audience - and with a degree of sophistication, indirection, qualification and playfulness which was always beyond the comprehension of at least half the student body.[13]

As in Quebec, most of the students gradually absented themselves, so that only one or two, or even none, might attend. But there was usually someone in the class who felt that he could not be left in the lurch, and he or she (usually she) would be treated to a solitary lecture.

Some people, however, got a great deal out of his teaching. As Williams and Wiggins go on to say: "Within another and smaller group ... his lectures and classes became the object of dogged and loyal persistence, even cult".[14] Kolnai usually took the second-year ethics class. After a time he also undertook a few graduate supervisions, where he might well again give what was in effect an improvised lecture to a solitary hearer unless the student concerned was particularly insistent on conducting some kind of dialogue. Where Kolnai always gave exceptionally good value for money was in his extensive written comments on a student's work. In his lectures he sometimes encouraged students to feed questions to him, which he would then sit back and consider in a leisurely fashion, and talk round them until he had produced answers that satisfied him. But any student who felt confined or disappointed by the prevailing understanding of philosophy in English universities might find Kolnai an inspirational teacher. Thus Peter Ayrton, a student with "revolutionary" tendencies whose views on many things differed greatly from Kolnai's, was one those drawn to him by his readiness to give due attention to important questions that many English philosophers would have dismissed as non-philosophical.

Kolnai approached his lack of teaching success by reifying it. "The attendance output is lugubrious", he reports to Professor Williams, "...even apart from the transfer of about one half of the students from Ethics to Political Philosophy".[15] But he observed his students minutely. "(Miss A) is studious but somewhat immature, and I am not sure that philosophy is what she is specially made for"; "I feel the presence in (Mr B) of some kind of incurable childishness and alienness; yet on the other hand he has done much reading and ... has been working diligently and with an effort to penetrate the matter"; "I credit (Mr C) with quite extraordinary gifts for philosophic thinking, ... and also with an earnestness of spirit, resolve and sustained interest that are probably exceptional". His communications with the head of department nearly all betray his lack of ease in face of his (much younger) superiors. Thus he begins his report to Bernard Williams: "May I submit my report about Lent and Easter terms. I am doing so with a shocking delay, and can only offer shamefaced apologies for this dereliction of duty." It then turns out that he has been "indulging in" "pneumonic fever". Nevertheless, he ends his report "with repeated apologies".[16] It must at times have been very difficult to discover whether Kolnai was being serious or not, though Williams and Wiggins' attribution to him of "an exact sense of the academic worth of individual students"[17] implies that they could completely rely on his assessments. If it is then asked why he did not impress very many people during his lifetime, we have surely to seek the answer in two things: his originality and his "timidity". Findlay made no bones about the former in his prepublication comment on *Ethics, Value and Reality*. "Kolnai's writings are of astonishing originality", he wrote. But originality by itself may be overlooked; coupled as it was with timidity and awkward mannerisms it would be surprising if it had been widely appreciated.

Acton found Kolnai "easy to get on with", as did most of Kolnai's Bedford colleagues, though he could sorely try their patience when buttonholing them, say, in the department office to tell them an anecdote that was fresh in his mind. He heartily disliked academic socialising, though would appear at official welcomes and farewells. But probably none of them got to know him intimately. David Lloyd-Thomas, for example, and his wife Anne, who was at one time taught by Kolnai, sometimes went to dinner with the Kolnais, and occasionally induced them to pay a return visit, but they learnt very little about them, and never knew that Kolnai had serious dietary problems. When Professor Acton left to take up his Scottish chair in 1964 he expressed the hope that the Kolnais would visit him and his wife in Edinburgh. But Kolnai himself never seems to have done so. However, when he sent his former chief "The Concept of Hierarchy" in 1970 he enclosed some of his drawings - though cannot have been over-pleased when Acton, with some justification, suggested their kinship with the figure-style of Francis Bacon. The main exception to all this was Doreen Tulloch, by whom and Ruby Meager (who lectured at Birkbeck College and shared a house with Tulloch) he was often treated to a convivial dram of whisky (Kolnai rarely over-indulged).

But, as I have already pointed out, he much enjoyed the company of intelligent and unconventional students especially if they were also good-looking. Most of these seem to have been women, with many of whom he enjoyed flirting - "outrageously", according to one of them - with a licentious twinkle of the eye. Whatever this kind of conduct really meant, it did not take any palpably physical form. With many of his student friends he seems to have talked very frankly and openly. He obviously talked far more to the handsome and revolutionary Peter Ayrton about his life (though avoiding "personal" questions) than to any of his older colleagues. Ayrton, for example, was perfectly familiar with his psychoanalytical phase, whereas Brian O'Shaughnessy, a Bedford philosophical colleague who lectured on Freud, and appreciated Kolnai, seems never to have heard of it. Ayrton and he had many political arguments, often in the café at the Wigmore Hall, or while walking in Regent's Park. Another postgraduate student at the college in the late sixties was Rose Dugdale, who was later imprisoned for robbing her parents to secure funds for the IRA. Before this, she too was a friend not only of Kolnai's but also of his wife. What makes all this especially remarkable was that "Student radicalism", rife at the time and outspokenly championed by both Ayrton and Dugdale, greatly upset Kolnai, and "affected (his) digestion".[18] Publicly, he might treat it in his usual calm and understated way. Yet, in a letter to the Lanyis he says that, unlike George, he can only live alongside the New Left by concealing his hatred and dissimulating.[19] After his heart attack in 1970, he tells Wiggins that he would be happy to attend the graduate seminar again, though he was "not, of course, willing to participate in neo-Marxist ideological propaganda".[20] It seems likely that, while he was prepared to keep company with student radicals, what he could not stomach were, say, university Marxists living comfortably on bourgeois salaries and at the same time corrupting their pupils through their teaching and writing.

Two female mature students he particularly liked were the mutual friends Doreen Vaughan and Cynthia Read. The three of them would occasionally have tea in a café in Baker Street, where Kolnai enjoyed using his Spanish to one of the waitresses ("what I really like about Spanish is the use of the subjunctive", he solemnly explained, in his deliberate and emphatic manner, provoking the ladies to peals of laughter). Cynthia Read used regularly to accompany him to art galleries, cinemas or theatres. She describes how he would suddenly stop in the gallery, or even in mid-street, if something struck him forcibly which he wanted to communicate, so that spatial advance was sometimes tardy. This was frequently exasperating, though his comments on art were always worth hearing. The first time Kolnai formally "took her out" he hastened to reassure her: "I shall tell my wife ... not that she will think I have committed adultery, even if I were capable of it, which I doubt!". The letters to Cynthia Read contain many variations on the theme of her eyes, like those of a certain rare breed of dachshund, and much play on the lunar associations of her Christian name. He once sent her a deep and subtle analysis of the saying "Honesty is the best policy". This contains the following passage on "duty for duty's sake":

I suggest that it is hardly logically possible to conform to Duty purely and simply for its own sake, as my love for Duty *necessarily* implies love for a number of goods, values, desirabilities, aesthetic appreciations, references to my own status, etc.; without the complex background formed by which, Duty would lose all meaning except that of an empty "command", obeyed blindly as it were because it is a command *and nothing else*. This is what makes the core of Kant's ethic so unnatural and inhuman - though he fails to uphold the principle consistently.

The legitimate meaning of the maxim is, to my mind, "To be ready to comply with the moral demand at the cost of unpleasantness and damage to one's interests if necessary"; but that is a vastly different thing.[21]

The sequence of letters to Cynthia Read up to May 1970 strongly suggests that Kolnai fell in love with her, though he never "declared himself". He told Doreen Vaughan that Cynthia meant even more to him than his wife, and "wondered whether he ought to take things further". Understandably, she could not make out whether he was serious or not.

Kolnai's address book names a good many Hungarians resident in London. These included Edith Bone, former member (as Edit Hajós) of Lukacs's "Sunday Circle", who was given seven years solitary confinement by the Hungarian Communists for her outspoken criticisms of the regime,[22] and the philosopher István Mészáros. There was also his old friend Bela Menczer, whom he saw regularly until his death, though constantly complaining about him in his letters to George. He would also quite often see the Vámbérys, as they passed through London, and occasionally his old class-mate György Kovács and his German-speaking Czech wife Sophie, for whom Kolnai once wrote a personal Hungarian text-book, larded with much scatological humour. Others who passed through included Erzsébet, widow of his friend Milán Füst. Kolnai composed for her a personal "cicerone", or guide, to London. He also wrote a "real English" grammar and course-book twelve years before for Eszter Kelemen, the daughter of Mrs Scheiber, an old friend of his boyhood. Eszter had visited him to talk about religion, but Kolnai was very much taken with "her original, tart and berry-like person",[23] and exchanged a few flirtatious letters with her. These contain some of Kolnai's risqué rhymes, but he knew that anything he wrote would be passed on to the circle of friends around her parents and the Kovácses, whom he had long entertained with his nonsense. He had already become firm friends with Vera Réz, who had come to London in 1956. She had been in Ravensbrück concentration camp during the war, where she was beaten up and suffered from typhus. She had professional psychological and educational interests, and had already given him first-hand news of this circle.

One well-known Hungarian he was most reluctant to meet again was Arthur Koestler. He was a friend of Paul Winkler, who repeatedly urged him to see this literary celebrity, from whom he might expect help in publishing something that would pay. Kolnai resisted this pressure for a time, but eventually gave in and went to see Koestler. There was no real meeting of minds, despite Winkler's predictions, but it seems likely that Kolnai's long article in the *Rheinischer Merkur*, which appeared the following September, was occasioned by this visit. The article laments the failure of the Austro-Hungarian Empire to reach its fulfilment in a

Danubian federation, or similar grouping.[24] Before this he was in contact with a couple of free Hungarian journals, *Látóhatár* (Munich) and *El Centinela Húngaro* (Buenos Aires), but he does not seem to have published in either. He did, however, address the Hungarian Catholic Academic Circle in London in 1967, treating them to a lecture on Christianity and Natural Science. The same year he got into contact[25] with an old gymnasium classmate in Budapest, Jenő Vértes, who regularly convened those of the class who took their *Abitur* together for a convivial evening. Vértes's letter[26] shows that Kolnai's original communication, with its vivid reminiscences and thumbnail portraits of individual boys, had caused a sensation when it was read out in the group, since, until then, they had had to rely on vague rumours of his doings. He had obviously been especially keen to hear about his old friend Andor Berei, who had lost much of his former political power in Hungary. Vértes's letter ends with his expression of surprise that Kolnai overlooked the one classmate of his who was resident in London, Jani Strasser. Four years later Dr Gáspár Soltész took over the convening, and wrote reminding Aurel of their meeting in Vienna in 1924, and of the literary competition described in the first chapter.[27]

Between 1958 and 1973 Kolnai went abroad every year except 1965, usually for about a fortnight, and sometimes more than once. He always went alone. When Spain ceased to be the obvious place to visit he turned to the Low Countries, and especially Belgium, which he had discovered in 1958. Belgium became for him "an ersatz Spain and Austrian Empire" (in accordance with its Habsburg past) and Brussels a substitute Madrid.[28] From there he made many excursions, even crossing the German frontier to Aachen to buy cheap German "Eckstein" cigarettes. His chief occupations abroad were city walks, very selective eating and drinking in cafés and restaurants, and visiting mediaeval churches. In 1966 he offered a communication to the French language philosophy conference at Geneva, and was able to revisit Bern and Fribourg. His Utopian Mind reading trip to Köln, Freiburg, Zürich and Strasbourg the following year was a business-only affair, and he had his annual holiday in the Low Countries in the early autumn. This urge to get away from England every year had, as its obverse, an indifference to holidaying in the British Isles. He would briefly explore the old Cathedral cities, if professional invitations made it possible, but the only extended visit he paid in England was to Cornwall in 1972. Kolnai had long wanted to see it, but it is doubtful if he would have done so had not Sarah Lumley-Smith, a favourite and very faithful student of his, persuaded him to come for a week. However, he would not stay in her parents' house on the edge of Bodmin Moor, but took up his quarters in a hotel in Fowey, and much disappointed her father by refusing to be drawn into philosophical discussions. On another occasion, when Ruby Meager took him and Alan Lacey, a Bedford College colleague, to Swansea by car for the Joint Meeting in 1967, she made a detour up the Wye Valley, a celebrated beauty spot. Lacey recalls his total indifference to the sylvan scene unfolded outside the vehicle for his own special benefit. His dislike of the country was rammed home to Kolnai's old boyhood friend, his cousin József Litván, who asked him where he would like to stay on a visit to Vienna, which he paid for. "Anywhere in the city centre or the third district, but, for God's sake, not in the country!", was Kolnai's answer.[29] He went in 1972, passing on to Graz and Innsbruck, and then unwinding at his home-from-home, Brussels. In a letter to Acton he says nothing about Vienna, but told him that he had

> fallen furiously and pathetically in love with Graz ... the City of Meinong ... and also, if certainly not the City of Moore, at any rate the City of the Mur ... the most marvellous of swift-running mountain streams I have ever seen.[30]

But his most exciting foreign trip was to Marquette University, Milwaukee, Wisconsin, during the first half of 1968, and the associated visits to Oberlin, Chicago, Quebec, Ottawa, Montreal, Providence, R.I., and New York. The person chiefly responsible for the university's invitation to his six-month Visiting Professorship was John Beach, Kolnai's Laval student and friend, who now taught in the Marquette philosophy department himself. He was soon beset by anxieties. All seven preparatory letters to Beach seem to raise some new worry, and an enormous amount of space is devoted to minutious specification of the kind of flat he considers desirable. He was anxious, too, about the content of his graduate course in Political Theory, a topic which, compared to ethics, seemed to him "boundless", primarily because

> the separation between the philosophical and the "materially scientific" is much more artificial and dubious in Politics, perhaps mainly because Politics constitutes a domain of Practice ("activities") whereas Morality does not, concerning as it does all Practice seen from one prominent valuational point of view.

He goes on to speculate why Professor Simmons should have dubbed him "quite a guy", and suggests it was probably because he had confessed (in his letter) to intemperance in Belgium "not in *Cerere* and *Baccho* and much less in *Venere*, but in walking". "Overwalking", he goes on, is perhaps the purest clinical example of Intemperance as such, since its intrinsic *materia* is altogether noble (at least in Spain or Belgium or in Bern) with no trace of baseness attaching to it..., wherefore it displays the blameworthiness of Excess merely in virtue of being Excess.

"There is further", he goes on somewhat inconsequentially,

a good deal of moral "problematicness" not in Fever itself (which lacks even an innuendo of agentiality) but its enjoyment (however reluctant) and now the occasional moods of woefully missing its unique and unmatched ecstasy, a kind of nostalgia incompatible with being "fully" virtuous. It is, no doubt, perilously germane to the vice of Sloth.[31]

Kolnai sailed on January 12th 1968 on the S.S. *United States*, arriving in New York on the 17th. He stayed a few days at the Henry Hudson Hotel, and spent some time with Elisabeth's cousins Yvonne and, especially, Vera Lanyi. Vera had married a man of the ancient family of Zolnay, but was now divorced. After the Hungarian Uprising she and her son Tom had left Hungary for Stockholm, where another cousin was Professor of Physics at the University; in 1957 they moved to the USA, where George Lanyi helped them towards gradual independence.

Once arrived in Milwaukee, Kolnai moved first into the Beaches' house while he looked for a suitable flat. He soon found a good ground-floor one, strategically situated for campus, public library ("fantastic Hungarian section"), cafetaria, supermarket and church, and secured the services of a Danish maid for three hours a week. His teaching duties comprised the two 75-minute sessions a week of his graduate political theory course and two one-hour sessions of ethics for undergraduates. A letter to George mentions two bad things, positivist and "hippy priest" colleagues, and two good, Hungarian apricot jam provided in the student "dive" where he breakfasted and freedom from breathlessness.[32] John Beach felt that the graduate students liked Kolnai, and the undergraduate student assessments, which followed him to England in the summer, seemed to indicate more positive than negative responses. Despite this, Kolnai himself felt he had "lost ground" as a college teacher. However, his special lecture to the Faculty, "Are there Degrees of Ethical Universality?", was well received, and there was a general feeling that he would be welcome to make a return visit. While he was at Marquette, the faculty paid for his attendance at a philosophy conference at Oberlin. Naturally he stayed with George - now a full Professor of Government - and Susi, in whose rural garden at one corner of the little planned town he was entranced by the beauty of a pair of cardinal-birds. Kolnai must have felt especially relaxed in the Lanyis' company. For all his occasional epistolary asides about George's being a "Central-European-type family-worshipper", and even a "trimmer",[33] he knew well enough what he owed to them, that they would never "let him down", and that George's "trimming" tolerance was based on genuine good will. He also admired, with not a little envy, the "normal" and successful career of a man who was "widely acknowledged to be a leading member of his field".[34] He also admitted some intellectual influence, and their mutual affection was continually strengthened by the exchange of doggerel verses and other nonsense.

On June 27th Kolnai left for New York, where he reported himself as "sweltering, boiling, sizzling".[35] He had earlier refused the Vámbérys' invitation to California, pleading, amongst other things, that the journey would be too difficult and that he wanted to see "old films".[36] After a short reunion with Elisabeth's cousins - "the Sisters, call them Merciful or Weird" - who took care of some of his baggage, he went on to Canada for two weeks. Although he was going to Quebec to stay with the Tremblays, he must have approached it with considerable apprehension. Yet he was later able to write: "the fortnight I spent in Canada was … something like a continuous state of bliss".[37] He had, of course, received reports of it in London. Jeanne Lapointe had visited the Kolnais while passing through in 1957; he had met some of the Germain family there in 1964. At some point Thomas DeKoninck, son of Kolnai's "boss", had called on the Kolnais with his fiancée; almost the first thing Kolnai did was to point "proudly" to London cats visible through the window, and wonder why they found this amusing. But an even more significant meeting had occurred at the French language philosophy conference in Geneva, where Kolnai had spent some time with two of his old enemies from the philosophy department, André Côté and Eugène Babin. Babin had given him a tie and Côté had called on the Kolnais in London on his way home.

Now, in 1968, despite his feeling that "the Thomist frenzy seems to have but very slightly abated",[38] his spirits were buoyed up by his Visiting Professorship. He was even able to meet Mgr Parent ("a bit aged and withered; 'more human', as Mrs Simard said") without any noteworthy recurrence of the old bitterness. He also met Côté, who now also gave him "a very fine tie", and one or two of his former friends, notably Jeanne Lapointe ("one of my greatest loves in spite of her abominable 'liberal' views") and, of course, his hosts. But he missed all the Germains and also DeKoninck, who was probably in Europe. But this "reconciliation" with Quebec - two years later he was admitting that he had "not been wholly guiltless" in the matter[39] - may well be one of the things that later prompted him to write his fine paper, "Forgiveness".

In Montreal, he spent much time with the Menzers and other friends, and was enthralled by the new rubber-tyred Metro. On his way home he stayed briefly with Mgr Ibrányi, now living at Providence. In New York he saw quite a lot of Elisabeth's two cousins and Yvonne's aged mother. In his letters to George all three women are portrayed as seriously neurotic, and Kolnai afterwards kept recalling various odd remarks the three had made (especially Vera, for whom he had a soft spot). The general opinion of the family was that he had "done Vera good"; he is sceptical, though does not think he did her any harm. Highlights of the dreaded sea voyage home (August 6th to 12th) were his discovery of Baked Alaska, and the chance to speak Spanish to a Catalan woman who was homesick for her country.

In the brief interlude between his arrival in London and departure again for his annual Brussels jaunt - drawing now for this on his "banker", George Lanyi, who was administering the $3,000-odd he had saved from his Marquette earnings - the Kolnais entertained Michael and Cate Beach, John and Sunny's children, to dinner. This was the first of several visits for Cate during her time at drama school. She recalls him talking away imperturbably at table, his head moving unpredictably about, while Elisabeth bustled in and out of the kitchen, frequently chiding him. Cate, who was very young at the time, felt she didn't get a lot from him, but always enjoyed Elisabeth's warm welcome.

The letters to John Beach during the next few years give a good picture of his concerns. There is firstly the question of another visit to Marquette in the year 1970-71, with at least one further year if everything went well. Kolnai accepted this in principle to Beach in November 1968, and, in his letter of Easter 1970, announced that he was "psychophysically fit" for at least a year, and ready to brave the Milwaukee winter. But now the Marquette department faced an unexpected financial shortfall, and Beach looked for ways of sharing the expense. Kolnai was eventually faced with the possibility of dispersal between philosophy, politics and theology. His letters express his impatience with Beach's apparent injunction to keep off "political controversies". He could either do "dry philosophical analysis of moral and even political topics", he writes, which in fact *is* anti-Communist, or, better, anti-totalitarian (as in ethics one cannot analyse special obligations and mankind's recognition of these without "some hint of a pro note") or else he could give "a more explicit defence of Constitutional Democracy ... against fashionable criticisms of it". What else could he be expected to do?[40] But by the time he wrote this last passage he was already recovering from his first heart attack, and writes as though there could now be no question of another visit, though Beach was all for keeping the question open. In the event, the complicated project had to be dropped. Kolnai naturally put the worst possible interpretation on all this, repeatedly expressing his - entirely erroneous - conviction that the head of department didn't want him.

Kolnai's letters also show very clearly why Beach might have felt anxious about "political controversy". For all his dry and sober analysis of politics as a form of human practice, and, for that reason, as bound to make room for legitimate differences of opinion, Kolnai always gives the impression of being ready to *fight* for his beliefs, as though some thematically moral issue was at stake, to which there could only be one rational answer. The political passages of his letters are often related to one or the other of two favourite quotations. One comes from Borchardt's novel *The Conspiracy of the Carpenters*, and identifies the most essential ability of a statesman as "The capacity to recognise Anti-Christ". The other comes from Julia Ward Howe's "Battle-Hymn of the Republic": "as ye deal with My contemners, so with you My grace shall deal" - which Kolnai takes to mean that nation-states and their rulers will primarily be judged by the measures they have taken to render "the enemy" harmless. At the time this could only be the Soviet Union, whose power and influence were spreading all over the world, and anyone who contributed in any way to this expansion. Thus, he writes much about United States Presidential candidates in the 1968 and 1972 elections, and their attitudes to the Vietnam war. This *unum necessarium* could lead him to some rather unexpected judgements, as a letter of April 21st 1970 shows. Having lamented the "great electoral victory of the socialist curs in London" in the local government elections, he says that if, *per impossibile*, the Conservative Norman St John Stevas and the Labour MP George Brown were to contest his constituency in the forthcoming general election he would vote for Brown - and this despite the facts that St John Stevas is "a highly intelligent 'liberal' [Catholic], in religious respects quite akin to me" and that Brown is a "loathsome cocky socialist". The reason is that Stevas, writing in the *Catholic Herald*, predicted the "smooth surrender of South Vietnam to the Reds" "with a smile of cynical approval", whereas George Brown

> was the only man to say literally and publicly to the Yanks: "Get on with the war and turn a deaf ear to their barking" ("They" were the people "morally indignant" at some American "atrocities" perpetrated on certain hapless, "neutral" Vietnamese civilians.)

As a result, he adds, he wouldn't mind "being clubbed to death ... in a Cheka cellar" if only Stevas were with him, so that he could enjoy the sight of the same fate being meted out to him; so "Three cheers for good old

Georgie Brown, and may his erring soul ultimately be cleansed and ascend to Glory!".[41]

As the 1972 Presidential election approached, Kolnai became convinced that the Democratic candidate, George McGovern, who advocated immediate and unconditional withdrawal from Vietnam, would win, since the Eastern Establishment media, the universities and the anti-authoritarian youth culture were all on his side. (In this he erred, and, as George Lanyi predicted, Nixon was reelected.) In the summer he wrote to John Beach as follows (the passage is strikingly similar to one in a letter to Robert Vámbéry a month before):

A military *coup d'État* preventing [McGovern] from being installed in office and the setting up of a severe military dictatorship ought to be prepared without delay ... Certain puerile excesses ... of the primitive fascisms of the past should be avoided. Thus, I would not persecute Negroes as such, only "professional Negroes", "emancipators", "civil rights" and "integration" people and the like. Hold down the Irish and the Jews discreetly but consistently. About 80 per cent of the universities and colleges I would transform into concentration camps with a very strict regime for former students, staff, leftist intellectuals and other traitors. The remaining universities and colleges I would place under firm and trigger-happy military rule. The speedy annexation of Canada and Mexico would seem advisable. I would establish a unitary Federal criminal law, with capital punishment not only for traitors and subversives but a great number of hippies, drug-addicts and perverts. I would drastically reduce public expenses for "cultural" muck and increase armament expenses six or sevenfold. Invade France and restore order there; not that the French deserve it, but the Russian occupation of western Fringe "Europe" would make "Fortress America" indefensible. I would refrain from palaeo-fascist person-worship à la Mussolini or Hitler, and justify all measures with references to the Founding fathers; also, use as a civilian façade some of the few honest politicians such as Goldwater, Agnew, Strom Thurmond, Buckley, perhaps Henry Jackson and Connally. It would be very important to show at an early date that McGovern owed his superabundant means largely to enemy subventions; some documents could be ferreted out, many others should be forged cleverly - without scruples.[42]

He then proceeds to sketch out his own "long-term programme", which is substantially the same as that projected in the unpublished Spanish papers described in chapter twelve, though in this case he has abandoned the monarchical element, and calls it "an entirely new type of republican-democratic constitution". It would be a mistake to think there was nothing serious in all this. The fan-letter addressed to "The Honorable Barry Goldwater, U.S. Senator from Arizona" (a "quixotic ideologue and ... extremist", says Paul Johnson),[43] a copy of which is among the letters to Beach, was actually sent. Four years before he had written: "Is America, is Western Civilization morally dead for ever? It seems likely." But, if there is still any hope, recovery will "require oceans of blood".[44] To George and Susi Lanyi he wrote:

> Like a man who stands essentially at a distance from the Bourgeoisie but who would pour out his blood and give his life for their defence and safety, I am naturally, in a formal but very essential sense a typical fascist. But I am anti-fascist in the sense that I put the Rechtsstaat [the Constitutional State], which only exists on civic soil, above everything ... I want to surpass the enemy in sternness, in the will to exterminate and in merciless persecutory rage ... but in lying and deceit, irrational sectarianism, self-worship, etc., perhaps in distinctive psychic structure, I am not willing to compete with them and imitate them. This is where I completely differ from fascist demagogues and leaders. Only where an *ad hoc* choice has to be made would I choose those things, with a bitter after-taste, in contrast to the real enemy, and thus with merely passive tolerance.[45]

Kolnai was clearly puzzled by the fact that so few of his fellow-thinkers seemed to share his views. Here is the substance of one brief meditation on the general topic: Why are intellectuals (almost of the essence) such fools and rogues [sc. In the matter of Vietnam]? Perhaps because thought raises man to a high plane and encourages the growth of unfulfillable, perhaps delusory, expectations. Again, pacifists hate defence more than attack because it is defence that generally brings about a state of war. And it is the reds that talk of perpetual peace, despite the unprecedented slaughter needed to attain it.[46]

Kolnai's first heart attack took place in the evening of May 24th 1970. He was rushed to hospital that night, and allowed home after about two weeks. When he wrote to Beach he says that if there *was* a psychic cause it was his sense of hopelessness at the world situation.[47] Although he had to ask the college for a ground-floor room because of the weight of his winter greatcoat (there was no lift), and had a slight relapse towards September, he was back at Bedford for the new term, and doing quite well by Christmas, though his projected inter-collegiate lectures had to be cancelled. By the following September Elisabeth reported him in quite good health, though getting tired easily.[48] The intercollegiate lectures took place as planned next

Lent term, but in the New Year of 1973 he wrote: "This is a bad winter for me and I feel very paralysed", but the problem now was not so much his heart, or the general feeling of hopelessness about the political situation, as "a tenacious febrile bronchitis". To make matters worse he was worried by the problem "how far physical weakness is grafted on characterological laziness".[49] Kolnai had hoped to write a German essay on "The Conservative View of Being and Value" for a collection edited by Gerd-Klaus Kaltenbrunner. This would have complemented the published paper "Konservatives und revolutionäres Ethos", which Kaltenbrunner published in a volume misleadingly entitled (in German) "The Reconstruction of Conservatism". But, despite much laudatory encouragement by Kaltenbrunner, and Kolnai's intention to write it, if possible, in January and February 1973,[50] he was never able to find the strength for this concentrated effort, and the only piece he published in his last half-year was the short conference communication "La Función Moralizadora del Derecho".[51] However, he did find the energy to make a selection from the works of the early nineteenth century French *idéologue*, Joseph-Marie De Gérando, for a Brazilian encyclopedia. He seems to have completed the selection very quickly, and was paid £58.20 for his pains. He continued to take his class at Bedford College, and occasionally to attend graduate seminars. His last, very "personal", paper in preparation for one of these, written some time in the early Spring, and consisting largely of his own reactions to the topic under discussion,[52] shows that he felt his end was approaching. In fact, he died in hospital of a second heart attack on June 28th and was buried in Hampstead Cemetery after a requiem mass at the Church of the Sacred Heart.

Elisabeth Kolnai survived her husband by about eight years, dying in 1982. She made up for her loss by devoting herself almost entirely to trying to get Kolnai's work better known. She had various helpers in this endeavour, but relied heavily on David Wiggins. Despite her poor state of health, she had an inward toughness that enabled her to keep going after countless disappointments. She was a sad figure, in many ways, but it must be said that, whatever was the exact nature of the relationship between Aurel and Elisabeth, he owed an enormous amount to her, possibly the last thirty-three years of his life. Whatever fundamental comfort she had during the time of her widowhood came from the practice of her religion.

***

Kolnai's writings during his last years show a wider range of topics than at any other time since his early days in journalism. His contact with the arts had always been intense and highly selective, but only now did he publish material on aesthetics. His first paper in this field is "The Concept of the Interesting".[53] There are parallels between it and his early paper "On the Mystical", the key to this link being his artistic preference for what he calls in a letter to Vicente Marrero "Magic Realism",[54] which is opposed to both Classicism and Romanticism. The new paper is an excellent example of how well Kolnai took to philosophising in the English mode, and combines conceptual analysis with well-argued claims to the effect that, though "interestingness" is more "reflective" and "cerebral" than beauty, it is nevertheless a genuine, objective, aesthetic category. After a detailed consideration of five "aspects", he asks whether there is a central principle of interestingness, and finds it in "the experiential mode of *transcendence*", our experience of "the fact that this world is so made as to render it possible for us to look beyond it; to stray, in fantasy, beyond its fragile and tremulous frontiers into outlying twilight zones". Thus, the interesting is set apart both from what is really important, and also from the amusing or entertaining, though there is a kinship with both the fantastic and the comic. The paper is enlivened with many examples. It was probably after he had submitted this paper to the *British Journal of Aesthetics* that the editor, Harold Osborne, successfully asked Kolnai to review Roman Ingarden's book, *Ontologie der Kunst*. Despite Kolnai's fears about his incompetence in aesthetics, both Ingarden and Osborne were full of praise for "The Concept of the Interesting", and Osborne encouraged Kolnai to produce the longer piece he had suggested, probably on the ontological aspects of art, which he felt Ingarden had mishandled. However, he did not return to aesthetics until, in 1970, he wrote his long paper "Aesthetic and Moral Experience", which was published in two parts in 1971 and 1972,[55] and then in unitary form in *Ethics, Value and Reality*. This densely written paper provides what is probably Kolnai's best general treatment of axiological questions. After an introductory passage on the tendency of many languages to conflate beauty and goodness, he compares moral and aesthetic values with four other types of value: instrumental values, ontological or metaphysical perfectional values, the values of "cognitive correctness, wealth and depth" and hedonic values. He then contrasts them under five heads: the range of their possible bearers, contemplative versus practical emphasis, the availability of rules (especially in relation to objectivity and disagreement), the thematic primacy of values and disvalues, and finally the "non-existential" character of the aesthetic as opposed to the urgent "existential" character of moral values. "The Dream as Artist",[56] Kolnai's third - and rather slight - paper in the aesthetic sphere, was composed as a short presentation for the annual conference of the British Society of Aesthetics, which, in 1972, was held at Bedford College. It is possible that the subject of dreaming occurred to him because he had, two years before, been provoked by Norman Malcolm's "preposterous" theory of dreaming - that the only reality possessed by dreams is that of the "dream reports" of waking persons - into writing a short sketch of refutation. Be that as it may, Kolnai starts with a formal ontogical claim of Hans Driesch, that dream is a third "domain of being" after reality and fantasy, but, unlike these two, has no proper indication of itself, but "usurps" that of reality. He then goes on to explore the similarities and differences between dreams and works of art.

Kolnai's two French "communications" for the francophone philosophers' conferences of 1964 and 1966 in Belgium and Switzerland respectively were probably both composed in connection with intended holidays. Like "The Sovereignty of the Object", they approach epistemological topics from a primarily ethical pont of view, though both, especially the first, contain echoes of contemporary academic issues current in the United Kingdom. "Error and Truth"[57] raises the question why we care so much for truth, when the very idea has been considered "redundant". The answer is that care for truth appears thematically as care to avoid error; in this sense it is part of the moral virtue of veracity, though it is usually only thematic in practical contexts. "Is linguistic integrity an indication of moral integrity?"[58] explores the sense in which a person's language is a general indication of his character. He clearly shows the link between veracity and clarity of expression, and hence of thought. Evil virtually always relies on confusion and obscurity, whereas moral purity involves making clear distinctions between good and evil. Kolnai does not overstate his case, but it seems likely that in both papers he was indirectly commenting on the modern tendency to de-moralise the life of the mind.

Amongst the moral philosophical papers Kolnai published in this period, the most important is undoubtedly "Moral Consensus",[59] which is an essential part of his whole "intuitional" or "intrinsicalist" undertaking. The idea received brief treatment towards the end of "Erroneous Conscience", and, a year or two later he read the first version of his paper at Birmingham in 1959, and benefited from the ensuing discussion. The published paper, revised ten years later, really has two parts. Most of it is concerned with establishing, refining and defending the idea of a "moral consensus of mankind". The first part, however, is more fundamental, since here he argues that moral judgements are, by their very nature, "consensual", and already contain an oblique appeal to "mankind". Kolnai is, despite his support for the intuitionists, very far from being an intuitionist in any purely intellectual sense. Moral judgements certainly "claim(ing) a cognitive status", but they also "include a factual reporting of (our) own emotive response", and are thus "essentially less objective" than, say, perceptual judgements, or even judgements of "the wrongness of an inference". When a person makes a moral judgement he does not speak simply for himself, but expects "others" to agree with him, since, after all, he learnt his morality from "others". This is bound up with the fact that there is a "very close though not quite simple or uniform connection between moral experience as such and the experience of reciprocity, mutual responsibility, and 'demands' both binding upon the moral agent and represented by him in relation with others". Underlying this opening section there is the idea of fundamental shared human concerns (hence the essential involvement of feeling), with which morality is in various ways closely intertwined, and which it is one of its "functions" to protect. But there is an essential openness about this relationship, precluding the idea that any formulation could ever fix it. Kolnai's brief outline of the content of moral consensus begins with quasi tautological formal principles, such as (I translate the Latin) "do good, avoid evil, keep your word", and with rules still seemingly grounded in abstract reason, such as the Golden Rule (especially in its negative form: "Pittakos's rule"). He then alludes to more concrete very general principles, such as: benevolence is good, malice bad; veracity right, mendacity wrong, and similarly with respect for others and arrogant self-assertion, self-respect and servile self-surrender, ... dignity and meretricious cynicism, magnanimity and cruelty, chastity and lust, self-control and intemperance, honesty and dishonesty, fidelity and treachery, loyalty and treason. Lastly, he stresses that moral appraisal primarily refers to intention rather than consequences or motivations. He then reminds us that moral laws cannot provide "sure and handy directives for doing right in every practical situation; what is absolute is the validity and claim for earnest consideration of all moral points of view, everywhere and in all circumstances". This basic consensus can of course be greatly distorted by factors of ethos, that is, the differential weight accorded by different groups to particular principles, because of the nature of their immensely variegated specific and local (practical) concerns. But despite the moral alienness afforded by some social milieux, the basic "person-to-person field subject to the claims and category-pattern of moral standards" is always somehow actualisable; where human beings meet, there is always the possibility of their penetrating the demands of local practice, and realising the fundamental moral bond which unites them. The anthropological base of Kolnai's thesis (a feature of his university dissertation) emerges once more in the claim that this consensus is a relative, not rigidly permanent, constant in the general perspective of human change. It is subject to "basic structural changes in the human condition". What we are faced with then, is a "quasi absolute".

Shortly before he read "Moral Consensus" in the Aristotelian Society he happened to meet his old friend **Ferenc Fejtő in Kingsway**. During the course of their conversation Fejtő scolded him for never having produced the definitive "Outline of Ethics" which, he told Kolnai, "only he could write". A week or so later Kolnai reported this incident in a letter to Claude (brother of Thérèse) Germain, whom he had also met about the same time. Among Kolnai's papers there is a photocopy of a hand-written manuscript entitled "Moral truth: inchoate sketch of a theory of Morality". Elisabeth Kolnai dated these notes to 1937, but it seems to me more likely that they were composed, or at least revised - they were certainly written out - much later, since the Moral Consensus theme is fully worked out here. They may well have something to do with the *magnum opus* Fejtő had scolded him for not having written. Kolnai argues here that the basic meaning of morality is "the affirmation of self-distance", and that this is expressed in both its formal and material aspects. Formally speaking, the moral agent must always stand lightly to his "concerns", to the "self" otherwise happily immersed in its own practical interests; the "split" in the human person must always be at least potentially activated. Materially speaking, self-distance works out as the demand to submit to what is not myself; to objective "fittingness" in justice, to the well-being of other beings in benevolence, to the needs of my "spiritual" as opposed to my "appetitive" self in temperance. Kolnai also shows that his continual insistence on the partial, or limited, rationality of morality is also accounted for by self-distance. If there were a rational key to morality we could make it our own, identify with it, or operate with it mechanically, in such a way as to eliminate the need to stand vigilantly back from ourselves. But this would be to fall asleep morally, and above all to renounce the sphere of positive moral performance and dedication to high ideals and lofty pursuits, which Kolnai calls the sphere of "self-transcendence", where no general rules can apply. Self-distance must ultimately be interpreted as the affirmation of moral status and true human worth, that "precious possession" that can be lost so easily by one vile act, and recovered only by an act of painful contrition.[60]

Another unpublished paper which seems to belong with the two papers just discussed is "Are there Degrees of Ethical Universality?", which he read to his colleagues at Marquette in 1968. As the title may suggest, there are many references to the earlier work of R.M. Hare, in which Kolnai was very interested. In the first section he argues that Hare's "universality", or "universalisability", should really be interpreted as material consensus, not as a mere "logical precondition". This is the first principle of ethical universality. He then suggests that pure universality, implying rigorous exclusion of particular references, cannot exhaust the moral sphere. He goes on to explore three kinds of "toned-down universality": supererogation, without which the ordinary universal morality of basic principles will very likely decay, moral authorities and paradigms, necessarily implying "particular affinity or proximity", and thirdly "loyalty rules", implying allegiance to particular persons, communities, and so on, to which no special note of moral superiority can be attached.

"Forgiveness"[61] was written in 1972, his last published paper in English. It is personally very significant, since Kolnai's moral style had, in general, little room for any "soft" response to injury. After some initial analysis of terms, the paper begins, in typically Kolnaian fashion, with the presentation of a "logical dilemma" of forgiveness: "Either the wrong is still flourishing, the offence still subsisting: then by 'forgiving' you accept it and thus confirm it and make it worse; or the wrongdoer has suitably annulled and eliminated his offence, and then by harping on it further you would set up a new evil, and by 'forgiving' you would only *acknowledge* the fact that you are no longer its victim". Forgiveness, then, seems to be either unjustified or pointless. However, after an examination of various cases he concludes that, in general, forgiveness is "legitimate and virtuous" when the injured party "has at least some reason to hope for *metanoia* on his injurer's part" and that this will indeed be made easier by the act of acceptance. This "venturesome pursuit of value" is, after all, an expression of *trust* in the world - an attitude which may denote "the epitome and culmination of morality", and one which is also given its due place in his dissertation.

"A Defence of Intrinsicalism against Situation Ethics"[62] was written in 1967 for a collection edited by R.L. Cunningham, a former Laval pupil. Although Situationism (which equates morally right action with "doing what is best in the particular situation with its peculiar circumstances" as opposed to "action in conformity to a moral law") was at the time primarily championed by Christian thinkers, Kolnai discusses it, with many useful comparisons and distinctions, alongside other varieties of "one-principle" and non-formal theories: antinomianism, existentialism, utilitarianism and especially neo-Thomist "Prudentialism". All these are "reformist" attempts to substitute a simplistic schema for ordinary moral experience. In the case of Situationism the single principle is usually "love" (or *agape*), a tricky psychological concept which, Kolnai argues, cannot provide the individual with adequate moral guidance without his having recourse to the principles whose intrinsic validity the situationist is so concerned to deny. The paper includes useful discussions of moral responsibility and its link with consensus, legalism, the relation between love and justice, and the special nature of sexual immorality.

Among other ethical papers, the short review-article of J.N. Findlay's *Values and Intentions*[63] is well worth reading, as is "Jottings on Personalism". This, and a companion lecture-outline of 1932, is of special interest as a condensed summary of Kolnai's own constant personal "ideology", though he never wrote a proper paper about it.[64] Among unpublished ethical papers so far unnoticed is a long and perhaps slightly laboured "draft" of 1965, which discusses "Two opposite ways of using descriptive-evaluative terms" (one person is, say, quite happy to talk about a "justified theft", another, agreeing in his non-negative evaluation of the act, refuses to call it theft at all), and goes on to discuss Aristotle's theory of "apparent good" (his attempt to cope with the fact that some goods are acquired by immoral means). He also left behind him his notes for the Intercollegiate Lectures he gave in March 1972. The first two are largely about one of Kolnai's great philosophical heroes, Franz Brentano; both "Brentano's Place in the History of Recent Philosophy" and "Brentano's Ethics" are largely expository and interpretative, the former containing a great deal of information about thinkers still largely unknown in the Anglo-Saxon world. The third lecture, "Some Features of Phenomenological Ethics", reveals more of his own preferences, especially in his exposition of the nature of phenomenology, and includes useful though brief discussions of the ethics of Scheler, von Hildebrand, Nicolai Hartmann and Hans Reiner.

"The Concept of Hierarchy", published in 1971,[65] had already been accepted for *Philosophy* when Kolnai was asked to read a paper at the annual conference of the British Society for Phenomenology in the early part of that year. Having no time to write something new he read a shortened version. The theme itself had constantly occupied him since at least 1941, especially the social need for multiple human "hierarchies" symbolising the various domains of value, which he regarded as an essential prophylactic against the otherwise almost inevitable tendency of democracy to collapse into totalitarianism. These views are certainly present here, but they occur almost incidentally alongside much other material, and his tone is more "philosophical" and less obviously *engagé* than, say, the parts of "Privilege and Liberty" that deal with social hierarchy. For instance, in a section called "The paradigm of the raised position", he discusses its dangers for mankind in general. Man's inherent spirituality and intellectuality makes him despise the "lower"; his "expanded and enriched conspectus" of things necessarily involves "a less intense contact with reality", and an unjustified "disdain" for the distinctive wisdom of "the common people". In a section on the Hierarchy of Values he offers a critical discussion of Scheler's treatment of "Nobility" values, and of Hartmann's thesis that the height and strength of values are in inverse proportion to each other. There is some connection between this paper and "Dignity",[66] which was first read in 1969 to a London University philosophy group, since Dignity is a response to "Height". When the paper was read, Gabrielle Taylor provided a reply, and Kolnai wanted to rewrite his own paper (which gives in part a somewhat rambling impression) in such a way as to deal with the points she raised in opposition to his own. But he never got round to it, and the paper was published posthumously in 1976, virtually unaltered. Though it is largely a straightforward analysis of the idea, the connection between human dignity and human rights provided a kind of political sub-plot, to which he alludes in a letter to the Lanyis.[67] While conceding the existence of "Human Dignity" (closely connected to human rights), a quality possessed by any human being whose humanity has not been in some way destroyed by, say, torture, drugs or disease, and whose recognition or preservation can therefore be "demanded" of others, he is perhaps more concerned to exhibit the independent importance of "Dignity as a Quality". This is a value whose presence, absence and degree depends rather on our conduct, going closely with things like rational self-control and a spiritual "centre of gravity" (the links with Kolnai's "Personalism" are clear). In an interesting section on the Undignified he claims that "the core of Un-Dignity ... is constituted by an attitude of refusal to recognize, experience and bear with, the tension between Value and Reality". As in "The Concept of Hierarchy", there is a substantial "axiological" section, in which he shows that Dignity as a Quality is an ontological value, with moral and aesthetical overtones. There also exists a substantial unpublished paper in Spanish, "La dignidad humana, hoy" (Human dignity today), dating from around 1960, where the religious background of the two concepts of dignity is also explored. He here makes the point that "human dignity", as opposed to "dignity as a quality", is primarily based on power.

"*Konservatives und revolutionäres Ethos*" was written in 1971,[68] and develops some of the material of "The Moral Theme in Political Division", written over ten years previously. Unusually for Kolnai, the paper has copious scholarly footnotes (the writing of which, he told Hartmann, brought him "torture and despair").[69] After surveying a few inadequate attempts to distinguish conservative ethos from that of the revolutionary, or leftist, in general, Kolnai approaches the contrast through the familiar opposition between affirmation of continuity, order, authority and hierarchy, and then pluralism, on the one hand, and criticism, progress, rational reordering and equality, on the other, exhibiting the underlying dialectical development of either set of axiological emphases and preferences. As far as morality itself goes, he finds no clear division, but, as regards moral theories, assigns both authoritarian and intuitional-axiological ethics to the right, whereas perfectionism can be both leftist and rightist, and each camp has its own differing interpretation of utilitarianism and monist formalist theories. The ethical difference can be summed up in the idea that the conservative moral critique of society is directed at human conduct *in* society, whereas the revolutionary criticises the institutions *of* society. Where the conservative proves himself superior to the revolutionary, says Kolnai, is in his ability to accept that the existence of his opponent's critique is a good thing. Thus, though the best contribution of the revolutionary is the critical spirit, the conservative is able to meet this not just *as* a conservative, but from a position of critical distance. The "patience" thus exemplified shows the ultimate superiority of this ethos. In the last section Kolnai develops what he takes to be the foundation of conservative thought - trust in God, which makes possible trust in man, with its power to create trustworthiness. The conservative version of the *Rechtsstaat* is "freedom and equality in the face of the moral law, which protects all in their differences and applies to all alike".

Kolnai's own conservative ability to accept the validity of his opponent's point of view comes out clearly in an unpublished manuscript sketch of 1957, "Waste-book: Political philosophy", which contains much discussion of the Moral Appraisal of Institutions, and the admission that the values of Justice and Injustice are not wholly confined to actual human conduct. Thus conservatism does not oppose the moral critique of existing conditions as much as the claim to create conditions out of moral demands. Among the many other topics discussed here are the limits of a sensible equalitarianism: the "moral demand for social justice" emerges as the demand that "the *de jure* stipulations of equality, as such, shall be *de facto* enforced". This practical defence of civic status derives from "awareness of the socio-economic marginal postulates of citizenship". Another unpublished political philosophical paper, "Universality and Political Attitudes", was read to a Bedford College seminar in 1964. It is related to "Games and Aims", described in chapter thirteen, though it begins with the relations between morality and politics. These are summed up as follows: "The proper principle of political taking-sides is not the weighing of greater and lesser obligations or even of non-moral objective goods but a weighing of the agent's greater and lesser concerns here and now, though in the typical and more developed forms of such a choice his relevant concerns will be other-regarding and specifically public-directed rather than merely self-regarding." This paper contains an interesting discussion of "Party", with some criticism of Hume's well-known essay. He then turns to the general paradox of competitiveness, especially in spiritual pursuits like philosophy: "Dissent as I may, say, from Plato and Spinoza, Nietzsche and Sartre, I would not only refrain from having them shot or forbidding them to publish, but even hesitate to wish they had never existed."

"Identity and Division as a Fundamental Theme of Politics" was first read to the Cerberus Club at Balliol College, Oxford, in 1967, and published posthumously.[70] This strongly analytical paper deals in fact with three "fundamental themes" of politics: "interests" or supposed "given" identities, where some self-regarding note is virtually inescapable, "ideas" or "ways of life", which involve response to value, and "identities" proper, in the sense of groups we identify ourselves with, the choice being almost necessarily arbitrary to some degree in the face of conflicting appeals. In a final section Kolnai sketches out his own "conservative-libertarian" preference for plurality, the play of tensions, and "qualified and multiple allegiances". This follows, he explains, as a consequence of his view of the individual as the "ultimate social reality", yet an inescapably social being who has to adopt some social identities. Among Kolnai's political papers, his substantial review of Michael Oakeshott's "Rationalism in Politics, and Other Essays"[71] must not be forgotten. Though an admirer of many aspects of Oakeshott's book, Kolnai could not overlook its "undeniable touch of obscurantism". Clean-slate "rationality" is indeed bad; but this must not lead to our banishing reflective thought altogether from practice.

Two further papers on aspects of Practice remain to be mentioned. In 1967 Kolnai read a paper to the London branch of the Philosophy of Education Society of Great Britain. The occasion of this invitation may have been a passage in "Games and Aims", where Kolnai says that the "pedagogical questions" (and commands) employed by teachers in their teaching exhibit "some manifestly game-like features" and are, to that extent (here he refers to the phenomenologist Adolph Reinach's book, *Die apriorischen Grundlagen des bürgerlichen Rechts*) un-genuine. "The Justification of Commands"[72] is a philosophical meditation on the "logical oddness" of teachers justifying their commands to their pupils. Understanding the reasons for commands is, of course, part of education, but so is "willing obedience to legitimate authority". There are no rules that will help the teacher to know when reasons are or are not appropriate. "Advising"[73] was written around the same time for a staff seminar at Bedford College. Though Kolnai says this was a "success" when read,[74] it was rejected by *Philosophy*, and probably not submitted by him elsewhere. It begins with a characteristic Kolnaian survey of various ways of getting other people to do things. Some of these are straightforward, but there is paradoxy in advising, since the adviser has to think in a practical mode "within a framework of another's concerns".

"The Standard Modes of Aversion: Fear, Disgust and Hatred" was also written for presentation at Bedford College in 1968.[75] It had been requested by Professor Wiggins for those of his colleagues who wished to know something of the untranslated "Der Ekel" (Disgust). Kolnai also added to the original material some of the contents of his paper on hatred ("Versuch über den Haß"). The later paper adds little to what he had already said in the original German papers, which are described in chapter 10, but forms a useful summary, and has now been published at Wiggins' suggestion twenty-five years after Kolnai's death. "Agency and Freedom" was written in 1966-67 as part of the annual lecture series on The Human Agent at the Royal Institute of Philosophy, and published in 1968.[76] It has very little in common with the earlier Spanish paper on the Positive Meaning of Liberty. There is, however, an unpublished paper called "Voluntas per se est Liberum Arbitrium", probably written around 1952 when Kolnai was writing his Memoirs, which anticipates most of the themes of the published paper. "Agency and Freedom" has a realist-phenomenological basis: our experience of free will cannot, "in common sense ... repose on mere illusion ..."; in so far as free action has to be "determined" by something, it is determined by the act (not "action") of free will - least misleadingly described as a sort of personal "decree" or "fiat" - and definitely not by, say, "the strongest reason". Reason never commands the will; it merely enlightens and informs it. He then goes on to defend the independent reality of an "act of will" against the thesis that this is merely the first phase of the action it is supposed to determine. Nor is "free will" the same as "agential power", despite the fact that "choice directly effective" is the "very core of free will"; it is in fact the expression of "a focal and unified 'self', set at a distance from desires and impulses", and capable of "sustained will". Kolnai then goes on to defend the metaphor of "decree" or "fiat"; free will is at least "decree-like", and even though there is no alien addressee to receive the decree, some element of experienced duality in the person is inescapable, especially in the phenomenon of commitment, where our decisions take on a kind of detached "law-likeness" by which we feel bound. The paper ends with the admission that there is "a kind of illusion" in free will - despite "an indestructible 'nucleus' of freedom", and that our wills do seem to be constrained in various ways.

"Actions and Inactions" was written for a staff seminar in 1970, and never published. Kolnai begins by defining an inaction as "the absence of an action or a system of actions which emerges as a possible theme in the agent's practice and which he might be expected or predicted to accomplish ..." The main types of inaction are failing to comply with a duty, resisting a temptation and rejecting an offer. In terms of significance, voluntariness and deliberateness, they are on a par with actions. This long and interesting discussion is followed by sections entitled "the problem of mutual translatability", "the limits of translatability", and "the reality of inactions". In "Right and Wrong Actions and Inactions" he shows the limits of translatability in the spheres of moral supererogation, ordinary beneficence, and certain very serious wrongs, and shows how some moral values and disvalues tend towards action rather than inaction, or the reverse. He also interpolates a section on the relation between interest in moral philosophy and personal moral status. In a final section he looks at his theme in relation to justice and special obligations, the sphere to which modern moral philosophers increasingly tend to confine morality, defending the claim that "right abstentions and wrong commissions" obtains throughout. Apparent exceptions, like promise-breaking, can be made to fall under the generalisation when we realise - Kolnai admits the slight artificiality here - that making and keeping a promise is really "a single unit of conduct drawn out in time", and "the germ of the broken promise" is present in the original act of promising.

Appendix

Kolnai's Attitude to the Catholic Faith

No reader of Kolnai's Memoirs, especially the original version, can fail to be struck by the huge amount of space he devotes to his conversion to the Faith and his attitude to the "Catholic World" in general. Anyone with an interest in Christianity will find this account enormously stimulating and illuminating. At the same time, there is an unmistakably "aestheticising" feel to some of it. This slightly jarring note can be compared with the "externality" and "perfunctoriness" which Doreen Vaughan, for whom he acted as sponsor on her reception into the Church, detected in his religious practice. Ferenc Fejtő, close friend of his Paris days, who emphasised the fundamentally religious nature of his character, added that he was an "anarchical heretic". Again, when Eszter Kelemen visited Kolnai to try to discover how a remorselessly objective thinker could combine this with religious belief, he was quite unable to enlighten her. There is, therefore, something undeniably puzzling in his approach, and I shall try here to indicate the best way of understanding it.[1]

Kolnai's chief aim as a thinker and writer was to promote and defend the moral and full "personal" stature of man, and the social and political conditions which foster it. Just as his political writings are mainly directed against dehumanising politics, so many of his pronouncements on religion outside the Memoirs are directed against its anti-human manifestations. During the Schuschnigg clericalist regime in Austria, for example, he bewails the

> dialectical tension between the "spiritual life" of moral conduct, justice, devotion, scholarship, etc, and the assumption of "objectified" spiritual entities (God, Christ, even the Soul, etc), which somehow come to be treated with familiarity, as magic, quietistically, and which thus become a *substitute* for real engagement in spiritual themes.[2]

Clericalism is also often attacked with great vehemence because it threatens the cultural and political importance of the Church "as a sovereign [spiritual] Authority, limited in its range but incontrovertible in its proper limits", and also as "the other organized society - besides civil society -

with the unique meaning for liberty, reason and morality inherent in this very claim of embodied spirituality and in the sociological fact of this dual division".[3]

Attacks on clericalism often go closely with attacks on Thomism. One corollary of the latter is his frequently repeated support of Molinism, "the central working principle of the Christian faith".[4] This is not the place to explore this highly complex issue, which is still disputed by Catholic thinkers today.[5] But Kolnai supported the Molinist position on Grace (almost to the extent of accepting the Pelagian heresy)[6] because he thought that it upheld the commonsensical meanings of free will, moral evil, rebellion against God's will, and God's judgement and retribution, whereas the Thomists made the moral life a sham by their false interpretation of these things in the interests of their metaphysical scheme. Thus, the Thomists say that Molinist thinkers detract from the majesty of God, and from his nature as "Universal Cause". But Kolnai insists that "the judge is determined by the accused". Therefore God cannot be omnipotent or omnicausatory, since in his judgement of men he must *depend* on their free decisions. We may add here that Kolnai never attempts any *defence* of the idea of Hell, but stresses its positive aspects. The existence of Heaven and Hell shows that what we human beings do really matters, and gives us "a positional value in the universe".[7]

A passage on Tragedy and Christianity in one of his letters to the Spanish Catholic Vicente Marrero betrays the passion with which he could argue about these matters:

> There is no way of by-passing the fact … that not even God himself, the God-Man who submitted to the Passion for the salvation of mankind, could, or could want to, do away with the reality of sin … and of our earthly life as a *vale of tears* …

Of course, he continues,

> this led to "redemption, *Hope*, the Gospel", but it did not touch pain and death, it did not end the actual commission of sin or abolish Hell … Naturally there is no tragedy for the ignoble Aristotelian "God", the "universal causality" of the Thomists, who is not in the least "disturbed" if I sin or am killed or tortured; whereas the crucifixion engulfs the Christian God in the Tragedy of the World …[8]

The overwhelmingly *moral* emphasis of Kolnai's faith is clearly expressed in the following passage, written towards the end of his life:

If God exists, which I believe to be the case and could perhaps argue, but certainly not prove, I see and revere in Him mainly the Moral Legislator (or rather the supreme fountain-head of our moral orientation) and above all the Supreme Judge (that is to say, the Guarantor of the decisive weight of moral values in the order of reality).[9]

Compare with this the fourth type of moral value experience Kolnai identifies in *Der ethische Wert und die Wirklichkeit* - "the experience of directness". Kolnai explains this as "the concentrated experience of the Ethical as having the solidity of an individual substance". In such contemplative or mystical experiences "nothing matters except the absolute Good". If "religious experience" meant anything to Kolnai, then it probably took this ethical form, which may remind one of the Old Testament prophets, especially Isaiah.

Kolnai's paper "The Humanitarian versus the Religious Attitude" makes it clear that his primarily ethical understanding of Christianity does not imply a religious *as opposed to* a secular approach to morals, but a deepening, purification and enlightening of ordinary moral consciousness. When he discusses "The ethics of the Gospel" he emphasises the same complexity and balancing of opposed principles as emerges from his examination of ordinary moral experience.[10] He is also prepared to amend pronouncements attributed to Jesus where they seem to go against moral common sense. Thus, he repudiates the saying "Judge not that ye be not judged", and substitutes for it "Judge, and submit to judgement yourself".[11] I have already implied above his scorn for any religious "love" ethic, as though "love" by itself were enough to guide conduct. Christian charity comprises and presupposes all other moral virtues. For the same reason he rejects the "social" interpretation of the Gospel, seeing in this a fatal concession to the spirit of revolution, which always tends towards an undue concentration on welfare values and our animal nature at the expense of responsible liberty and personal life.

But an even bigger stumbling-block to the Faith among philosophers is probably doctrine, such as those of redemption, the Trinity, Christ's dual nature and the sacraments. Kolnai never attempts either a "critique" or a thorough explication of these things.[12] Indeed, he mistrusted the attempt to systematise the Supernatural, and, as he does in philosophy, professes his adherence to a "Religion of the Fragmentary". He seems to have accepted the sacramental life of the Church as the main instrument of salvation, and, provided his central moral and personalist insights were respected,[13] to have assented to the Church's teachings (albeit sometimes "uneasily and restlessly").[14] He would (as he does in the Memoirs) enlarge on them if they had some personal appeal or particular significance, as, for example, the doctrine of papal infallibility:

> I welcomed the dogma ... precisely in view of the sharp contours it gave to supernatural beliefs and the limits it set to their range. This I took to be the proper antithesis of an indefinite open attitude of "credulity" which, I thought, was liable to the most various kinds of insidious abuse.[15]

As for theism itself, this was barely more than common sense, and strongly indicated by a virtual consensus of mankind. But many of the doctrines which have often been considered to raise serious difficulties for the Christian thinker are hardly mentioned.

The fact is that Kolnai's understanding of faith is one not generally shared by philosophers, including the Thomists. The latter set much store by theoretical "reasoning" and "proofs", and are savagely attacked by Kolnai for doing so. For Kolnai, a believer's faith is not dispassionate conviction, "on its intrinsic merits and independently of [his] will, preferences and desire for happiness", of the truth of supernatural claims. But nor is faith "a pragmatic affair, a matter of the will dictating to the intellect". Rather, "faith implies a decision of the person as well as a self-contained operation of his mind". "We trust that God has actually and explicitly spoken to mankind and that the teaching authority of the Church does represent God's word", though of course this acceptance is continuously bolstered by "arguable evidences".[16] Should the church teach something contrary to all reason, or directly opposed to man's moral consciousness, Kolnai would reject it.

But are not, say, the Doctrines of the Trinity (God as three Persons, and yet a unity) and Incarnation (Jesus Christ as fully God and fully man) "contrary to all reason"? So far as I know Kolnai never presents an apology for these doctrines, but points (explicitly in the first case) to the function of dogma in excluding heresy, with all the moral and other corruptions it gives rise to. If pressed, he would probably have argued that these doctrines are attempts - based on Greek metaphysics - to formulate mysteries; they do not violate the rational life. In the same way he accepts the "real presence" of Christ in the Eucharist, but rejects any attempt to "rationalise" it. Once Kolnai had seen the personal necessity for belief in God and the Church, and the "intellectual suicide" of most modern philosophy, the rest followed - provided nothing fundamental to human experience was violated.

Notes

Abbreviations

Books

BM Memoirs	Béla Menczer's unpublished Memoirs, *Bread far from my Cradle*
EWW	*Der ethische Wert und die Wirklichkeit*
FP	*The Fallacies of Pacifism*
Notes	*Notes on the Hungarian Revolution of 1918* (see Ch.1, note 27)
PM	*Political Memoirs*
SE	*Sexualethik*
WAW	*The War against the West*

Newspapers and periodicals

ASPS	*Archiv für systematische Philosophie und Soziologie* (Berlin)
BJA	*British Journal of Aesthetics*
BMU	*Bécsi Magyar Ujság* (Vienna Hungarian News)
DV	*Der Deutsche Volkswirt* (The German Economist)
HS	*Húszadik Század* (Twentieth Century)
IZP	*Internationale Zeitschrift für Psychoanalyse* (International Journal of Psychoanalysis)
OS	*Der Oesterreichische Ständestaat* (The Austrian Corporative State)
OV	*Der Oesterreichische Volkswirt* (The Austrian Economist)
PAS	*Proceedings of the Aristotelian Society*
PJGG	*Philosophisches Jahrbuch der Görres-Gesellschaft* (Philosophical Yearbook of the Görres Society) (Munich)
ULTP	*Université Laval Théologique et Philosophique* (Quebec)
RUL	*La Revue de l'Université Laval* (Quebec)

Writers and recipients of letters

AK	Aurel Kolnai
BM	Béla Menczer
BW	Bernard Williams
CR	Cynthia Read
CDK	Charles DeKoninck
DW	David Wiggins
EG	Elisabeth Gémes, who in 1940 becomes
EK	Elisabeth Kolnai
EKW	Ernst Karl Winter
ES	Esther Simpson
GL	George Lanyi
GS	Gáspár Soltész
GSL	George and Susi Lanyi
GSz	George Szell
HBA	Harry Acton
IG	Irene Grant
IK	Imre Kinszky
JL	József Litván
KH	Klaus Hartmann
LG	Lisbeth Gombrich
MF	Milán Füst
OJ	Oszkár Jászi
RV	Robert Vámbéry
SL	Susi Lanyi
SP	Salvador Pons
TZ	Tom Zolnay
VM	Victor Marrero

Kolnai's memoirs

Kolnai's memoirs, originally entitled *The Barmecide Feast: Twentieth Century Memoirs*, underwent many abbreviations and alterations before Mrs Kolnai's death. They were then abbreviated once more by Dr Francesca Murphy, who produced the published edition under the title *Political Memoirs*. My references to these memoirs appear in varying form, as follows:

PM p.*n.*   reference to the published text
PM p.*n*   reference to the published text as it was when Mrs Kolnai died
(original)
PM   reference to a part of the text left by Mrs Kolnai which I have
(original)   not found in any form in the published text
PM   reference to a part of the text already detached or deleted
(omitted)   before Mrs Kolnai's death

Notes to Introduction

1   Kolnai kept very few letters written to him.
2   *Political Memoirs*, ed. Dr Francesca Murphy, Lanham, Boulder, New York, Oxford: Lexington Books, 1999.
3   AK to GL 6/12/52.

Notes to chapter 1

1   John Lukacs, *Budapest 1900: a Historical Portrait of a City and its Culture*, London: Weidenfeld & Nicholson, 1988, p.45.
2   A glimpse of it can be seen behind its more famous neighbour, the "Babocsay Villa", in a photograph in Gábor Eszter, "Ízlesváltas a Századfordulón", *Ars Hungarica*, 1989, 2, pp.169-78.
3   John Lukacs, op. cit. p.44.
4   PM p.4.
5   Ibid. (original).
6   AK to MF Christmas 1923.
7   PM p.3.
8   József Litván, *Ítéletidő*, Hungary, Tekintet, n.d. The quoted passages are on p.14, the photo on p.153.
9   Op. cit. p.15.
10 AK to GL 29/11/50.
11 John Lukacs, op. cit., pp.xiii and 64.
12 PM p.5.
13 Marginal note in *Situationism and the New Morality*, ed. R.L. Cunningham.
14 PM p.5.
15 This survives in an unpublished school exercise book entitled "1919-1920".
16 AK to GSL, New Year 1970.
17 AK to GSL 28/1/70.
18 PM p.4 (original).
19 PM p.5 (original).
20 Marginal note in Egon Friedell's *Kulturgeschichte des Ägyptens und des alten Orients*.
21 The writer is Arthur Bryant in his book *The Age of Elegance*. Kolnai's annotation follows. Kolnai bought the copy in London with money sent him by a Quebec friend, Jeanne Lapointe. It was understood that he would write comments in the margin of this and other books and send them to her. He also made this arrangement with other people.
22 AK to GL 10/7/48.
23 TZ to me 3/3/97.

[24] AK to GSL, New Year 1970.

[25] Ibid.

[26] PM p.10.

[27] PM p.14f.

[28] From *Notes on the Hungarian Revolution of 1918: Memories of the 1914-1918 World War: the Story of my first published article in H[uszadik] Sz[ázad]* (henceforth referred to as *Notes*). An incomplete version of the Hungarian text, edited by George Litván, was published in *Világosság*, XXXVIII, 5-6, 1997, pp.51-61. Other quotations from the unpublished English text follow below.

[29] AK to GSL, New Year 1970.

[30] AK to CR 3/5/70.

[31] Claude Winkler to me 19/2/95.

[32] József Litván, op. cit. p.14.

[33] "Universality and Political Attitudes", unpublished paper.

[34] *Notes*.

[35] PM p.20f.

[36] PM (original). Kovács was still alive when these were written.

[37] PM p.22.

[38] AK to GL n.d.

[39] I shall call it *1915-1916*.

[40] GS to AK 15/12/71.

[41] *Notes*.

[42] *1915-1916*.

[43] G.K. Chesterton's *The Napoleon of Notting Hill*, a novel based on similar ideas, only came his way in 1925.

[44] BM Memoirs.

[45] *Notes*.

Notes to chapter 2

[1] "Reflexiones sobre el Alzamiento Húngaro", *Oriente Europeo*, 27, 1957, pp.259-74.

[2] PM p.40.

[3] Polanyi, Karl, "Count Michael Károlyi", *Slavonic and East European Review*, XXIV, 63, January 1946, pp.92-97, p.96.

[4] PM p.39 (original).

[5] PM p.51.

[6] PM p.36 (original).

[7] Ibid. (original).

[8] Kolnai says he was a distant relation of his mother, AK to GL 19/8/50.

[9] Jászi, Oszkár, *Revolution and Counter-revolution in Hungary*, New York: Howard Fertig, 1969, p.23.

[10] Karl Polányi was brother of Michael Polányi, chemist, economist and philosopher.

[11] Karl Polányi, Karl, "Ötven Év", *Irodalmi Ujság*, 1/5/59 and *A Galilei Kör ötven Év Távlatából*, unpublished typescript from the Karl Polanyi Archive, Concordia University, Montreal.

[12] Kari Polanyi-Levitt and Marguerite Mendell, "Karl Polanyi: His Life and Times", *Studies in Political Economy* (Ottawa), 22, Spring 1987, pp.17f.

[13] Karl Polanyi, op. cit.

[14] Compare this comment on Jászi's editorial policy in *Huszadik Század*: contributions from many different positions were welcome provided they were "scientific" in

approach, a condition which, according to him, ruled out a priori any contributions from "reactionary" writers. Mary Gluck, *Georg Lukács and his Generation 1900-1918*, Harvard U.P., 1985, p.90.

15 PM p.46.
16 Mary Gluck, op. cit.
17 PM p.49.
18 PM p.21.
19 Francis Körmendi, *The Happy Generation*, translated by Claud W. Sykes, London: Nicholson & Watson, 1945.
20 Though Kolnai says in PM that they "had hardly any contact" at school, he had a little to do with him in the immediate post-school years.
21 *The Happy Generation.*
22 AK to IK 20/8/[17].
23 BM Memoirs.
24 PM p.47f.
25 *The Happy Generation.*
26 AK to IK 20/8/[17].
27 PM p.27.
28 *Notes.*
29 József Litván, op. cit., p.19.
30 *Notes.*
31 Mary Gluck, op. cit., p.102, emphasises the "intellectual fastidiousness" of the Radicals.
32 *Notes.*
33 Ibid.
34 Ibid.
35 Ibid.
36 Ibid.
37 PM p.48 (original). The full reference of Kolnai's first paper is "Aktivitás és passzivitás a kulturfejlődésben", *Huszadik Század*, XIX, November/December 1918, pp.309-22.
38 "Végcélprogramm és átmeneti programm", *Huszadik Század*, XX, March/April 1919, pp.156-58.
39 "Az állandó és változékony álláspont lélektanához", *Huszadik Század*, XX, May/June 1919, pp.217-22.

Notes to chapter 3

1   Tibor Hajdú, author of Ch XVI, Pt I, in *A History of Hungary*, London and New York: I.B. Tauris & Co Ltd, 1990, eds Peter Sugar et al., p.304.
2   AK to OJ 25/6/41.
3   PM p.55.
4   Ibid.
5   PM p.56 (original).
6   Ibid.
7   BM Memoirs.
8   PM p.58.
9   PM p.62 (original).
10 PM p.59 (original).
11 György Litván, "Vienne: capitale de la pensée hongroise en exil" (see note 1, ch. 2) p.203, says this was a 200-page ms on Marxism, Bolshevism and the possibility of a peaceable "Liberal socialism". It was never published.

[12]   This information and the quotations from Jászi's unpublished diary appear in György Litván, "'Sorai Ismét Választ Követelnek': Jászi Oszkár és Kolnai Aurél levelezéséből", *Világosság*, XXXVIII, 5-6, 1997, p.74.

[13]   AK to IK 8/2/20.

[14]   "Gnade und Gerechtigkeit", *Neue Gemeinschaft*, I, 7, 1919 (17th-24th November), p.1f.

[15]   "Entwurf eines Verhältniswahlsystems nebst persönliche Bezirksvertretung", *Nord und Süd*, Apr-Jun, 1920, pp.257-62.

[16]   Professor Michael Dummett.

[17]   "Ist das Volk zur Demokratie reif?", *Nord und Süd*, July-September, 1920, pp.18-23.

[18]   Personal communication from Ferenc Fejtő.

[19]   Kolnai probably called his imaginary kingdom after the Polish Jagellonian King who ruled Hungary in the 15th century.

[20]   Weininger's *Über die letzten Dinge* makes ethical concepts fundamental for all world-interpretation.

[21]   Paul Johnson, *A History of the Jews*, London: Orion Books, 1993, p.233.

[22]   I owe this assessment to the English-Hungarian poet and critic, Mr George Szirtes.

[23]   The influence of L.F. Ward is acknowledged here.

[24]   See Ray Monk, *Ludwig Wittgenstein: the duty of genius*, London: Jonathan Cape, 1990.

[25]   "Ki   : Otto Weininger" (Who was Otto Weininger?), *Tűz*, October 22nd 1922, p.3f.

[26]   Weininger's claim is also reflected in the "Ethical Aphorisms of 1919". One of them reads as follows: "In sex man is either the woman's plaything or makes the woman his plaything. It is the ruin of both".

[27]   Aurel Kolnai, *EWW*, p.116.

[28]   BM Memoirs.

Notes to chapter 4

[1]   PM p.73f.

[2]   Ferenczi to Freud 18/4/20. *The Correspondence of Sigmund Freud and Sándor Ferenczi*, vol. III, 1920–33, ed. Ernst Falzeder and Eva Brabant, Cambridge Ma.: Harvard University Press, 2000, p.16. I have used my own translations from the German.

[3]   Freud to Ferenczi 31/10/20. Op. cit., p.37.

[4]   The full references are: *Psychoanalyse und Soziologie: zur Psychologie von Masse und Gesellschaft*, Wien-Leipzig: Psychoanalytischer Verlag, 1920, p.115, and *Psycho-analysis and Sociology*, London and New York: Allen & Unwin, 1921, translated by Eden and Cedar Paul.

[5]   Theodor Reik, "Internationale Psychoanalytische Bibliothek", *Imago*, 7, 1921, p.196.

[6]   Aurel Kolnai, "A Tömegpszichológus Freud", *BMU*, III, 287, 1/12/21, p.6.

[7]   PM p.74.

[8]   Op. cit., p.76.

[9]   Paul Federn, *Zur Psychologie der Revolution. Die vaterlose Gesellschaft*, Wien-Leipzig, 1919.

[10]   PM p.76.

[11]   Ibid. (original). H.J. Sandkühler, in his introduction to *Psychoanalyse und Marxismus: Dokumentation einer Kontroverse*, Frankfurt a.M. 1970, where the article by W.Jurinetz, referred to below, is reprinted, also thought Kolnai's book was nothing more than an example of the possibly counter-revolutionary role of psychoanalysis.

[12]   PM p.78.

[13]   AK to MF 11/2/21.

[14] Jászi's diary entry of 17/6/21 mentions only "a young Englishman", but the fact that he gave Jászi some printed matter about Chesterton makes the identification almost certain.

[15] PM p.79.

[16] *IZP*, 7, 1921, p.531.

[17] "Az 'én' és a tudattalan lélek", *BMU*, V, 128, 3/6/23, p.8.

[18] Apart from the two articles already mentioned, he published a review of *Populäre Vorträge über Psychoanalyse* by S. Ferenczi, BMU, IV, 171, 23/7/22, p.6 and "A Zsidógyőlölet Pszichoanalizise" (The Psychoanalysis of anti-Semitism), BMU, V, 142, 20/6/23, p5f.

[19] "Zur psychoanalytischen Soziologie", *Imago*, VIII, 1922, pp.242-50.

[20] "Die geistesgeschichtliche Bedeutung der Psychoanalyse", IZP, IX, 1923, pp.345-56.

[21] Op. cit. p.355.

[22] Op. cit. p.349.

[23] Op. cit. p.354.

[24] "Gontscharows 'Oblomow'", *Imago*, IX, 1923, pp.485-494.

[25] Review of Franz Werfel, *Nicht der Mörder, der Ermordete ist schuldig*, in *Imago*, VII, 1921, pp.218-221.

[26] AK to MF 12/11/23.

[27] "Max Schelers Kritik und Würdigung der Freudschen Libidolehre" (Max Scheler's treatment of Freud's theory of Libido), *Imago*, XI, 1925, pp.135-46.

[28] Op. cit. p.146.

[29] Ibid.

[30] See note 20 for reference.

[31] AK to MF 5/11/24.

[32] Ferenczi to Freud 31/1/26. Op. cit., p.248.

[33] *Der ethische Wert und die Wirklichkeit* (Ethical Value and Reality), Freiburg i. Br.: Herder, 1927, pp.171.

[34] Op. cit. p.114.

[35] Op. cit. p.118.

[36] Op. cit. p.115.

[37] Ibid.

[38] Op. cit. p.116.

[39] "Eine Illusion der Zukunft", *Volkswohl*, XIX, 2, 1928, pp.53-56.

[40] *Die Zukunft einer Illusion*.

[41] "Thomas Mann, Freud und der Fortschritt" (Thomas Mann, Freud and Progress), *Volkswohl*, XX, 9, 1929, pp.321-27.

[42] "Die Stellung Freuds in der modernen Geistesgeschichte", *Die psychoanalytische Bewegung*, I, 1, 1929, pp.3-32.

[43] "Psychoanalyse und Marxismus", *Unter dem Banner des Marxismus*, I, 1, 1925, pp.90-133.

[44] H.J. Sandkühler, op. cit., p.296.

[45] "Über das Mystische", *Imago*, VII, 1, 1921, pp.40-70.

[46] PM p.77.

[47] Op. cit. p.68. "The Mystical" always remained important to Kolnai. Much later, he once jotted down a set of headings contrasting the Mystical with the Romantic. A few examples may suffice to convey his drift: "Mysticism as central religious-philosophical system" [R]: "Mysticism as aura surrounding the central content" [M]; "Irrationality as substance" [R]: "Irrationality as corrective" [M]; "Exalted irrationality" [R]: "Irrationality of secondary accents" [M]. The two basic categories are also coordinated with Utopian [R] and with non-Utopian motifs [M], e.g. "Community of Identity" and "Community of Alterity" respectively.

Notes to chapter 5

1   This is how Kolnai usually refers to him in later life. "Bácsi", literally "uncle", is (or was) frequently used by Hungarians when referring to older men, especially where there was some personal tie between speaker and subject.

2   At 11 Webgasse.

3   PM p.72 (original).

4   Quoted in György Litván, "Vienne: capitale de la pensée hongroise en exil", in *Vienne-Budapest 1867-1918*, eds, Dieter Hornig and Endre Kiss, Paris: Ed. Autrement, 1996, p.208.

5   Nevertheless, his diary records that he had time to write to Franz Oppenheimer on 12/12/21 in his efforts to promote Kolnai's book on Liberal Socialism.

6   György Litván, "Oszkár Jászi's Vienna Years and his Attempts to Build Contacts with the Democratic Left in the Successor States", *Danubian Historical Studies*, I, 3, 1987, p.15f.

7   Pacifista nevelés: review of *Erziehung zur Friedensgesinnung* by W. Börner, HS, XIX, December 1918, pp.348-49.

8   PM (original).

9   *Kulturpolitik, Weltkrieg und Sozialismus* by Paul Weisengrün, *Aurora*, II, 2, February 1921, p.176.

10 "Gefia" was an acronym: "Gesellchaft für allgemeine Industrie-Anlagen".

11 PM (omitted).

12 AK to MF 4/11/22.

13 Verbal communication György Litván.

14 Many of these details are from Györgyi Markovits, "Egyetemes kultúrvilágról álmodott: A Modern Könyvtár szerkesztője", Magyar Hírlap, 24/8/80, and László Sándor, "A *Tűz* évfordulójára", Magyar Nemzet, 13/12/81.

15 AK to MF 14/3/23.

16 Kolnai's articles are reprinted on pp.495-573 of a collection entitled *Egy gazdaságelmélet küszöbén Polányi Károly - Cikkek a Bécsi magyar ujságban 1922-1923*, ed Gyurgyák János (Budapest, 1985), where they were mistakenly ascribed to Karl Pólanyi.

17 BM Memoirs.

18 PM p.82 (original).

19 Jászi's diary for 13/1/22 records a visit from Kolnai with a letter from Franz Oppenheimer, who expresseed approval of part of the work (see note₅ above).

20 "A liberális szocializmus erkölcsi kiindulópontjai", *Aurora*, II, 2, February 1921, pp.91-98.

21 "A liberális szocializmus társadalomtudományi kiindulópontjai", *Aurora*, II, 3, March 1921, pp.208-22.

22 *Tűz*, I, 1-2, 1921, p.79f.

23 "Füst Milán: az Aranytál", *Tűz*, II, 1-3, 1922, pp.144-6.

24 "Krisztianizmus vagy keresztény kultúra?", *Tűz*, II, 1-3, 1922, pp.64-67.

25 Ibid. p.66f.

26 Ibid. p.67.

27 PM p.112 (original).

28 "A katolikus forradalmár" (The Catholic Revolutionary), *BMU*, 26/6/21, pp.495-97 (all *BMU* page references are to the reprinted collection referred to above).

29 "A destruktiv apát és az óvatos püspök" (The Destructive Abbot and the Cautious Bishop), *BMU*, 6/10/21, pp.507-11.

30 "Mereskovszki, az orosz katolikus", *BMU*, 16/2/22, pp.521-23.

[31] "Szocialista kereszténység", *BMU*, 14/7/22, pp.539-42.
[32] "Engels és Dühring", *BMU*, 23/4/22, pp.529-33.
[33] József Litván, op. cit., p35f.
[34] PM (omitted).
[35] József Litván, op. cit., p.36f.
[36] AK to OJ 5/3/44.
[37] For example, *In Quest of the 'Miracle Stag': the Poetry of Hungary*, ed. Adam Makkai, Korvina, Budapest and Atlantis-Centaur, Chicago, 1996, p.535.
[38] Another critic has likened Füst to Jeremiah.
[39] AK to MF 11/1/22.
[40] AK to MF 26/2/22.
[41] AK to MF 4/4/22.
[42] AK to MF 22/4/22.
[43] BM Memoirs.
[44] PM (omitted).
[45] AK to MF 27/7/22.
[46] AK to MF 3/8/22.
[47] AK to MF 4/11/22.
[48] AK to MF 20/11/22.
[49] AK to MF 1/12/22.
[50] AK to MF 14/1/23.
[51] AK to MF 14/3/23.
[52] AK to MF 9/7/23.
[53] AK to MF 2/10/23.
[54] AK to MF 3/11/23.
[55] AK to MF 12/11/23.
[56] AK to MF 11/12/23.
[57] AK to MF Christmas 1923.
[58] AK to MF 23/2/24.

Notes to chapter 6

[1] AK to MF 2/10/23.
[2] AK to MF 3/11/23.
[3] Lantos was an important bookshop in Budapest.
[4] PM (original).
[5] PM p.129 (original).
[6] PM p.130.
[7] This means, very roughly, the claim that thought, as opposed to sensation, always involves mental reference to objects outside the mind, rather than the treatment of ideas inside it.
[8] PM p.129 (original).
[9] PM p.131 (original).
[10] AK to MF 23/2/25.
[11] All objectivists, and, if not all phenomenologists, then closely allied thinkers.
[12] PM p.129.
[13] PM p.109.
[14] PM p.107 (original).
[15] *Der ethische Wert und die Wirklichkeit*, Freiburg i.Br.: Herder & Co, 1927.
[16] April 1928, p.468.

[17] EWW p.v.
[18] EWW p.122, note; although the quoted passage refers to experiences of value, it holds good for the work as a whole.
[19] Roughly the idea that there is an ideal order of values for each person in addition to the universal order; two values may be equal in rank in the universal order, but a particular individual will ideally prefer one of them.
[20] EWW p.vi.
[21] EWW p.5.
[22] EWW p.50.
[23] EWW p.57.
[24] The German word is *Bedürfnis.*
[25] EWW p.55.
[26] EWW p.14f.
[27] EWW pp.66-71.
[28] EWW p.97.
[29] EWW p.103.
[30] EWW p.108.
[31] EWW p.110.
[32] EWW p.130f.
[33] EWW p.142.
[34] EWW p.148.
[35] EWW p.154.
[36] EWW p.160.
[37] "Neigung, Pflicht und Gesinnung", *ASPS*, XXX, 1 and 2, 1927, pp.55-65.
[38] Op. cit. p.63.
[39] "Der Aufbau der ethischen Intention", PJGG, XLI, 1, 1928, pp.1-16.
[40] Op. cit. p.6.
[41] PM p.85.
[42] PM (original).
[43] PM (original).
[44] PM p.117.
[45] PM p.85 (original).
[46] See the appendix to this book for some more remarks about Kolnai's attitude to Catholicism.
[47] RV to me.
[48] AK to GSL, New Year 1970.
[49] There is a marked change of tone in the letters to Füst from January 1925, if not earlier, and the correspondence breaks off in April of that year until 1934.
[50] AK to IK, November 1926.
[51] Friends and relations assumed that it was sexually consummated, and knew that Irma herself would not have had serious moral scruples about this.
[52] *Sexualethik: Sinn und Grundlagen der Geschlechtsmoral* (Sexual Ethics: the Meaning and Foundations of Sexual Morality), Paderborn: Schöningh, 1930, pp.447.
[53] AK to MF 5/5/24.
[54] Including an interest in "the basic mathematics of [homo]sexual relations (numbers and combinations)"!, AK to RV 4/8/66.
[55] *Literarischer Handweiser*, 1930/31, 5, quoted in the publisher's blurb.
[56] SE p.2.
[57] SE p.3.
[58] In terms of EWW, it is a form of the "exclusion experience".
[59] SE pp.12-16.
[60] SE pp.16-18.

[61] SE pp.19-21.
[62] SE p.21.
[63] SE p.29.
[64] SE p.31.
[65] SE pp.34-42.
[66] SE p.42f.
[67] SE pp.43-49.
[68] SE pp.53-60.
[69] SE pp.60-67.
[70] SE p.72.
[71] SE pp.72-97; phrases in inverted commas indicate section headings.
[72] Weininger, he says, "has clearly seen something important, but irresponsibly 'absolutised' it through his failure to see still more important things". Footnote to SE p.109f.
[73] SE pp.97-123.
[74] SE pp.123-28
[75] SE pp.128-32.
[76] SE p.156.
[77] SE p.157.
[78] SE pp.160-66.
[79] SE pp.330-39.
[80] SE p.336f.
[81] SE pp.370ff. For "Corporativism", etc. see next chapter. Kolnai ascribes his book's greater success in Germany than in Austria to this polemical emphasis.
[82] SE pp.378ff.
[83] "Das sexualethische Weltbild der Gegenwart: Literatur der Sexual- und Ehefragen", *Berichte zur Kultur- und Zeitgeschichte* (Vienna), Vol VI, 1932 (24th April), pp.605-711. The characterisation of the journal comes from the original version of PM.
[84] This is one of the functions of "moral disgust"; see the discussion of "Der Ekel" (Disgust) in Ch. 7.

Notes to chapter 7

[1] That is, incorporation into an expanded Germany.
[2] PM p.46.
[3] Felix Schaffer, unpublished Memoir of the Polányis and their circle; Karl Polanyi Archive, Concordia University, Montreal.
[4] Polanyi, Kari (ed.), *The Life and Work of Karl Polanyi*, Montreal: Black Rose Books, 1990, p.39.
[5] PM (original).
[6] PM (original).
[7] Peter Drucker, *Adventures of a Bystander*, London: Heinemann, 1979, p.9.
[8] "Antifascistische Enzyklika", *OV*, XXIII, 41, 11/7/31, p.1086f.
[9] PM p.119 (original).
[10] PM (original).
[11] "Fascismus und Bolschewismus", *DV*, I, 7, 12/11/26, pp.206-13.
[12] PM p.135.
[13] AK to OJ 5/3/44.
[14] For full reference, see note 38.
[15] PM p.136 (original).

[16]   AK to CDK, n.d.

[17]   AK to GL 19/2/57.

[18]   PM (original).

[19]   "Max Scheler und der Kapitalismus", III, 43, 22/7/28, pp.924-26 and "Bellocs Vision vom Sklavenstaat" (Belloc's Vision of the Servile State), IV, 6, 4/11/28, pp.116-18.

[20]   PM p.141 (original).

[21]   See G. Silberbauer, *Oesterreichs Katholiken und die Arbeiterfrage*, Wien: Verlag Styria, 1966, pp.237-40.

[22]   In "Die Ideologie des Ständestaates", written for the main socialist monthly *Der Kampf*, (XXVII, 1, 1934, pp.13-23) he actually allies himself with the early Marx.

[23]   PM p.130.

[24]   Ibid. (omitted).

[25]   "Fascismus und Bolschewismus", I, 7, 12/11/26, pp.206-13.

[26]   "Rechts und links in der Politik", I, 22, 25/2/27, pp.665-71.

[27]   "Die Ideologie des sozialen Fortschritts", I, 30, 22/4/27, pp.933-36, and "Kritik des sozialen Fortschritts", I, 31, 29/4/27, pp.965-69.

[28]   "Tote und lebendige Demokratie", II, 26, 30/3/28, pp.854-7.

[29]   "Jugend und fascistische Reaktion", V, 20, 13/2/31, pp.640-45.

[30]   "Der Abbau des Kapitalismus: die Soziallehren G.K.Chestertons", I, 44, 29/7/27, pp.1382-86, and "Max Scheler als sozialphilosoph", II, 38, 22/6/28, pp.1300-3.

[31]   "Die christlichen Gewerkschaften im Kampf gegen den Kapitalismus", XX, 11, 1929, pp.405-15.

[32]   Op. cit. p.409.

[33]   "Versuch einer Klassifizierung der allgemein-sozialen Machtideen", *ASPS*, XXXI, 1 and 2, 1929, pp.125-41.

[34]   There is an obvious anticipation here of some of the themes of "Az emberek egyenlöségéröl" (On Human Equality), *Századunk*, IX, 5-6, Aug/Sep 1934, pp.211-222, pp.211-222, described in the next chapter.

[35]   Marginal note to a copy of his paper "Hochmut"; the note certainly dates from the fifties, or later.

[36]   "Die Machtideen der Klassen", *Archiv für Sozialwissenschaft und Sozialpolitik* (Tübingen), LXII, 1, 1929, pp.67-110.

[37]   "Gegenrevolution", *Kölner Vierteljahrshefte fur Soziologie* (München), X, 2 and 3 ,1931 and 1932, pp.171-99 and 295-319.

[38]   "Der Ekel", *Jahrbuch für Philosophie und Phänomenologische Forschung*, X, 1929, pp.515-69.

[39]   See Robert Radford, "Aurel Kolnai's 'Disgust': a source in the art and writing of Salvador Dalí", *The Burlington Magazine*, January 1999, p32f.

[40]   In 1968, when Kolnai was teaching in London, he was asked by Professor Wiggins if he would read a paper incorporating the main points of "Der Ekel" to his colleagues. This he did, adding some of the material on Hatred. Thirty years after its composition "The Standard Modes of Aversion: Fear, Disgust and Hatred", appeared in *Mind* (CVII, July 1988).

[41]   Ekel p.520.

[42]   Kolnai's unusual claims about the importance of physical disgust for moral health can be compared with C.S. Lewis's treatment of the topic in his novel of ideas, *That Hideous Strength* (London: The Bodley Head, 1945), where Mark's diabolical training in immoralist "objectivity" involves overcoming physical disgust.

[43]   "Der Hochmut", *PJGG*, XLIV, 2 and 4, 1931, pp.153-70 and 317-31.

[44]   "Versuch Über den Hass", *PJGG*, XLVIII, 2/3, 1935, pp.147-87.

Notes to chapter 8

1   PM p.153 (original).
2   EK to GL 19/4/39.
3   PM p.159.
4   Kolnai's account of the setting up of the CDV in Political Memoirs, p.152f. differs in certain respects from that of Josef Aussermair, *Kirche und Sozialdemokratie: der Bund der religiösen Sozialisten*, 1926-34, Wien-München-Zürich: Europaverlag, 1979.
5   PM p.153.
6   AK to IG 5/11/34.
7   Marginal annotation to Lord David Cecil's *Poets and Story-Tellers*, one of the books he sent to Jeanne Lapointe.
8   PM p.153.
9   "Neuösterreichische Staatslehre", OS, XXIX, 3, 17/10/36, pp.51-54.
10   PM p.163.
11   Ibid. (original).
12   AK to GL 25/9/51. Lisbeth Gombrich, who had a legal training, eventually moved to England, where she lived in what was for some time a kind of "Austro-Hungarian colony" in Wellington Square, Oxford, until her death in the mid 1990s. Here she became good friends with Irma Gémes, and became a professional translator.
13   PM p.153 (original).
14   Now published with a later summary of his Personalism in *Appraisal* ("A journal of constructive and post-critical philosophy and interdisciplinary studies", edited and published by Richard Allen), II, 2, October 1998 (ISSN 1358-3336).
15   PM (omitted).
16   PM p.150 (original).
17   PM (omitted).
18   PM p.152.
19   PM (omitted).
20   RV to me.
21   AK to IG 11/12/34.
22   AK to IG 8/5/34.
23   "Marxistisches und Liberalistisches im Nationalsozialismus", OS, I, 29, 24/6/34, pp.4-7.
24   "Heidegger und der Nationalsozialismus", OS, I, 28, 17/6/34, pp.5-7.
25   This subject was taken up again in *The War against the West*, and in Kolnai's much later Aristotelian Society paper "Existence and Ethics", *Aristotelian Society Supplementary Volume* XXXVII, 1963, pp.27-50.
26   "Staatsidee und Staatsform", OS, I, 37, 19/8/34, pp.4-6.
27   "Der Mißbrauch des 'Vitalen'", OS, I, 38, 26/8/34, pp.11-14.
28   "Othmar Spanns Ganzheitslehre", OS, I, 49, 11/11/34, pp.4-8 and "Othmar Spanns 'organische' Staatslehre", OS, I, 50, 18/11/34, pp.7-10.
29   Two further related articles are "Die Ideologie des Ständestaates", written for the leading socialist monthly, *Der Kampf*, XXVII, 1, 1934, pp.13-23, and a sequel, "Sozialismus und Ganzheit". As *Der Kampf* was by then closed, along with all other socialist organizations, E.K. Winter published it in his own *Wiener soziologisch-politische Blätter*, II, 1, 1934, pp.37-48, which was itself frequently subject to censorship, and also soon closed altogether.
30   "A józan ész mágusai: K. Kraus és G.K. Chesterton" (The Magicians of Common Sense: Karl Kraus and G.K. Chesterton), XI, 6-7, July/August 1936, pp.233-55.
31   PM (original).

[32] "Az emberek egyenlöségéröl" (On Human Equality), IX, 5-6, August/September 1934, pp.211-222.

[33] For a later, and more conservative, discussion, see "The Meaning of the 'Common Man'", *The Thomist*, July 1949, pp.272-335.

[34] "Democrácia és valóság", X, 7, September 1935, pp.261-270. At the end of his life Kolnai thought this the best of his *Századunk* papers (AK to JL 18/2/72).

[35] *Zeitschrift fur die Gesamte Staatswissenschaft* (Tübingen), XCIV, 1, 1933, pp.1-38.

[36] A letter to GL of 29/11/50 suggests that, despite his very critical approach to Schmitt's book, he nevertheless found in it a strong stimulus towards his later ideas about "the primacy of the negative".

[37] *The War against the West*, London: Gollancz and New York: Viking Press, 1938, pp.711.

[38] 1st February 1933, pp.107-109.

[39] PM (original).

[40] John Macmurray, Christian Socialist, (non-Kolnaian) Personalist philosopher and friend of the Polányis, had been brought in to help with Kolnai's project.

[41] PM p.165 (original).

[42] PM p.166.

[43] Ibid. (original).

Notes to chapter 9

[1] EK to DW 16/2/77.

[2] AK to OJ 5/3/44.

[3] AK to IG 23/2/39.

[4] BM Memoirs.

[5] AK to OJ 21/3/37.

[6] The handwritten ms survives.

[7] AK to OJ 5/3/44.

[8] AK and EK to BM.

[9] Typed excerpt by EK from a letter from AK to "a friend in Hungary" in 1938.

[10] PM (omitted).

[11] PM p.171.

[12] AK to IG 18/7/38.

[13] See note 9.

[14] See note 9.

[15] AK to IG 23/2/39.

[16] PM p.171.

[17] PM p.172 (original).

[18] AK to IG 16/1/39.

[19] *WAW* p.5.

[20] 711 pages.

[21] AK to BM 18/8/38.

[22] *WAW* p.5.

[23] *John O'London's Weekly*, 5/8/38.

[24] PM (original). In a later "list of publications" AK says: "Not valueless as a collection of texts; but drowned in verbose and dubious critical comments".

[25] PM (original).

[26] *WAW* p.57.

[27] *WAW* p.673.

28 *WAW* p.91.
29 *WAW* p.109.
30 *WAW* p.189.
31 *WAW* p.278.
32 *WAW* p.298.
33 *WAW* p.310f.
34 *WAW* pp.480-83.
35 *WAW* p.495.
36 *WAW* p.536.
37 *WAW* p.520.
38 *WAW* p.421.
39 AK to IG 18/7/38.
40 PM p.174.
41 PM (original).
42 PM (original).
43 PM p.173.
44 FP (unpublished manuscript) p.18.
45 FP p.20.
46 FP p.21.
47 FP p.32.
48 FP p.135.
49 *The Nation* (New York), CXLVIII, 4, 21 January 1939, pp.86-88. The general title of the debate was "Must Democracy Use Force?". Niebuhr's and Russell's contributions are in the same volume, nos 5, pp.117-19, and 7, pp.173-75, respectively.
50 AK to OJ 9/7/44.
51 PM (original).
52 "Dignity", *Philosophy*, 51, 1976, pp.251-71, esp p.265f.
53 Undated letter fragment, possibly to Irma Gémes, written in the last few months of 1938.
54 AK to IG 16/1/39.
55 His American earnings from the Viking Press edition were no more than £22/10/- per 1500 copies.
56 Elisabeth gives the same picture of his position in a letter to her cousin GL of early 1939. She even toys with the idea of returning to her mother in Hungary and thus escaping her – onerous - responsibility for Aurel; perhaps he'll find someone else who can look after him without being a financial burden.
57 Zsigmond Lányi, proprietor of the popular daily *Friss Ujság.*
58 AK to IG 23/2/39.
59 In March the Germans had coolly annexed Bohemia and Moravia.
60 EG to GL 19/4/39.
61 Fejtő's reminiscences of Kolnai have been published both in his *Memoárok*, Budapest: Megvető 1991, pp.198-203, and, at much greater length, in a recorded interview in *Világosság*, 1997, 5-6, though I also draw on an uncut version of the latter. It was conducted on 21/7/95.
62 He did so in *Korunk* (4, 1939, pp.362-65), a Hungarian periodical published in Cluj, Romania (formerly Kolozsvár). It was probably the only review in Hungarian.
63 Leader of the Octobrists of 1918.
64 In AK to JL 20/9/72 he explains that he began his gradual swing back towards the Right (completed in 1943) to the Munich agreement, and his feeling that Western Democracy would always incline him to take the pacifist option.
65 PM p.175f. (original).
66 EG to IG 9/11/39.
67 AK to BM 4/9/39.

68 Joseph Aufricht, *Erzähle damit du dein Recht erweist*, Berlin: Propyläen Verlag, 1966, pp.164ff. Aufricht, the great theatrical producer, under whom Lolo Vámbéry worked in Berlin, was also interned twice like Kolnai. He too was initially called to the Stade de Colombe, and he was also sent to the same camp as Kolnai during the second internment. It is clear from his descriptions that conditions were rather more uncomfortable than Kolnai says.

69 EG to IG 16/9/39.

70 PM p.178.

71 IG to Rennie Smith 14/11/39.

72 EG to IG 27/10/39.

73 AK to OJ 5/3/44.

74 AK to BM 27/11/39.

75 EG to IG 13/10/39.

76 "Shall it be German or Western 'Imperialism'?", II, 14, 17/5/40, p.14.

77 AK to IG 10/4/40.

78 Harold Nicolson to IG 8/6/40.

79 PM p.182.

80 Ibid.

81 EK to Olga Forbát 22/10/40.

82 PM p.185.

83 AK to OJ 5/3/44.

84 PM p.187 (original).

85 EK to GL 6/10/40 & 12/10/40.

86 AK to OJ 5/3/44.

87 AK to GL 6/12/40.

88 PM p.191.

Notes to chapter 10

1 AK to RV 14/12/40.

2 *The Nation*, CLII, 22, 31/5/41, pp.636-39.

3 PM p.194 (original). America entered the war when the Japanese attacked Pearl Harbor in December 1941.

4 AK to OJ 14/1/41.

5 PM p.195.

6 AK to OJ 14/1/41.

7 OJ to EK 24/6/41.

8 PM (omitted).

9 OJ to BM 8/2/41 & 20/2/41.

10 EK to GL 27/12/40.

11 Many of the details in this paragraph from Aufricht, op. cit.

12 AK to EKW 13/2/41.

13 BM to OJ 21/3/42 (probably a mistake for 41).

14 PM p.200.

15 AK to OJ 5/3/44.

16 Both these passages come from documents preserved in the Jászi Archive at Columbia University, New York.

17 *The American Teacher*, May 1941, pp.28ff (probably pp.28-30).

18 AK to OJ 25/6/41.

19 AK to OJ 15/9/42.

[20] PM p.197 (original).

[21] OJ to BM 29/6/42.

[22] OJ to BM n.d.

[23] OJ to Arnold Dániel 10/12/42.

[24] AK to OJ 15/9/42.

[25] "The Problem of Austrian Nationhood", *Journal of Central European Affairs*, II, 3, 1942, pp.290-309.

[26] AK to OJ 13/11/42.

[27] AK to OJ 11/2/44.

[28] PM p.197 (original).

[29] AK to Lewis Mumford 7/12/40.

[30] AK to OJ 24/8/44.

[31] Kolnai's attitude to the USA is brilliantly summed up in *Political Memoirs*, pp.200-206 (though the original has here been drastically abbreviated). In later life he felt that "The Kingdom of the Common Man" was perhaps the best section of the whole book.

[32] That is, in the human social and cultural environment.

[33] AK to OJ 13/12/44.

[34] AK to OJ 24/8/44 & 13/12/44.

[35] "Slaves of the Immaculate Heart of Mary".

[36] AK to OJ 8/4/45.

[37] AK to Rusztem Vámbéry 16/1/43.

[38] RV to me.

[39] "Collective Insecurity", *Liberation*, July 1943, pp.9-11.

[40] AK to Franz Klein 24/7/43.

[41] AK to OJ 11/2/44.

[42] RV to me.

[43] PM (omitted).

[44] OJ to AK 25/2/44.

[45] AK to OJ 5/3/44.

[46] OJ to AK 14/3/44.

[47] AK to OJ 12/4/44.

[48] OJ to AK 25/6/44.

[49] AK to OJ 9/7/44.

[50] OJ to AK 10/8/44.

[51] AK to OJ 24/10/44.

[52] *Free Europe*, 30/6/44, p.202f.

[53] Ibid.

[54] AK to OJ 14/11/44.

[55] Count István Bethlen was Horthy's Prime Minister, 1922-1931.

[56] AK to OJ 13/12/44.

[57] OJ to AK 21/3/45.

[58] AK to OJ 8/4/45.

[59] PM p.214.

[60] PM (omitted).

[61] *The Thomist*, October 1944, pp.429-57.

[62] AK to OJ 14/11/44.

Notes to chapter 11

[1] PM (original).
[2] Written communication to me.
[3] AK to GL 22/1/51.
[4] PM (original).
[5] EK to GL 12/1/49.
[6] AK to OJ 15/5/46.
[7] OJ to AK 2/8/47.
[8] AK to MF 20/4/47.
[9] An old honorific title for addressing university deans.
[10] AK to MF 28/4/48. Mgr Parent became University Rector in 1951.
[11] PM p217 (original).
[12] PM p218 (original).
[13] AK to OJ 15/5/46.
[14] AK to EKW 1/2/46.
[15] However, many clergy supported the province's "Quiet Revolution", which began in 1960.
[16] AK to GSL, New Year 1970.
[17] PM p.215 (original).
[18] PM (original).
[19] AK to GL 12/4/51.
[20] EK to GL 7/4/53.
[21] In Boston Elisabeth had painted her own designs on glass and "children's cups" (EK to GL 10/4/46). In Quebec she made a fine sculpture of Aurel's head, of which a small photograph survives.
[22] AK to MF 28/4/48.
[23] AK to MF 21/9/47.
[24] EK to Mrs DeKoninck 20/8/48.
[25] However, Jeanne Lapointe told me that on one occasion Elisabeth consulted DeKoninck about how she should deal with Kolnai's sexual demands.
[26] *ULTP*, I, 2, 1945, pp.199-205.
[27] AK to OJ 21/3/46.
[28] *ULTP*, II, 1, 1946, pp.74-116. This paper was translated in an abridged version as "The Cult of the Common Man and the Glory of the Humble", *Integrity* (New York), VI, 2, 1951, pp.3-43.
[29] *La Nouvelle Relève* (Montreal), Jan.1946 and June 1947, pp.533-46 and 644-56.
[30] RUL, I, 4, 1946, pp.269-71.
[31] "Necesidad de la Filosofía", *Estilo* (San Luis Potosí, Mexico), VII, 3, 1947, pp.151-64.
[32] AL to GL 30/5/47.
[33] *Actes, Congrès de Sociétés Philosophiques de la Langue Francaise*, Geneva, 1952, pp.91-95.
[34] *Appraisal* (ISSN 1358-3336), II, 1, 1998, pp.4-11.
[35] Op. cit. p.5.
[36] Op. cit. p.9.
[37] Ibid.
[38] Op. cit. p.10.
[39] Op. cit. p.11.
[40] AK to F.A. Hayek 23/10/58.
[41] *The Thomist*, July 1949, pp.272-335.
[42] Unpublished typescript (6 pp).

43 Op. cit. p.274.
44 Op. cit. p.282.
45 Op. cit. p.288.
46 Op. cit. p.294.
47 Op. cit. p.299.
48 Op. cit. p.310.
49 ULTP, V, 1, 1949, pp.66-110.
50 Op. cit. p.68.
51 Op. cit. p.69.
52 Op. cit. p.70.
53 Op. cit. p.73.
54 Ibid.
55 Op. cit. p.82.
56 Op. cit. p.87.
57 Op. cit. p.91.
58 Op. cit. p.93.
59 Op. cit. p.94.
60 AK to MF 5/9/48.
61 AK to EKW 7/9/48.
62 AK to EKW 26/1/49.
63 AK to GL 30/10/51.
64 AK to GL 8/2/50.
65 In AK to ES 19/3/57, Rehmke is coupled with Brentano and Meinong in a list of influences on his own thinking.
66 AK to GL 24/5/51.
67 That is, apart from "special courses", which included Positivism, Non-Scholastic ethics, Contemporary political philosophies and Phenomenology. He might give two of these in a year.
68 AK to GL 22/1/51.
69 AK to GSL, New Year 1970.
70 *Integrity* (New York), V, 11, 1951, pp.40-45.
71 AK to EKW 6/12/51.
72 *Commonweal* (New York), 14/9/51, p.554.
73 RUL, IV, 8, V, 1, V, 4, V, 5 and V, 7, 1950-51, pp.681-93, 1-19, 323-37, 388-97 and 626-38 respectively. For an account of this see next chapter.
74 *The Tablet*, 17/5/52, p.397. In this interesting little paper high praise is balanced by the exposure of serious defects.
75 "Edmund Husserl", *The Tablet*, 30/1/54, p.117, "On fidelity to Scholasticism in philosophy", 13/3/54, p.258, and "Approaches to Philosophy", 10/4/54, p.354.
76 AK to CDK 22/12/52.
77 AK to various colleagues 3/5/53.
78 General draft letter for university teaching applications 11/8/56.
79 PM (original).
80 PM (original).
81 *Cité Libre* (Montreal), 13, 1955, pp.9-20.
82 *Cité Libre*, 12, 1961, pp.5-10.

Notes to chapter 12

[1]   PM (original).
[2]   AK to GL 9/11/52 and 6/12/52.
[3]   PM p.227.
[4]   PM (omitted).
[5]   Madrid: Ateneo, 1952, p.40.
[6]   Madrid: Rialp, S.A., 1952, p.167 (translated by Salvador Pons).
[7]   PM p.229 (original).
[8]   For this see previous chapter.
[9]   PM p.229 (original).
[10] AK to CDK 19/8/52.
[11] AK to GL 8/11/52.
[12] AK to GL 6/12/52.
[13] Ibid.
[14] Karl Popper to AK 29/9/52.
[15] It is dated 19/4/57 and is now in the research department of the Bodleian Library, Oxford, MS SPSL 574/6.
[16] "Revolución y Restauración", *Arbor* (Madrid), LXXXV, 1953, pp.125-34.
[17] They did not stay with the Grants, though did visit them in 1956. But the change in AK's political views made a gradual drifting apart almost inevitable.
[18] *Philosophical Quarterly*, VI, 1956, pp.27-42.
[19] AK to ES 24/3/58.
[20] PM pp.219-22 (much abbreviated).
[21] Published in Spanish as *Crítica de las Utopías Políticas*, Madrid: Ateneo, 1959. The English (slightly expanded) version appears as Ch. 1 of "The Utopian Mind", in *The Utopian Mind and Other Papers*, London: Athlone, 1995, pp.xxxvi and 217, ed. Francis Dunlop, introduction by Pierre Manent.
[22] AK to Nuffield Foundation 12/5/56.
[23] Then Professor of Philosophy, King's College, University of London.
[24] AK to SP 8/8/56.
[25] 1823-1925. Maura was a prominent Spanish statesman at the beginning of the 20th century.
[26] AK to GL 13/5/56.
[27] ES to Karl Popper 25/4/57 (Bodleian Library, Oxford, MS SPSL 574/6).
[28] John Macmurray to AK 6/7/57.
[29] John Macmurray to EK 16/11/57.
[30] Karl Popper to ES 19/4/57 (Bodleian Library, Oxford, MS SPSL 574/6).
[31] AK to SP 20/10/56.
[32] AK to GL 19/2/57.
[33] "Despedida a Aurele Kolnai", *Ateneo: las Ideas, el Arte y las Letras*, 18, 27/9/52, p.12f. This article is illustrated by a very flattering photograph.
[34] SP to AK 28/11/56.
[35] AK to SP 12/12/56.
[36] AK to GL, n.d.
[37] "Reflexiones sobre el Alzamiento Húngaro", *Oriente Europeo* (Madrid), 27, 1957, pp.259-74.
[38] The characteristic detail in AK to GL 26/4/57.
[39] "Notas sobre la utopía reaccionaria", *Punta Europa*, I, 10, 1956, pp.71-86.
[40] "El Sentido Positivo de la Libertad", *Punta Europa*, 18/19, 1957, pp.105-22.
[41] AK to SP 28/2/61.

[42] "Ocho Tesis en torno a la Restauración", unpublished.
[43] Kolnai found the traditionalist "atmosphere" of Carlism very congenial, and enjoyed the company of the staunch Carlist Professor Rafael Gambra Cuidad, but he could not take his politics seriously, considering them a recipe for fanatical clericalism.
[44] AK to VM 18/2/62.
[45] José Luis Arangúren, *Ética*, Madrid: Revista de Occidente, 1958.
[46] AK to VM 25/6/57.
[47] "Los Intereses Políticos y no Políticos", *Atlantida* (Madrid), 14, March/April 1965, pp.147-61.
[48] "Objetividad y Tecnicismo", *In* (Madrid), 22, 1965, pp.71-78.
[49] AK to KH 21/2/70.
[50] "La Función Moralizadora del Derecho", in *Anuario de Filosofía del Derecho*, Instituto Nacional de Estudios Juridicos, Madrid, 1973, pp.205-9.
[51] See *El Juicio y el Ingenio y Otros Ensayos*, Madrid: Editorial Prensa Española, 1967, pp.179-86.
[52] "La Filosofía Británica Actual y sus Aspectos Políticos", *Punta Europa*, 41, 1959, pp.70-90.
[53] New Series, no. 33, p.9.

Notes to chapter 13

[1] Gilbert Ryle to AK 24/4/57.
[2] AK to VM 11/1/57.
[3] G.E.M. Anscombe, "Modern Moral Philosophy", *Philosophy*, 1958, pp.1-19.
[4] *PAS*, 1957-58, pp.171-98.
[5] Stuart Hampshire to AK 16/7/(58).
[6] *Philosophy*, XXXV, 1960, pp.234-54.
[7] Elizabeth Anscombe to AK n.d., but probably April 1958.
[8] *La Table Ronde* (Paris), 153, Sept 1960, pp.62-84. Kolnai's Spanish friend Calvo Serer prompted the invitation.
[9] AK to VM 16/6/59.
[10] Austin Duncan-Jones to HBA 15/5/59.
[11] HBA to Austin Duncan-Jones 19/5/59.
[12] Austin Duncan-Jones to HBA 29/5/59.
[13] GL to GSz 18/10/59.
[14] AK to ES 2/8/61.
[15] Professor Goetz Briefs, whom Kolnai got to know as a visitor to Laval, used at one time to send a regular Christmas cheque, and at some point got an episcopal friend of his to offer Kolnai "a chair at his seminary at Essen"; at the time Kolnai said he was not well enough to accept, but it is quite likely that he would not have accepted in any case because of his dislike of Germany. Goetz Briefs to EK 21/11/73.
[16] AK to J.L.Arangúren 16/4/64.
[17] Very probably "The Logic of Sex". See next chapter.
[18] GL to GSz 12/4/64.
[19] HBA to Daiches Raphael 28/4/64.
[20] GL to GSz, undated draft, probably June 1964.
[21] From 5/12/70 Kolnai received an OAP of about £460 p.a.
[22] Kolnai paid income tax of £102 in 1971-2 and £201 in 1972-73. On 17/6/72 George Lanyi was still holding $940 belonging to him - the remainder of his savings from his

Marquette University Visiting Professorship (see below). At his death £1,228 was passed to his estate account.

23   For the relevant parts of this letter see Aurel Kolnai, *The Utopian Mind and other papers*, ed. Francis Dunlop, London: Athlone, 1995, pp.viii-ix.

24   "The Moral Theme in Political Division", originally intended for it, does not always appear in later synopses.

25   "Utopia Plans and Notes", unpublished.

26   This might almost be taken as a motto for Kolnai's philosophy.

27   AK to JB 30/11/69.

28   AK to Elizabeth Anscombe 23/3/58.

29   See pp.183-95 of UM.

30   In *Scientiis Artibusque*, Hungarian Academy of Science and Arts, Rome: Herder & Co., 1958, pp.49-60.

31   *Philosophical Quarterly*, VI, 1956, pp.27-42.

32   *PAS*, 1957-58, pp.171-98.

33   *The Human Person and the World of Values*, ed. Balduin V. Schwarz, New York: Fordham University Press, 1960, pp.57-81.

34   See note 6 above for reference.

35   *PAS*, 1961-62, pp.195-218.

36   Kolnai's paper is of value whether or not Aristotle actually held the view Kolnai attributes to him.

37   *Ethics, Value and Reality: selected papers of Aurel Kolnai*, eds Francis Dunlop and Brian Klug, London: The Athlone Press, 1977, pp.63-94 and 95-122 respectively.

38   *PAS*, 1965-66, pp.103-28.

39   An unpublished Spanish paper, still shorter, may be the version actually read in Madrid or Tortosa.

40   See note 8 above for reference.

41   UM pp.155-75.

42   Pp.176-82.

43   *Aristotelian Society Supplementary Volume XXXVII*, 1963, pp.27-50.

44   *Philosophy*, LV, 1980, pp.5-16.

Notes to chapter 14

1   AK to GL 17/2/68.

2   On the other hand Emily Brontë's fault is that "there is no society and no morality" in her books. These comments come from book annotations.

3   Hearing that CDK needed a doctor in New York, he strongly recommended his friend Dr Julius Holló, the only doctor he knew who took a "sapiential" approach to medicine.

4   I was put right on this matter by conversations with Peter Ayrton and Dr A.de Tószeghi.

5   AK to KH 21/2/70.

6   AK to GL 23/7/59.

7   In *The Nature of Metaphysics*, ed. D.F. Pears, London: Macmillan, 1957, pp.99-123.

8   Kolnai's letters to Vicente Marrero frequently mention his "religion of the Fragmentary", e.g. 31/5/57.

9   Two long unpublished papers on this general topic, "Existentialism, Libertarian or Anti-libertarian?" and "Testability, Universality: 'Emphasis on the Individual' (Existentialist Ethics)" certainly existed in about 1976, but no trace of them was found after EK's death.

10   AK to DW 1/4/69.

[11] AK to RV 4/8/66. No copy of this was found among Kolnai's papers after EK's death.

[12] Personal communication to me.

[13] Op. cit. p.x.

[14] Ibid.

[15] AK to BW 1/5/66.

[16] AK to BW 30/7/65.

[17] Op. cit. p.xi.

[18] AK to HBA 17/4/69.

[19] AK to GSL, New Year 1970.

[20] AK to DW 27/9/70.

[21] AK to CR 21/10/65.

[22] See her superb account, free from self-pity: Edith Bone, *Seven Years Solitary*, London: Hamish Hamilton, 1957.

[23] AK to Eszter Kelemen, Xmas 1957.

[24] "Das unvollendete Völkerreich: die hundertjahres Feier eines fünfzigjährigen Reiches", *Rheinische Merkur*, 29/9/67, p.32f.

[25] Probably as a result of a meeting with György Kovács.

[26] Jenő Vértes to AK 9/2/67.

[27] GS to AK 15/12/71. In his letter of 11/2/72 he says that of the original 51 boys in the class who took their Abitur together, 21 still survived.

[28] AK to JB 28/8/67.

[29] Litván József, *Ítéletidő*, Budapest: Tekintet, n.d., p.14. In a letter to Litván about this trip (20/9/72) he calls himself a "small or medium town ghetto inhabitant".

[30] AK to HBA 12/10/72.

[31] AK to JB 21/10/67.

[32] AK to GL 7/2/68.

[33] AK to JB 1/12/67.

[34] Memorial minute by Paul Dawson, Professor of Government, adopted by the General Faculty of Oberlin College April 30th 1981.

[35] AK to JB 1/7/68.

[36] AK to RV 28/4/68.

[37] AK to David Lloyd-Thomas 27/8/68.

[38] AK to JB 1/8/68.

[39] AK to JB 5/8/70.

[40] AK to JB 25/7/70.

[41] AK to JB 21/4/70.

[42] AK to JB 7/7/72.

[43] *A History of the American People*, London: Weidenfeld & Nicholson, 1997, p.729.

[44] AK to JB 20/8/68.

[45] AK to GSL, New Year 1970.

[46] AK to RV 8/5/67.

[47] AK to JB 25/7/70.

[48] EK to Sunny Beach 26/9/71.

[49] AK to JB 23/1/73. In his letter to Jozsef Litván of 24/5/72 he bewails his inability to give up smoking, though says he tries not to inhale.

[50] G.K. Kaltenbrunner to AK 20/1/73.

[51] Described in ch. 12.

[52] Thomas Nagel's book *The Possibility of Altruism*.

[53] *BJA*, IV, 1964, pp.22-39.

[54] AK to VM 16/4/59.

55 "Aesthetic and Moral Experience", *BJA*, XI, 1971, pp.178-88; "Contrasting the Ethical and the Aesthetical", *BJA*, XII, 1972, pp.331-44. The two were reprinted as one paper with the title "Aesthetic and Moral Experience".

56 *BJA*, XII, 1972, pp.158-62.

57 "Erreur et Verité", *Actes du XIIe Congrès des Sociétés de Philosophie de la Langue Francaise*, Brussels-Louvain, 1964, pp.108-11.

58 "La Pureté du Langage est-elle Signe de Pureté Morale?", *Actes du XIIIe Congrès des Sociétés de Philosophie de la Langue Francaise*, Geneva, 1966, pp.340-43.

59 *PAS*, 1969-70, pp.93-118.

60 This idea also occurs in earlier papers, for example, "The Thematic Primacy of Moral Evil".

61 *PAS*, 1973-4, pp.91-106.

62 In *Situationism and the New Morality*, ed. R.L. Cunningham, New York: Appleton-Century-Crofts, 1970, pp.232-71.

63 *Philosophy*, XXXIX, 1964, pp.75-79.

64 They are both published in *Appraisal*, II, 1, March 1998 (ISSN 1358-3336), pp.12-14.

65 *Philosophy*, XLVI, 1971, pp.203-22.

66 *Philosophy*, LI, 1976, pp.251-71.

67 AK to GSL, New Year 1970.

68 In *Rekonstruktion des Konservatismus*, ed. G.K. Kaltenbrunner, Freiburg i. Br.: Rombach, 1972, pp.95-136.

69 AK to KH 31/11/71.

70 In *Structure and Gestalt: Philosophy and Literature in Austria-Hungary and her Successor States*, ed. Barry Smith, Amsterdam: John Benjamins B.V., 1981, pp.317-46.

71 *Philosophy*, XL, 1965, pp.68-71.

72 *British Journal of Educational Studies*, XVI, 1968, pp.258-70.

73 *Appraisal*, II, 1, March 1998 (ISSN 1358-3336), pp.14-19.

74 AK to JB 23/11/67.

75 *Mind*, CVII, 1998, pp.581-95.

76 In *The Human Agent*, Royal Institute of Philosophy Lectures, I, 1966-67, London: Macmillan and New York: St Martin's Press, 1968, pp.20-46.

Notes to Appendix

1 I shall leave virtually untouched here the question of Jewish influence.

2 AK to EG 10/5/36.

3 PM p.98.

4 PM p.241.

5 The omitted portion of Kolnai's Memoirs devoted to this issue can be found as Appendix 1 of PM.

6 Marginal note in *A Handbook of Heresies*, by M.L.Cozens.

7 PM p.104.

8 AK to VM 3/8/60.

9 "Aesthetic and Moral Experience", *BJA*, II, 2, p.183.

10 PM p.102.

11 AK to EG 10/5/36.

12 A defence of personal survival after death is part of Natural Theology; AK to LG 6/3/55.

13 The correspondence with JB contains savage outbursts against Pope Paul VI for his reaffirmation of the ban on artificial contraception.

14 AK to VM 3/8/60.

[15] PM p.88f.; the quoted passage recalls Kolnai's life-long war with "Occultism", and any belief-system which blurred the clear distinction between Good and Evil.

[16] PM (original).

Select Bibliography of Kolnai's Published Works and of Works about Kolnai

Books

Der ethische Wert und die Wirklichkeit, Freiburg i. Br.: Herder, 1927, pp.171.
Sexualethik: Sinn und Grundlagen der Geschlechtsmoral, Paderborn: Schöningh, 1930, pp.447.
The War against the West, London: Gollancz and New York: Viking Press, 1938, pp.711.
Errores del Anticomunismo, Madrid: Rialp, S.A., 1952, pp.67 (translated from French by Salvador Pons).
La Divinización y la Suma Esclavitud del Hombre, Madrid: Ateneo, 1952, pp.40.
Political Memoirs, ed. Francesca Murphy, Lanham, Md: Lexington Books, 1999, pp.xliii, 253.

Posthumously published collections

(EVR) *Ethics, Value and Reality*, London: Athlone Press, 1977, pp.xxv+251, eds Francis Dunlop and Brian Klug, introduction by Bernard Williams and David Wiggins (contains two chapters of an unfinished book entitled "Morality and Practice", and published papers nos 24, 27, 30, 32, 40, 42, 43, 44, 46).
(UM) *The Utopian Mind and Other Papers*, London: Athlone, 1995, pp.xxxvi+217, ed. Francis Dunlop, introduction by Pierre Manent (contains Kolnai's unfinished book, published papers 28 and 29 - the latter in translation - and other unpublished material).
(PLO) *Privilege and Liberty and Other Essays in Political Philosophy*, ed. and introduced by Daniel J. Mahoney, foreword by Pierre Manent, Lanham, Maryland: Lexington Books, 1999 (contains published papers

17, 18, 45, 50, 53, 56 and another unpublished paper on the Utopian Mind).

Published papers

Abbreviations:
ASPS   *Archiv für systematische Philosophie und Soziologie* (Berlin)
PJGG   *Philosophisches Jahrbuch der Görres-Gesellschaft* (Munich)
PE   *Punta Europa* (Madrid)
PAS   *Proceedings of the Aristotelian Society*
BJA   *British Journal of Aesthetics*

1   "Über das Mystische", *Imago* (Vienna), VII, 1, 1921, pp.40-70.
2   "Gontscharows 'Oblomow'", *Imago*, IX, 1923, pp.485-94.
3   "Max Schelers Kritik und Würdigung der Freudschen Libidolehre", *Imago*, XI, 1/2, 1925, pp.135-46.
4   "Neigung, Pflicht und Gesinnung", *ASPS*, XXX, 1/2, 1927, pp.55-65.
5   "Der Aufbau der ethischen Intention", *PJGG*, XLI, 1, 1928, pp.1-16.
6   "Versuch einer Klassifizierung der allgemein-sozialen Machtideen", *ASPS*, XXXI, 1/2, 1929, pp.125-41.
7   "Die Machtideen der Klassen", *Archiv für Sozialwissenschaft und Sozialpolitik* (Tübingen), LXII, 1, 1929, pp.67-110.
8   "Der Ekel", *Jahrbuch für Philosophie und phänomenologische Forschung*, X, 1929, pp.515-69. Reprinted Tübingen: Max Niemeyer, 1974.
9   "Der Hochmut", *PJGG*, XLIV, 2 and 4, 1931, pp.153-70 and 317-31.
10 "Gegenrevolution", *Kölner Vierteljahrshefte für Soziologie* (Munich), X, 2 and 3, 1931 and 1932, pp.171-99 and 295-319.
11 "Der Inhalt der Politik", *Zeitschrift für die gesamte Staatswissenschaft* (Tübingen), XCIV, 1, 1933, pp.1-38.
12 "Die Ideologie des Ständestaates", *Der Kampf* (Vienna), XXVII, 1, 1934, pp.13-23.
13 "Versuch über den Hass", *PJGG*, XLVIII, 2/3, 1935, pp.147-87.
14 "The Humanitarian versus the Religious Attitude", *The Thomist* (Baltimore, Md), Oct.1944, pp.429-57.
15 "Les Ambiguités Nationales", *La Nouvelle Relève* (Montreal), Jan.1946 and June 1947, pp.533-46 and 644-56.
16 "Necesidad de la Filosofía", *Estilo* (San Luis Potosí, Mexico), VII, 3, 1947, pp.151-64.
17 "The Meaning of the 'Common Man'", *The Thomist*, July 1949, pp.272-335 (reprinted in PLO).

18 "Privilege and Liberty", *ULTP*, V, 1, 1949, pp.66-110 (reprinted in PLO).

19 "Le Conditionnement Historique de la Pensée Humaine et la Philosophie de l'Expérience Commune", in *Actes, Congrès de Sociétés Philosophiques de la Langue Francaise*, Geneva, 1952, pp.91-5.

20 "Revolución y Restauración", *Arbor* (Madrid), LXXXV, 1953, pp.125-34.

21 "Notes sur l'Utopie Réactionnaire", *Cité Libre* (Montreal), 13, 1955, pp.9-20.

22 "The Thematic Primacy of Moral Evil", *Philosophical Quarterly*, VI, 1956, pp.27-42.

23 "El Sentido Positivo de la Libertad", *PE*, 18/19, 1957, pp.105-22.

24 "Erroneous Conscience", *PAS*, 1957-8, pp.171-98 (reprinted in EVR).

25 "A Note on the Meaning of Right and Wrong", in *Scientiis Artibusque, Hungarian Academy of Science and Arts*, Rome: Herder & Co., 1958, pp.49-60.

26 "La Filosofía Británica Actual y sus Aspectos Políticos", *PE*, 41, 1959, pp.70-90.

27 "The Sovereignty of the Object: Notes on Truth and Intellectual Humility", in *The Human Person and the World of Values*, ed. Balduin V. Schwarz, New York: Fordham University Press, 1960, pp.57-81 (reprinted in EVR).

28 "The Moral Theme in Political Division", *Philosophy*, XXXV, 1960, pp.234-54 (reprinted in UM).

29 "La Mentalité Utopienne", *La Table Ronde* (Paris), 153, 1960, pp.62-84 (translated in UM).

30 "Deliberation is of Ends", *PAS*, 1961-2, pp.195-218 (reprinted in EVR).

31 "Existence and Ethics", in Symposium: "Existentialism", *Aristotelian Society Supplementary Volume XXXVII*, 1963, pp.27-50 (reprinted in EVR).

32 "The Concept of the Interesting", *BJA*, IV, 1964, pp.22-39 (reprinted in *Aesthetics and the Modern World*, ed. Harold Osborne, pp.166-87, New York: Weybright and Talley).

33 "Los Intereses Políticos y no Políticos", *Atlantida* (Madrid), 14, March/April 1965, pp.147-61.

34 "Objetividad y Tecnicismo", *In* (Madrid), 22, 1965, pp.71-78.

35 "Games and Aims", *PAS*, 1965-6, pp.103-28.

36 "La Pureté du Langage est-elle Signe de Pureté Morale?", in *Actes du XIIIe Congrès des Sociétés de Philosophie de la Langue Francaise*, Geneva, 1966, pp.340-3.

37 "Agency and Freedom", in *The Human Agent*, Royal Institute of Philosophy Lectures, I, 1966-67, London: Macmillan and New York: St Martin's Press, 1968, pp.20-46.

38 "The Justification of Commands", *British Journal of Educational Studies*, XVI, 1968, pp.258-70.

39 "Moral Consensus", *PAS*, 1969-70, pp.93-118 (reprinted in EVR).

40 "A Defence of Intrinsicalism against Situation Ethics", in *Situationism and the New Morality*, ed. R.L. Cunningham, New York: Appleton-Century-Crofts, 1970, pp.232-71.

41 "The Concept of Hierarchy", *Philosophy*, XLVI, 1971, pp.203-22 (reprinted in EVR).

42 "Aesthetic and Moral Experience", *BJA*, XI, 1971, pp.178-88 (reprinted in EVR).

43 "Contrasting the Ethical and the Aesthetical", *BJA*, XII, 1972, pp.331-44 (reprinted in EVR as continuation of 43).

44 "Konservatives und revolutionäres Ethos", in *Rekonstruktion des Konservatismus*, ed. G.K. Kaltenbrunner, Freiburg i.Br: Rombach, 1972, pp.95-136 (translated in PLO).

45 "Forgiveness", *PAS*, 1973-74, pp.91-106 (reprinted in EVR).

46 "Dignity", *Philosophy*, LI, 1976, pp.251-71.

47 "The Ghost of the Naturalistic Fallacy", *Philosophy*, LV, 1980, pp.5-16.

48 "Identity and Division as a Fundamental Theme of Politics", in *Structure and Gestalt: Philosophy and Literature in Austria-Hungary and her Successor States*, ed. Barry Smith, Amsterdam: John Benjamins B.V., 1981, pp.317-46.

49 "Three Riders of Apocalypse", *Appraisal*, II, 1, March 1998 (ISSN 1358-3336), pp.4-11 (reprinted in PLO).

50 "Advising", *Appraisal*, II, 1, March 1998, pp.14-19.

51 "The Standard Modes of Aversion: Fear, Disgust and Hatred", *Mind*, CVII, 1998, pp.581-95.

Book reviews

52 "Man and the State by Jacques Maritain", *Integrity* (New York), V, 11, 1951, pp.40-45 (reprinted in PLO).

53 "Findlay on Ethics", review of "Values and Intentions" by J.N.Findlay, *Philosophy*, XXXIX, 1964, pp.75-79.

54 "Untersuchungen zur Ontologie der Kunst by Roman Ingarden", *BJA*, IV, 1964, pp.164-66.

55 "Rationalism in Politics by Michael Oakeshott", *Philosophy*, XL, 1965, pp.68-71 (reprinted in PLO).

56 "Die Lebenswelt; eine Philosophie des konkreten Apriori by Gerd Brand", *Journal of the British Society for Phenomenology*, IV, 1973, pp.76-78.

Selected journalism

Volkswohl (Vienna)
"Thomas Mann, Freud und der Fortschritt", XX, 9, 1929, pp.321-27.
"Geistige und politische Voraussetzungen der Wirtschaftsdemokratie", XXII, 1, 1931, pp.4-16.

Schönere Zukunft (Vienna)
"Max Scheler und der Kapitalismus", III, 43, 22/7/28, pp.924-26.

Der Deutsche Volkswirt (Berlin)
"Fascismus und Bolschewismus", I, 7, 12/11/26, pp.206-13.
"Rechts und links in der Politik", I, 22, 25/2/27, pp.665-71.
"Die Ideologie des sozialen Fortschritts", I, 30, 22/4/27, pp.933-36.
"Kritik des sozialen Fortschritts", I, 31, 29/4/27, pp.965-69.
"Tote und lebendige Demokratie", II, 26, 30/3/28, pp.854-57.
"Max Scheler als sozialphilosoph", II, 38, 22/6/28, pp.1300-3.

Der Oesterreichische Volkswirt (Vienna)
"Der Sinn des Liberalismus", XXV, 52, 23/9/33, pp.249-52.
"Totaler Staat und Zivilisation", XXVI, 5, 28/10/33, pp.113-16.
"Persönlichkeit und Massenherrschaft", XXVI, 20, 10/2/34, pp.442-44.
"Das Problem des Konservatismus", XXVI, 42, 14/7/34, pp.903-6.
"Die Aufgabe des Konservatismus", XXVI, 44, 28/7/34, pp.943-46.

Der Christliche Ständestaat: Österreichische Wochenhefte (Vienna)
"Heidegger und der Nationalsozialismus", I, 28, 17/6/34, pp.5-7.
"Der Mißbrauch des 'Vitalen'", I, 38, 26/8/34, pp.11-14.
"G.K.Chesterton", III, 26, 28/6/36, pp.619-21.

The Nation (New York)
"Pacifism means Suicide", CXLVIII, 4, 21 Jan 1939, pp.86-88 (Kolnai's article was the first in a series of three with the general title "Must Democracy Use Force?". The 2nd was by Reinhold Niebuhr, the 3rd by Bertrand Russell, same vol., nos 5, pp.117-19, and 7, pp.173-75).

Works about Kolnai

The introductory material to the posthumously published collections, EVR, UM and PLO (see above), will be found very useful.

I also mention here, for those who can read Hungarian, the extremely interesting double issue of *Világosság* (XXXVIII, 5-6, 1997, Budapest), which is devoted to Kolnai's life and work.

Otherwise I recommend:

Beach, John D., "The Ethical Theories of Aurel Kolnai", *The Thomist*, 45, 1, 1981, pp.132-43.

Congdon, Lee, "Aurel Kolnai: in Defence of Christian Europe", *The World and I*, September 1988, pp.631-45.

Dunlop, Francis, "The Philosophy of Aurel Kolnai", *Journal of the British Society for Phenomenology*, IX, 1, 1978, pp.56-58.

Dunlop, Francis, "Aurel Kolnai" [his views on conservative restoration], *The Salisbury Review*, XVI, 1, 1997, pp.8-11.

Dunlop, Francis, "Kolnai's 'Inchoate Sketch of a Theory of Morality'", *Appraisal*, II, 1, 1998 (ISSN 1358-3336), pp.20-25, 42.

Hittinger, John, "Approaches to Democratic Equality" (on Kolnai and Maritain), in *Freedom in the Modern World*, ed. Michael Torre, Notre Dame Press, 1989.

Mahoney, Daniel J., "The Recovery of the Common World: an Introduction to the Moral and Political Reflection of Aurel Kolnai", *Perspectives on Political Science*, XXVI, 2, 1997, pp.77-84.

Manent, Pierre, "La Philosophie Morale d'Aurèle Kolnai" (Review Article of EVR), *Commentaire*, I, 3, 1978, pp.442-45.

Manent, Pierre, "Aurel Thomas Kolnai (1900-1973)", *The Chesterton Review*, VIII, 2, 1982, pp.162-69.

Pons, Salvador, "Despedida a Aurèle Kolnai", *Ateneo: las Ideas, el Arte y las Letras* (Madrid), 18, 27/9/52, p.12f.

Index

All references to Kolnai as "AK"
Titles of all Kolnai's works referred to are in inverted commas; where the original language is not English they are translated.
Dates in brackets are dates of publication or (in the case of unpublished work) composition. Where published works were written a long time before publication, I give date of composition.

"*1915-1916*" (autobiographical notes)
15-17
"*1919*" (notebook) 47
"*1919-1920*" (notebook) 48-50, 307

AK (=Aurél, Aurélka, Auluska,
    Großvater)
    attitudes: charity 83-84; Czarist
        Russia 8, 10, 48; England 10, 82,
        87, 112, 145, 149, 151-54, 156,
        169-70, 234-35, 254, 272,
        281-82; First World War 6, 9-11,
        18, 22, 26; France 10, 155-57,
        165-66, 234; French Revolution
        165, 194, 223; Germany 10, 13,
        42, 100, 110, 114, 157-61, 174,
        198, 246, 281, 325; Hungarian
        revolution of 1918 42-44;
        New Left 279; USA 188, 321;
        women and sex 24, 50, 79-80,
        82-83, 99-102, 108, 123-24,
        132-33, 144-46, 172, 183,
        209-10, 243, 275, 278-80, 310,
        314, 322
    career problems 79, 113-14, 152, 166
    change of surname 11-12
    character and personality viii-ix, 1,
        4-9, 11-14, 17, 21, 27, 30-33, 45,
        48-50, 64, 66, 78-79, 99, 111-12,
        129, 143-47, 151-52, 157, 162,
        166, 168, 170-73, 176, 181,
        186-87, 192-95, 205, 208, 210,
        223-24, 226-27, 230, 235,
        242-43, 246-48, 255, 258, 260,

264, 272, 275-80, 282, 284-89,
    294, 296, 301, 307;
    precociousness 5, 12, 15-16, 26,
    35; predominantly moral
    orientation 10, 23, 77, 80-81,
    165, 169, 286
correspondence ix, 65-66, 78, 131,
    220, 187, 245-47, 255, 307
economic and financial matters 149,
    165-67, 176-77, 180-81, 185-86,
    191, 238, 253, 255-59, 285, 289,
    325-26
education at home 13-14
emigration to the West 141-43,
    149-53, 170; dangers of his
    personal situation (1938-40) 149,
    152, 165-66, 168, 176; escape to
    Spain and the USA 174-78;
    expulsion from Switzerland 156;
    failure to settle in England in
    1939 and 1940 171, 173, 177
family prosperity and connections
    2-3, 8, 18, 82, 253
foreign trips from London 281-82;
    significance of Belgium 281-83
grants and scholarships, 187, 196,
    227, 238, 249, 253, 257, 255-56,
    255, 257
health and illness, viii, 7, 13, 17-18,
    28, 31, 65, 130, 144, 157,
    166-68, 170-71, 173-74, 196,
    206, 234, 243, 259, 272-73, 277,
    279, 283, 285, 288-89, 326-27;

National Health Service 273;
    fatal heart attack, 289
holiday in Cornwall 281
internment: Méslay 170-72, 174;
    La Braconne 173-74
Jewish background of, viii, 1-4, 6-7,
    9-10, 14, 17, 21-24, 39, 41-42,
    45-46, 48-49, 65, 82-83, 87,
    98-99, 102, 107, 161, 176, 193,
    230, 287, 327-28
lectures: Hungarian Catholic
    Academic Circle (London) 281;
    Left Book Club Summer School
    169; London Logos Circle 235,
    240; on National Socialism
    (Budapest, 1933) 141; suggested
    topics for American Lecture
    Bureau 183
Lloyd-Muirhead Fellowship at
    Birmingham 257, 276
marriage to Elisabeth Gémes 171-73
nationality changes 72, 156-57, 183,
    187, 189, 220, 234, 273
on the arts 74, 279, 289-90
"original sin at Basle" 11
philosophical allegiances 42, 64,
    147, 221, 241
physical appearance 111, 168, 226,
    276, 285
places of residence 1, 50, 66, 113,
    154-55, 165, 179, 181, 185, 203,
    210, 237, 272, 312
politics: activity, viii, 25-27, 42-43,
    144, 183-84, 252; as a subject
    282, 285-86; beliefs and
    allegiances 21-22, 28-29, 45, 50,
    110, 113, 115, 136, 141-42,
    148-49, 157, 159, 181, 184,
    186-87, 191-95, 207, 214, 221,
    236-37, 239-40, 286-88, 298,
    319
relations with his parents 5-11, 27,
    30-31, 43, 45, 50, 65-66, 70-72,
    79, 81-83, 101, 149, 152, 167,
    172, 174, 253
religion: conversion 98-99; early
    attitudes 2, 13-14, 25, 33, 57-58,
    62, 64, 68, 74, 76, 82, 98-99;
    post-conversion attitudes 226,
    301-4; "religion of the
    fragmentary" 233, 263, 303;
    "second conversion" 188, 201,

schooling 13; *Abitur* exam 18, 327;
    editing *On Both Sides* 15-16;
    "Problem Bureau" 43; trouble
    with the staff 15, 26-27
search for employment 69, 170,
    179-80, 185, 192, 222-24, 229,
    240-43, 245, 253-58, 325
special interests 1, 6-7, 12-13, 15-17,
    29, 32, 34-35, 46, 63-64, 73-74,
    102, 123, 169-70, 206, 209, 226,
    273, 275, 279, 281-84
university studies: Budapest 18, 44;
    German and Swiss enquiries
    69-71; term in Freiburg 114-15;
    Vienna 58, 71-72, 86;
    examinations 86; subjects
    studied 86-87, 89
university teaching, viii, 86, 196,
    203, 205, 211, 220, 222, 225,
    253, 256-59, 276-77, 283,
    288-89, 323; relations with
    students 204, 209, 221, 226, 278,
    283; teaching ability 203-4, 226,
    258-59, 276-77, 283
visit to Berlin 101, 113-14
Visiting Professorship at Marquette
    University 282; preparations
    282; journeys out and back 283;
    possibility of another visit 283,
    285-86; trip to Canada 284-85
work other than teaching:
    as sub-editor 70, 80, 112,
    114-15, 184; commercial
    traineeship 69, 71, 82, 85;
    translating 182, 192, 196, 205,
    255, 258
"A Complete Rhymed Course of
    Medical Science" (c.1950) 206
"A Critique of Political Utopias" (1959)
    238, 270
"Actions and Inactions" (1970) 299-300
"Activity and Passivity in the
    Development of Civilisation"
    (1918) 30-32, 53
Acton, H.B. 254-56, 258-60, 274, 278,
    282
"A Defence of Intrinsicalism against
    Situation Ethics" (1970) 294
"Advising" (c.1967) 298
Ady, Endre 78
"Aesthetic and Moral Experience"
    (1971) 290
"Agency and Freedom" (1966) 299

Agnew, Spiro 287
"A Half Hour's Journey around Moral
    Radicalism" (1919) 48
Allen, Richard 317
America
    Civil War 187
    Federation of Labour 176
    Phenomenological Association 123
    philosophy 251
    way of life 188, 192
"An Attempt to Classify the General
    Social Ideas about Power"
    (1929) 119-20
"An Illusion of the Future" (1928) 61
"A Note on the Meaning of Right and
    Wrong" (1958) 264-65
Anscombe, Elizabeth 245, 255, 264
    correspondence with, 254-55
    "Modern Moral Philosophy" 245,
    254
Antal, Géza 191
Arangúren, José 247, 249
    Ethics 247, 249, 251, 257
Arbor (Madrid traditionalist periodical)
    230, 236, 241, 247
"Are the People Mature Enough for
    Democracy?" (1920) 47
"Are there Degrees of Ethical
    Universality?" (1968) 283,
    293-94
Aristotelian Society 238, 242, 264, 273,
    276, 292
Aristotle 219, 222, 246-47, 251, 265-69,
    295, 302, 326
"A Song of Leave-Taking" (c.1951,
    poem) 222
"A Synthesis of Christ and Anti-Christ"
    (1951) 223
atheism, the meaning of 233
Atlantida (Madrid monthly) 248
"At Lunch" (1920) 66
Aufricht, Joseph 100-101, 174, 181-82,
    320
Augustine 88
Aurora (Budapest monthly) 69, 72
Aussermair, Josef 317
Austen, Jane 272
Austin, J.L. 274
Austria
    AK's journalistic writings 117
    AK's political hopes for 184
    AK revisits 282
    Anschluss 110, 136, 184

Austrofascism 144, 147, 229;
    "The Fatherland Front" 136-37
Christian Democratic Union (CDV)
    132, 142, 144, 317
Christian Social Party (CSP) 109,
    115, 135; "Solidarists" vs "Social
    Romantics" in 115-16
Communist Party 65
historical background 3, 13, 19-20,
    38, 65, 109-10, 115-16, 130,
    135-36, 147; *see also* Habsburg
League of Religious Socialists
    (BRS)119, 131-33, 135, 144,
    their leader, "little" Otto Bauer,
    132, 135
monarchist (Legitimist) movement
    109-11, 134, 184-85; "Austrian
    Action" 134
Nazi Party 130, 135-36
"Paramilitaries" 110, 116;
    Volksbund 116; Heimwehr 116,
    130, 136
Social Democratic Party (SDP) 65,
    109, 111, 115-16, 119, 131-32,
    134-35, 184; Otto Bauer, party
    leader 135
wartime politics among the
    American émigrés 184-85
Ayrton, Peter 277-79, 326

Babin, Eugène 284
Back, Kató (cousin of AK) 5
Bacon, Francis 278
Baroja, Pio 243
Barth, Karl 156
Beach, John 204, 221-22, 224, 282-83,
    285, 287-88
Bécsi Magyar Ujság (Vienna daily) 56,
    68, 71, 74, 98, 111
Bedford College, University of London
    256-58, 290
Béguin, M. (director of *Esprit*) 225
Belloc, Hilaire 75
"Belloc's Vision of the 'Servile State'"
    (1928) 115
Berei, Andor 14, 18, 26, 28-9, 42-44,
    47-48, 76, 281
Bergson, Henri 15
Bern, 234, 281, 283
    AK's long stay there 155-56
    attitude towards 156, 167
Bertha, Aunt 8
Bethlen, Count István 195, 321

Bichlmair S.J., Fr Georg 98-99, 131
Biel, Egon 174-75
Binet, Alfred 17, 32
Biró, Pál 113
Blüher, Hans 144
Bochenski, Joseph 221
Boden, Margaret 276
Bódog, Somló 48
body, the human, attitudes to 160
Bolshevism, *see* Communism
Bone, Edith (née Hajós) 280, 327
"Book-shortage" (1921) 76
Borchardt, Herrmann, 182, 190, 221-22
    The Conspiracy of the Carpenters
      286
Börner, Wilhelm 68-69
Braun, Robert 43
Brendel, Rudolph 133
Brentano, Franz 89, 91, 182, 221, 295,
    323
Briefs, Goetz 223, 226-27, 325
British Academy 273
British Empire 196
British Journal of Aesthetics 273, 290
British Society for Phenomenology 123,
    273, 295
Brontë, Emily 326
Brown, George 286-87
Bruno, Giordano 127
Bryant, Arthur 307
Bühler, Karl 87, 89
Burns, Tom 241

Calvo Serer, Rafael, 239, 243, 245,
    249
    Teoría de la Restauración 236, 325
Canadian Anti-Communist League 221
Capitalism 4, 23, 39, 75, 115, 117-18,
    121, 145, 207, 220, 232
Catholic Committee for Refugees 187,
    192
Catholicism, Catholic Church 82, 150,
    196, 207, 301, 303
    faith 61, 75, 82, 98-99, 301-4
    political orientations 115-16, 185,
      226, 240, 242
Chamberlain, Houston Stewart 161
Chesterton, G.K. 58, 64, 74-76, 78,
    89, 114, 138, 149, 152, 308,
    311
Chilver, Sally 259

Christian
civilisation (Christendom) 74-75, 83,
    185-86, 196, 198-201, 213-15,
    234, 236-37, 263, 286, 301-2
philosophy 62, 75-76, 117, 160, 186,
    213, 221-22, 232, 240, 247, 263,
    302; "love" ethics 294
social gospel 113, 303
Socialism 75, 103, 116, 119, 131,
    169, 182
Christian Course 41, 74
Christianism 74, 77
Christianity
    and democracy 95, 117-19, 132, 245
    and tragedy 302
Cité Libre (Montreal liberal monthly)
    227
    AK's letter to 251
clericalism 133, 136, 182, 207, 229,
    301-2
Clerk, Sir George 41
"Collective Insecurity" (1943) 191
Committee for Christian Refugees
    180-81
common good 216-18
"Common Mistakes about Communism"
    (1950) 223, 232-34, 241, 250
common sense 57, 138, 140, 160, 248,
    261-64, 266, 274, 295, 302
    moral 193, 274, 303-4
Commonweal (American Catholic
    journal) 223
Communism (and Bolshevism) 3, 25-28,
    33, 36, 39-47, 51-53, 77, 79, 81,
    94, 107, 119-20, 150, 158, 201,
    210, 212-14, 216, 219, 221, 225,
    231-34, 236, 251
community 159
Comte, Auguste 33
Connally, John B. 287
Conservatism 157, 169, 182, 188, 190,
    213-14, 219, 243, 251, 263,
    296-97
    its foundation in trust 297
"Conservative and Revolutionary Ethos"
    (1972) 289, 296-97
"Contemporary British Philosophy and
    its Political Implications" (1959)
    250-51
"Contemporary Sexual Ethics:
    Publications on problems of sex
    and marriage" (1932) 108

Cooper, Duff 173
corporativism 107, 115, 117, 119, 123, 135
Côté, André 284
"Counter-revolution" (1931) 123-24
"Courtesy towards Women" (1919) 49
"Critique of the Creed of Progress" (1927) 118

Dalí, Salvador 123
Dániel, Arnold 72, 185
Danubian federation, idea of 23, 75, 184, 186
Das Neue Reich (Vienna weekly) 114
Dawson, Christopher 193
DeKoninck, Charles 203-8, 210-11, 221-22, 224-26, 234, 255, 284, 322
DeKoninck, Mrs (m. to CDK) 210, 222
DeKoninck, Thomas (s. of CDK) 204, 210, 284
"Deliberation is of Ends" (1962) 250, 267
democracy 21, 26, 37, 42-43, 46-47, 72, 74, 115-19, 132, 136, 142-43, 150, 157, 159, 162, 169, 182, 190-92, 194, 196, 198-200, 212-14, 216, 219, 225, 250, 295
"Democracy and Reality" (1935) 139
"*Democracy and Value*" (1936-37, unfinished book) 152, 155, 166, 174, 318
"Democracy Dead and Alive" (1928) 118
Der Christliche Ständestaat (Vienna weekly) 136, 149, 161
Der Deutsche Volkswirt (Berlin weekly) 113, 118
Der Oesterreichische Volkswirt (Vienna weekly) 111-12, 114, 117, 137, 143-44, 184
De Sade, Marquis de 193
Descartes 220
"Design for a System of Proportional Representation with Personal Representation of Districts" (1920) 46
dictionary knowledge 148
"Dignity" (1969) 165, 295-96
dignity as a quality 296
Dion, Léon 208, 226, 253
"Disgust" (1929) 64, 114, 123-25, 298
 its moral aspects 124-25

Distributivism 75
Dollfuß, Engelbert 118, 130, 135, 147, 182, 195, 223-24, 229
Dormándi, László 165, 168
Dostoievsky 74
Dracula, by Bram Stoker 137
Driesch, Hans 91, 113, 221, 291
Drucker, Peter 315
Duczynska, Ilona (=Helen, m. Karl Polányi) 111, 131, 144-45, 149, 151, 154, 159, 173, 192, 195
Dugdale, Rose 278-79
Dühring, Karl 72, 76
Dummett, Michael 310
Duncan-Jones, Austin 256-57, 276
Duns Scotus 268
Duplessis, Maurice 207, 221, 228
Durham, Bishop of (Hensley Henson) 159
Durkheim, Émil 35, 46-47, 53, 72
duty for duty's sake 279-80

Eastern Switzerland, idea of, *see* Danubian Federation
Eckhardt, Tibor 185
egalitarianism, *see* equality
Eibl, Hans 87-89, 137
"Eight Theses about the Restoration" (c.1957) 245-46
El Centinela Húngaro (free Hungarian journal) 281
"*Elements of Personalist Ethics*" (1920-21, unpublished book) 68-69, 72, 73
Emergency Rescue Committee 177, 179
"Engels and Dühring" (1922) 76
"Epistolary Memorandum" (1956) 236, 238-41, 245
Equality and egalitarianism 20, 53, 76, 119-20, 123, 134, 138-9, 141, 200, 215-16, 297, 316
Erdélyi, Klára (m. Robert Vámbéry) 136, 154, 178-79, 190, 280
"Erroneous Conscience" (1958) 254-56, 265-66, 291
"Error and Truth" (1964) 291
"Essay on Hatred" (1935) 127-29, 298
"*Ethical Value and Reality*" (1927) 90-96, 197, 303
 critique of psychoanalysis 60
 composition 88, publication 90, reception 90, 113

"*Ethics, Value and Reality*" (1977,
    posthumous collection) 278, 290
Eugenics 161
Europe, post-war, hopes and fears for
    172, 185-86, 193-94, 196
    central Europe, the same 186, 194,
    197
Evans, Mrs 172
Ewald, O. 87
"Existence and Ethics" (1963) 246,
    270-71
Existentialism 225, 248, 271, 274-75

faith, religious 304
Falk, Dr 133
Fascism 61, 112-13, 122, 137, 145, 147,
    150, 164, 211, 288
"Fascism and Bolshevism" (1926) 118
"Fate or Freedom?" (1941) 179
Federn, Paul 53-54, 310
Feeney, Fr Leonard S.J. 188-89, 224
Fejtő, Ferenc 129, 165, 168-69, 292-93,
    301, 310, 319
Ferrero, Guglielmo 15
Ferenczi, Sándor 18, 46, 51-52, 56, 59
Fernández, Gonzalo 242-43, 245
Fichte 198, 210
"Final Goal and Provisional Programmes
    in Politics" (1919) 34
Findlay, J.N. 238, 254, 256-57, 274-75,
    278
"Findlay on Ethics" (1964) 294
Fisher, Alec 276
Fisher, H.A.L. 158
Fleischer, Georg, and the
    "Fleischerkreis" 133
Fokschaner, Dr 55
Foot, Philippa 274, 276
Forbát, Elemer (later "Ford", AK's
    brother-in-law) 235
"Forgiveness" (1972) 284, 294
free choice 270-71
Free Europe (wartime weekly) 173, 191
"Freud, the Social Psychologist" (1921)
    53
Freud, Sigmund 18, 32, 51-63
free will 299
Friedrich, István 41
Friedrich, Prof 194
Fumet, Stanislas 171
Füst, Milán 27, 47, 54, 58-59, 66, 70-71,
    74, 77-86, 88, 90, 98, 101, 205,

209, 220, 280
Erzsébet (m. to MF) 280

Gábor, Eszter 307
Galilei Circle (G Kör) 15, 24-28, 33, 42,
    110-11, 174
    AK's "arrest" 27
Gambra, Rafael 325
"Games and Aims" (1966) 269, 297-98
Gaudron, Fr 208
Geiger, Moritz 221
Gémes, Elisabeth (=Bözsi), *see* Kolnai,
    Elisabeth
Gémes, Irma (mother of Elisabeth and
    Olga) 98, 100-102, 131, 135-36,
    145-46, 152, 167, 190, 235,
    256-58, 317
Gémes, Olga (later Forbát, then Ford)
    100, 167-68, 173, 235
George, Henry 23, 34, 42, 48, 72, 76
George, Lloyd 159
George, Stefan, 144, 158
Gérando, Joseph-Marie de 289
Germain, Claude 293
Germain, Stanislas 209-10
Germain, Thérèse 209, 293
German Idealism 182
Germania (Berlin Catholic daily) 113
Germanus, Gyula 46
Gestapo 174-77
Geyser, Josef 91
Gluck, Mary 309
Goebbels, Joseph 144, 246
Gogarten, Friedrich 144
Goldwater, Barry 287-88
Gollancz, Victor 145, 149, 151, 153-54,
    157, 162, 166-67
Gombrich, Ernst 133, 235
Gombrich, Lisbeth 133, 235, 317
Gömöri, Jenő (first cousin of AK) 3,
    70, 80
Gomperz, Heinrich 87-88, 116, 136
"Goncharovs 'Oblomow'" (1923) 57-58
good and evil, analyses of, 268
Grant, Donald 131, 141, 150, 167, 169,
    180, 324
Grant, Irene (m. to DG) 131, 141-46,
    151, 154-55, 157, 162, 166-67,
    169-70, 172-74, 324
Gyurgyák, János 312

Habsburg
   Empire 19-20, 36-38, 41, 109, 186;
     movement for a revival of 183,
     185-86, 191
   Empress Zita 205
   Otto von 184-85
Hadik, Count 37-38
Hajdú, Tibor 309
Hall, Noble 171
Haller, Sigmund 55
Hampshire, Stuart 255
Harc (free Hungarian periodical) 192
Hare, R.M. 273, 293
Hartmann, Klaus 249, 273, 296
Hartmann, Nicolai 97, 113, 295
Hayek, F.A. 214
Hegel 198, 210
Heidegger, Martin 114, 123, 137, 139,
   161, 247, 270
Herbertz, Prof 155-56
Hertzka, Theodor 48, 72
hierarchy 76, 91, 117, 120, 183, 200,
   215, 218, 220, 232, 236, 295-96
Hildebrand, Dietrich von 91, 136-37,
   146-47, 182-84, 187, 209, 221,
   266, 295
Hiller, Eric 54-56, 58, 75, 84
Hitler, Adolph 112, 135-36, 144, 149,
   156, 167, 229, 287
Hollis & Carter 235, 238, 241
Horthy, Nicholas 41-42, 138
Howe, Julia Ward, her "Battle-hymn of
   the Republic" 286
Huebsch, Mr 180
Hug-Hellmuth, Dr 59
"Human Dignity Today" (c.1960) 296
human
   condition 160, 164, 201, 216-17,
     225, 232-34, 239, 249, 262-63,
     267, 269-70, 293, 299
   dignity 296
   normality 232, 243
   rights 295
humanitarianism 201
Hume, David 297
Hungary
   Astoria Hotel, Budapest 38
   Awakening Magyars 41, 185
   Communist Party 39-41, 111
   government, 1945 and after 195
   historical background 3-4, 10-13,
     19-20, 22-23, 26, 28-29, 33-34,
     36-42, 44, 71-72, 243, 253

Independence Party
   ("Independentists") 27, 37-39
liberalism 19-23, 25
National Citizens Radical Party 23,
   26, 28-29, 33, 37, 39-40, 42-43
Octobrists 39, 44, 46, 75, 186, 319
radicalism (progressivism) 21-29,
   32-33, 36-37, 39, 41-42, 46, 54,
   75, 309
Social Democratic Party 37-41
Husserl, Edmund 89, 91, 114, 123, 182,
   221, 224, 266, 308-9
Huszadik Század (progressive Budapest
   monthly) 22, 29-30, 33, 43, 46,
   308
Huxley, Aldous 193
Huxley, Brigadier 240
Huxley, Julian 193

Ibrányi, Mgr 208, 227, 285
Ibsen's *Rosmersholm* 28
"Identity and Division as a Fundamental
   Theme of Politics" (1967)
   297-98
Imago (psychoanalytical cultural
   monthly) 51, 58, 63
immoralism 104, 274
"Inclination, Duty and Cast of Mind"
   (1927) 96-97
Indig, Otto 168
individualism 217
Ingarden, Roman 290
"In Praise of Alienation" (probably
   c.1950) 270
"Is Linguistic Integrity an Indication of
   Moral Integrity?" (1966) 291
Integrity (American Catholic journal)
   223
intellectuals 288, 295
intemperance 182-83
internationalism 198-99
intuitionism 268, 291
Isolde (probably =Ilse von Scholey)
   132-34, 142
Italy, Abyssinian invasion 146

Jackson, Henry 287
Jászi, Oszkár (Oscar) 21-25, 28-34,
   37-40, 43-45, 54, 66, 68, 72, 78,
   111, 114, 129, 154, 158, 162,
   164, 171, 176, 179-83, 185-89,
   191-96, 204-5, 224, 308, 311-12

Johnson, Alvin 179
Johnson, Paul 288, 310
Jolly, Douglas 173
Jones, Ernest 54, 56, 58
"Jottings on Personalism" (c.1963)
    294-95
Journal of Central European Affairs 184
Jurinetz, W. 62

Kaltenbrunner, Gerd-Klaus 289
Kant and Kantianism 60, 88, 94, 96-97,
    251, 264, 268, 279
Karinthy Frigyes, 68, 70
Károlyi, Mihály (Michael) 25, 34, 37-40,
    68, 168
Karpoviches, Mr and Mrs 192, 195, 207,
    210
Kaufmann, Felix 87, 89, 117
Kelemen, Eszter 280, 301
Kierkegaard 248
King's College, London 256-57
Kinszky, Imre (first cousin of AK) 15,
    26, 28, 30-32, 44-46, 48, 51-52,
    66, 68-70, 73, 77, 87, 98, 100
Kirchwey, Freda 179
Klages, Ludwig 139, 144, 158
Klein, Franz 184, 186, 191-92
Klein, Melanie 56
Kneale, William 114
Koestler, Arthur 154, 280
Kolnai, Mrs (Elisabeth Kolnai, née
    Gémes) ix, 100-101, 131, 142,
    147, 153-55, 162, 164, 166,
    168-72, 176, 178, 180-81, 183,
    185, 188, 190-91, 194, 196,
    204-5, 208, 210, 222-23, 229,
    238, 240, 242-43, 253-54,
    257-58, 278, 285, 288, 289, 293,
    319, 322
    AK's attitude to 145-51, 172-73, 194,
    210
    her miscarriage 210
    searches for AK after German
    invasion 175
    prepared for baptism by Fr Castaing
    175
Koppányi, Theodore 98, 180, 187
Körmendi, Francis 14, 26, 309
    The Happy Generation 26-27, 29
Kornfeld, S. 87
Kosztolányi, Dezső 70
Kovács, György 14, 18, 43, 47-48, 77,
    87, 280, 308, 327

Kovács, Sophie (m. to GK) 280
Kraus, Karl 136, 138, 149-50
Külpe, Oswald 89, 91
Kun, Béla 4, 39-41, 43-44, 46, 80, 110
Kurz, Trude 111

Lacey, Alan 282
Lándor, Béla 77
Lányi, György (=George Lanyi, s. of
    ZsL) 101, 113, 133, 154, 172,
    176-81, 185, 209-10, 221-23,
    229, 235, 240, 251, 255-59, 273,
    275, 279-80, 283-85, 287-88,
    296
Lányi, Susi (m. to GL) 101-2, 179, 209,
    283-84, 288, 296
Lányi, Yvonne (EK's and GL's cousin)
    173, 175-76, 283-85
Lányi, Zsigmond (Irma Gémes's brother)
    319
Lapointe, Jeanne 208, 226-27, 284, 307,
    317, 322
Laski, Harold 193
La Table Ronde (French monthly) 256
Látóhatár (free Hungarian journal) 281
Laval Philosophique et Théologique
    205
Laval University, Quebec 196, 205,
    223-25
Leftism 120, 122, 137, 150, 169, 186,
    199, 213, 296-97
Lerner, Max 167-68
Levin, Harry 192, 197
Levinas, Emanuel 114
Lévy-Bruhl, Lucien 32
Lewis, C.S. 316
Lewis, John 151, 154, 157, 162
    The Case against Pacifism 162
"Liberal Socialism" (1920-21,
    unpublished book) 45, 66, 68-69,
    72, 312
liberalism 94, 117, 119-20, 160, 169,
    186, 189-90, 200, 219, 231, 233,
    246-47, 274
Liberation (successor to The Voice of
    Austria) 191
liberty 197-98, 214, 218-20, 231-32,
    239, 302
    versus emancipation from God
    231-34
"Liberty and the Heart of Europe"
    (1943-44, unfinished book) 187,
    191-92, 194, 197-201, 211, 236

"*Liberty or Equality* by Erik von
  Kuehnelt-Leddhin" (1952) 224
linguistic analysis 251, 273-75
Litván, György (s. of JL) 5, 67-68,
  308-10, 312
Litván, József (first cousin of AK) 2-3,
  10-12, 15, 18, 28, 44, 48, 76-77,
  282, 307-9, 313, 327
Lloyd-Thomas, David and Anne 278
logic of moral discourse 251
love and hate 128-29
Löwenherz, Herr 102
Lukacs, John 307
Lukács, György, 25, 43-44
Lumley-Smith, Sarah 281
Luther, Martin 158

McGovern, George 287
Mach, Ernst 17
Macmurray, John 144, 167-68, 227, 237,
  240-41, 318
Makkai, Adam 313
Malcolm, Norman 291
Maluf, Dr Fakhri (later Br Francis
  S.I.H.M.) 189
Maniu, Julius 22
Mann, Thomas 61-62
Mannheim, Karl 43-44, 115, 117
Manser, A.R. 270
Maritain, Jacques 169, 171, 182, 185,
  188, 193, 211, 223
Markovits, Györgyi 312
Marrero, Vicente 129, 243-49, 251, 254,
  256, 290, 302
Martindale SJ, Fr 98
Marx 23-24, 33, 56, 198, 231, 270, 316
Marxism 21, 23, 25, 28, 33-34, 39, 42,
  51, 53, 56, 62, 74, 117, 168, 183,
  210, 225, 279
  and psychoanalysis 62-63
"Marxist and Liberal Elements in
  National Socialism" (1934) 137
Masaryk, Thomas 22, 33, 46, 134, 191
Mathews, Basil 170-71
Matthiesen, Prof 192
Maura, Antonio 239, 324
Mayo, Bernard 273, 275-76
"Max Scheler and Capitalism" (1928)
  115
"Max Scheler as Sociologist" (1928) 118
"Max Scheler's Treatment of Freud's
  Theory of Libido" (1925) 58, 60
Meager, Ruby 278, 281-82

mediaeval (scholastic) philosophy 88-89,
  182, 189
Meinong, Alexius 89, 91, 125, 221, 282,
  323
Memoirs, AK's, see "*Political Memoirs*"
Menczer, Béla 26, 43, 50, 72, 79, 84,
  133, 146-48, 150, 154-55, 158,
  170-71, 181-82, 185, 235, 280
Mendell, Marguerite 308
Mendl, Irma (cousin of AK) 3
Menzer, Reginald 209, 285
"Mercy and Justice" (1919) 46
"Merezhkovsky, the Russian Catholic"
  (1922) 76
Mészáros, István 280
Mind 254
Mindszenty, Cardinal 208, 221
Mises, Ludwig von 86
Missong, Alfred 134
modern philosophy 89, 304
modernity 250, 260
Molinism 302
Molnár, Ferenc, 81
  The Paul Street Boys 11
monarchy 47, 181, 184, 190, 200, 231,
  239, 245-46
  and "compenetration" 239, 246
Monk, Ray 310
Monléon, Jacques de 208, 234
Moore, G.E. 271, 282
"Moral Consensus" (1970) 256, 264,
  291-92
moral
  conscience 228
  consensus 103, 264, 266, 293;
    content of, 292
  emphasis 265, 268
  judgement, its nature and cognitive
    status 291
  laws 292
  relativism 104
  status 293, 300, 328
"Morality and Practice" (begun 1962)
  257, 267-69
morality, thematic and implicit 265
  basic meaning of 293
  and politics 267, 269, 297
  and religion 201, 268, 302-3
"Moral Truth: inchoate sketch of a
  Theory of Morality" (date
  uncertain) 293
Mounier, Emmanuel 193, 225
Mullins, Cate 285

Mumford, Lewis 168, 176, 178, 180, 187
Munich Pact 162
Murdoch, Iris 274-75
Murphy, Francesca ix
Mussolini, Benito 136, 246, 287
mysticism 63, 311

nationalism 198-99
National Socialism (Nazism) 88, 113, 123, 136, 141-42, 158-62, 167, 186, 201, 211-14
naturalism 88, 142, 268, 271, 274
Naturalistic Fallacy 271
Nazi-Soviet Pact, the 162, 169
Negative, thematic primacy of the 124
Németh, Andor 67, 168, 183
New School of Social Research 179-80, 182
Nicolson, Harold 174
Niebuhr, Reinhold 164, 211, 223
Nietzsche 139, 158, 162, 210, 297
nobility 216, 218
Nock, O.S. 192
"Notes on Reactionary Utopia" (1955) 227-28, 244
"Notes on the Hungarian revolution of 1918, etc" (1919) 29-30, 34, 99, 308
Noth, Erich 174
Nowell-Smith, P.H. 273
Nunberg, Hermann 59
Nuremberg Trials 197
Nyugat (progressive literary periodical) 25, 77

"Objectivity and Technicism" (1965) 249
occultism 74, 329
Oesterreicher, the Revd John M. 223
"On the Equality of Man" (1934) 138-39
"On the Mystical" (1921) 63-4, 74, 77, 290, 311
Oppenheimer, Franz 72, 312
Ortega y Gasset, José 123, 247-48
Osborne, Harold 290
O'Shaughnessy, Brian 278
"Othmar Spann's Theory of the Organic State" (1934) 138
"Othmar Spann's Theory of the 'Total State'" (1934) 138
"Outlines of a Personalist Conception of State and Society" (1932) 134

"Pacifism Means Suicide" (1939) 164, 319
Palacios, Carmen (m. to LP) 223
Palacios, Leopoldo 223, 227, 237, 241, 250
pantheism 127
Parent, Mgr 205, 226, 284, 322
Pareto, Vilfredo 139
Paulsen, Ernő 68-69
perfection 261-62
Perry, R.B. 197
personalism 29, 73, 103, 105, 117, 119-20, 132, 136, 141, 150, 164-65, 181-82, 200, 225, 246, 292, 294-96, 301, 303, 317
"Personalism, the Spiritual Basis of Democracy" (1941, unpublished and possibly unfinished article) 183, 186
"*Phenomenological Ethics*" (1932, unpublished "textbook") 112, 141
phenomenology 60, 64, 73, 88-89, 91-92, 103, 112, 114, 123, 146-47, 248, 251, 272, 295, 299
phenomenology of cats 226
Phillips, D.Z. 260
Philosophical Quarterly 273
Philosophical Review 275
Philosophy 255, 298
philosophy, nature and method of 147-48, 224, 266
Pikler, Gyula 22, 24, 308
Plato 134, 189, 246, 268, 297
Plotinus 127
"Pluralism and the Correlation of Ends" (1959) 250
Polányi, Ilona (=Helen), *see* Duczynska
Polányi, Karl (=Karli) 24-25, 56, 80-81, 110-12, 116, 131, 134-35, 142-45, 151-54, 167, 173, 180, 224, 274, 308, 312
Polányi, Kari (d. of KP, later Kari Polanyi-Levitt) 24, 131, 144, 308, 315
Polanyi, Michael 274, 308
Pole, David 275
"Political and Non-political Interests" (1965) 248-49
"*Political Memoirs*" (=Memoirs, 1952-55) ix, 10, 22, 44, 52, 66, 133, 204, 224, 227, 235, 237, 240-42, 301, 304, 317, 321

Polya, Mrs 102
Pons, Salvador 238, 241-45, 247, 249, 324
Popper, Karl 227, 235-37, 240-41, 255, 274
positivism 42, 60
poverty and wealth 29, 136, 149-50, 220
practice 267, 269
and morality 269
Pribram, Francis 87
"Privilege and Liberty" (1949) 214, 216-20, 236, 244, 295
prudence 267, 269
Prussianism 161
psychoanalysis 18, 21, 46, 51-63, 278
"Psychoanalysis and Sociology" (1920) 52, 62, 66, 69
"Psychoanalytical Sociology" (1922) 56
Punta Europa (Madrid monthly) 244-45, 247, 250
AK's relations with 244-45

Quadragesimo Anno 116, 131
Quebec
townscape 206, climate 206, culture 206-7, 227
AK's excursions from 209-10; return in 1968 225, 284; summer school of 1945 196, 207; visit to France and England in 1952 234-36
"Québecisme", 207-8, 210, 222, 226-28, 237, 284, 322

Rácz, László 14-15
Radford, Robert 316
Radó, Sándor 52
Rambaud, Prof 243
Ramírez, Fr Santiago 247
Rank, Otto 18, 51, 54-56, 58, 63
Raphael, Daiches 258
"Rationalism in Politics by Michael Oakeshott" (1965) 298
Read, Cynthia 279-80 ǝo6
reason 140, 216, 263, 302
and feeling 247-48
and will 299
and religion 304
in ethics 254, 293
Rédei, Dr 48
Redler, Richard 132, 134, 142, 209
"Reflections on the Hungarian Uprising" (1957) 243
Rehmke, Johannes 221-22, 323

Reid, Thomas 221
Reik, Theodor 52, 55, 310
Reinach, Adolf 221, 298
Reiner, Hans 295
Reininger, Robert 87-88
religion, presupposition of 188
Renner, Karl 135
review of Freud's *The Ego and the Id* (1923) 55
"Revolution and Restoration" (1953) 236-37, cf 200
Réz, Vera 280
Rightism 199, 213-14
"Right and Left in Politics" (1927) 118
Röhm, Ernst 144
Roosevelt, F.D. 147
Röpke, Wilhelm 227
Rousseau, Jean Jacques 119, 239, 270
Roy, Archbishop 226
Royal Institute of Philosophy 273, 299
Russia, *see* USSR
Russell, Bertrand 91, 164
Ryle, Gilbert 254

St Benedict Centre 187-90, 196
St John of St Thomas 208
Sándor, László 312
Sangnier, Marc 169
Sandkühler, H.J. 310-11
Santayana, George 152
Sartre, Jean-Paul 123, 270, 275, 297
Sbrik, Heinrich 86
Schaffer, Felix 111
Scheiber, Mrs 280
Scheler, Max 49, 58-59, 87, 89, 91, 96-97, 105, 113-14, 126, 136-37, 161-62, 275, 295
Schiller 96
Schiller, Zsigmond (m. an aunt of AK) 3, 30
Schleß, Maurice 189
Schlick, Moritz 87
Schmitt, Karl, on politics 139, 318
Schönere Zukunft (Vienna weekly) 115, 136
Schopenhauer, Artur 107
"Should the State Promote a Single Religion or be Completely Neutral?" (1961) 228
Schulze-Gävernitz, Ruth von 146
Schuschnigg, Kurt von 136, 182, 229, 301
Schuster, George 180

Schwarz, Balduin 183, 209, 326
Schwarzwald, Eugenia 110-11
Science 160, 264, 266
Scitovsky, Tibor 179
Sebba, Gregor 133
Second World War
    seeing it coming 147, 151
    German invasion of and armistice
        with France 173-76
Seipel, Ignaz 110, 116, 134
Seton-Watson, R.W. 154
"Sexual Ethics: the Meaning and
    Foundations of Sexual Morality"
    (1930) 88, 102-8, 112, 315
sexual morality 50, 79, 82-83, 102-7,
    150, 201
Silber, Prof 275
Silberbauer, G. 116
"Silvesterlandschaft" (1924, poem) 100
Simard, M. and Mme 208, 284
Simmons, Prof 282
Simpson, Esther 240-41, 255
Sinkó, Ervin 80
Smith, Rennie 170-71, 173
social aspect of morality, the 106-7
social Darwinism 57
social justice 233, 297
social reform, 235-36, 261
Socialism 160, 286
"Socialist Christianity" (1922) 76
Society for the Protection of Science and
    Learning (SPSL) 236, 240
Soloviev, Vladimir 91
Soltész, Gáspár 16, 281
"Some Features of Phenomenological
    Ethics", Intercollegiate Lectures
    (1972) 295
"Song of the Dog" (c.1933, poem) 130
Sonnenschein, Karl 113
Sorel, Georges 139
Spain, 237, 241-42; its "reality" 230;
    "generation of '98" 243
    Civil War 151, 229, 245
    Franco Regime, 229-31, 238-39,
        245, 251
    AK's journey through (1940) 176,
        229; lecture tours: (1952) 224,
        229-31, (1956) 237-38, 241,
        (1957) 242-43, (1959) 249-51,
        255-56, (1961) 246-47, 249
    AK's attitude to 234-35, 241-42, 249,
        251-52, 282, 325; hopes for 214,
        229-30, 236-37, 239-40, 251

Spanish Institute (London) 242
Spann, Prof Othmar, and AK's
    anti-Spann campaign 117-18,
    141
Spencer, Herbert 21, 32-35, 46-47, 51,
    57, 72
Spengler, Oswald 139, 144, 158
Spinoza 127, 297
"Spiritual Pride" (1931) 126
Stapel, Wilhelm, his *Der christliche*
    Staatsmann 144
Starhemberg, Rüdiger von 171
Steed, Wickham 154, 158, 171, 173
Stein, Ármin (=Hermann, AK's father)
    1-2, 4-6, 9, 11, 44-45, 64, 71,
    196, 253
Stein, Dora (AK's sister-in-law) 9
Stein, László (=Laci, AK's brother) 8-9,
    11, 30-31, 46, 65
Stein, Valéria (*née* Glück, AK's mother)
    1-6, 11, 196, 253
Steiner, Árpád 180
Steinitz, Imre 18, 26, 48
Stevas, Norman St John 286
"Still Life at Trenčanteplice" (1919) 6
Stoicism 127
Stoljarov, A. 62-63
Storfer, A.J. 59
Strasser, Jani 281
Strawson, P.F. 264
student radicalism 279
Stumpf, Carl 221
Stux, Ilia 231
Sunday Circle 25, 280
Switzerland 114-15, 155-57, 167
Szamuely, Tibor 41
Századunk (successor to *Huszadik*
    Század) 72, 138, 149
Székács, Béla 47
Szell, George (s. of SG; the famous
    conductor) 3, 54, 66, 114, 209,
    253, 255-59
Széll, György (cousin of AK's mother)
    55, 66, 71-72
Széll, Olga (m. to SG the younger) 66
Szende, Pál 28
Szép, Ernő 70
Szirtes, George 310

Tawney, R.H. 141
Taylor, Gabrielle 295
Teleki, Count 42
teleological ethics 91-92

Terhaar, Jost 90
"The Accursed Café" (c.1932, poem)
130
"The Ambiguities of Nationalism"
(1946) 211
"The American Mind and the Problem of
Europe" (1944) 194
"The Austrian Coffee-House" (1940) 67
"The Beginnings of Formalism in
Modern Philosophy" (1946) 211
"*The Case against False Pacifism*"
(1937-8) (unpublished book,
later entitled "*The Fallacies of
Pacifism*") 155, 157, 162-64,
166-68, 173, 180
"The Catholic Revolutionary" (1921) 75
"The Christian Trade Unions in their
Fight against Capitalism" (1929)
118-19
"The Concept of Hierarchy" (1971) 278,
295
"The Concept of Practical Error" (1959)
256-57, 269-70
"The Concept of the Interesting" (1964)
290
"The Cult of the Common Man and the
Glory of the Humble" (1946)
211
"The Cultural Importance of
Psychoanalysis" (1923) 56, 59
"The Destructive Abbot and the Cautious
Bishop" (1921) 75
"*The Divinisation and Complete
Enslavement of Man*" (1952) 231
"The Dream as Artist" (1972) 290-91
"The Ethical Foundations of Liberal
Socialism" (1921) 72
"The Ghost of the Naturalistic Fallacy"
(1962) 271
The Globe (Boston daily) 221
"The Historical Conditioning of Thought
and the Philosophy of Common
Sense" (1952) 212
"The Humanitarian versus the Religious
Attitude" (1944) 201-2, 303
"The Idea and the Form of the State"
(1934) 137
"The Ideology of Progress" (1927) 118
"The Indispensability of Philosophy"
(1947) 211-12
"The Justification of Commands" (1967)
298

"The Logic of Sex" (1963) 275
"The Magicians of Common Sense:
K. Kraus and G.K. Chesterton"
(1936) 138
"The Meaning of the 'Common Man'"
(1949) 211, 214-16
"The Misuse of the 'Vital'" (1934)
118-19
The Montreal Gazette 221, 227
"The Morally Improving Function of
Law" (1973) 249-50, 289
"The Moral Theme in Political Division"
(1960) 255, 267, 296
"The Myth of the 'Children of Light'"
(1945) 211
The Nation (American liberal weekly),
167, 179, 183, 186, 193
The New Republic (American periodical)
193
"The Pivotal Principles of National
Socialist Ideology" (1938,
lecture notes) 169
"The Positive Conception of Liberty"
(1957) 244, 299
"The Problem of Austrian Nationhood"
(1942) 186
"The Psychology of Anarcho-
Communism" (1920) 52
"The Psychology of continuity and
change in political positions"
(1919) 34-35
"The Relevance of Psychoanalysis to
Sociology" (1920) 51
"The Social Classes' Ideas of Power"
(1929) 120-22
"The Sociological Foundations of
Liberal Socialism" (1921) 72
"The Songs of Bern" (1940-41, poem
sequence) 156-57
"The Sovereignty of the Object" (1951)
212, 223, 266, 291
"The Standard Modes of Aversion: Fear,
Disgust and Hatred" (1968)
298-99
"The Structure of Moral Intention"
(1928) 97-98
The Tablet (London Catholic weekly)
224, 235
"The Techniques of Fascism" (1941)
183
"The Thematic Primacy of Moral Evil"
(1956) 237, 265

"The Three Riders of Apocalypse:
    Communism, Naziism and
    Progressive Democracy"
    (c.1950) 212-14
"The Unfulfilled Multinational Empire"
    (1967) 280-81
"The Universality of Loyalty Rules"
    (1957) 254
"The Utopian Mentality" (1960) 256,
    270
"The Utopian Mind" (1960, paper)
    270
"The Utopian Mind" (begun 1956;
    unfinished book on Utopian
    thought) 237, 242, 250, 253,
    255-57, 260-63, 281
The Utopian Mind and other papers
    (1995, posthumous collection)
    270, 324, 326
"The Utopian Negation of Fundamental
    and Ineliminable Distinctions"
    (probably 1956) 264
The Voice of Austria (free Austrian
    monthly) 184, 186, 191
"*The War against the West*" (1938,
    ="War") 112, 133, 137, 141,
    143-46, 150-52, 154, 158-62,
    166, 168-69, 176, 180, 256, 318
    improving the English of, 146, 154
Thomas Aquinas 99, 196, 207, 221, 266,
    268
"Thomas Mann, Freud and Progress"
    (1929) 61-62
Thomism 99, 188, 196, 207-8, 221-26,
    247, 266, 302, 304
Thompson, Dorothy 180
Thurmond, Strom 287
Tisza, István 37-38
Tolstoy 74
Tószeghi, Dr and Mrs de 272, 326
totalitarianism 169, 185, 188, 190-91,
    198, 212-14, 216, 218-19, 239,
    261, 295
Tóth, Kálmán 14
traditionalism 227-28, 247
Tremblay, Arthur 196, 207, 227, 284
Tremblay, Pauline (m. to AT) 196, 207,
    227, 284
Trendelenburg, Adolf 221
Trépanier, Prof 208
Tulloch, Doreen 278
Tűz (Vienna monthly, then weekly)
    0-71, 73, 80-82, 98

"Two Opposite Ways of Using
    Descriptive-evaluative Terms"
    (1965) 295
Tyrannicide (by Oscar Jaszi) 193

Ulászló (imaginary kingdom of
    Hungary) 47, 169, 181, 310
Ulman, Elinor 167
Unamuno, Miguel 248
"'Universalisability' and 'Totality' Types
    of Ethics" (c.1963) 274-75
"Universality and Political Attitudes"
    (1964) 297
USSR 53-54, 194-95, 221, 233, 286
utilitarianism, 72-73, 94
"Utopia and Alienation" (c.1960) 270
utopianism, 75, 122, 203, 254, 260-64,
    266, 269
    AK's critical writings on 92, 118,
    197, 227, 237, 249, 260-61, 264,
    266-67
    departmental 57, 262
    Rightist (reactionary) 189, 227-28,
    237

Vámbéry, Robert (=Lolo) 99-101, 108,
    113-15, 131, 136, 150, 154, 179,
    182, 190, 192, 280, 284, 287
Vámbéry, Rusztem (father of RV) 138,
    162, 179, 189, 192
Vaughan, Doreen 279-80, 301
Veblen, Thorstein 152
Vértes, Jenő 281
Vienna
    AK's feelings for 50, 66-67, 72, 98,
    114, 147, 151
    coffee-houses 67
    Ethical Society 56, 69
    Leo Society 133-34
    Logos Verein 133-34
"Vienna District Wars" (poems of
    various dates) 130-31, 142
Vienna School (of Philosophy) 87
Vierkandt, Alfred 32
Vietnam War 286, 288
Viking Press 162, 180, 319
Voegelin, Eric 117, 133
Volkswohl (Viennese monthly) 61, 116,
    118
Vyx, Colonel 40

Wahle, R. 87
Ward, L.F. 32, 310

"Waste-book: Political Philosophy"
(1957) 297
Weininger, Otto 48-50, 79, 105, 310,
315
Weisengrün, Paul 68-69, 72
Weiss, Rudolph 259
Werfel, Franz 58, 67, 182
Western civilisation, essential features of
236-37
"What Politics is About" (1933) 139-41,
318
Whitehead, A.N. 192
"Who was Otto Weininger?" (1922)
49-50
Wiggins, David ix, 259, 271, 276-77,
279, 289, 299
"Will German Catholics Go Left?"
(1933) 141-42
Williams, Bernard 259, 276-77
"Will in itself is Free Will" (c.1952) 299
Winch, Peter 264

Winkler, Claude 308 (d. of PW)
Winkler, Pál (=Paul, maternal cousin of
AK), 3, 12, 54, 68, 165, 173,
177, 179-80, 258-59, 280
Winspear, Hugh 98
Winter, Ernst Karl 134-35, 141, 182,
184, 220, 224, 317
"Aktion Winter" 135-36
Wittgenstein, Ludwig 49
Woodruff, Douglas 224, 235

York, Archbishop of (William Temple)
171
"Your Three Questions" (1961) 245
"Youth and Fascist Reaction" (1931)
118
Youth Movement 142

Zolnai, Tom (s. of VZ) 9, 257
Zolnai, Vera (G. Lányi's sister) 257, 259,
283-85